THE NEW AMERICAN SUBURB

Katrin Anacker and the authors advance detailed research into associations, causes, and consequences of diverse socio-economic and poverty trajectories affecting thousands of suburbs. The researchers explore important policy effects, such as urban containment policies, on suburban poverty, and whether urban sustainability policies can be implemented to increase equity among income and racial groups.

William H. Lucy, University of Virginia, USA

Once depicted as a refuge for the white middle class, American suburbs now display a puzzling mosaic of income and demographic diversity. The New American Suburb *presents a broad and insightful portrait of this new social and economic geography. Addressing topics that range from the suburban foreclosures and immigration to the prospects for revitalization, this sophisticated collection probes the variation that characterizes contemporary suburbs in the United States.*

Margaret M. Weir, University of California, Berkeley, USA

American suburbs are changing like never before. A small portion of the suburbs are becoming hip, walkable, urban places, whether revitalizing 19th century town centers or a dead regional mall being bulldozed, replaced by a grid of streets lined with retail beneath office and residential. The surrounding neighborhoods of both these models will prosper from proximity. However, much of suburbia will have social problems reminiscent of declining center cities 50 years ago. Higher poverty rates in a fiscal monoculture reliant on residential property taxes in decline point to serious problems. As The New American Suburb *authors point out, this will be the most important social challenge of the early 21st century.*

Christopher Leinberger, George Washington University
School of Business, USA

Für Mama und Papa

The New American Suburb

Poverty, Race and the Economic Crisis

Edited by
KATRIN B. ANACKER
George Mason University, Arlington, USA

ASHGATE

Published by
Ashgate Publishing Limited
Wey Court East
Union Road
Farnham
Surrey, GU9 7PT
England

Ashgate Publishing Company
110 Cherry Street
Suite 3-1
Burlington, VT 05401-3818
USA

www.ashgate.com

British Library Cataloguing in Publication Data
A catalogue record for this book is available from the British Library

The Library of Congress has cataloged the printed edition as follows:
The new American suburb : poverty, race and the economic crisis / [edited] by
    Katrin B. Anacker.
        pages cm
    Includes bibliographical references and index.
        ISBN 978-1-4094-4259-2 (hardback) -- ISBN 978-1-4094-4260-8 (ebook) --
    ISBN 978-1-4724-0180-9 (epub) 1. Suburbs--United States. 2. Metropolitan areas--United States. 3. Poverty--United States. 4. Racism--United States. 5. Suburbs--United States--Economic conditions. I. Anacker, Katrin B.

    HT352.U6N477 2015
    307.760973--dc23

                                                                                2014028901

ISBN 9781409442592 (hbk)
ISBN 9781409442608 (ebk – PDF)
ISBN 9781472401809 (ebk – ePUB)

Printed in the United Kingdom by Henry Ling Limited,
at the Dorset Press, Dorchester, DT1 1HD

Contents

List of Figures   *vii*
List of Tables   *xi*
Notes on Contributors   *xv*
Acknowledgments   *xix*

1   Introduction   1
     Katrin B. Anacker

SECTION I: SUBURBAN POVERTY

2   The Resurgence of Concentrated Poverty in America: Metropolitan
     Trends in the 2000s   15
     Elizabeth Kneebone and Carey Anne Nadeau

3   Debunking the "Cookie-Cutter" Myth for Suburban Places
     and Suburban Poverty: Analyzing Their Variety and Recent Trends   39
     Karen Beck Pooley

SECTION II: RACIAL, ETHNIC, AND NATIVIST CHANGE

4   The Washington, DC Metropolitan Region—Traditional No More?   81
     Carolyn Gallaher

5   Local Immigration Legislation in Two Suburbs: An Examination of
     Immigration Policies in Farmers Branch, Texas, and Carpentersville,
     Illinois   113
     Bernadette Hanlon and Thomas J. Vicino

SECTION III: SUBURBAN DECLINE—OR NOT?

6   Beyond Sprawl: Social Sustainability and Reinvestment in the
     Baltimore Suburbs   133
     Bernadette Hanlon

7   Metropolitan Growth Patterns and Inner-Ring Suburban Decline: A
     Longitudinal Analysis of the 100 Largest U.S. Metropolitan Areas   153
     Sugie Lee, Nancey Green Leigh and Andrew McMillan

SECTION IV: SUBURBAN FORECLOSURES

8   Responses to Foreclosure and Abandonment in Cleveland's
     Inner Suburbs: Three Case Studies   177
     W. Dennis Keating

9   Punctuated Equilibrium: Community Responses to Neoliberalism
     in Three Suburban Communities in Baltimore County, Maryland   187
     Gregory Smithsimon

SECTION V: SUBURBAN POLICY

10   Revitalizing Distressed Older Suburbs: Case Studies in Alabama,
     Michigan, Ohio, and Pennsylvania   213
     *Kathryn W. Hexter, Edward W. (Ned) Hill, Benjamin Y. Clark,
     Brian A. Mikelbank and Charles Post*

11   The Response of the Nonprofit Safety Net to Rising
     Suburban Poverty   247
     Benjamin J. Roth and Scott W. Allard

Index   *285*

List of Figures

2.1   Share of Total and Poor Population in Extreme-Poverty Tracts, 1990 to 2005–2009   21

3.1   Breakdown of Tract Types by Region   45

3.2   Breakdown of all Suburban Tracts and Higher Poverty Suburban Tracts by Tract Type, 2005–2009   51

3.3   Percent of Type 1 Tracts in Growing MSAs with Moderate or High Poverty Rates by Suburb Type, 2005–2009   58

3.4   Percent of Type 1 Tracts in Exurban Suburbs of Growing MSAs by Poverty Level, 2005–2009   59

3.5   Year Housing Units Built in Growing MSAs' Type 1 Tracts in Non-Exurban Suburbs by Region and Poverty Level, 2005–2009   60

3.6   Proportion of Suburban Tracts in Shrinking Metros by Suburb Type and by Poverty Level, 2005–2009   61

3.7   Comparison of Tract- and MSA-Level Median Owner Incomes in Type 1, 2, and 3 Tracts, 2005–2009   63

3.8   Comparison of Tract- and MSA-Level Median House Values in Type 1, 2, and 3 Census Tracts, 2005–2009   63

3.9   Tract Type of Suburban Homeowners by Race and Ethnicity in the 100 Largest MSAs, 2005–2009   66

3.10   Racial and Ethnic Breakdown in Type 3 Tracts by Region, 2005–2009   68

3.11   Predominant Racial and Ethnic Groups in Type 3 Tracts by Region and Poverty Level, 2005–2009   68

3.12   Number of Bedrooms in Owner-Occupied Housing Units by Tract Type, 2005–2009   71

3.13   Age of Housing by Tract Type, 2005–2009   71

3.14   Percent of Counties with Higher Proportion of Type 5 than Type 4 Tracts, by Market Strength, 2005–2009   73

4.1   Washington, DC Metropolitan Area   89

4.2   Frequency Distribution, Percent Black/African American, Washington, DC Metropolitan Area, 2010   90

4.3   Census Tracts with Proportion Black/African Population Greater Than One Positive Standard Deviation from Mean, Washington, DC Metropolitan Area, 2010   91

4.4   Census Tracts with Proportion Black/African American Population Greater Than Two Positive Standard Deviations from Mean, Washington, DC Metropolitan Area, 2010   92

4.5   Weighted Spatial Mean and Standard Distance, Black/African
       American Proportion of the Population, Washington, DC
       Metropolitan Area, 2010   93
4.6   Frequency Distribution, Latino Proportion of the Population,
       Washington, DC Metropolitan Area, 2010   94
4.7   Census Tracts with Latino Proportion of the Population Greater
       Than One Positive Standard Deviation, Washington, DC
       Metropolitan Area, 2010   95
4.8   Census Tracts with Latino Proportion of the Population Greater
       Than Two Positive Standard Deviations, Washington, DC
       Metropolitan Area, 2010   96
4.9   Weighted Spatial Mean and Standard Distance, Latino Proportion
       of the Population, Washington, DC Metropolitan Area, 2010   97
4.10   Frequency Distribution, Non-Hispanic White Proportion of the
       Population, Washington DC Metropolitan Area, 2010   98
4.11   Census Tract Overlap of Non-Hispanic White and Black/African
       American Population with Greater Than One and Two Positive
       Standard Deviations, Washington, DC Metropolitan Area, 2010   99
4.12   Spatial Means in Comparison   100
4.13   Census Tracts with Non-Hispanic White Proportion of the
       Population Greater Than One Positive Standard Deviation,
       Washington, DC Metropolitan Area, 2010   102
4.14   Top Ten Tracts with Greatest Positive Change in Proportion
       Non-Hispanic White Population, District of Columbia, 2010   103
4.15   Frequency Distribution Proportion, Persons Age 25–29,
       Washington, DC Metropolitan Area, 2010   105
4.16   Young Worker Proportion of the Population Greater Than One
       Standard Deviation, Washington, DC Metropolitan Area, 2010   106
4.17   Weighted Spatial Mean and Standard Distance, Young Worker
       Proportion of the Population, Washington, DC Metropolitan Area,
       2010   107
6.1   Example of Mansionization in Baltimore County, Maryland   141
6.2   Priority Funding Areas in the Baltimore Region   142
6.3   Number of Permits Issued for Single-Family Residential
       Redevelopment in the Baltimore Suburbs, 1999 to 2011   143
6.4   Location of Single-Family Residential Redevelopment Permits
       Issued in the Baltimore Suburbs, 1999 to 2011   144
6.5   Dollar Amount for Single-Family Residential Development in the
       Baltimore Suburbs by Census Block Group, 1999 to 2011   145
7.1   Transformation of the Metropolitan Spatial Structure and Inner-
       Ring Suburbs   154
7.2   Metropolitan Growth Patterns and Inner-Ring Suburban Decline   157
7.3   Trends of Relative Per Capita Income (PCI) for the 100 largest
       CBSAs by Sub-area (1970–2007)   161

7.4   Poverty Rate for the 100 Largest CBSAs by Sub-area (1970–2007)   161
7.5   Proportion of Population of Color for the 100 Largest CBSAs by
       Sub-area (1970–2007)   163
7.6   Ratio of the Proportion or College Graduates to the Average for the
       100 Largest CBSAs by Sub-area (1970–2007)   165
7.7   Scatterplots of Sprawl Index and Per Capita Income (PCI) for
       Inner-Ring Suburbs (1980–2007)   169
7.8   Scatterplots Comparing Sprawl Index and Inner-Ring Suburban
       Poverty for the 100 Largest CBSAs (1980–2007)   170
9.1   Locations of Liberty Road, Bel Air Road, and Reisterstown Road
       in Baltimore County, Maryland   190
10.1   General Fund Balance per Capita for Case Study Cities, 2005–09
       (2011 Dollars)   224
10.2   Common Size Ratio for All Governmental Funds, Case Study
       Sites, 2005–09   225

List of Tables

2.1 Total and Poor Population in Extreme-Poverty Tracts, 1990 to 2005–2009 21

2.2 Total and Poor Population in Extreme-Poverty Tracts by Community Type, 2000 to 2005–2009 23

2.3 Total and Poor Population in Extreme-Poverty Tracts by Census Region, 100 Metro Areas, 2000 to 2005–2009 24

2.4 Top and Bottom Metro Areas for Change in Concentrated Poverty Rate, 2000 to 2005–2009 25

2.5 Change in Extreme-Poverty Neighborhoods in Cities and Suburbs, 100 Metro Areas, 1990 to 2005–2009 27

2.6 Change in Extreme-Poverty Neighborhoods by Suburban Type, 2000 to 2005–2009 28

2.7 Top and Bottom Metro Areas for Change in Concentrated Poverty Rate by City and Suburb, 2000 to 2005–2009 30

2.8 Change in Neighborhood Characteristics in Extreme-Poverty Tracts, 100 Metro Areas, 2000 to 2005–2009 33

2.9 Neighborhood Characteristics by Poverty Rate Category, 100 Metro Areas, 2005–2009 34

3.1 Typology of Suburban Census Tracts in the Largest 100 Metropolitan Statistical Areas 41

3.2 Number and Proportion of Tracts by Type, 2000 and 2005–2009 47

3.3 Prevalence of High and Low Homeownership Suburban Census Tracts, 2005–2009 48

3.4 Proportion of the Population in the 100 Largest MSAs Living in Suburban Census Tracts by Race and Ethnicity, 1990, 2000, and 2009 49

3.5 Number and Proportion of Suburban Census Tracts by Tract Type and by Poverty Rate, 2005–2009 50

3.6 Number and Proportion of Suburban Census Tracts with Moderate or High Poverty Rates by Tract Type, 2005–2009 51

3.7 Population Trends in Type 1, 2, and 3 Tracts by Poverty Level, 1990–2005–2009 54

3.8 Proportion of Long-Time Households in Type 1, 2, and 3 Tracts by Poverty Level, 2005–2009 54

3.9 Proportion of Households in Type 1, 2, and 3 Tracts by Mortgage Status and by Poverty Level, 2005–2009 55

3.10 Average and Median Owner Incomes for Households in Type 1, 2, and 3 Tracts by Mortgage Status and by Poverty Level, 2005–2009 55

3.11	Year Housing Units Built in Type 1, 2, and 3 Tracts by Poverty level, 2005–2009	57
3.12	Comparison of Tract- and MSA-level Median Value-to-Median Household Income Ratios for Type 1, 2, and 3 Tracts, 2005–2009	64
3.13	Proportion of Type 1, 2, and 3 Tracts where Median Value-to-Median Household Income Ratio is Less Than or More Than Their MSA's Ratio, by Poverty Level, 2005–2009	65
3.14	Homeownership Rates by Race and Ethnicity in High Homeownership Tracts, 2005–2009	65
3.15	Regional Breakdown of Type 1, 2, and 3 Tracts, 2009	67
3.16	Age of Housing in Type 4 Tracts by Region, 2005–2009	72
5.1	Socioeconomic Characteristics of Farmers Branch, Texas, 1970–2005–2009	114
5.2	Socioeconomic Characteristics of Carpentersville, Illinois, 1970–2005–2009	115
6.1	Coefficient Results from Stepwise Regression. Dependent Variable: Total Dollar Amount for Redevelopment Permits Issued by Census Block Group	147
7.1	100 Largest CBSAs by Urban Containment Policy Type	159
7.2	Average Relative Per Capita Income (PCI) and Relative PCI Change of the 100 Largest CBSAs by Sub-area (1970–2007)	160
7.3	Poverty Rate for the 100 Largest CBSAs by Sub-area (1970–2007)	160
7.4	Proportion of Population of Color for the 100 Largest CBSAs by Sub-area (1970–2007)	162
7.5	Proportion of College Graduates for the 100 Largest CSBAs by Sub-area (1970–2007)	164
7.6	ANOVA Mean Difference Test for the 100 Largest CBSAs by Metropolitan Growth Policy	166
7.7	Sprawl Index by Containment Type for the 100 Largest CBSAs (1970–2007)	168
9.1	Median Property Values of Single-Family Owner-Occupied Homes in Liberty Road, Bel Air Road, and Reisterstown Road, 1970–2006–2010 (in 2010 Dollars)	197
9.2	Median Household Incomes in Liberty Road, Bel Air Road, and Reisterstown Road, 1970–2006–2010 (inflation-adjusted)	198
10.1	Most-Distressed Suburbs Classification by Per Capita GDP and Total Population Change	219
11.1	Characteristics of Nonprofit Suburban Social Service Providers Surveyed in Metropolitan Chicago, Los Angeles, and Washington, DC	254
11.2	Demographic Characteristics: Population by Race and Ethnicity, Metropolitan Los Angeles, 2005–2009	255
11.3	Demographic Characteristics: Population by Race and Ethnicity, Metropolitan Chicago, 2005–2009	256

11.4   Demographic Characteristics: Population by Race and Ethnicity,
        Metropolitan Washington, DC, 2005–2009   258
11.5   Proportion and Number of Immigrant Population, Suburban Los
        Angeles Counties and Select Cities, 2005–2009   259
11.6   Characteristics of Immigrant Population, Select Cities in Three
        Metro Areas, 2005–2009   260
11.7   Demographic Characteristics: Population below the Federal
        Poverty Line, Metropolitan Los Angeles, 2005–2009   263
11.8   Demographic Characteristics: Population below the Federal
        Poverty Line, Metropolitan Chicago, 2005–2009   264
11.9   Demographic Characteristics: Population below the Federal
        Poverty Line,Metropolitan Washington, DC, 2005–2009   266
11.10   Survey Respondents' Space Usage in 2010   271
11.11   Type of Coping Strategy Being Considered for Coming Year   275

Notes on Contributors

Scott W. Allard is Professor at the Daniel J. Evans School of Public Affairs at the University of Washington, USA. He has a Ph.D. from the University of Michigan. His research focuses on issues of place, poverty, and safety net provision. He is author of the book, *Out of Reach: Place, Poverty, and the New American Welfare State* that explores the spatial contours of the modern safety net.

Katrin B. Anacker is Associate Professor at George Mason University, Arlington, Virginia, USA. She earned her Ph.D. in City and Regional Planning from The Ohio State University. She is the author of the book *Analyzing Mature Suburbs in Ohio through Property Values* and numerous articles published in peer-reviewed academic journals.

Karen Beck Pooley is a Senior Associate at czb LLC and teaches at Lehigh University. She was previously the Executive Director of the Allentown (PA) Redevelopment Authority and a Deputy Director with New York City's Department of Housing Preservation and Development. She has a Ph.D. in City Planning from the University of Pennsylvania. Both her research and professional work focus on neighborhood revitalization strategies and the evolution of federal, state and local housing policy.

Benjamin Y. Clark is Assistant Professor in the Levin College of Urban Affairs at Cleveland State University. He has a Ph.D. from the University of Georgia. His research interests include public budgeting and finance, city management, and co-production. He has published in journals including *Public Administration Review*, *Journal of Policy Analysis & Management*, *Policy Studies Journal*, and *Policy Sciences*.

Carolyn Gallaher is an Associate Professor at American University. She is a political geographer by training, but her research interests also include metropolitan areas. She is currently working on a project about the politics of condo conversion and gentrification in Washington DC. She has published two books and numerous journal articles in high ranking geography journals including *Antipode, Society and Space*, and *ACME* among others.

Bernadette Hanlon is Assistant Professor in the City and Regional Planning program at Ohio State University. She is author of *Once the American Dream: Inner-ring Suburbs of the Metropolitan United States*. Professor Hanlon recently co-authored *Global Migration: The Basics* with Thomas J. Vicino (Routledge). Her research focuses on the growth, decline and redevelopment of diverse communities.

Kathryn W. Hexter directs the Center for Community Planning and Development at the Levin College of Urban Affairs, Cleveland State University, Cleveland, Ohio. She has a M.C.R.P. from Harvard. A public policy analyst, she conducts program evaluations, research and technical assistance projects in the public, philanthropic and non-profit sectors. Her research interests include suburban poverty, community and neighborhood development, affordable housing and foreclosure prevention. She is an author of two books and numerous articles on these issues.

Edward (Ned) Hill is Dean, Professor and Distinguished Scholar at the Levin College of Urban Affairs; Nonresident Senior Fellow of The Brookings Institution; and Adjunct Professor of Public Administration at the South China University of Technology. Ned writes on economic development and urban public policy and edited *Economic Development Quarterly*.

W. Dennis Keating is a Distinguished Professor of Planning and Director, Master of Urban Planning, Design and Development Program in the Department of Urban Studies, Levin College of Urban Affairs, at Cleveland State University. His research interests and publications include urban policy, housing policy and programs, neighborhood development and land use planning law.

Elizabeth Kneebone is a Fellow at the Metropolitan Policy Program at Brookings. She has a Master's in Public Policy from the University of Chicago. Her research primarily focuses on urban and suburban poverty and metropolitan demographic and economic trends. Her publications include *Confronting Suburban Poverty in America* (Brookings Press, 2013).

Sugie Lee is Associate Professor at Hanyang University in Seoul, Korea. He has a Ph.D. from the School of City and Regional Planning at Georgia Institute of Technology in Atlanta, Georgia, USA. His research interests include land use, urban spatial structure, smart growth and New Urbanism, and urban design. He has published numerous articles, including several that focus on metropolitan growth patterns and inner-ring suburban decline.

Nancey Green Leigh, Professor of City and Regional Planning and an Associate Dean for Research at Georgia Institute of Technology, co-edits the *Journal of Planning Education and Research*. Specializing in economic development planning, she has published more than 50 articles and three books, *Stemming Middle Class Decline: The Challenge to Economic Development Planning* (1994); *Economic*

Revitalization: Cases and Strategies for City and Suburb (2002 with J. Fitzgerald); and *Planning Local Economic Development*, 5th edition (2013 with E.J. Blakely).

Brian A. Mikelbank is an Associate Professor of Urban Studies in the Maxine Goodman Levin College of Urban Affairs at Cleveland State University. He is an urban geographer whose research focuses on the spatial analysis of metropolitan housing markets and the dynamics of urban-suburban change.

Andrew McMillan is a Ph.D. student in the Department of Urban and Regional Planning at the University of Illinois at Urbana-Champaign. His research interests include affordable housing, land use, and quantitative spatial analysis.

Carey Anne Nadeau, formerly a Research Analyst with the Brookings Institution, is a Master's in City Planning Candidate (2015) at Massachusetts Institute of Technology and a Research Assistant to Professor Amy Glasmeier, quantifying a living wage and assessing access to economic opportunity for low-income families in U.S. metropolitan areas.

Charles Post has been a Project Manager/Research Associate in the Maxine Goodman Levin College of Urban Affairs at Cleveland State University since 1992. He has an MA from Washington University and an MS from Carnegie-Mellon University. Charlie's research interests include urban sprawl, tax base disparity, and housing trends.

Benjamin J. Roth is Assistant Professor at the University of South Carolina in Columbia, South Carolina. He has a Ph.D. from the University of Chicago. His research interests include urban and suburban poverty, the nonprofit safety net, and immigrant integration. He has authored several articles and book chapters that examine the intersection of poverty and immigrant adaptation.

Gregory Smithsimon is Associate Professor of Sociology at Brooklyn College, CUNY. He is the author of *September 12: Community and Neighborhood Recovery at Ground Zero* (NYU Press) and, with Benjamin Shepard, *The Beach beneath the Streets: Contesting New York City's Public Spaces* (SUNY Press). His current project is *Liberty Road: African American Middle-Class Suburbs between Civil Rights and Neoliberalism*, on how suburban space reframes political conflicts for middle-class African Americans.

Thomas J. Vicino is Associate Professor of Political Science at Northeastern University. He has a Ph.D. in Public Policy from the University of Maryland. His research interests focus on the political economy of metropolitan America, and he is the co-author most recently of the book *Global Migration: The Basics* (Routledge, 2014).

Acknowledgments

This project was supported by a seed grant from the Faculty Research Funding for Tenure-Track and Tenured Faculty program, awarded by the Office of the Provost of George Mason University. Dr. Roger Stough, former Vice President of Research and Economic Development, supported my application and thus made this project possible. I would like to thank Matthew Ogborn for his superb copy editing efforts, and the three anonymous reviewers for their constructive comments. Katy Crossan, Margaret Younger, and other team members were a pleasure to work with over the many months it took to bring this volume together.

Books, including edited volumes, are an outcome of collaborative efforts over many years, sometimes decades. I became interested in mature suburbs during my time at The Ohio State University thanks to Dr. Hazel Morrow-Jones, who first competently supervised my research on mature shopping centers and then my further research on property values in mature suburbs in the Cleveland, Columbus, and Cincinnati metropolitan statistical areas and was an utmost pleasure to work with. Over the past several years I have been honored to receive constructive feedback on my work on suburbs at numerous conferences, including the annual conferences of the Association of Collegiate Schools of Planning (ACSP), the Urban Affairs Association (UAA), the Association of American Geographers (AAG), and the Association of Public Policy and Management (APPAM). In addition to these regular conferences I have been privileged to benefit from intellectually stimulating comments at several suburban conferences, for example, "A Suburban World? Global Decentralization and the New Metropolis" hosted by Virginia Tech Alexandria in April 2008; "The Diverse Suburb: History, Politics, and Prospects" conference at Hofstra University in October 2009; the "From the Outside In: Sustainable Futures for Global Cities and Suburbs" conference at Hofstra University in March 2013; the "Out of Control Suburbs? Comparing Representations of Order, Disorder, and Sprawl" conference at Hofstra University (co-hosted with the University of Exeter) in June 2013; and the "Global Suburbanisms: Governance, Land and Infrastructure in the 21st Century" conference at York University in September 2013.

Over the years some of these conference attendees have not only remained colleagues but become close collaborators for whose intellectual stimulations I have been grateful. These are scholars such as Scott Allard, Victoria Basolo, Thomas Bier, Jim Carr, John Carruthers, Karen Chapple, Rachel Franklin, Robert Freestone, Todd Gardner, Jill Grant, Nicole Gurran, Bernadette Hanlon, Kingsley Haynes, Sonia Hirt, Kathryn Howell, Elena Irwin, Yuki Kato, W. Dennis Keating, Roger Keil, Tom Kingsley, Jim Klein, Marti Klein, Robert

Lake, John Landis, Sugie Lee, Christa Lee-Chuvala, Larry Levy, Thomas Ludden, Paul Maginn, Sarah Mawhorter, Ali Modarres, Markus Moos, Stephen Mulherin, Darla Munroe, Alexandra Murphy, Christopher Niedt, Myron Orfield, Burcu Ozuduru, Rolf Pendall, Kathy Pettit, Haifeng Quian, David Phillips, David Rain, Bill Randolph, Gillad Rosen, Benjamin Roth, Upal Basu Roy, Deni Ruggeri, Laurie Schintler, Alex Schwartz, Roger Stough, Ayse Tekel, Margery Austin Turner, Thomas Vicino, Alan Walks, June Williamson, Elvin Wyly, and Becky Yust, among others.

One of my closest collaborators in the field of suburban studies has been Christopher Niedt, who has been incredibly inspiring, fiercely ambitious, and wildly supportive. I hope to continue our rewarding and productive collaboration for many decades to come. Lastly, I wish to thank my parents Jürgen and Erika Anacker, who have supported my academic journey, which started at the University of Kiel/ Germany, led me to The Ohio State University thanks to a Fulbright Fellowship, continued at Virginia Tech Alexandria thanks to a postdoctoral fellowship, and has a current stop at George Mason University in Arlington, Virginia. I could not have been luckier to have their stalwart support. *Nein, ihr braucht das Buch nicht lesen.*

Chapter 1

Introduction

Katrin B. Anacker

Over the past several decades some suburban picture windows in the United States have developed cracks (Jackson 1985, Baxandall and Ewen 2000). Many suburbs are no longer places with high proportions of home-owning non-Hispanic Whites and native borns with relatively high household incomes, high levels of education, and without any problems (Teaford 2008, Keil 2013, Kneebone and Berube 2013). Indeed, some suburbs have never had these characteristics (Nicolaides 2002, Wiese 2004). Interestingly, perception has been lagging behind. As Bier (1991) stated, "Suburbanites have had the mistaken belief that an impenetrable wall stands between them and the problems and threats in the city […]" (48). Denton and Gibbons (2013) referred to the difference between reality and perception as the "'hidden frame' that many carry around in their heads of suburban areas as places with single-family detached houses occupied by two white parents and their children" and state that "[w]hat is perhaps more surprising is the perseverance of that image, and, more importantly, the fact that the desirability of suburbs as a place to live is still rooted in the images found in that frame" (29).

Communities of concern have been suburbs located outside central cities and inside metropolitan statistical area (MSA) boundaries, especially those built from World War II until the late 1960s. Different labels have been used to designate these suburbs, ranging from mature suburbs (Anacker 2009), first ring suburbs (Rokakis and Katz 2001), inner-ring suburbs (First Suburbs Consortium Housing Initiative 2002), inner-ring cities (Advisory Commission on Intergovernmental Relations 1984), inner suburbs (Sutker 1974), first suburbs (Puentes and Orfield 2002, Puentes and Warren 2006), first-tier suburbs (Hudnut 2003), older suburbs (Kotkin 2001, Lucy and Phillips 2001, and others), or older hubs (Listokin and Beaton 1983). Despite these different labels, concerns have remained the same or even increased among an interdisciplinary body of contributing authors in disciplines and professional fields such as sociology, political science, history, economics, urban studies, urban and regional planning, and public policy.

Since the mid-1980s the literature on suburbs has repeatedly discussed changes in their demographics, socioeconomics, and housing stock. While earlier works have focused on suburban decline and diversity, more recent works have focused on poverty and the possible end of suburbs, possibly indicating a reduced gap between reality and perception (Baldassare 1986, Kunstler 1993, Lucy and Phillips 2000, 2006, Vicino 2008, Hanlon 2010, Hanlon et al. 2010, Gallagher 2013, Kneebone and Berube 2013). In regard to methods, descriptions, anecdotal evidence, archival research, expert interviews, and descriptive statistics were common from the 1980s to the mid-2000s. Expert interviews, typologies, and quantitative (especially regression) analyses have been utilized since the mid-2000s. Examples of works that fall within the two categories of suburban decline and diversity, and poverty and the possible end of suburbs, are discussed in some detail below, followed by a section on suburban policy.

One of the first analyses on suburban decline and diversity was provided by Baldassare (1986), who utilized two surveys in Orange County, California, in 1982 and 1983 to establish four hypotheses. First, homeownership by suburban residents is largely a function of the length of residence; second, recent homeowners have higher housing costs than other homeowner groups; third, suburban residents continue overwhelmingly to favor the single-family home, and most renters desire to own a home although most who desire to own a home are pessimistic that this goal will be reached; and fourth, most suburban renters are willing to compromise their ideal housing for a small and affordable home that they can own. Baldassare's observations were continued by Bier (1991) and Lucy and Phillips (2000). The latter analyzed select suburbs in terms of the age of the housing stock and median family incomes from 1960 to 1990 and concluded that the studied older suburbs declined in population and income (although income decline was not associated with housing age) and that many suburbs declined faster than central cities.

Adding to these observations, Hudnut (2003) provided portraits of select U.S. first-tier suburbs, based on expert interviews and field visits, that are "stressed and, in some instances, distressed" (xii), illustrating a declining and aging population; rapid racial, ethnic, and nativist change; an increasing proportion of residents in or near poverty who thus have an increasing need for social services; an aging housing stock and infrastructure; and a declining tax base. A few years later Lucy and Phillips (2006) updated their analyses of select suburbs based on 1990 and 2000 data and found (again) a decline in terms of population; an increase in terms of Blacks/African Americans, immigrants, and senior citizens, and thus more diversity; and housing vacancies. Also, Lucy and Phillips found indicators of poverty in terms of lower incomes and lower income growth relative to their metropolitan areas from 1990 to 2000, as well as an increase in concentrated poverty in suburban neighborhoods from 1980 to 2000.

While these contributions illustrated that select suburban communities faced challenges, the question remained whether these descriptions and analyses were generalizable. Thus, regional or national suburban typologies were established. One of the first suburban typologies was created by Orfield (2002), who identified six different types of suburbs: at risk, segregated; at risk, older; at risk, low density; bedroom developing; affluent job center; and very affluent job center. He found that the three types of at-risk suburbs were communities with relatively high poverty rates that had only two-thirds of the fiscal capacity of their respective central cities and that their fiscal capacity was growing slowly. "Once poverty and social instability permeate communities just outside the central city and begin to grow in older satellite cities, decline accelerates and intensifies" (Orfield 2002: 35). Another example of these national suburban typologies is the one suggested by Mikelbank (2004), who conducted a national study and identified ten distinct types of suburbs: seasonal wealth, traditional, small retail, Black, struggling, prosperity, working stability, aging, South/Western diversity, and central diversity, pointing out that there is an increasing diversity in population, especially in terms of race as well as function in these communities.

Hanlon (2010) established a national typology of inner-ring suburbs, identifying four types: elite, middle class, vulnerable, and ethnic, again concluding that "inner-ring suburbs, first built as bedroom communities in the postwar period and earlier, have evolved into places with varied characteristics, assets, and problems" (131). The typology of inner-ring suburbs was followed by a more recent model called The New Metropolitan Reality by Hanlon et al. (2010). This model encompassed the following metropolitan forms: (1) central cities, (2) early suburbs, (3) exurbs, (4) edge cities, (5) edgeless cities, (6) megalopolis, (7) boomburbs, (8) metroburbia, and, in sum, (9) The New Metropolitan Reality model, which reflects the complexities of the current and future changes. This model is characterized by influences from politics, economics, and social and spatial components.

In a study on Ohio, Anacker (2009) established a typology based on suburbs in three counties in Ohio, Cuyahoga County, Franklin County, and Hamilton County, where Cleveland, Columbus, and Cincinnati are located, respectively. Based on quantitative and qualitative analyses, she classified suburbs in mature and developing suburbs and defines the former as having at least two of the following three characteristics: first, it shares a boundary with the adjacent central city of the area; second, it does not share a boundary with an adjacent unincorporated area (called a township in Ohio); and third, it falls in the lower half of all municipalities in each county ranked by proportion of vacant residential parcels. In other words, it has little land available for development.

In a national study, Kneebone and Berube (2013) differentiated among four types of suburban jurisdictions that experienced growing poverty from 2000 to 2008/10. First, rapid growth suburbs had above average population growth and above average change in regional employment. Second, strained suburbs had above average population growth but below average change in regional employment. Third, at risk suburbs had below average population growth yet above average change in regional employment. Fourth, distressed suburbs had below average population growth and below average change in regional employment.

Quantitatively, regression analyses that focus on suburbs have been utilized for more than a decade. Many works have focused on demographic and socioeconomic factors. For example, Vicino (2008) analyzed patterns of suburban change in the first-tier suburban communities of Baltimore at two data points, 1970 and 2000, and presented evidence of suburban decline in terms of (a) population characteristics, (b) income dynamics, (c) the nature of the housing stock, and (d) labor force structure based on a principal component analysis. At a broader level, Vicino concludes that suburban decline is fundamentally an income problem (i.e., a regional problem), as income earners are mobile, but also a housing problem (i.e., a local problem), as housing units are fixed.

Some work has focused on suburban housing, especially property values, in the suburbs. For example, Anacker (2009) analyzed property values in mature and developing suburbs in three metropolitan areas in Ohio and found a high degree of unevenness of property values and their appreciation rates within mature suburbs, countering the myth that property values increase to a greater degree in suburbs compared with central cities. Also, she found that space, operationalized as square footage and the number of bathrooms, is of particular importance in mature suburbs in Ohio. Thus, design approaches should be continued and improved to address this issue (First Suburbs Consortium Housing Initiative 2002). National analyses showed that suburban census tracts that are predominantly non-Hispanic White are better off in terms of the analyzed characteristics than suburban census tracts with high proportions of residents of color (Anacker 2010). More specifically, Black/African American and Latino suburbs have relatively low property values and low appreciation rates. In contrast, non-Hispanic White and Asian suburbs have relatively high property values and high appreciation rates, controlling for many factors (Anacker 2010, 2012). Follow-up national work on suburbs in immigrant gateways also illustrated variety (Anacker 2013).

The works discussed above focus on suburban decline and diversity. More recently, a strand of the suburban literature has discussed poverty and the possible end of suburbs, consistent with the literature on community lifecycles (Gallagher 2013). One of the first who fall into this group is Leinberger (2008), who argues that mixed-use walkable urban areas will see an increase in demand and that major changes are ahead for the suburbs. "If gasoline and heating costs continue to rise, conventional suburban living may not be much of a bargain in the future," (Leinberger 2008: n.p.). He states that it is difficult if not impossible to convert cheaply built suburban homes to nonresidential uses. Thus, homes could be converted into rental units, "which would herald the arrival of the poor" for some suburbs (Leinberger 2008: n.p.).

Kneebone and Berube (2013) explore "the complicated changes occurring in suburban communities that for several decades defined the middle-class American dream. Why is poverty on the rise there? What are the consequences for those places and their residents?" (3). The authors stress that suburban poverty is not necessarily better or worse but "aim to understand how it is *different* in its origins, its consequences, and its implications for policy" (12, italics in original). They conclude that suburban neighborhoods are safer and that suburban schools are of higher quality, yet many residents are isolated in terms of transportation, social services, employment, and community support. They also conclude that, compared to the urban poor, the suburban poor are different in terms of race and the homeownership rate.

Interestingly, many of the suburban changes discussed above have been assisted by policies, as Bier (1991) observed, stating that "public policy is working against itself" (43) for the Cleveland area. While some policies push people outward and invite city decline, others combat decline through revitalization and community development. As the policies working against the city are more powerful than the policies working for it, cities face an uphill battle when it comes to combating decline.

Similarly, Puentes and Orfield (2002) pointed out that first suburbs are caught in a policy blindspot.

> Unlike central cities, they are not poor enough to qualify for many federal and state reinvestment programs and not large enough to receive federal and state funds directly. Unlike newer suburbs, they are ill suited to federal and state programs that focus on building new infrastructure and housing rather than maintaining, preserving and removing what is already built. (3)

Hudnut (2003) pointed out the existence of federal, state, and county programs that benefit these communities yet concluded that "first-tier suburbs do not benefit from the wider tax base or more numerous services in the big city nearby, or from the substantial tax base and low need for services of their newer and more affluent neighbors in the outer suburbs" (xiii).

There seems to be agreement that cities and suburbs are interdependent (Ledebur and Barnes 1992, Voith 1992, Ledebur 1993, Savitch et al. 1993, but see also Garreau 1991, Blair and Zhang 1994 for alternative findings). Thus, regional strategies have been suggested to address issues that not only affect principal cities but increasingly the suburbs. Rusk (1999) divides urban policy efforts into two categories, the "inside game" and the "outside game." The former encompasses many antipoverty initiatives that the federal government has implemented to target challenged principal city neighborhoods, for example, Community Action Grants, Model Cities Programs, Community Development Block Grants, Urban Development Action Grants, Empowerment Community and Enterprise Zone Funds, and Tax Credits. Being part of the "inside game," according to Rusk (1999), means looking to Washington for "subsidy" or assistance. The latter denotes establishing regional strategies, for example, (1) helping control sprawl by requiring regional land use planning; (2) helping dissolve concentrations of poverty and ensuring that all suburbs provide their fair share of low- and moderate-income housing; and (3) helping reduce fiscal disparities by implementing regional revenue sharing. Therefore, "for both poverty-impacted cities and poverty-impacted neighborhoods, even the strongest 'inside game' must be matched by a strong 'outside game'" (Rusk 1999: 13).

Whereas Rusk is primarily concerned with central cities in the Northeast and Midwest, most of which cannot annex or consolidate, Orfield (1997, 2002) is primarily concerned with the entire metropolitan region in any part of the country and pays special attention to declining suburbs. He argues that "once [regional] polarization occurs, the concentration of poverty, disinvestment, middle-class flight, and urban sprawl grow more and more severe […] There is essentially no federal urban policy left to deal with this polarization or its costs" (Orfield

1997: 1). Orfield suggests six substantive reforms and one structural reform at the metropolitan level to stabilize principal cities and older suburbs. In terms of socioeconomic stability of the core, he proposes (1) fair housing, (2) property tax-base sharing; (3) reinvestment; (4) land planning and growth management; (5) welfare reform and public works; and (6) transportation and transit reform (see also Downs 1994, Dodge 1996, Pastor et al. 2000, Calthorpe and Fulton 2001, Pastor et al. 2009).

Hanlon (2010) points out the existing federal programs, for example, the Community Development Block Grant (CDBG), Urban Action Grants, Empowerment Zone funding, and HOPE VI projects, yet concludes that "little in the way of national urban policy is aimed specifically at curbing decline in U.S. metropolitan areas, and, since the 1980s, federal assistance to declining cities has been greatly reduced" (133). She discusses state policies in the realms of growth management, the rehabilitation of aging housing stock, and community redevelopment, although these policies are not directly and exclusively aimed at suburbs of concern. Lastly, she discusses inner-ring suburban coalitions in the Midwest that were formed from 1969 until 2003.

Lastly, Kneebone and Berube (2013) focus on issues of lower-income suburban households and discuss the jobs mismatch, the transportation challenge, the strained safety net (along with the fact that social welfare and philanthropy infrastructure is located in inner cities), access to quality schools, and the problem of perceptions. They argue that the U.S. is "fighting today's poverty with yesterday's policies" (77) and suggest modernizing the metropolitan opportunity agenda within the current fiscal and political environment through several organizational strategies.

This book has five sections. Section I focuses on suburban poverty, Section II focuses on racial, ethnic, and nativist suburban change, Section III focuses on suburban decline, Section IV focuses on suburban foreclosures, and Section V focuses on suburban policy. In Section I, Suburban Poverty, Elizabeth Kneebone and Carey Anne Nadeau analyze data from the 1990 and 2000 decennial censuses and the 2005–2009 American Community Survey (ACS) to assess the extent to which concentrations of poverty have changed within the United States in the 2000s. They conclude that the economically turbulent 2000s saw much of the progress against concentrated poverty during the booming economy of the late 1990s erased, with suburbs witnessing the steepest increases in the poor population over the decade.

Karen Beck Pooley utilizes the same datasets Kneebone and Nadeau use and argues that suburban communities in general and moderate- and high-poverty suburban communities in particular are not homogeneous. Instead, they are based on a typology of five types of suburban census tracts in the top 100 MSAs. Beck Pooley presents several stories behind these five types. First, some suburbs are struggling to attract new households or new construction; second, some suburbs have housing markets that undervalue racially and ethnically diverse neighborhoods; third, some suburbs are characterized by poverty with significant rental housing and weak housing markets while other suburbs have strong housing markets. She concludes that policymakers should tailor their responses to specific suburban problems. The more tailored the response, the more likely it is to succeed.

In Section II, racial, ethnic, and nativist suburban change are analyzed. Carolyn Gallaher looks at the spatial distribution of key demographic data from the 2010 Census in the Washington, DC Metropolitan Area, comparing and contrasting it with the Traditional Model of urban form. She focuses on the proportions of non-Hispanic Whites, Blacks/African Americans, Latinos, and population 25 to 29 years of age. Gallaher finds that Washington, DC deviates from the Traditional Model for some variables but also conforms to the Traditional Model for others.

Bernadette Hanlon and Thomas Vicino look at the devolution of immigration policy and examine local immigration policies in Farmers Branch, Texas, and Carpentersville, Illinois, arguing that suburbs are socially constructed spaces where fervent ideas around safety, socioeconomic stability, homeownership, and immigrant assimilation exist and where, in the case of Farmers Branch and Carpentersville, the dominant group and power structure was able to mobilize support for the introduction of local exclusionary immigrant legislation.

In Section III, Suburban Decline, Bernadette Hanlon points out that the debate on suburban sustainability has neglected aspects of social sustainability and argues that reinvestment in the suburbs increases social inequity within the metropolis more broadly, using the case of the Baltimore Metropolitan Area.

Sugie Lee and Andrew McMillan analyze metropolitan growth patterns and inner-ring suburban decline, focusing on urban containment policies for the 100 largest U.S. metropolitan areas based on 1970, 1980, 1990, and 2000 Censuses and 2005–2009 ACS data. They find that inner-ring suburbs experienced observable demographic and socioeconomic symptoms of decline, and that metropolitan areas with greater levels of sprawl tended to have inner-ring suburbs with relatively lower per capita incomes, but that metropolitan areas with containment policies do not show relatively lower rates of inner-ring suburban decline. Lee and McMillan conclude that there is a need for strategic initiatives that encourage revitalization in inner-ring suburbs.

In Section IV, Suburban Foreclosures, W. Dennis Keating discusses responses to foreclosure and abandonment in three inner suburbs in the Cleveland metropolitan area. He finds that these responses are similar to the responses provided in communities with blighted houses and vacant lots. While the Neighborhood Stabilization Program (NSP) has provided some much needed resources to address these issues in the past, the question remains how these resource-constrained communities will solve these issues in the future.

Greg Smithsimon analyzes community responses to demographic and economic change in three suburban communities in Baltimore County, Maryland. He shows that decline in median property values and median household incomes does not necessarily occur, although long periods of stability may be interrupted by moments of crisis, for example, the recent foreclosure crisis.

In Section V, Suburban Policy, Kathryn Hexter, Edward (Ned) Hill, Benjamin Clark, Brian Mikelbank, and Charles Post introduce strategies to revitalize select distressed older suburbs in Alabama, Michigan, Ohio, and Pennsylvania, based on a literature review, site visits, interviews, and data analyses. They recommend making programs funded by the U.S. Department of Housing and Urban Development (HUD) more flexible to spend dollars in ways that meet each suburb's most pressing needs and to support economic development projects.

Benjamin Roth and Scott Allard analyze the response of the nonprofit safety net to rising suburban poverty based on an extensive survey and site visits in suburbs of the Chicago, Illinois, Los Angeles, California, and Washington, DC metropolitan areas. They find that over the past decade many suburbs have experienced unprecedented increases in their poor population but that the nonprofit social service sector has faced numerous obstacles in its efforts to keep up with these demographic and socioeconomic changes, illustrating a spatial mismatch. As these issues will most likely persist, Roth and Allard predict a suburban geography that continues to be increasingly unequal.

All contributors utilize the term "suburbs" in their chapters, although the U.S. Bureau of the Census does not explicitly define suburbs. Some researchers define a suburb as a municipality that is not a central city but inside a metropolitan area, others define a suburb as a municipality that is not a principal city, similar to the definition of the U.S. Office of Management and Budget (U.S. Office of Management and Budget 2009). In other words, while there is consensus that a central city is not a suburb, there is much less consensus about whether some principal cities should be considered suburbs. For example, the Washington-Arlington-Alexandria, DC-VA-MD-WV Metropolitan Statistical Area officially has Washington, DC; Alexandria, Arlington, and Reston, Virginia; and Bethesda, Rockville, Frederick, and Gaithersburg, Maryland as principal cities. While the vast majority of researchers would agree that Washington, DC is not a suburb, some would argue that all the other principal cities enumerated above are.[1] The contributing chapters in this volume range from national studies to regional or local case studies. As different researchers define suburbs differently, the Editor of this volume left the definition of "suburb" to each contributor or contributing team. Thus, there is lack of consistency and thus some effect on comparability across the various chapters. Overall, however, the differences are not sufficient to detract from the value of the overall findings about suburbs.

---

1   The concept of a central city and a principal city is generally the same. In 2000, the Office of Management and Budget (OMB) adopted a new standard, which resulted in a broadening of the types of places that qualified as principal cities, allowing for the recognition of census-designated places (CDPs, which are unincorporated places) as principal cities. Previous to 2000, only incorporated municipalities could qualify as central cities (although there were exceptions). The new standard also changed the term from "central city" to "principal city." In 2003, the OMB announced the metropolitan and micropolitan statistical areas resulting from the application of the 2000 standard to 2000 Census data. In 2010, the OMB adopted a revised standard.

References

Advisory Commission on Intergovernmental Relations. 1984. *Fiscal Disparities: Central Cities & Suburbs, 1981*. Washington, DC: U.S. Government Printing Office.

Anacker, K.B. 2013. Immigrating, assimilating, cashing in? Analyzing property values in suburbs of immigrant gateways. *Housing Studies*, 28, 720–45.

Anacker, K.B. 2012. Shaky palaces? Analyzing property values and their appreciation rates in minority first suburbs. *International Journal of Urban and Regional Research*, 36, 791–816.

Anacker, K.B. 2010. Still paying the race tax? Analyzing property values in homogenous and mixed-race suburbs. *Journal of Urban Affairs*, 32, 55–77.

Anacker, K.B. 2009. *Analyzing Mature Suburb in Ohio through Property Values*. Saarbrücken/Germany: Verlag Dr. Müller.

Baldassare, M. 1986. *Trouble in Paradise: The Suburban Transformation in America*. New York, NY: Columbia University Press.

Baxandall, R. and Ewen, E. 2000. *Picture Windows: How the Suburbs Happened*. New York, NY: Basic Books.

Bier, T.E. 1991. Public policy against itself: Investments that help bring Cleveland (and eventually suburbs), down in *Cleveland Development: A Dissenting View*, edited by A.L. Schorr. Cleveland, OH: David Press.

Blair, J.P. and Zhang, Z. 1994. Ties that bind revisited. *Economic Development Quarterly*, 8, 373–77.

Calthorpe, P. and Fulton, W. 2001. *The Regional City: Planning for the End of Sprawl*. Washington, DC: Island Press.

Denton, N.A. and Gibbons, J.R. 2013. Twenty-first-century suburban demography: Increasing diversity yet lingering exclusion, in *Social Justice in Diverse Suburbs: History, Politics, and Prospects*, edited by C. Niedt. Philadelphia, PA: Temple University Press.

Dodge, W.R. 1996. *Regional Excellence: Governing Together to Compete Globally and Flourish Locally*. Washington, DC: National League of Cities.

Downs, A. 1994. *New Visions for Metropolitan America*. Washington, DC: The Brookings Institution.

First Suburbs Consortium Housing Initiative. 2002. *Bungalows: Unit Designs and Neighborhood Improvement Concepts*. Cleveland, OH: First Suburbs Consortium Housing Initiative.

Gallagher, L. 2013. *The End of the Suburbs: Where the American Dream is Moving*. New York, NY: Portfolio.

Garreau, J. 1991. *Edge City: Life on the New Frontier*. New York, NY: Anchor Books.

Hanlon, B. 2010. *Once the American Dream: Inner-Ring Suburbs of the Metropolitan United States*. Philadelphia, PA: Temple University Press.

Hanlon, B., Short, J.R., and Vicino, T.J. 2010. *Cities and Suburbs: New Metropolitan Realities in the US*. New York, NY: Routledge.

Hudnut, W.H. 2003. *Halfway to Everywhere: A Portrait of America's First-Tier Suburbs.* Washington, DC: Urban Land Institute.

Jackson, K.T. 1985. *Crabgrass Frontier: The Suburbanization of the United States.* Oxford: Oxford University Press.

Keil, R. 2013. Welcome to the suburban revolution, in *Suburban Constellations: Governance, Land, and Infrastructure in the 21st Century*, edited by R. Keil. Berlin/Germany: jovis Verlag.

Kneebone, E. and Berube, A. 2013. *Confronting Suburban Poverty in America.* Washington, DC: Brookings Institution Press.

Kotkin, J. 2001. *Older Suburbs: Crabgrass Slums or New Urban Frontier?* Los Angeles, CA: Reason Public Policy Institute.

Kunstler, J.H. 1993. *The Geography of Nowhere: The Rise and Decline of America's Man-Made Landscape.* New York, NY: Touchstone.

Ledebur, L.C. 1993. *"All in it Together": Cities, Suburbs and Local Economic Regions.* Washington, DC: National League of Cities.

Ledebur, L.C. and Barnes, W.R. 1992. *Metropolitan Disparities and Economic Growth: City Distress and the Need for a Federal Local Growth Package.* Washington, DC: The National League of Cities.

Leinberger, C. 2008. The Next Slum? The Subprime Crisis is just the Tip of the Iceberg. Fundamental Changes in American Life May Turn Today's McMansions into Tomorrow's Tenements. Available at: http://www.theatlantic.com/magazine/archive/2008/03/the-next-slum/306653/ [accessed: February 15, 2014].

Listokin, D. and Beaton, W.P. 1983. *Revitalizing the Older Suburb.* New Brunswick, NJ: Center for Urban Policy Research.

Lucy, W.H. and Phillips, D.L. 2006. *Tomorrow's Cities, Tomorrow's Suburbs.* Chicago, IL: Planners Press.

Lucy, W.H. and Phillips, D.L. 2001. Suburban Population and Income Change: 554 Suburbs in 24 Metropolitan Areas, 1960 to 2000. Draft.

Lucy, W.H. and Phillips, D.L. 2000. *Confronting Suburban Decline: Strategic Planning or Metropolitan Renewal.* Washington, DC: Island Press.

Mikelbank, B.A. 2004. A typology of U.S. suburban places. *Housing Policy Debate*, 15, 935–64.

Nicolaides, B.M. 2002. *My Blue Heaven: Life and Politics in the Working-Class Suburbs of Los Angeles, 1920–1965.* Chicago, IL: The University of Chicago Press.

Orfield, M. 2002. *American Metropolitics: The New Suburban Reality.* Washington, DC: The Brookings Institution Press.

Orfield, M. 1997. *Metropolitics: A Regional Agenda for Community and Stability.* Washington, DC: Brookings Institution Press.

Pastor, M., Benner, C., and Matsuoka, M. 2009. *This Could Be the Start of Something Big: How Social Movements for Regional Equity Are Reshaping Metropolitan America.* Ithaca, NY: Cornell University Press.

Pastor, M., Dreier, P., Grigsby, J.E., and Lopez-Garza, M. 2000. *Regions That Work: How Cities and Suburbs Can Grow Together*. Minneapolis, MN: University of Minnesota Press.

Puentes, R. and Orfield, M. 2002. *Valuing America's First Suburbs: A Policy Agenda for Older Suburbs in the Midwest*. Washington, DC: The Brookings Institution Press.

Puentes, R. and Warren, D. 2006. *One-Fifth of America: A Comprehensive Guide to America's First Suburbs*. Washington, DC: The Brookings Institution Press.

Rokakis, J. and Katz, H. 2001. *One Tool in Revitalization of First Ring Suburbs—Cuyahoga County's Home Enhancement Loan Program (HELP)*. Cleveland, OH: Cuyahoga County.

Rusk, D. 1999. *Inside Game/Outside Game: Winning Strategies for Saving Urban America*. Washington, DC: Brookings Institution Press.

Savitch, H.V., Collins, D., Sanders, D., and Markham, J.P. 1993. Ties that bind: Central cities, suburbs, and the new metropolitan region. *Economic Development Quarterly*, 7, 341–57.

Sutker, S. 1974. New settings for racial transition, in *Racial Transition in the Inner Suburb: Studies of the St. Louis Area*, edited by S. Sutker and S.S. Sutker. London: Praeger Publishers.

Teaford, J.C. 2008. *The American Suburb: The Basics*. New York, NY: Routledge.

U.S. Office of Management and Budget. 2009. *OMB Bulletin No. 10–02*. Washington, DC: Executive Office of the President: Office of Management and Budget.

Vicino, T.J. 2008. *Transforming Race and Class in Suburbia: Decline in Metropolitan Baltimore*. New York, NY: Palgrave Macmillan.

Voith, R. 1992. City and suburban growth: Substitutes or complements? *Business Review* (Federal Reserve Bank of Philadelphia), September/October, 21–33.

Wiese, A. 2004. *Places of Their Own: African American Suburbanization in the Twentieth Century*. Chicago, IL: The University of Chicago Press.

SECTION I
Suburban Poverty

Chapter 2

The Resurgence of Concentrated Poverty in America: Metropolitan Trends in the 2000s

Elizabeth Kneebone and Carey Anne Nadeau

Introduction[1]

As the first decade of the 2000s drew to a close, the two downturns that bookended the period, both followed by weak recoveries, clearly took their toll on the nation's less fortunate residents. Over a ten-year span, the country saw the population living below the federal poverty line grow by 12.3 million, driving the total number of Americans in poverty to a historic high of 46.2 million in 2010. By the end of the decade, over 15 percent of the nation's population lived below the federal poverty line—$22,314 for a family of four in 2010—an increase of almost 3 percentage points over 2000, though these increases did not occur evenly throughout the country (Kneebone and Berube 2011).

The poverty data released each year by the U.S. Census Bureau show us the aggregate level of disadvantage in America, as well as what parts of the country are more or less affected by poverty. Less clear, until now, is how these trends changed the location of poor households within urban, suburban, or rural communities.

Why does the geographic distribution of the poor matter? Rather than spread evenly, the poor tend to cluster and concentrate in certain neighborhoods or groups of neighborhoods within a community. As discussed in more detail below, very poor neighborhoods face a whole host of challenges that come from concentrated disadvantage—from higher crime rates and poorer health outcomes to lower-quality educational opportunities and weaker job networks. A poor person or family in a poor neighborhood must then deal not only with the challenges of individual poverty but also with the added burdens that stem from the place in which they live. This double burden affects not only the families and individuals bearing it but also complicates the jobs of policymakers and service providers working to promote connections to opportunity and to alleviate poverty (Jargowsky 2003, Federal Reserve System Community Affairs Offices and the Brookings Institution 2008).

After decades of growth in the number of high-poverty neighborhoods and increasing concentrations of the poor in such areas, the booming economy of the 1990s led to a significant de-concentration of American poverty (Jargowsky

---

1   This chapter was adapted from Kneebone, Nadeau, and Berube (2011).

1997, 2003). Shortly after the onset of the 2000s, however, that progress seemed to erode as the economy slowed, though until recently researchers have lacked the necessary data to fully assess the changes in the spatial organization of the poor over the past decade (Kneebone and Berube 2008, Pendall et al. 2011).

After a brief overview of the methods, this chapter uses data from the decennial census and American Community Survey to update previous analyses and assess the extent to which concentrations of poverty have changed within the United States in the 2000s. We first analyze the trends for the nation as a whole, as well as metropolitan and nonmetropolitan communities, but focus primarily on changes in concentrated poverty within and across the nation's 100 largest metropolitan areas, which are home to two-thirds of the nation's residents and over 60 percent of the country's poor population.

Why Does Place Matter?

Being poor in a poor neighborhood subjects residents to costs and limitations above and beyond the burdens of individual poverty. Summarized in part below, research has shown the wide-ranging social and economic effects that result when the poor are concentrated in economically segregated and disadvantaged neighborhoods.[2]

Education

Children in high-poverty communities tend to go to neighborhood schools where nearly all the students are poor and at greater risk of failure, as measured by standardized tests, dropout rates, and grade retention (Century Foundation Task Force on the Common School 2002, Wodtke, Harding, and Elwert 2011). Low performance owes not only to family background but also to the negative effects high-poverty neighborhoods have on school processes and quality. Teachers in these schools tend to be less experienced, the student body more mobile, and additional systems must often be put in place to deal with the social welfare needs of the student body, creating further demands on limited resources (Lupton 2004).

Crime Rates and Health Outcomes

Crime rates, and particularly violent crime rates, tend to be higher in economically distressed inner-city neighborhoods (Ellen and Turner 1997). Faced with high crime rates, dilapidated housing stock, and the stress and marginalization of poverty, residents of poor neighborhoods demonstrate a higher incidence of poor

---

2   For a more detailed review of this literature, see Federal Reserve System Community Affairs Offices and the Brookings Institution (2008) and Berube and Katz (2005).

physical and mental health outcomes, like asthma, depression, diabetes, and heart ailments.[3]

Assets and Wealth Building

Some residents in extreme-poverty neighborhoods own their homes, yet neighborhood conditions in these areas can lead the market to devalue these assets and deny them the ability to accumulate wealth through the appreciations of house prices (Rusk 2001). Moreover, the presence of high-poverty neighborhoods can affect residents of the larger metropolitan area generally, depressing values for owner-occupied properties in the region by 13 percent on average (Galster, Cutsinger, and Malega 2008).

Private Sector Investment and Prices of Goods and Services

High concentrations of low-income and low-skilled households in a neighborhood can make the community less attractive to private investors and employers, which may limit local job opportunities and ultimately create a "spatial mismatch" between low-income residents and employment centers (Ihlanfeldt and Sjoquist 1998). In addition, lack of business competition in poor neighborhoods can drive up prices for basic goods and services—like food, car insurance, utilities, and financial services—compared to what families pay in middle-income neighborhoods (Fellowes 2006).

Costs for Local Government

The concentration of poor individuals and families—which can result in elevated welfare caseloads, high rates of indigent patients at hospitals and clinics, and the need for increased policing—burdens the fiscal capacity of local governments and can divert resources from the provision of other public goods. In turn, these dynamics can lead to higher taxes for local businesses and nonpoor residents (Pack 1998).

Methodology

To analyze recent changes in the spatial organization of poverty across the United States, we draw on a well-established body of research to define geographic units of analysis, data sources, and key measures of these trends over time.[4]

---

3 See, e.g., Cohen et al. (2003).

4 See, e.g., Jargowsky and Bane (1990), Jargowsky and Bane (1991), Danziger and Gottschalk (1987), Kasarda (1993), Kingsley and Pettit (2003).

Geographies

Census tracts make up the base units of analysis in this study.[5] The Census Bureau divides the entire United States into tracts, which are meant to delineate relatively homogeneous areas that contain roughly 4,000 people on average. They do not always align perfectly with local perceptions of neighborhood boundaries, but they provide a reasonable proxy for our purposes. Tract boundaries change over time to reflect local population dynamics; we use contemporaneous boundaries for each year of data to avoid introducing bias in the neighborhood-level analysis.[6]

Based on the location of its centroid, each tract is assigned to one of three main geography types using GIS mapping software: large metropolitan areas, small metropolitan areas, and nonmetropolitan communities. The U.S. Office of Management and Budget identified 366 metropolitan statistical areas (MSAs) in 2008. *Large metropolitan areas* include the 100 most populous based on 2008 population estimates, while the remaining 266 regions are designated as *small metropolitan areas*. Any tract in a county that falls outside of a metropolitan statistical area is considered *nonmetropolitan*.

Within the 100 largest metro areas, we designate primary city and suburban tracts. *Primary city* tracts include those with a centroid that falls within the first city in the official metropolitan statistical area name or within any other city in the MSA name with a population over 100,000. In the top 100 metro areas, 137 cities meet the primary city criteria. *Suburban* tracts make up the remainder of the metropolitan area. We also assign suburban tracts a type based on the urbanization rate of the county (net of the primary city) in which it is located. *High density* suburbs are counties where more than 95 percent of the population lived in an urbanized area in 2000; *mature* suburbs had urbanization rates of 75 to 95 percent; in *emerging* suburbs between 25 and 75 percent of the population lived in an urbanized area; and *exurbs* had urbanization rates below 25 percent in 2000.[7]

Key Measures

Throughout this study, we use the federal poverty thresholds to measure poverty. The shortcomings of the official poverty measure have been well documented.[8]

---

5   We use the terms "tracts" and "neighborhoods" interchangeably throughout the analysis.

6   For a more detailed discussion of potential bias that can result for using standardized tract boundaries across years, see Jargowsky (2003).

7   For a more detailed discussion of geography types, see Brookings Metropolitan Policy Program (2010).

8   See, e.g., National Academy of Sciences (1995). The Census Bureau recently began releasing a supplemental poverty measure that takes into account recommendations from the 1995 NAS study; however, because the estimates are based on the Current Population Survey data, the sample size is not sufficient to report estimates for sub-state geographies.

However, the measure provides a stable benchmark—and is reported at a level of detail—that allows for tracking changes in the spatial organization of the poor over time.

To do so, we first measure the incidence of tracts with poverty rates of 40 percent or more in each year, referred to here as *extreme-poverty neighborhoods.*[9] Though any absolute threshold will have its shortcomings (neighborhoods with poverty rates of 39 percent may not differ significantly from those with poverty rates of 41 percent), previous research and policy practice have established the 40 percent parameter as a standard measure by which to designate areas of very high poverty (Jargowsky 2003).

In addition to measuring the total number of residents in extreme-poverty neighborhoods and the extent to which their characteristics change over time, we also calculate the rate of *concentrated poverty*, or the share of the poor population located in extreme-poverty tracts. Together these metrics describe not only the prevalence and location of very poor areas within a community but also the extent to which poor residents in the community are subjected to the double burden of being poor in a highly disadvantaged neighborhood.

In addition, we examine trends and characteristics in *high-poverty neighborhoods*, or those with 20 to 40 percent poverty rates. These tracts do not register in the concentrated poverty rate but may also experience heightened levels of place-based disadvantage and signal increased clustering of low-income residents in lower-opportunity neighborhoods.

Data Sources

Census tract data for this analysis come from the decennial censuses in 1990 and 2000 and the American Community Survey (ACS) five-year estimates for 2005–2009.

Key differences exist between the decennial census and the ACS that could affect comparisons. First, the decennial census is a point-in-time survey that asks recipients to report their income for the previous year. For example, Census 2000 was administered in April of that year, and its long form asked respondents to report on income in 1999. In contrast, the American Community Survey is a rolling survey that is sent out every month and asks participants to report on their income "in the last 12 months." The 12 months of data are then combined and adjusted for inflation to create a single-year estimate. The 2008 ACS estimates, for example, represent a time period that spans from January of 2007 to December of 2008.

Second, the ACS surveys a significantly smaller population (3 million households per year) than the decennial census long form (roughly 16 million households in 2000). To produce statistically reliable estimates for small geographies—like census

---

9   We exclude tracts where at least 50 percent of residents are enrolled in college or graduate school, as these individuals likely have only temporarily low incomes. We also exclude tracts with small populations (i.e., 500 people or less).

tracts—multiple years of data must be pooled. The only ACS data set that contains sufficient sample size to report on census tracts is the five-year estimates. These estimates are based on 60 months' worth of surveys that ask about income in the past 12 months, meaning they span from January of 2004 through December of 2009. They do not represent any given year but provide an adjusted estimate for the entire five-year period. This period bridges vastly different points in the economic cycle, starting with a period of recovery and modest growth and ending two years after the onset of the worst downturn since the Great Depression. The combination of such different periods likely mutes the trends studied here. For example, according to ACS single-year estimates, in 2005 the nation's poverty rate was 13.3 percent. In 2009 it was 14.3 percent. The five-year estimates place the nation's 2005–09 poverty rate at 13.5 percent, much closer to the 2005 estimate.[10]

To address the margins of error that accompany the 2005–09 data, we calculate the Z score and note where changes are significant at the 90 percent confidence level.

Findings

The Resurgence of Concentrated Poverty in the United States

The 1970s and 1980s saw high-poverty neighborhoods proliferate—in fact, they roughly doubled, along with the population living in such areas—due to a combination of economic forces and policy decisions (Jargowsky 1997). In contrast, Census 2000 recorded a significant reversal in the spatial location of the poor population.[11] Between 1990 and 2000, the number of extreme-poverty tracts declined by 29 percent, from 2,921 to 2,075 (see Table 2.1). As pockets of poverty diminished, the number of Americans living in these neighborhoods also fell, and the poor population in extreme-poverty tracts fell faster still.

These changes did not simply result from a decline in poverty (Jargowsky 2003). Over the same time period, the nation's poverty rate dropped from 13.1 to 12.4 percent—a smaller decline than the decrease in pockets of extreme poverty— but the actual number of poor individuals increased from 31.7 to 33.9 million. Thus the changes signaled a real shift in the types of neighborhoods occupied by poor individuals over that decade.

---

10   In addition, as Jargowsky pointed out in a presentation at Johns Hopkins University (9/19/2011), a region could have the same number of extreme-poverty tracts in each month for 60 months, but the exact tracts that are high poverty could change over time due to factors like gentrification or the demolition of housing units. It would then be possible, after pooling 60 months of data, that zero tracts show up as extreme poverty in the 2005–09 estimates, thereby understating concentrated poverty in the region.

11   For an analysis of concentrated poverty trends since 1970, see Jargowsky (1997) and Berube and Katz (2005).

Table 2.1   Total and Poor Population in Extreme-Poverty Tracts, 1990 to 2005–2009

Extreme-Poverty Tracts*	1990	2000	2005–09	Percent Change		
				1990 to 2000	2000 to 2005–09	1990 to 2005–09
Total Population	9,101,622	6,574,815	8,735,395	-27.8%	32.9%	-4.0%
Poor Population	4,392,749	3,011,893	4,050,538	-31.4%	34.5%	-7.8%
Number of Tracts	2,921	2,075	2,822	-29.0%	36.0%	-3.4%

*Extreme-poverty tracts have poverty rates of 40 percent or higher.
**All changes significant at the 90 percent confidence level.
Source: Brookings analysis of decennial census and ACS data.

Very different poverty dynamics marked the 2000s, however. The poor population climbed to 39.5 million in 2005–09, pushing the nation's poverty rate up to 13.5 percent. The number of neighborhoods with at least 40 percent of residents in poverty climbed by 747. By 2005–09, these neighborhoods housed 8.7 million Americans—2.2 million more than at the start of the decade, a one-third increase. Almost half of those residents—4.1 million—were poor. In 2005–09, 10.5 percent of the poor population lived in extreme-poverty tracts (see Figure 2.1). While the

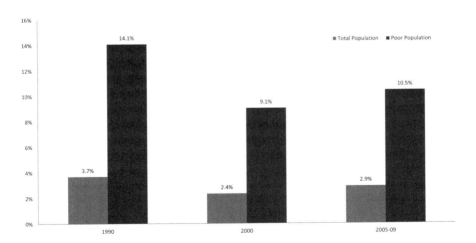

Figure 2.1   Share of Total and Poor Population in Extreme-Poverty Tracts, 1990 to 2005–2009
Source: Brookings analysis of decennial census and ACS data.

2005–09 concentrated poverty rate did not reach its 1990 level (14.1 percent), it represents a significant increase over 2000 (9.1 percent) and signals an emerging reconcentration of the poor.

Moreover, increasing concentrations of poverty over the decade were not confined to urban areas (see Table 2.2). Over 60 percent of the nation's poor lived in the 100 most populous metropolitan areas in 2005–09, with the remaining 40 percent roughly split between smaller metropolitan areas and nonmetropolitan communities. While large metropolitan areas experienced the largest absolute increases in extreme-poverty neighborhoods and concentrated poverty, small metropolitan areas were home to the fastest growth in extreme-poverty tracts and the number of residents living in them, followed by nonmetropolitan communities. However, the nation's most populous metro areas continued to house a disproportionate share of the nation's extreme-poverty neighborhoods in 2005–09 and retained the highest concentrated poverty rate (11.7 percent, compared to 10.9 percent in small metropolitan areas and 6.3 percent in nonmetropolitan communities). The remainder of the analysis focuses on changes in the spatial location of poverty within and across these large regions.

Regional Impacts

During the 2000s, roughly three-quarters of the nation's largest metro areas saw their number of extreme-poverty neighborhoods grow, along with the number of poor living in them, compared to just 16 metro areas that experienced decreases. The largest increases and decreases tended to cluster in different parts of the country, illuminating larger regional patterns in these trends and tracking with broader changes in poverty across different regions.

The Midwest experienced the most rapid decline in the incidence of extreme-poverty neighborhoods in the 1990s (Jargowsky 2003). Much of that progress was erased in the 2000s as the Midwest led other regions for growth in pockets of extreme poverty (see Table 2.3). Taken together, Midwestern metro areas registered a 79 percent increase in extreme-poverty neighborhoods in the 2000s. The number of poor living in these tracts almost doubled over the decade, pushing the concentrated poverty rate in the region's metro areas up by a staggering 5 percentage points to a level that surpassed that in Northeastern metro areas. While large metro areas like Detroit (30 percent) and Chicago (13 percent) drove some of the growth in the number of poor in extreme-poverty tracts, the majority of the growth was shared across the other 17 large metro areas in the Midwest.

Southern metro areas recorded a substantial 33 percent growth in the number of poor individuals in extreme-poverty neighborhoods, though this figure masks the steep declines in places like New Orleans and Baltimore that somewhat offset large gains in places like the Texas metro areas of El Paso, Dallas, and Houston. Given the region's fast growth in overall population and poor residents in the 2000s, and the mixed trajectories of metro areas in different parts of the South, the region's concentrated poverty rate rose by a modest 0.8 percentage points.

Table 2.2 Total and Poor Population in Extreme-Poverty Tracts by Community Type, 2000 to 2005–2009

Type of Geography	Number of Extreme-Poverty Tracts			Total Population in Extreme-Poverty Tracts			Poor Population in Extreme-Poverty Tracts		
	2000	2005–09	% Change	2000	2005–09	% Change	2000	2005–09	% Change
100 Metro Areas	1,536	1,898	23.6%	4,935,506	5,903,264	19.6%	2,277,193	2,764,587	21.4%
Small-metro	351	616	75.5%	969,828	1,746,883	80.1%	432,643	802,089	85.4%
Non-metro	188	308	63.8%	669,481	1,085,248	62.1%	302,057	483,862	60.2%
Distribution Across Geography Types	2000	2005–09	Change	2000	2005–09	Change	2000	2005–09	Change
100 Metro Areas	74.0%	67.3%	-6.8%	75.1%	67.6%	-7.5%	75.6%	68.3%	-7.4%
Small-metro	16.9%	21.8%	4.9%	14.8%	20.0%	5.2%	14.4%	19.8%	5.4%
Non-metro	9.1%	10.9%	1.9%	10.2%	12.4%	2.2%	10.0%	11.9%	1.9%

*All changes significant at the 90 percent confidence level.

Source: Brookings analysis of decennial Census and ACS data.

Table 2.3   Total and Poor Population in Extreme-Poverty Tracts by Census Region, 100 Metro Areas, 2000 to 2005–2009

Region	Number of Extreme-Poverty Tracts			Poor Population in Extreme-Poverty Tracts				Concentrated Poverty Rate			
	2000	2005–09	% Change	2000	2005–09	% Change		2000	2005–09	Change	
Top 100 Metro Areas	1,536	1,898	23.6%	2,277,193	2,764,587	21.4%	*	11.2%	11.7%	0.5%	*
Midwest	344	617	79.4%	344,958	672,262	94.9%	*	10.3%	15.5%	5.2%	*
Northeast	452	475	5.1%	738,579	752,393	1.9%		15.4%	15.2%	-0.2%	
South	465	576	23.9%	697,649	930,420	33.4%	*	10.6%	11.4%	0.8%	*
West	275	230	-16.4%	496,007	409,512	-17.4%	*	8.8%	6.6%	-2.2%	*

*Change is significant at the 90 percent confidence level.

Source: Brookings analysis of decennial Census and ACS data.

Table 2.4 **Top and Bottom Metro Areas for Change in Concentrated Poverty Rate, 2000 to 2005–2009**

Metro Areas	2000 to 2005–09		
With Greatest Increases in Concentrated Poverty	**Concentrated Poverty Rate Change**	**Change in Poor Population in Extreme-Poverty Tracts**	**Change in Number of Extreme-Poverty Tracts**
Toledo, OH	15.3%	16,918	15
El Paso, TX	14.5%	33,953	16
Youngstown-Warren-Boardman, OH-PA	14.3%	12,390	11
Baton Rouge, LA	13.5%	16,150	7
Detroit-Warren-Livonia, MI	13.2%	98,940	73
Jackson, MS	12.2%	12,383	11
New Haven-Milford, CT	11.3%	10,834	9
Poughkeepsie-Newburgh-Middletown, NY	10.5%	8,334	0
Dayton, OH	9.9%	11,959	8
Hartford-West Hartford-East Hartford, CT	9.5%	11,023	11
With Greatest Decreases in Concentrated Poverty			
New Orleans-Metairie-Kenner, LA	-9.3%	-29,524	-14
McAllen-Edinburg-Mission, TX	-7.3%	11,229	-3
Virginia Beach-Norfolk-Newport News, VA-NC	-6.7%	-10,234	-7
Fresno, CA	-6.6%	-11,064	-5
Provo-Orem, UT	-6.0%	-1,725	1
Bakersfield, CA	-5.8%	-4,291	-3
Baltimore-Towson, MD	-5.5%	-13,051	-14
Charleston-North Charleston-Summerville, SC	-4.9%	-2,552	-1
Stockton, CA	-4.8%	-4,373	0
San Diego-Carlsbad-San Marcos, CA	-4.6%	-15,641	-8

*All changes significant at the 90 percent confidence level.

Source: Brookings analysis of decennial Census and ACS data.

Northeastern metro areas held steady on these indicators over the decade, while the West actually experienced a drop in concentrated poverty. The Northeast's trend resulted almost entirely from New York's significant decrease in the number of poor in extreme-poverty tracts. From 2000 to 2005–09, the number of extreme-poverty tracts in the New York metro area alone dropped by 64, and poor residents of its extreme-poverty neighborhoods declined by 108,000, effectively canceling out increases in almost every other Northeastern metro area. Similarly, steep declines in the number of poor in extreme-poverty tracts in Los Angeles, and to some extent places like San Diego and Riverside, outweighed increases in metro areas like Phoenix, Tucson, Las Vegas, and Denver.

Between 2000 and 2005–09, all but 12 of the nation's 100 largest metro areas experienced a statistically significant change in their concentrated poverty rate. The majority (67 metro areas) saw their concentrated poverty rates increase, while 21 regions experienced a decline. Among individual metro areas, the largest increases in the rate of concentrated poverty occurred in the Great Lakes metro areas of Toledo, Youngstown, Detroit, and Dayton and the Northeastern metro areas of New Haven and Hartford (see Table 2.4). Many of these areas saw poverty rise throughout the decade amid the continuing loss of manufacturing jobs.

On the other end of the spectrum, some metro areas in the West and South, like Virginia Beach, Bakersfield, Baltimore, and Stockton, exhibited among the largest declines in concentrated poverty rates over the decade.[12] However, many of these regions were on the front lines of the housing market collapse and downturn that followed, and recent poverty trends suggest these gains may have been short lived (Kneebone and Berube 2011). McAllen and Fresno also led for decreases in their concentrated poverty rates in the 2000s, but even with that progress, they rank first and fifth, respectively, for metropolitan concentrated poverty rates in 2005–09. They are joined in this regard by other Southern metro areas like El Paso, Memphis, and Jackson, as well as Midwestern metro areas like Detroit, Cleveland, Toledo, and Milwaukee.

City and Suburban Trends

Historically, pockets of extreme poverty have been a largely urban phenomenon, though the geography may be slowly changing for large metro areas. Cities reaped the benefits of deconcentrating poverty in the 1990s to a much greater extent than their surrounding suburbs (see Table 2.5).

Extreme-poverty neighborhoods grew in cities and suburbs alike during the 2000s, though the phenomenon remained a majority-urban one. In 2005–09, cities contained over two-thirds of extreme-poverty tracts within the nation's 100 largest

---

12   New Orleans' significant decline in concentrated poverty was largely the result of natural disasters, with the evacuations and destruction following Hurricanes Katrina and Rita driving this region's trend (Berube and Katz 2005).

Table 2.5 Change in Extreme-Poverty Neighborhoods in Cities and Suburbs, 100 Metro Areas, 1990 to 2005–2009

Extreme-Poverty Tracts	City			Change		Suburb			Change	
	1990	2000	2005–09	1990 to 05–09	2000 to 2005–09	1990	2000	2005–2009	1990 to 05–09	2000 to 05–09
Total Population	5,174,783	4,027,578	4,662,473	-9.9%	15.8%	900,842	907,928	1,240,791	37.7%	36.7%
Poor Population	2,529,484	1,871,337	2,193,858	-13.3%	17.2%	429,081	405,856	570,729	33.0%	40.6%
Tracts	1,701	1,313	1,554	-8.6%	18.4%	262	223	344	31.3%	54.3%
Share of Total Population	9.5%	6.9%	7.7%	-1.8%	0.8%	0.9%	0.8%	0.9%	0.0%	0.2%
Share of Poor Population	26.6%	18.3%	20.0%	-6.6%	1.7%	5.1%	4.0%	4.5%	-0.6%	0.5%

*All changes significant at the 90 percent confidence level.

Source: Brookings analysis of decennial Census and ACS data.

Table 2.6   Change in Extreme-Poverty Neighborhoods by Suburban Type, 2000 to 2005–2009

Type of Suburb	Number of Extreme-Poverty Tracts			Total Population in Extreme-Poverty Tracts			Poor Population in Extreme-Poverty Tracts		
	2000	2005–09	% Change	2000	2005–09	% Change	2000	2005–09	% Change
Suburban Total	223	344	54.3%	907,928	1,240,791	36.7%	405,856	570,729	40.6%
High Density	79	114	44.3%	304,745	342,375	12.3%	132,628	158,883	19.8%
Mature	100	156	56.0%	450,095	629,557	39.9%	204,842	288,460	40.8%
Emerging	36	58	61.1%	121,603	193,436	59.1%	56,089	93,353	66.4%
Exurb	8	16	100.0%	31,485	75,423	139.6%	12,297	30,033	144.2%

*All changes significant at the 90 percent confidence level.

Source: Brookings analysis of decennial Census and ACS data.

metro areas and had a concentrated poverty rate more than four times higher (20 percent) than suburbs (4.5 percent).

However, just as suburbs outpaced cities for growth in the poor population as a whole over the decade, they also saw the number of poor living in extreme-poverty neighborhoods grow faster than in cities (Kneebone and Berube 2011). The number of extreme-poverty neighborhoods in suburban communities grew by 54 percent, compared to 18 percent in cities, and the poor population living in these suburban neighborhoods rose by 41 percent—more than twice as fast as the 17 percent growth in cities. As a result, though cities still remained better off on these measures in 2005–09 than in 1990, suburbs had surpassed 1990 levels on almost every count.

Growth rates differed across suburbs as well. Higher-density, older suburbs were home to a larger number of extreme-poverty neighborhoods and poor residents living in concentrated poverty than newer, lower-density communities (see Table 2.6). Interestingly, mature suburbs—those that largely developed in the middle decades of the twentieth century, in contrast to older streetcar suburbs bordering central cities—are home to more extreme-poverty tracts and poor population in those tracts than their more urbanized neighbors. But newer emerging and exurban suburbs experienced the fastest pace of growth among suburbs in concentrated poverty over the decade, albeit from a low base. The trends underscore that just as no category of suburb was immune to broader growth in poverty over the decade, the challenges of concentrated poverty became more regional in scope as well (Kneebone and Garr 2010).

Increases in concentrated poverty were widespread among both cities and suburbs in the 100 largest metro areas during the 2000s. Altogether, 61 experienced significant increases in city concentrated poverty rates, compared to 20 with significant decreases (19 remained unchanged). Suburban concentrated poverty rates rose in 55 metro areas and declined in 16 (see Table 2.7). By and large, city and suburban rates moved together over time, but Poughkeepsie and Fresno experienced among the steepest drops in cities' concentrated poverty rates even as they topped the list for increases in suburban concentrated poverty rates.

Different factors can cause concentrated poverty to rise or fall in a region: a change in the number of extreme-poverty neighborhoods, growth or decline in the poor population living in these neighborhoods, or a combination of the two. Fifty-eight percent of extreme-poverty tracts in cities in 2000 remained extreme-poverty tracts in 2005–2009. However, these tracts shed total population and poor residents over the 2000s. The increase in concentrated poverty in cities was thus driven by growth of new pockets of poverty in these urban centers. Just as in cities, 58 percent of suburban extreme-poverty tracts in 2000 remained above the 40 percent threshold in 2005–2009. Unlike in cities, those neighborhoods added total residents and poor population over the decade. The rise in suburban concentrated poverty thus reflected growth in both existing pockets of poverty and the development of new extreme-poverty neighborhoods.

Table 2.7 Top and Bottom Metro Areas for Change in Concentrated Poverty Rate by City and Suburb, 2000 to 2005–2009

Metro Areas	Change in Concentrated Poverty Rate	Metro Areas	Change in Concentrated Poverty Rate
With Greatest Primary City Increases:		**With Greatest Suburban Increases:**	
• Bradenton-Sarasota-Venice, FL	36.7%	• New Haven-Milford, CT	13.8%
• Youngstown-Warren-Boardman, OH-PA	36.3%	• Poughkeepsie-Newburgh-Middletown, NY	13.1%
• Portland-South Portland-Biddeford, ME	25.4%	• Palm Bay-Melbourne-Titusville, FL	10.2%
• Dayton, OH	25.2%	• Cleveland-Elyria-Mentor, OH	8.0%
• Detroit-Warren-Livonia, MI	24.3%	• Baton Rouge, LA	7.0%
• Hartford-West Hartford-East Hartford, CT	23.0%	• Greenville-Mauldin-Easley, SC	6.9%
• Jackson, MS	22.4%	• El Paso, TX	6.7%
• Baton Rouge, LA	22.0%	• Toledo, OH	6.6%
• Greenville-Mauldin-Easley, SC	19.6%	• Fresno, CA	6.5%
• Toledo, OH	19.4%	• Youngstown-Warren-Boardman, OH-PA	6.4%

With Greatest Primary City Decreases:

- Provo-Orem, UT   -15.4%
- Fresno, CA   -13.9%
- Poughkeepsie-Newburgh-Middletown, NY   -12.2%
- New Orleans-Metairie-Kenner, LA   -11.6%
- Providence-New Bedford-Fall River, RI-MA   -9.6%
- Scranton--Wilkes-Barre, PA   -9.4%
- San Diego-Carlsbad-San Marcos, CA   -9.3%
- Charleston-North Charleston-Summerville, SC   -8.4%
- Virginia Beach-Norfolk-Newport News, VA-NC   -8.1%
- Baltimore-Towson, MD   -7.2%

With Greatest Suburban Decreases:

- Tucson, AZ   -9.3%
- McAllen-Edinburg-Mission, TX   -9.0%
- Bakersfield, CA   -6.4%
- Ogden-Clearfield, UT   -5.1%
- Virginia Beach-Norfolk-Newport News, VA-NC   -4.4%
- Miami-Fort Lauderdale-Pompano Beach, FL   -3.8%
- Sacramento--Arden-Arcade--Roseville, CA   -3.6%
- Charleston-North Charleston-Summerville, SC   -3.2%
- Cape Coral-Fort Myers, FL   -2.5%
- Los Angeles-Long Beach-Santa Ana, CA   -2.1%

*All changes significant at the 90 percent confidence level.

Source: Brookings analysis of decennial Census and ACS data.

New pockets of poverty that developed in these communities may have been tracts hovering just below the 40 percent threshold in 2000 or others that experienced more significant increases in their poverty rates over the course of the decade. Not reflected in these numbers are the neighborhoods that saw significant increases in poverty but did not top the 40 percent threshold in 2005–2009. Overall, cities saw the ranks of the poor in neighborhoods with 20 to 40 percent poverty rates grow by 36 percent over the decade, while suburban poor populations in neighborhoods at those poverty levels grew by 86 percent—even faster than the growth experienced in extreme-poverty neighborhoods since 2000. Research indicates that residents of these neighborhoods experience disadvantages that, while not of the same severity as those afflicting extreme-poverty neighborhoods, may nonetheless limit opportunities and negatively affect their quality of life (Galster 2010).

In short, concentrated poverty trends in the 2000s appear to have erased some of the progress made in central cities during the 1990s while accelerating and spreading the growth of higher-poverty suburban communities witnessed that decade.

Demographic Shifts

As concentrations of poverty increased and spread in the 2000s, the makeup of extreme-poverty neighborhoods shifted across a number of characteristics (see Table 2.8). In particular, the traditional picture of extreme-poverty neighborhoods has been colored by research and public discussion of the urban "underclass," a term that has fallen out of favor in recent years but, according to Ricketts and Sawhill, is meant to describe a subset of the population that "suffers from multiple social ills that are concentrated in depressed inner-city areas" (Ricketts and Sawhill 1988: 321, Sawhill and Jargowsky 2006).

Past research has identified four factors to proxy "underclass" characteristics at the neighborhood level: the share of teenagers dropping out of high school, the proportion of households headed by single mothers, the share of able-bodied men not in the labor force, and the proportion of households on public assistance. During the 2000s, the share of working-age men not in the labor force in extreme-poverty neighborhoods fell by 7 percentage points, as did the share of teenagers in these neighborhoods not in school and without a diploma. The share of households receiving public assistance dropped by more than 8 percentage points, and a smaller share were headed by single mothers than at the start of the decade. These shifts underscore an observation made by Ricketts and Sawhill that, while "extreme poverty areas can reasonably be used as a proxy for concentrations of social problems … they are not the same thing" (Ricketts and Sawhill 1988: 322–3).

In addition, by 2005–2009, residents of extreme-poverty neighborhoods were more likely to be non-Hispanic White and less likely to be Latino than in 2000, though African Americans remained the single largest group in these areas (44.6

Table 2.8 Change in Neighborhood Characteristics in Extreme-Poverty Tracts, 100 Metro Areas, 2000 to 2005–2009

Share of Individuals:	2000	2005–09
Who are:		
• Non-Hispanic White	11.2%	16.5%
• Black	45.6%	44.6%
• Latino	37.4%	33.9%
• Other	5.9%	5.1%
• Foreign born	20.0%	17.9%
25 and over who have completed:		
• Less than High School	50.0%	37.9%
• High School	25.9%	31.9%
• Some College or Associates Degree	17.4%	20.5%
• BA or Higher	6.7%	9.7%
22- to 64-year-old males not in the labor force	39.8%	32.4%
16- to 19-year-olds not in school and without a diploma	20.6%	13.6%
Share of Households:		
That are owner occupied	24.4%	29.3%
That receive public assistance	18.0%	9.6%
That are headed by women with children	26.8%	22.5%

*All changes significant at the 90 percent confidence level.

Source: Brookings analysis of decennial Census and ACS data.

percent).[13] The population in extreme-poverty tracts was also less likely to be foreign-born, and residents were more likely to own their homes than at the start of the decade, though the majority (61 percent) remained renters. Compared to 2000, by the last half of the decade residents of these neighborhoods were also better educated—a higher proportion had finished high school (31.9 percent) and a higher share held bachelor's degrees (9.7 percent).

These changes may capture in part the rapid growth of concentrated poverty in the Midwest, which accompanied the economic struggles of regions like Detroit, Toledo, Chicago, and Dayton across the decade. Concentrated poverty in these metro areas spread beyond the urban core to what might previously have been

---

13 Research has also found that the share of all Whites, of all Blacks, and of all Latinos living in high-poverty tracts largely stayed the same over the decade, meaning the shifts in the racial and ethnic composition of these neighborhoods were driven by changes in the composition of the larger population. See Pendall et al. (2011).

Table 2.9   Neighborhood Characteristics by Poverty Rate Category, 100 Metro Areas, 2005–2009

Share of Individuals:	In Extreme-Poverty Tracts	In High Poverty Tracts	Total Population
Who are:			
• White	16.5%	29.9%	59.7%
• Black	44.6%	27.5%	13.7%
• Latino	33.9%	35.6%	18.4%
• Other	5.1%	6.9%	8.2%
• Foreign born	17.9%	23.4%	16.2%
25 and over who have completed:			
• Less than High School	37.9%	29.2%	14.8%
• High School	31.9%	30.8%	26.8%
• Some College or Associates Degree	20.5%	23.9%	27.3%
• BA or Higher	9.7%	16.1%	31.1%
22- to 64-year-old males not in the labor force	32.4%	20.1%	14.4%
16- to 19-year-olds not in school and without a diploma	13.6%	11.5%	6.5%
Share of Households:			
That are owner occupied	29.3%	42.8%	65.1%
That receive public assistance	9.6%	5.2%	2.4%
That are headed by women with children	22.5%	13.7%	8.1%

*All differences significant at the 90 percent confidence level.
Source: Brookings analysis of ACS data.

considered working-class areas. Poor local labor market conditions may have pushed up poverty rates across a more demographically and economically diverse set of neighborhoods than traditional "underclass" areas. The same may apply to the South, where the rapid spread of high-poverty neighborhoods to suburban areas amid the housing market downturn further alters long-held notions of concentrated poverty. At the same time, "underclass" characteristics may themselves have become less concentrated as broader swaths of metropolitan areas diversified economically and demographically.

Within major metro areas, extreme-poverty neighborhoods in cities and suburbs share a similar overall demographic and economic profile. An exception is their racial and ethnic makeup—reflecting larger differences in the racial and ethnic profile of cities and suburbs, in that suburban residents of extreme-poverty neighborhoods are more likely to be non-Hispanic White and Latino than their counterparts in cities—and a higher homeownership rate in the suburbs.

Greater demographic and economic differences emerge between neighborhoods with poverty rates of at least 40 percent on the one hand and those with poverty rates between 20 to 40 percent on the other. The latter group housed more than one-third of the metropolitan poor population in 2005–2009, compared to about one-tenth of metropolitan poor in the former group.

Residents of high-poverty neighborhoods in 2005–2009 were more likely to be non-Hispanic White and Latino and less likely to be African American than the population in extreme-poverty tracts (see Table 2.9). They were also more likely to be foreign born. Residents of high-poverty neighborhoods exhibited higher levels of education than those in extreme-poverty tracts, with a much higher share of college graduates as well as those who attended some college or held an associate's degree. And high-poverty tract residents are much less likely to exhibit the four "underclass" characteristics than their counterparts in extreme-poverty neighborhoods. However, when the benchmark is the metropolitan population as a whole, high-poverty neighborhoods continue to exhibit higher use of public assistance and trail behind the general population on educational attainment, dropout rates, single-mother households, and male attachment to the labor force.

Conclusion

The findings here confirm what earlier studies this decade suggested: After substantial progress against concentrated poverty during the booming economy of the late 1990s, the economically turbulent 2000s saw much of those gains erased. In cities, concentrated poverty had not yet returned to 1990 levels by 2005–2009. However, suburbs—home to the steepest increases in the poor population over the decade—cannot say the same: By 2005–2009 the number of residents living in extreme-poverty neighborhoods had risen by a third compared to 1990.

What is more, the five-year estimates likely downplay the severity of the upturn in these trends because they pool such different time periods together. In particular, many Sun Belt metro areas continue to struggle with steep poverty increases in the wake of the housing market collapse and the deep recession that followed, such that the positive shifts in concentrated poverty seen in many of these regions through 2005–2009 may have since evaporated if not reversed.

There is also evidence that as poverty has increasingly suburbanized this decade, new clusters of low-income neighborhoods have emerged beyond the urban core in many of the nation's largest metro areas. The proposition of being poor in a suburb may bring benefits to residents if it means they are located in neighborhoods that offer greater access to opportunities—be it higher-quality schools, affordable housing, or better jobs—than they would otherwise find in an urban neighborhood. But research has shown that, instead, the suburban poor often end up in lower-income communities with less access to jobs and economic opportunity compared to higher-income suburbanites (Raphael and Stoll 2010, Covington, Freeman, and Stoll 2011). Thus, rather than increased opportunities and connections, being poor in poor suburban neighborhoods may mean residents face challenges similar to those that accompany concentrated disadvantage in urban areas but with the added complication that even fewer resources are likely to exist than one might find in an urban neighborhood with access to a more robust and developed safety net. However, as poverty continues to suburbanize and to concentrate, absent policy intervention the suburbs are poised to become home to the next wave of concentrating disadvantage.

Given that a strong economic recovery has failed to materialize and threats of a double-dip recession loom, it is unlikely the nation has seen the end of poverty's upward trend. Trends from the past decade strongly indicate that it is difficult to make progress against concentrated poverty while poverty itself is on the rise. It is also unlikely that without fundamental changes in how regions plan for things like land use, zoning, housing, and workforce and economic development that the growth of extreme-poverty neighborhoods and concentrated poverty will abate. With cities and suburbs increasingly sharing the challenges of concentrated poverty, regional economic development strategies must do more to encourage balanced growth that includes opportunities for workers up and down the economic ladder. Metropolitan leaders must also actively foster economic integration throughout their regions and forge stronger connections between poor neighborhoods and areas with better education and job opportunities so that low-income residents are not left out or left behind in the effort to grow the regional economy.

References

Berube, A. and Katz, B. 2005. *Katrina's Window: Confronting Concentrated Poverty Across America.* Washington, DC: Brookings Institution.

Brookings Metropolitan Policy Program. 2010. *State of Metropolitan America: On the Front Lines of Demographic Transformation.* Washington, DC: Brookings Institution.

Century Foundation Task Force on the Common School. 2002. *Divided We Fall: Coming Together Through Public School Choice.* New York, NY: Century Foundation Press.

Cohen, D., Mason, K., Bedimo, A., Scribner, R., Basolo, V., and Farley, T. 2003. Neighborhood physical conditions and health. *Journal of American Public Health*, 93(3), 467–71.

Covington, K., Freeman, L., and Stoll, M. 2011. *The Suburbanization of Housing Choice Voucher Recipients.* Washington, DC: Brookings Institution.

Danziger, S. and Gottschalk, P. 1987. Earnings inequality, the spatial concentration of poverty, and the underclass. *American Economic Review*, 77(2), 211–15.

Ellen, I. and Turner, M. 1997. Does neighborhood matter? Assessing recent evidence. *Housing Policy Debate*, 8(4), 833–66.

Federal Reserve System Community Affairs Offices and the Brookings Institution. 2008. *The Enduring Challenge of Concentrated Poverty in America: Case Studies from Communities Across the U.S.* Washington, DC: Federal Reserve System and Brookings Institution.

Fellowes, M. 2006. *From Poverty, Opportunity: Putting the Market to Work for Lower-Income Families.* Washington, DC: Brookings Institution.

Galster, G., Cutsinger, J., and Malega, R. 2008. The costs of concentrated poverty: Neighborhood property markets and the dynamics of decline, in *Revisiting Rental Housing: Policies, Programs, and Priorities,* edited by N. Retsinas and E. Belsky. Washington, DC: Brookings Institution.

Galster, G. 2010. *The Mechanism(s) of Neighborhood Effects: Theory, Evidence, and Policy Implications*, ESRC Seminar, St. Andrews University, Scotland, United Kingdom, 4–5 February.

Ihlanfeldt, K. and Sjoquist, D. 1998. The spatial mismatch hypothesis: A review of recent studies and their implications for welfare reform. *Housing Policy Debate,* 9(4), 849–92.

Jargowsky, P. and Bane, M. 1990. Ghetto poverty: Basic questions in *Inner-City Poverty in the United States*, edited by L. Lynn and M. McGeary. Washington, DC: National Academy Press.

Jargowsky, P. and Bane, M. 1991. Ghetto poverty in the United States, in *The Urban Underclass,* edited by C. Jenks and P. Peterson. Washington, DC: Brookings Institution.

Jargowsky, P. 1997. *Poverty and Place: Ghettos, Barrios, and the American City.* New York, NY: Russell Sage Foundation.

Jargowsky, P. 2003. *Stunning Progress, Hidden Problems.* Washington, DC: Brookings Institution.

Kasarda, J. 1993. Inner-city poverty and economic access, in *Rediscovering Urban America: Perspectives on the 1980s*, edited by J. Sommer and D. Hicks. Washington, DC: U.S. Department of Housing and Urban Development.

Kingsley, T. and Pettit, K. 2003. *Severe Distress and Concentrated Poverty: Trends for Neighborhoods in Casey Cities and the Nation.* Washington, DC: Urban Institute.

Kneebone, E. and Berube, A. 2008. *Reversal of Fortune: A New Look at Concentrated Poverty in the 2000s.* Washington, DC: Brookings Institution.

Kneebone, E. and Berube, A. 2011. *The Rapid Growth of the Suburban Poor.* [Online: The Atlantic Cities]. Available at: http://www.theatlanticcities.com/jobs-and-economy/2011/09/rapid-growth-suburban-poor/190/ [accessed: 18 November 2011].

Kneebone, E. and Garr, E. 2010. *The Suburbanization of Poverty: Trends in Metropolitan America, 2000 to 2008.* Washington, DC: Brookings Institution.

Kneebone, E., Nadeau, C., and Berube, A. 2011. *The Re-Emergence of Concentrated Poverty: Metropolitan Trends in the 2000s.* Washington, DC: Brookings Institution.

Lupton, R. 2004. *Schools in Disadvantaged Areas: Recognising Context and Raising Quality*. London: Centre for the Analysis of Social Exclusion.

National Academy of Sciences. 1995. *Measuring Poverty: A New Approach*. Washington, DC: National Academy Press.

Pack, J. 1998. Poverty and urban public expenditures. *Urban Studies*, 35(11), 1995–2019.

Pendall, R., Davies, E., Freiman, L., and Pitingolo, R. 2011. *A Lost Decade: Neighborhood Poverty and the Urban Crisis of the 2000s*. Washington, DC: Joint Center for Political and Economic Studies.

Raphael, S. and Stoll, M. 2010. *Job Sprawl and the Suburbanization of Poverty*. Washington, DC: Brookings Institution.

Ricketts, E. and Sawhill, I. 1988. Defining and measuring the underclass. *Journal of Policy Analysis and Management,* 7(2), 316–25.

Rusk, D. 2001. *The Segregation Tax: The Cost of Racial Segregation to Black Homeowners*. Washington, DC: Brookings Institution.

Sawhill, I. and Jargowsky, P. 2006. *The Decline of the Underclass*. Washington, DC: Brookings Institution.

Wodtke, G., Harding, D., and Elwert, F. 2011. Neighborhood effects in temporal perspective: The impact of long-term exposure to concentrated disadvantage on high school graduation. *American Sociological Review*, 76(5), 713–36.

Chapter 3

Debunking the "Cookie-Cutter" Myth for Suburban Places and Suburban Poverty: Analyzing Their Variety and Recent Trends

Karen Beck Pooley

Introduction

For over 100 years, and particularly in the years since World War II, Americans have been suburbanizing. In 1910, just 7 percent of all Americans, or roughly 6.5 million people, lived in suburbs. By 2000, about 50 percent of Americans were suburbanites, and the suburban population had reached nearly 141 million (Hobbs and Stoops 2002). Today, not only do most Americans live in suburbia, they also rely on suburban retail establishments and recreational and cultural venues (Teaford 1990, Bradley 2001, Palen 2005). Nationally, more commuters head to suburban jobs than urban ones (Bowman 2008); in the country's 100 largest metropolitan areas, there are 1.8 times as many jobs in the suburbs as in the central cities (Bajaj, Kingsley, and Pettit 2005).

But what is suburbia?[1] Up until recently, popular perception saw suburban communities as uniformly non-Hispanic White, upper-income, primarily residential, and dominated by homeowners living in detached single-family homes (Frey 2011a). While this may be true of some suburbs, it is certainly not true of all suburbs. These places—having grown up around the streetcar, the train, or the car—take a range of physical forms, from walkable to sprawling. These places house a variety of uses, ranging from primarily residential places to job centers or retail hubs. In addition, while some suburbs are home to nearly all-non-Hispanic White and all upper-income populations, most are not. As of the 2005–2009 American Community Survey, in the nation's 100 largest Metropolitan Statistical Areas (MSAs), 56 percent of residents of color and 54 percent of people with incomes below the poverty line lived in the suburbs.

The decentralization of poverty is presenting a whole new array of challenges for poor people and the communities in which they now live. Suburban communities typically have far less experience than central cities providing social services.

---

[1] Suburbs are not explicitly classified by the U.S. Bureau of the Census. The common practice among researchers is to consider any zip code, municipality, or census tract outside the primary city or cities in a Metropolitan or Micropolitan Statistical Area to be suburban.

Unlike cities, they often lack the public agencies and nonprofit institutions to oversee such programming and also the philanthropic organizations to support them (Weir 2011). As a result, "the capacity of [the] suburban safety net and nonprofit service providers has likely lagged behind the dramatic demographic changes that have caught many [suburban] communities by surprise" (Allard and Roth 2010: 7). Few suburbs with significant poor populations can offer assistance sufficient to meet local needs; fewer still can do so in a way that is comparable with the outreach efforts of urban centers (Allard and Roth 2010).

On the one hand, suburban governments must increase their capacity to deliver a wider array of public services. On the other hand, local leaders face the challenge of retaining existing and attracting new higher-income households as their communities' numbers and proportions of lower-income homeowners and renters increase. Popular and long-held assumptions predict that lower-income households will negatively affect area property values. These tend to fuel most not-in-my-backyard (NIMBY) opposition to proposed affordable housing projects in suburban neighborhoods (Galster et al. 2003) and, subsequently, the outmigration of higher-income households once these projects and populations move to town. Countering these expectations may require that municipal governments play a more active role in addressing housing conditions (for example, increasing code enforcement efforts) or more aggressively respond to real or perceived upswings in violent or property crimes than many suburban officials have needed to do in the past.

While conventional wisdom suggests that incomes and property values decline together, this analysis found that socioeconomic changes instead interact with local real estate market conditions in incredibly complicated and highly varied ways from one place to the next. To better understand this complexity, this study first created a typology of suburban census tracts in the nation's largest 100 metropolitan statistical areas (MSAs), grouping suburban tracts based on homeownership rates, degrees of racial and ethnic diversity, and housing market strength.[2] These tracts fell into one of five categories (see Table 3.1).

Before addressing poverty levels, this typology shows how heterogeneous suburbia is. For example, just 23 percent of suburban tracts were classified as Type 1 Tracts (all non-Hispanic White with high homeownership rates) or would fit with popular perceptions of suburbia. Nearly twice as many (39 percent) had low homeownership rates (Types 4 and 5). Type 2 and Type 3 Tracts illustrate conditions reinforced by more recent data from the 2010 Census: the degree to which people of color, particularly Latinos, are driving population growth (Frey 2011b), how "global neighborhoods" are largely replacing all-non-Hispanic White enclaves in suburbia (Logan and Zhang 2010), and how these situations differ, in some cases dramatically, by region.

---

2   This typology only includes suburban tracts as identified by Kneebone and Nadeau (see Chapter 2 in this volume). What is "suburban" in their chapter is also "suburban" in this chapter.

Table 3.1   Typology of Suburban Census Tracts in the Largest 100 Metropolitan Statistical Areas

	Tracts with High Homeownership Rates	Tracts with Low Homeownership Rates
	(70 percent or higher)	**(less than 70 percent)**
Type 1	At least 90 percent of residents were non-Hispanic White	
Type 2	65 to 89.9 percent of residents were non-Hispanic White	
Type 3	Less than 65 percent of residents were non-Hispanic White	
Type 4		More than 30 percent of all single-family units were either renter-occupied or vacant
Type 5		Less than 30 percent of all single-family units were either renter-occupied or vacant

Sources: 2005–2009 American Community Survey, The Brookings Institution, author.

This study then identified suburban census tracts with moderate poverty rates (any tracts with poverty rates from 10 percent to 19.9 percent)[3] and high poverty rates (20 percent or more)[4] (Kneebone and Nadeau, this volume). Tracts with moderate or high poverty rates were collectively defined as "moderate/high-poverty" tracts in this analysis. Within each suburb type, moderate/high-poverty tracts (those with poverty rates of 10 percent or more) were then compared to low-poverty tracts (those with poverty rates below 10 percent) to see how these otherwise similar tracts differed—for example, in terms of their housing stock and MSA or regional profile. This analysis yielded several important findings.

First, while moderate and high poverty levels exist in all five types of suburban census tracts, some types are more likely to have higher poverty rates than others. Overall, 37 percent of suburban census tracts in the largest 100 MSAs had poverty rates at or above 10 percent, according to the 2005–2009 American Community Survey (ACS). The percentages ranged, though, from roughly 15 percent among high homeownership tracts that were either All-Non-Hispanic White and Diverse or Diversifying (Type 1 or Type 2) to 38 percent among high homeownership tracts classified as Melting Pots[5] (Type 3), 51 percent of low homeownership tracts with less than 30 percent of their single-family stock either renter-occupied or

---

3   Ten percent of all suburban residents in the top 100 MSAs lived below the poverty rate.

4   The U.S. Bureau of the Census uses the 20 percent threshold to qualify tracts as "poverty areas."

5   This label is borrowed from Frey (2011a).

vacant (Type 5), to 84 percent of low homeownership tracts with higher renter-occupancy or vacancy rates in their single-family units (Type 4).

A second discovery was that moderate and high poverty rates manifested themselves differently in different types of suburbs, in different types of metropolitan areas, and in different regions. Some moderate/high-poverty suburban areas with high levels of homeownership and largely homogeneous populations are failing to attract new buyers and seeing poverty increase among long-time residents as their incomes fall during retirement or stretches of under- or unemployment. Other suburbs are increasingly home to poor residents priced out of expensive adjacent primary cities, such as New York City, Boston, or Washington, DC. Some suburbs, particularly those with high poverty rates (rates over 20 percent), are facing substantial distress, such as declining home values, homeownership rates, and overall quality of life. Others, though, are maintaining strong for-sale housing markets even as poverty levels rise, in many cases buoyed by healthy countywide or regional housing markets.

The varying experiences of moderate/high-poverty suburbs offer important lessons to those looking to intervene on behalf of these people and places— by revitalizing communities with declining property values and deteriorating property conditions and neighborhood quality; by helping poor residents rise out of poverty; or by constructively integrating affordable units into suburban neighborhoods. Understanding suburban poverty and its implications for different types of places is especially important in the current economic climate. While the data used for this analysis captures the beginnings of the economic downturn, it predates the more serious consequences of the Great Recession. The 2005–2009 ACS, for example, reported a national poverty rate of 13.5 percent and estimated a total of 39.5 million people living below the poverty line. However, the nation's poor population and overall poverty rate have both skyrocketed since 2008. By 2010, according to Census data from that year, 15.2 percent of Americans, or roughly 46.6 million people, lived below the official poverty line (Short 2011). Poverty rates rose not only nationally but in the vast majority of metropolitan areas between 2000 and 2010 (Berube and Kneebone 2011).

These increases are by no means bypassing suburbs. In fact, Berube and Kneebone (2011) discovered that in the largest 100 MSAs poverty rates in cities and suburbs increased to the same degree, by 3.0 and 2.9 percentage points, respectively, between 2000 and 2010. Over the course of the decade, the number of people living below the poverty line in these MSAs' suburbs increased by 53 percent, nearly double the rate of growth (23 percent) as in these MSAs' cities (Berube and Kneebone 2011).

At the same time, the current housing market crisis has had not just *people*-based consequences but also *place*-based consequences for communities throughout the country. These include declining property values, a dramatic decrease in new construction, and a rash of foreclosures and property abandonment. Many of the localities facing the most serious ramifications of the downturn are not cities but suburbs (Leinberger 2008). This analysis, then, and the recommendations it suggests to address poverty in different types of suburbs, is likely to resonate with even more communities in the years ahead as more suburban communities experience rising poverty rates.

Data and Methodology

To fully understand the complexity of suburban census tracts, the prevalence of poverty in different types of suburban tracts, and the distinctions between low-poverty and moderate/high-poverty tracts that share other characteristics, this analysis utilized data from the 1990 and 2000 Censuses and the 2005–2009 American Community Survey 5-Year Estimates (the most recent data available at the census tract level as of this writing). Census data was downloaded using American Factfinder and also extracted from the CensusCD Neighborhood Change Database (NCDB), which weights prior year data to correspond with 2000 census tract boundaries, making it possible to calculate trends at the tract level even though roughly half of all census tract boundaries changed between 1990 and 2000.

To ensure that findings from this study complemented other work currently underway on the changing nature of America's suburbs (see Berube and Kneebone 2011, Frey 2011a, Kneebone and Nadeau, this volume), this analysis focused solely on census tracts within the country's 100 largest metropolitan statistical areas (MSA), as defined by the U.S. Office of Management and Budget (OMB), based on a data set provided by The Brookings Institution (see Kneebone and Nadeau, this volume). This analysis also relied on The Brookings Institution's labeling of tracts as either urban or suburban, which considers urban census tracts to be those within either the primary city listed in the official MSA name or in other cities listed in the MSA names that have populations of at least 100,000. Suburban census tracts are those whose center point falls within the MSA boundary but outside the MSA's city or cities.

Of the 40,350 census tracts in the largest 100 MSAs, The Brookings Institution classified 64 percent (or 25,795 tracts) as suburban. This analysis arrayed these 25,795 suburban census tracts into a typology made up of five different categories.[6] As homeownership has long been a central feature of the suburban experience, tracts' homeownership rates factored prominently into where they fit within the author's typology. Since the 1970s, the national homeownership rate has largely hovered between 64 percent and 66 percent, and at the peak of the recent housing boom, the national homeownership rate reached a high of 69 percent (U.S. Bureau of the Census, n.d.). Among all suburban tracts within these MSAs, the average homeownership rate was 71 percent according to the

---

6 Nearly all (99.7 percent, or 25,724 out of 25,795) suburban census tracts were categorized. The 71 tracts that were not classified either lacked a geographic identification number or had less than 100 housing units.

2005–2009 ACS. Therefore, this study used a 70 percent cutoff to separate high homeownership tracts from low homeownership tracts.[7] Tracts with high homeownership rates (70 percent or more) were split into (a) Primarily Non-Hispanic White Tracts, i.e., those where at least 90 percent of residents were non-Hispanic White[8] (Type 1 Tracts; n = 5,808); (b) Diverse or Diversifying Tracts, i.e., those where 65 to 89.9 percent of residents where non-Hispanic White (Type 2 Tracts; n = 6,651); and (c) following Frey (2011a), Melting Pot Tracts, i.e., those where less than 65 percent of residents were non-Hispanic White (Type 3 Tracts; n = 3,271). Low homeownership tracts were split into two groups: (a) those with more than 30 percent of all single-family units either renter-occupied or vacant, considered to have a weak housing stock (Type 4 Tracts; n = 3,834); and (b) those with less than 30 percent of all single-family units either renter-occupied or vacant, considered to have a strong housing stock (Type 5 Tracts; n = 6,160).[9]

Within these types, the census tracts were then classified as either low-poverty tracts (those with poverty rates below 10 percent) or moderate/high-poverty tracts (those with poverty rates of 10 percent or more). The 10 percent poverty threshold was selected for several reasons. First, according to the 2005–2009 ACS, suburban tracts in these MSAs averaged a poverty rate of 10 percent, and 9.5 percent of all suburban residents in the 100 largest MSAs lived below the poverty rate.[10] Second, prior research (Galster 2009) has found that poverty levels of 10 percent or more exert negative neighborhood effects on children's educational achievement and families' upward mobility. Third, a sufficient sample size of poor tracts, within each of the typology's categories, was necessary to meaningfully compare and contrast them to low-poverty tracts.[11]

This analysis relied on a range of descriptive statistics and Z-scores to illustrate the prevalence of moderate/high poverty rates within each tract type and to identify the ways in which moderate/high-poverty tracts differed from low-poverty tracts, also within each tract type. The results of that analysis are discussed below.

---

7   The median homeownership rate among suburban census tracts in the largest 100 MSAs was 76 percent.

8   Ninety percent was one standard deviation from the mean percent non-Hispanic White for all census tracts in the largest 100 MSAs.

9   Low homeownership tracts in which less than 30 percent of single-family units were either renter-occupied or vacant averaged median values equivalent to their MSA median; low homeownership tracts in which more than 30 percent of single-family units were either renter-occupied or vacant averaged median values equal to just 73 percent of their MSA median.

10   The median poverty rate for these census tracts was 7.4 percent.

11   Several suburb types had too few tracts with poverty rates of 20 percent or more to meet this threshold. While 3,118 suburban census tracts in the largest 100 MSAs (representing 12 percent of all suburban tracts in these MSAs) had poverty rates at or above 20, this was true of just 107 (or 1.6 percent of) Type 2 tracts and only 65 (or 1.1 percent of) Type 1 tracts.

A Typology of Suburban Census Tracts

The stereotypical view of suburbs as being racially and ethnically homogeneous (overwhelmingly non-Hispanic White), economically homogeneous (primarily middle and high income), and politically homogeneous (largely conservative) is now out of date (Dreier, Mollenkopf and Swanstrom 2001, Jones-Correa 2006). In fact, suburbs come in "countless varieties" (Kruse and Sugrue 2006: 8). There are non-Hispanic White suburbs and non-Hispanic Black/African American suburbs and Latino suburbs, as well as those that house immigrant communities or a diverse mix of people. There are rich suburbs and poor suburbs, white collar suburbs and blue collar suburbs, inner ring suburbs and outer ring suburbs. There are municipalities made up nearly entirely of single-family detached houses that are occupied by homeowners and others with a mix of building types and tenure choices. There are suburbs that serve as bedroom communities and others that house regional employment and retail hubs (Dreier, Mollenkopf and Swanstrom 2001, Kruse and Sugrue 2006, Murphy 2007).

The typology of suburban census tracts utilized in this analysis underscores this present variety and also illustrates how suburbs tend to vary by region. Type 1 Tracts, for example, are most common in the Northeast and Midwest, where they account for 35 percent and 40 percent, respectively, of all suburban tracts in the 100 largest MSAs in these regions (see Figure 3.1).

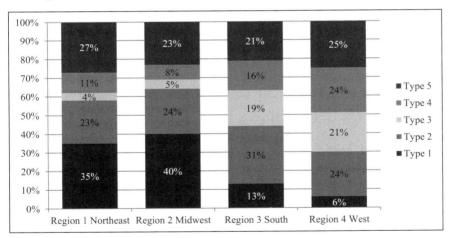

Figure 3.1   Breakdown of Tract Types by Region

Sources: 2005–2009 American Community Survey, The Brookings Institution, author.

In contrast, Type 1 Tracts account for only 13 percent of all suburban tracts in the South and just 6 percent of all suburban tracts in the West. In the South and West, Type 2 and Type 3 Tracts (more diverse, high homeownership suburban census tracts) are far more common: roughly half of all suburban tracts in these regions are Type 2 or Type 3 Tracts, the case with fewer than one-third of all suburban tracts in the Northeast and Midwest. Concerning low homeownership tracts, Type 4 Tracts, like Type 2 and Type 3 Tracts, represent a larger share of all suburban tracts in the South and West than in the Northeast and Midwest; Type 5 Tracts account for a similar share of suburban tracts in all regions.

To put this variety into further context and illustrate how it has only increased in the past decade, the author utilized data from the 2000 Census to array all census tracts within the largest 100 MSAs into the same typology framework as was done with data from the 2005–2009 American Community Survey. This provided a snapshot of suburbia from the recent past to compare and contrast with the present one. In addition, by assessing a tract's type in 2000 against its type in 2005–2009, it was thus possible to further highlight the changes underway in suburbia.

For example, even though the vast majority of non-Hispanic Whites within the nation's 100 largest MSAs live in suburban census tracts (and have consistently done so for decades), the stereotypical "lily-White" suburb predominated by homeowners is becoming far less common. Back in 2000, 61 percent of suburban census tracts in the 100 largest MSAs had homeownership rates of 70 percent or more. That year, 50 percent of these high homeownership tracts were more than 90 percent non-Hispanic White (or Type 1 Tracts). Type 1 Tracts actually slightly outnumbered the more diverse high homeownership tracts (those classified as either Diverse or Diversifying (Type 2) tracts, where non-Hispanic White residents account for 65 percent to 89.9 percent of all residents, or Melting Pot (Type 3) tracts, where people of color represent more than 35 percent of all residents) that year (7,978 versus 7,827) (see Table 3.2).

While the percentage of high homeownership suburban census tracts within the largest 100 MSAs remained at 61 percent in 2005–2009, the demographic profile of these tracts changed dramatically. Between 2000 and 2005–2009, the number of Type 1 Tracts fell by nearly 2,200 as these communities became increasingly racially and ethnically diverse.[12]

By 2005–2009, Type 1 Tracts—the non-Hispanic White homeowner enclaves that match popular perceptions of suburbia—accounted for only 37 percent of high homeownership tracts (down from 50 percent in 2000) and only 23 percent of all suburban census tracts in these MSAs (down from 31 percent in 2000) (see Table 3.3). That year, more diverse high homeownership tracts (Type 2 and Type 3 Tracts) outnumbered Type 1 Tracts nearly two-to-one (9,922 versus 5,807) (see Table 3.2). This shift occurred in nearly all of the largest 100 MSAs: 88 of them had fewer Type 1 suburban census tracts and more Type 2 and/or Type 3 Tracts in 2005–2009 than they did in 2000.[13]

---

12   Among tracts classified as Type 1 in 2000, only 68 percent remained Type 1 Tracts in 2005–2009: 28 percent were reclassified as Type 2 Tracts and 4 percent became low homeownership tracts (Type 4 or Type 5). Just two percent of all tracts classified as Type 2, Type 3, Type 4, or Type 5 in 2000 (408 of 17,739) were reclassified as Type 1 Tracts in 2005–2009.

13   Of the remaining 12 MSAs, six had no Type 1 Tracts either year, three had just one Type 1 Tract both years, and another had just two Type 1 Tracts both years. In addition, one

Table 3.2   Number and Proportion of Tracts by Type, 2000 and 2005–2009

Suburban Tract Type	Number of Tracts			Proportion of Tracts		
	2000	2005–2009	Change (2000–2005–2009)	2000	2005–2009	Change (2000–2005–2009)
All High Homeownership Rate Tracts	**15,805**	**15,729**	**-76**	**61.5%**	**61.1%**	**-0.3%**
Type 1 – High Homeownership Rate, Primarily non-Hispanic White	7,978	5,807	-2,171	31.0%	22.6%	-8.4%
Type 2 – High Homeownership Rate, Diverse/Diversifying	5,542	6,651	1,109	21.5%	25.9%	4.3%
Type 3 – High Homeownership Rate, Melting Pot	2,285	3,271	986	8.9%	12.7%	3.8%
All Low Homeownership Rate Tracts	**9,908**	**9,994**	**86**	**38.5%**	**38.9%**	**0.3%**
Type 4 – Low Homeownership Rate, Weak Single-family Stock	3,080	3,834	754	12.0%	14.9%	2.9%
Type 5 – Low Homeownership Rate, Strong Single-family Stock	6,828	6,160	-668	26.6%	23.9%	-2.6%
All Suburban Census Tracts	**25,717**	**25,723**		**100.0%**	**100.0%**	

Sources: 2000 Census, 2005–2009 American Community Survey, The Brookings Institution, author.

Population trends captured in analyses of the 2010 Census help explain these changes. From 2000 to 2010, for example, "Non-whites and Hispanics accounted for *98 percent* of population growth" in the 100 largest MSAs (Frey 2011b: 1 [author's emphasis]). Specifically in the suburbs of these metropolitan areas, Latinos were responsible for 49 percent of all population growth in the 2000s, while non-Hispanic Whites were responsible for just 9 percent of all growth (Frey 2011a: 4).

MSA gained Type 1 Tracts while also gaining Type 2 Tracts and losing Type 3 Tracts; the other lost Type 1 Tracts and had no change in Type 2 or Type 3 Tracts.

Table 3.3   Prevalence of High and Low Homeownership Suburban Census Tracts, 2005–2009

Suburban Tract Type	Number of Tracts	Tracts as a Proportion of All Suburban Tracts	Tracts as a Proportion of High or Low Homeownership Tracts
All High Homeownership Rate Tracts	**15,730**	**61.1%**	**100.0%**
Type 1 – High Homeownership Rate, Primarily non-Hispanic White	5,808	22.6%	36.9%
Type 2 – High Homeownership Rate, Diverse/Diversifying	6,651	25.9%	42.3%
Type 3 – High Homeownership Rate, Melting Pot	3,271	12.7%	20.8%
All Low Homeownership Rate Tracts	**9,994**	**38.9%**	**100.0%**
Type 4 – Low Homeownership, Weak Single-family Stock	3,834	14.9%	38.4%
Type 5 – Low Homeownership, Strong Single-family Stock	6,160	23.9%	61.6%
All Suburban Census Tracts	**25,724**	**100.0%**	

Sources: 2005–2009 American Community Survey, The Brookings Institution, author.

In addition, Black flight from cities, the ongoing dispersal of the Latino population, and immigrants' increasing tendency to bypass core cities altogether and instead move directly to suburban communities have greatly increased the share of people of color living in suburbs (Dreier, Mollenkopf, and Swanstrom 2001, Jones-Correa 2006). By 2005–2009, 50 percent of non-Hispanic Blacks/African Americans and 58 percent of Latinos in these metro areas lived in suburbs (see Table 3.4). In both cases, this represented a roughly ten percentage point increase from 1990.

In contrast, between 1990 and 2005–2009, the percentage of all residents of the largest 100 MSAs living in suburban census tracts increased by only three percentage points (from 66 percent to 69 percent); among non-Hispanic Whites, it rose by just four percentage points (from 74 percent to almost 78 percent).

As mentioned above, a substantial number of suburban census tracts in the largest 100 MSAs have a significant presence of renter households and multifamily housing. In fact, the number of these tracts (Type 4 and Type 5 Tracts, or those

Table 3.4   Proportion of the Population in the 100 Largest MSAs Living in Suburban Census Tracts by Race and Ethnicity, 1990, 2000, and 2005–2009

Race/Ethnicity	1990	2000	2005–2009	Change (1990 to 2005–2000)	Change (2000 to 2009)	Change (1990 to 2005–2009)
Proportion of All Residents	65.8%	67.8%	69.2%	2.0%	1.4%	3.4%
Proportion of Non-Hispanic Whites	74.2%	77.1%	77.9%	2.9%	0.8%	3.7%
Proportion of Non-Hispanic Blacks/African Americans	38.1%	44.7%	49.8%	6.6%	5.1%	11.7%
Proportion of Latinos	49.9%	54.1%	58.0%	4.2%	3.9%	8.1%

Sources: Neighborhood Change Database, 1990 and 2000 Census, 2005–2009 American Community Survey, The Brookings Institution, author.

with homeownership rates under 70 percent) remained constant between 2000 and 2005–2009, inching up from 9,908 to 9,994 and consistently representing almost 39 percent of all suburban census tracts in these MSAs (see Tables 3.2 and 3.3). There were some changes, however: The number of Type 4 Tracts (those in which more than 30 percent of single-family units are either renter-occupied or vacant) rose by roughly 750 between 2000 and 2005–2009 while the number of Type 5 Tracts (those in which less than 30 percent of single-family units are either renter-occupied or vacant) declined by nearly 670 (see Table 3.1). These adjustments, though, were minor, and the vast majority of tracts classified as Type 4 Tracts in 2000 remained Type 4 Tracts in 2005–2009; the same was true among Type 5 Tracts. At both points in time, Type 5 Tracts accounted for roughly two-thirds (69 percent in 2000 and 62 percent in 2005–2009) of low homeownership rate suburban tracts.

In sum, by 2005–2009, most suburban census tracts proved to be far different from popular perceptions of suburbia. What follows in the next several sections is a more in-depth discussion of the various tract types (Types 1 to 5). That discussion identifies key issues and forces at play in each type of suburban census tract. It also reviews the degree to which poverty is impacting each tract type.

Suburban Census Tracts with Moderate or High Poverty Rates across Tract Types

Just as all suburban census tracts run the gamut—from high to low homeownership and homogeneous to heterogeneous in terms of housing stock, tenure, and people—so, too, do moderate/high-poverty suburban census tracts. In the top 100 MSAs, 37 percent of all suburban census tracts have moderate/high poverty rates (rates at or above 10 percent); and 12 percent have high poverty rates (rates at or above 20 percent). Among all suburban tract types, Type 1 and Type 2 Tracts are the least likely to have moderate or high poverty rates: 13 and 14 percent of these tracts, respectively, have moderate poverty rates and just 1 and 2 percent of these tracts, respectively, have high poverty rates. While Melting Pot Tracts (Type 3 Tracts) are more likely to have moderate or high poverty rates, most (62 percent) have poverty rates below 10 percent (see Table 3.5).

Table 3.5   Number and Proportion of Suburban Census Tracts by Tract Type and by Poverty Rate, 2005–2009

Low Poverty Rate (<10%)		Moderate Poverty Rate (10% to 19.9%)		High Poverty Rate (≥20%)		Total
Number	Prop.	Number	Prop.	Number	Prop.	Number
12,617	80.2%	2,651	16.9%	462	**2.9%**	**15,730**
4,993	86.0%	750	12.9%	65	1.1%	5,808
5,584	84.0%	960	14.4%	107	1.6%	6,651
2,040	62.4%	941	28.8%	290	8.9%	3,271
3,604	**36.1%**	**3,734**	**37.4%**	**2,656**	**26.6%**	**9,994**
610	15.9%	1,336	34.8%	1,888	49.2%	3,834
2,994	48.6%	2,398	38.9%	768	12.5%	6,160
16,269	**6310.0%**	**6,393**	**24.8%**	**3,134**	**12.1%**	**25,796**

Sources: 2005–2009 American Community Survey, The Brookings Institution, author.

Type 4 Tracts are the most likely to have moderate or high poverty rates: 35 percent have moderate poverty rates and 49 percent have high poverty rates, leaving just 16 percent with low poverty rates. The reverse is the case in Type 5 Tracts, 49 percent of which have low poverty rates and just 13 percent of which have high poverty rates.

Together, while Type 4 and Type 5 Tracts account for just 39 percent of all suburban census tracts, they make up 67 percent of those suburban tracts with poverty rates at or above 10 percent (see Figure 3.2). Type 4 Tracts are particularly overrepresented among moderate/high-poverty tracts: Only 15 percent of all suburban census tracts are Type 4 Tracts but fully 34 percent of moderate/high-poverty tracts are Type 4 Tracts.

This means, though, that high homeownership rate tracts make up fully one-third of all moderate/high-poverty suburban tracts. And this third is fairly evenly split between Type 1, Type 2, and Type 3 Tracts, which each account for roughly 10 percent of all census tracts with poverty rates at or above 10 percent (see Table 3.6).

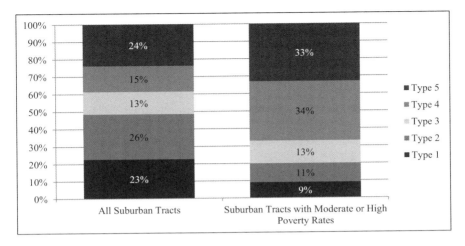

Figure 3.2   Breakdown of All Suburban Tracts and Higher Poverty Suburban Tracts by Tract Type, 2005–2009

Sources: 2005–2009 American Community Survey, The Brookings Institution, author.

Table 3.6   Number and Proportion of Suburban Census Tracts with Moderate or High Poverty Rates by Tract Type, 2005–2009

Suburban Tract Type	Suburban Tracts with Moderate or High Poverty Rates	
	Number	**Proportion**
All High Homeownership Rate Tracts	**3,113**	**32.8%**
Type 1 – High Homeownership Rate, Primarily non-Hispanic White	815	8.6%
Type 2 – High Homeownership Rate, Diverse/Diversifying	1,067	11.2%
Type 3 – High Homeownership Rate, Melting Pot	1,231	13.0%
All Low Homeownership Rate Tracts	**6,390**	**67.2%**
Type 4 –Low Homeownership Rate, Weak Single-family Stock	3,224	33.9%
Type 5 – Low Homeownership Rate, Strong Single-family Stock	3,166	33.3%
All Suburban Census Tracts	**9,503**	**100.0%**

Sources: 2005–2009 American Community Survey, The Brookings Institution, author.

While these suburban census tracts do have moderate or high poverty rates, the vast majority of residents in these neighborhoods are not poor. (Only 1 percent of suburban census tracts, for example, have poverty rates over 40 percent.). As a result, these places are not overrun with the issues commonly associated with poverty, such as homelessness or widespread reliance on public entitlement or welfare programs. While these issues are not overwhelming these communities, they are becoming an increasing reality in several of these places (Brookings Institution 2010). And moderate or high poverty rates further suggest that these places are struggling to a certain degree to attract households who have choices and/or to raise sufficient revenue to fund high quality local services, which only further reduces their competitiveness.

Focusing on the *people* in these communities, the poor populations within suburban census tracts with moderate or high poverty rates are just as varied as the places in which they live. Over the past decades, several factors have pushed or pulled poor people to suburban communities or reduced the incomes of households already living in them. These factors range from in-migration and out-migration patterns, to public programs that encourage or enable the mobility of low-income households into higher-income neighborhoods, to the ongoing suburbanization of jobs, to region-wide economic decline, to the aging and declining of older suburban housing stocks (Berube and Kneebone 2011). Certain forces are more or less present in particular MSAs and in different regions. For example, between 2000 and 2005–2009, immigrants accounted for "almost a quarter (22%) of the growth in the suburban poor population in the South," a region where 76 percent of the MSAs had overall population increases between 2000 and 2005–2009 and also saw gains within their core city or cities. Immigrants accounted for just half that share (11 percent) in the Midwest, where just 47 percent of all MSAs grew along with their core cities (Suro, Wilson, and Singer 2011: 7). In the Midwest, poverty rates increased more for native-born Americans than for immigrants over the past decade, reflecting the influence of the region's declining economy on poverty levels there (overall and in suburbia) (Murphy 2007, Suro, Wilson, and Singer 2011).

In regards to a *place's* perspective, as a result of the wide variety of poorer communities and the wide variety of factors behind increasing poverty rates and growing poor populations, the moderate/high-poverty tracts described in this study present a range of challenges for policymakers. For example, they show the need to stabilize neighborhoods facing housing market weaknesses as well as the need to stabilize owner and renter households facing shrinking economic capacity and therefore the reduced ability to purchase, rent, or maintain their housing. On a more positive note, the moderate/high-poverty tracts discussed here also provide key insights for how affordable housing (and lower-income residents) can successfully be integrated into suburban communities and, as a result, gain access to higher quality services and economic opportunity.

Distinctions between High Homeownership Tracts with Low versus Moderate or High Poverty Rates

Moderate- and high-poverty Type 1, Type 2, and Type 3 suburban census tracts offer important insights into the degree to which certain neighborhoods and regions are attracting new households or new construction; how tract-level and MSA-level conditions contribute to tracts' moderate or high poverty level; the degree to which the market values racially and ethnically diverse neighborhoods relative to homogeneous ones; and also how the demographic makeup of diverse tracts varies considerably between regions. The stories that emerge about Type 1, Type 2, and Type 3 Tracts, the three types of high homeownership tracts, are discussed in detail below.

The Story behind Moderate/High Poverty in Type 1 Tracts: Struggling to Attract New Households or New Construction

Most Type 1 census tracts with moderate or high poverty rates are not gaining population to the degree that other tracts are. As this analysis shows, moderate/high-poverty Type 1 Tracts typically experienced smaller population gains and less in-migration than low-poverty Type 1 Tracts and, to an even greater degree, than Type 2 and Type 3 Tracts. The likely causes of these distinctions might be a dearth of a competitive housing stock and amenities that many households look for when buying homes or renting apartments and also the fact that many moderate/high-poverty Type 1 Tracts are located in metropolitan areas with stagnating or declining populations that are struggling to attract new residents.

Between 1990 and 2005–2009, moderate/high-poverty Type 1 Tracts collectively registered a population increase of just 14.5 percent, well below the rate in low-poverty Type 1 Tracts (23 percent) and a far slower pace than in Type 2 Tracts and Type 3 Tracts, both of which grew roughly three times as fast (see Table 3.7). These disparities only grow when looking just at population trends since 2000. In the past decade, moderate/high-poverty Type 1 Tracts grew at half the rate of low-poverty Type 1 Tracts, one-fourth of the rate of Type 2 Tracts, and one-fifth of the rate of Type 3 Tracts.

Further evidence of low population growth appears in Table 3.8 below, documenting the levels of resident mobility. For example, moderate/high-poverty Type 1 Tracts are more likely than low-poverty Type 1 Tracts, Type 2 Tracts, and Type 3 Tracts to have higher percentages of households who have lived in their current homes longer. Fully 20 percent of households in moderate/high-poverty Type 1 Tracts moved into their current homes prior to 1980, compared to 18 percent in low-poverty Type 1 Tracts and just 13 percent in all Type 2 Tracts and 12 percent in all Type 3 Tracts (see Table 3.8).

An illustration of the prevalence of long-term owners in moderate/high-poverty Type 1 Tracts is the high proportion of households without mortgages. In moderate/high-poverty Type 1 Tracts, nearly 39 percent of all households do not have an

Table 3.7 Population Trends in Type 1, 2, and 3 Tracts by Poverty Level, 1990–2005–2009

	Type 1 Tracts			Type 2 Tracts			Type 3 Tracts		
	All	Low Poverty Rate	Moderate or High Poverty Rate	All	Low Poverty Rate	Moderate or High Poverty Rate	All	Low Poverty Rate	Moderate or High Poverty Rate
Population Change 1990–2005–2009	5,020,337	4,568,208	452,129	12,144,935	10,980,061	1,164,874	7,153,783	5,075,521	2,078,262
Percent Population Change 1990–2005–2009	22.1%	23.3%	14.5%	46.4%	50.0%	27.7%	53.9%	62.4%	40.5%
Population Change 2000–2005–2009	1,887,354	1,744,387	142,967	5,504,945	5,036,680	468,265	3,527,483	2,577,623	949,860
Percent Population Change 2000–2005–2009	7.3%	7.8%	4.2%	16.8%	18.0%	9.5%	20.9%	24.2%	15.2%
Number of Tracts	**5,807**	**4,992**	**815**	**6,651**	**5,584**	**1,067**	**3,271**	**2,040**	**1,231**

Sources: Neighborhood Change Data Base, 1990 and 2000 Census, 2005–2009 American Community Survey, The Brookings Institution, author.

Table 3.8 Proportion of Long-Time Households in Type 1, 2, and 3 Tracts by Poverty Level, 2005–2009

	Type 1 Tracts			Type 2 Tracts			Type 3 Tracts		
	All	Low Poverty Rate	Moderate or High Poverty Rate	All	Low Poverty Rate	Moderate or High Poverty Rate	All	Low Poverty Rate	Moderate or High Poverty Rate
Proportion of Owner Households who Moved in 1979 or Earlier	17.9%	17.6%	20.0%	12.7%	12.4%	14.9%	12.2%	11.2%	14.2%
Total Number of Tracts	**5,808**	**4,993**	**815**	**6,651**	**5,584**	**1,067**	**3,271**	**2,040**	**1,231**

Sources: 2005–2009 American Community Survey, The Brookings Institution, author.

Table 3.9 Proportion of Households in Type 1, 2, and 3 Tracts by Mortgage Status and by Poverty Level, 2005–2009

	Type 1 Tracts			Type 2 Tracts			Type 3 Tracts		
	All	Low Poverty Rate	Moderate or High Poverty Rate	All	Low Poverty Rate	Moderate or High Poverty Rate	All	Low Poverty Rate	Moderate or High Poverty Rate
Proportion of Owner Households without Mortgages	30.6%	29.5%	38.7%	25.5%	23.9%	35.1%	22.2%	18.7%	29.1%
Total Number of Tracts	**5,808**	**4,993**	**815**	**6,651**	**5,584**	**1,067**	**3,271**	**2,040**	**1,231**

Sources: 2005–2009 American Community Survey, The Brookings Institution, author.

Table 3.10 Average and Median Owner Incomes for Households in Type 1, 2, and 3 Tracts by Mortgage Status and by Poverty Level, 2005–2009

	Type 1 Tracts		Type 2 Tracts		Type 3 Tracts	
	Low Poverty Rate	Moderate or High Poverty Rate	Low Poverty Rate	Moderate or High Poverty Rate	Low Poverty Rate	Moderate or High Poverty Rate
Average Income, Owner Households with a Mortgage	$105,312	$73,804	$116,312	$77,776	$103,781	$73,042
Average Income, Owner Households without a Mortgage	$75,892	$49,815	$86,102	$51,585	$75,591	$49,428
Total Number of Tracts	**4,993**	**815**	**5,584**	**1,067**	**2,040**	**1,231**

Sources: 2005–2009 American Community Survey, The Brookings Institution, author.

outstanding mortgage, compared to just under 30 percent in low-poverty Type 1 Tracts, 26 percent in all Type 2 Tracts, and only 22 percent in all Type 3 Tracts (see Table 3.9).

That larger percentages of households without a mortgage coincide with higher poverty rates is not surprising given that, in general, the incomes of households without a mortgage are typically well below those of households with a mortgage. Nationwide, the median income of households with a mortgage is nearly twice the median income of households without a mortgage ($73,892 versus $41,797) (2010 American Community Survey 1-Year Estimates). This disparity between households with and without an outstanding mortgage holds in low- and moderate/high-poverty Type 1, Type 2, and Type 3 Tracts (see Table 3.10).

In addition to smaller population gains, moderate- and high-poverty Type 1 Tracts also saw less new construction than other tracts. These tracts have the lowest share of new housing of all high homeownership tracts: Just under 10 percent of units were built since 2000 in these tracts—significantly less than the share in low-poverty Type 1 Tracts and roughly half the share found in low-poverty Type 2 and low-poverty Type 3 Tracts (see Table 3.11).

Alternatively, more than 15 percent of all units in moderate/high-poverty Type 1 Tracts were built before 1940 (equivalent to roughly three times the share in Type 2 Tracts and five times the share in Type 3 Tracts) and 32 percent were built prior to 1970 (twice the share in Type 2 and Type 3 Tracts).

In sum, these population trends and past construction patterns highlight the fact that Type 1 Tracts with moderate and high poverty rates seem to be struggling to attract new households and new construction. The failure to attract residents may be due to issues specific to these particular census tracts such as a less central location, an outdated housing stock, or a dearth of popular amenities for those who have choices.

A Closer Look at Type 1 Tracts: Tract-level and MSA-level Conditions Contributing to Tracts' Moderate or High Poverty Levels in Growing versus Shrinking MSAs

In growing MSAs (those that gained population between 2000 and 2005–2009), this analysis found that tract-level characteristics, namely location within the metropolitan area and age of housing, seemed to influence Type 1 Tracts' power to draw households willing and able to buy or rent local housing and, in turn, these tracts' housing values and poverty levels. Among the 5,043 suburban census tracts analyzed in growing metros, "exurban" suburban Type 1 census tracts[14] have

---

14   These categorizations are based on a data set provided by the Brookings Institution. According to that research, "High Density Suburbs" are those in which more than 95 percent of the population lives in an urbanized area; "Mature Suburbs" have a 75 to 95 percent urbanization rate; "Emerging Suburbs" have a 25 to 75 percent urbanization rate; and "Exurbs" have an urbanization rate of less than 25 percent.

Table 3.11   Year Housing Units built in Type 1, 2, and 3 Tracts by Poverty Level, 2005–2009

Year Built	Type 1 Tracts		Type 2 Tracts		Type 3 Tracts	
	Low Poverty Rate	Moderate or High Poverty Rate	Low Poverty Rate	Moderate or High Poverty Rate	Low Poverty Rate	Moderate or High Poverty Rate
Units Built Since 2000	12.1%	9.9%	18.8%	13.4%	21.9%	16.8%
Units Built Since 1980	42.7%	39.9%	56.1%	47.1%	57.8%	50.1%
Units Built in the 1960s, 1970s	28.0%	27.9%	25.7%	31.2%	25.4%	29.7%
Units Built in the 1940s, 1950s	17.3%	16.9%	12.6%	14.9%	13.4%	16.0%
Units Built in 1939 or Earlier	12.0%	15.4%	5.6%	6.8%	3.3%	4.2%

Sources: 2005–2009 American Community Survey, The Brookings Institution, author.

higher proportions of moderate or high poverty rates than Type 1 Tracts in all other suburban types: 37 percent of exurban suburban Type 1 census tracts have poverty rates of at least 10 percent, compared to just 9 percent of Type 1 Tracts in other suburb types (see Figure 3.3).

This disparity holds across all four regions of the country, especially in the South, where 61 percent of exurban suburbs in growing MSAs have moderate or high poverty rates. In all regions, exurban Type 1 census tracts were at least two and a half times as likely as Type 1 Tracts in other suburb types (High Density, Mature, and Emerging) to have moderate or high poverty rates. As a result, exurban tracts are overrepresented among moderate- and high-poverty Type 1 census tracts in growing MSAs. While exurban tracts account for 13 percent of all Type 1 Tracts in these metros, they account for 39 percent of Type 1 Tracts with moderate or high poverty rates (see Figure 3.4).

Frey (2012) points out that these exurban places were being overbuilt during the housing boom and, as a result, were particularly hard-hit by the recent recession. The "end-of-decade economic doldrums—and especially the declining housing market—had substantial impacts on" exurban communities across the country (Frey 2012: 12). The exurban Type 1 census tracts in growing MSAs identified in this study together had 67,798 more poor residents in 2005–2009 than in 2000, a 32 percent increase. During the same time period, the number of single-family units occupied by renters increased by 9,616 (up 11 percent) and

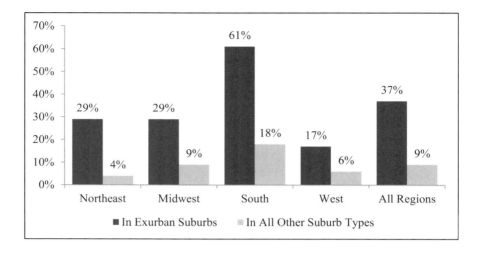

Figure 3.3 **Percent of Type 1 Tracts in Growing MSAs with Moderate or High Poverty Rates by Suburb Type, 2005–2009**

Sources: 2005–2009 American Community Survey, The Brookings Institution, author.

the number of vacant single-family homes rose by 31,905 (bumping the vacancy rate among single-family homes in these tracts from 9.9 percent in 2000 to 11.4 percent in 2005–2009). By 2005–2009, 65 percent of these tracts had median values that trailed their MSA's median.

Among non-exurban Type 1 census tracts in growing metropolitan areas, weak demand and moderate or high poverty rates tended to vary not based on tracts' locations within the MSA but rather tracts' housing stock characteristics, most notably the year units were built (see Figure 3.5).

In the Northeast, moderate- or high-poverty Type 1 Tracts in non-exurban suburbs have higher proportions of housing built prior to 1940; in the Midwest, they have higher proportions of housing built prior to 1960; and in the South and West, they have higher proportions of housing built prior to 1980 than in the other housing age cohorts. These housing cohorts (pre-1940 in the Northeast, pre-1960 in the Midwest, and pre-1980 in the South and West) may be more difficult to market and therefore may place the non-exurban tracts in which they predominate at a disadvantage when it comes to attracting and keeping households both willing and able to invest in local housing.

In shrinking MSAs (those that lost population between 2000 and 2005–2009), moderate/high-poverty Type 1 Tracts' difficulty attracting households who are both willing and able to invest in local housing is more often the result of MSA-wide weaknesses. Moderate- and high-poverty Type 1 Tracts are especially common in MSAs with shrinking overall populations and shrinking core cities. This group of shrinking MSAs is made up nearly entirely of Rust Belt cities in

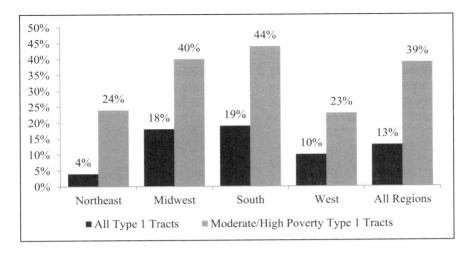

Figure 3.4   Percent of Type 1 Tracts in Exurban Suburbs of Growing MSAs by Poverty Level, 2005–2009

Sources: 2005–2009 American Community Survey, The Brookings Institution, author.

the Midwest and Northeast (such as Buffalo, Rochester, and Syracuse in Upstate New York; Cleveland, Dayton, and Youngstown in Ohio; and Pittsburgh and Scranton in Pennsylvania). While just 18 percent of all Type 1 suburban census tracts are in these weakest MSAs, 27 percent of moderate/high-poverty Type 1 Tracts are in such areas (see Figure 3.6).

The Pittsburgh MSA, for example, has more moderate/high-poverty Type 1 Tracts (89 tracts, representing 16 percent of all suburban tracts in the MSA) than any other of the 100 largest MSAs; in the Youngstown-Warren-Boardman MSA, nearly 24 percent of all suburban tracts (30 out of 127) are Type 1 Tracts with a moderate or high poverty rates.

In addition, moderate/high-poverty Type 1 Tracts in the weakest MSAs represent extreme examples of these tracts in terms of their inability to attract households with residential choices. Type 1 Tracts with moderate or high poverty rates located in shrinking MSAs with shrinking core cities have a higher proportion of owners with no outstanding mortgage (43 percent versus 38 percent) and a larger share of owners who have resided in their home since 1979 (30 percent versus just 17 percent) than in moderate/high-poverty Type 1 Tracts in stronger MSAs. Owners in moderate/high-poverty Type 1 Tracts in these weakest MSAs also have lower average incomes than those in stronger MSAs' moderate/high-poverty Type 1 Tracts ($60,090 versus $65,730).

Going forward, the inability of certain Type 1 Tracts to attract households who have residential choices is likely to have serious consequences for these communities: Places where not enough of these households are willing to in-

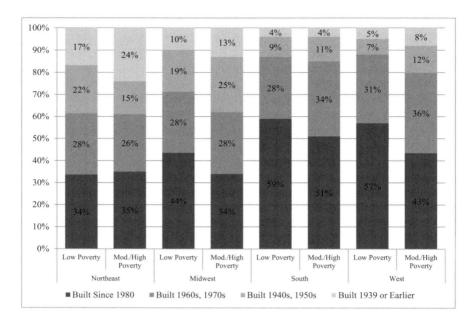

Figure 3.5   Year Housing Units built in Growing MSAs' Type 1 Tracts in Non-Exurban Suburbs by Region and Poverty Level, 2005–2009

Sources: 2005–2009 American Community Survey, The Brookings Institution, author.

migrate—due to the nature of the local housing stock or tracts' locational disadvantages—face stagnating or declining property values and increasing property abandonment (Anacker and Morrow Jones 2011). Such a drag on housing values is already evident: On average, the median value in moderate/high-poverty Type 1 Tracts increased by just 14 percent during the housing boom (between 2000 and 2005–2009), adjusted for inflation. In contrast, the typical median value rose by 29 percent, adjusted for inflation, in low-poverty Type 1 census tracts during the same time frame.

The Story behind Moderate/High Poverty in Type 2 and 3 Tracts: The Market's Undervaluing of Racially and Ethnically Diverse Neighborhoods

The population trends and past construction patterns described above show that nearly all non-Hispanic White Type 1 Tracts are struggling to attract new households or new construction. Those places where new housing is being built and where new residents are moving are diverse ones. In other words, new construction and population growth, and increasing racial and ethnic diversity, currently tend to go hand in hand in the analyzed suburbs.

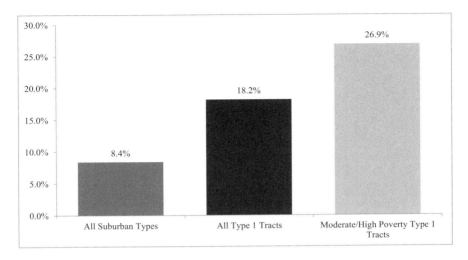

Figure 3.6   Proportion of Suburban Tracts in Shrinking Metros by Suburb Type and by Poverty Level, 2005–2009

Sources: 2005–2009 American Community Survey, The Brookings Institution, author.

While the growth trends are substantially different between Type 1 Tracts on the one hand and Type 2 and Type 3 Tracts on the other, what sets Type 2 and Type 3 Tracts apart from Type 1 Tracts is in how the median property values of their owner-occupied housing compare to the median household incomes of their owners. Typically, there is a high positive correlation between property values and household incomes. But race, ethnicity, and in some cases nativity tend to disrupt this positive correlation, as will be discussed below.

In the 100 largest MSAs, the median household incomes of owners in Type 1 Tracts correlate with their overall MSA median household incomes nearly identically to the way that those among owners in Type 2 Tracts correlate. Most Type 1 and Type 2 Tracts have median household incomes between 90 percent and 149.9 percent of their MSA's median, although less than 20 percent of all Type 1 and Type 2 census tracts in these MSAs have median incomes equal to less than 90 percent of their MSA's median household income. Some Type 2 Tracts actually have median household incomes well above their MSA's median: 18 percent of Type 2 Tracts have median incomes equal to at least 150 percent of their MSA's median compared to just 12 percent of Type 1 Tracts (see Figure 3.7).

If property values and household incomes are positively correlated, one would expect median property values in Type 1 and Type 2 Tracts relative to their MSA's median property value to break down similarly, too. However, there are fewer Type 2 Tracts that have median property values that exceed their respective MSA's median house value: 32 percent of Type 2 Tracts have median property values equal to less than 90 percent of their MSA's median property value, compared to just 26 percent of Type 1 Tracts. Among Type 3 Tracts, while only 40 percent have median household incomes equal to less than 90 percent of their MSA's median, 57 percent have median property values equal to less than 90 percent of their MSA's median property value (see Figure 3.8).

Given the expected high correlation between property values and household incomes, the two bars for each tract type in Figures 3.7 and 3.8 should be equally split; median property values should compare to MSA medians just as median household incomes do. However, as Figures 3.7 and 3.8 illustrate, this is not the case. This discrepancy will be discussed below.

Race, ethnicity, and long-standing patterns of residential segregation play a part in influencing the real estate market in these census tracts (Anacker 2010 and 2012, among others). For decades, these segregation patterns were encouraged and reinforced by discriminatory housing practices, such as redlining, steering, and blockbusting. While these practices were outlawed by the Fair Housing Act of 1968, segregation levels have declined only slightly and at a very slow pace in the decades since (Logan and Stults 2011).

Early twentieth-century thinking on how neighborhoods change, codified into several New Deal Programs and the post-World War II federal homeownership programs, including the Federal Housing Administration (FHA), continue to powerfully affect not only popular attitudes about race and ethnicity but also households' preferences for certain neighborhoods and neighbors. In the 1920s, scholars at the Chicago School of Sociology advanced the life-cycle theory of neighborhood change. According to this theory, neighborhoods change from birth to death (or abandonment) as housing densities increase, local income levels fall, and residents become increasingly diverse (Ahlbrandt and Brophy 1975, Goetze 1979, Downs 1981, Aitken 1990, Lauria 1998, Temkin 2000, Cohen 2001). Federal homeownership policies, specifically the FHA's mortgage insurance program that made homeownership possible for millions of American households from the 1930s through the 1960s, used these expectations about neighborhood change to identify supposedly risky investment areas (Jackson 1985). The label attached to these typically urban and diverse places discouraged banks from lending to them and encouraged non-Hispanic White households to leave for them for homogeneous suburban neighborhoods.

These negative connotations and pessimistic expectations have stuck with many: Research has shown that non-Hispanic Whites tend to move into new neighborhoods as the percentage of Blacks/African Americans in those neighborhoods increases, particularly as it reaches roughly one-third of all residents (Massey and Denton 1993). As a result, the demand for housing among non-Hispanic Whites decreases as neighborhood diversity increases, ultimately dragging down property values in diverse neighborhoods.

Rusk (2001) defines this drag—or the difference between where property values would be if race were not a factor in housing choices and where property values are since race *is* a factor—as the segregation tax that households of color, particularly Black/African American ones, are forced to bear. Rusk calculates the

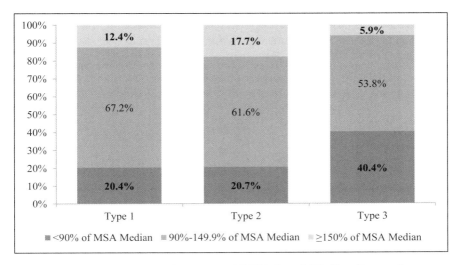

Figure 3.7   Comparison of Tract- and MSA-Level Median Owner incomes in Type 1, 2, and 3 Tracts, 2005–2009

Sources: 2005–2009 American Community Survey, The Brookings Institution, author.

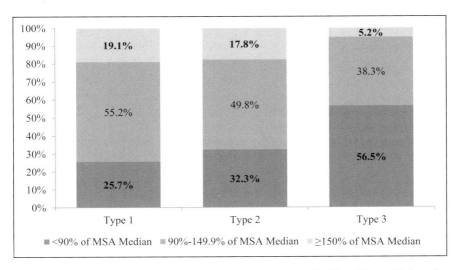

Figure 3.8   Comparison of Tract- and MSA-Level Median House Values in Type 1, 2, and 3 Census Tracts, 2005–2009

Sources: 2005–2009 American Community Survey, The Brookings Institution, author.

Table 3.12   Comparison of Tract- and MSA-Level Median Value-to-Median Household Income Ratios for Type 1, 2, and 3 Tracts, 2005–2009

Tract Type	Tract Ratio (Median Value/Median Owner Household Income) ÷ MSA Ratio (Median Value/Median Owner Household Income)	Proportion of Tracts where Value-to-Income Ratio is less than the MSA's Ratio
Type 1 Tracts	1.04	47%
Type 2 Tracts	0.96	64%
Type 3 Tracts	0.92	73%

Sources: 2005–2009 American Community Survey, The Brookings Institution, author.

segregation tax by comparing the median property value-to-median owner income ratios for majority-non-Hispanic White neighborhoods to those for majority-non-Hispanic Black/African American neighborhoods. The difference between these ratios is the segregation tax.

This analysis used a similar methodology to calculate median property value-to-median household income ratios for each census tract; a similar ratio was calculated for each MSA. Dividing a tract's ratio from its MSA's ratio, it was determined whether median property values were lower (relative to median household incomes) in tracts compared to their MSAs as a whole. If property values increase with household incomes, one would expect fewer low-poverty tracts to have ratios that trail their respective MSA's ratio than higher poverty ones. However, this is not the case, as analyses below show.

First, median property value-to-median household ratios were compared at the tract and MSA level for Type 1, 2, and 3 Tracts; second, the proportion of tracts where the median property value-to-median household income ratio deviates from their respective MSA ratios for Type 1, 2, and 3 Tracts was calculated. In regard to the former, the ratio in a Type 1 Tract (a tract that is at least 90 percent non-Hispanic White) exceeds its respective MSA ratio, meaning that median property values are higher, relative to household incomes, in these neighborhoods than they are MSA-wide. Type 2 Tracts (tracts that are 65 percent to 89.9 percent non-Hispanic White) have a ratio equal to just 96 percent of their MSA's ratio and Type 3 Tracts (tracts that are less than 65 percent non-Hispanic White) have a ratio equal to only 92 percent of their MSA's ratio (see Table 3.12).

Put another way, only 47 percent of all Type 1 Tracts have ratios that trail their MSA's ratio. This is the case, however, of 64 percent of all Type 2 Tracts and 73 percent of all Type 3 Tracts (see Table 3.12).

In regard to the latter, about 46 percent of Type 1 Tracts that had a low poverty rate had a tract ratio that was less than their respective MSA ratio. In contrast, 57 percent of Type 1 Tracts with a moderate or high poverty rate did so. Yet this larger

Table 3.13   Proportion of Type 1, 2, and 3 Tracts Where Median Value-to-Median Household Income Ratio is Less Than or More Than Their MSA's Ratio, by Poverty Level, 2005–2009

Tract Median Value-to-Income Ratio Relative to MSA Median Value-to-Owner Household Income Ratio	Type 1 Tracts			Type 2 Tracts			Type 3 Tracts		
	Low Poverty Rate	Moderate/High Poverty Rate	Diff.	Low Poverty Rate	Moderate/High Poverty Rate	Diff.	Low Poverty Rate	Moderate/High Poverty Rate	Diff.
Tract Ratio Less than MSA Ratio	45.7%	57.1%	-11.4%	62.6%	68.9%	-6.3%	73.7%	73.1%	0.6%
Tract Ratio More than MSA Ratio	54.3%	42.9%		37.4%	31.1%		26.3%	26.9%	

Sources: 2005–2009 American Community Survey, The Brookings Institution, author.

Table 3.14   Homeownership Rates by Race and Ethnicity in High Homeownership Tracts, 2005–2009

Tenure	Type 1 Tracts		Type 2 Tracts		Type 3 Tracts	
	Low Poverty Rate	Moderate or High Poverty Rate	Low Poverty Rate	Moderate or High Poverty Rate	Low Poverty Rate	Moderate or High Poverty Rate
Homeownership Rate	86.8%	80.5%	85.5%	79.5%	82.9%	78.6%
Homeownership Rate, Non-Hispanic White	87.2%	81.1%	87.0%	82.1%	85.2%	83.6%
Homeownership Rate, of Color	76.8%	64.9%	77.3%	66.1%	80.3%	74.8%

Sources: 2005–2009 American Community Survey, The Brookings Institution, author.

percentage among moderate/high-poverty Type 1 Tracts was still less than the portion of *low-poverty* Type 2 Tracts (63 percent) and *low-poverty* Type 3 Tracts (74 percent) that had a tract ratio that was less than their respective MSA ratio (see Table 3.13). In addition, while Type 1 and Type 2 Tracts with moderate or high poverty rates, compared to their low-poverty counterparts, had ratios that trailed their MSA's ratio (57 percent versus 46 percent, and 69 percent versus 63 percent), there was almost no difference between low-poverty Type 3 Tracts (74 percent) and moderate/high-poverty ones (73 percent).

The presence of these disparities has negative consequences for the ability of many residents in diverse (particularly Type 3) tracts to build wealth through homeownership, as higher household incomes do not necessarily translate into higher property values the same way they do in largely non-Hispanic White tracts (Rusk 2001).

This is particularly troubling because Type 3 Tracts—even moderate/high-poverty Type 3 Tracts—have homeownership rates comparable to those in Type 1 and Type 2 Tracts and have even higher homeownership rates among households of color. In moderate/high-poverty Type 3 census tracts, 75 percent of all households of color own their homes, compared to just 65 percent in moderate/high-poverty Type 1 and 66 percent in moderate/high-poverty Type 2 Tracts (see Table 3.14).

Fifty-eight percent of suburban households of color who own their homes live in Type 2 or Type 3 Tracts (see Figure 3.9). Another 38 percent live in suburban census tracts with low overall homeownership rates (Type 4 and Type 5 Tracts).

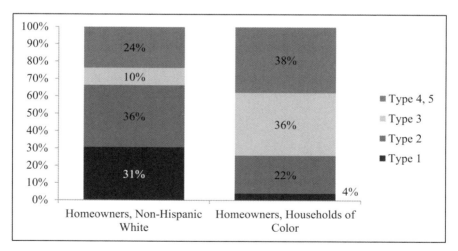

Figure 3.9   Tract Type of Suburban Homeowners by Race and Ethnicity in the 100 Largest MSAs, 2005–2009

Sources: 2005–2009 American Community Survey, The Brookings Institution, author.

As a result, most owners reside in neighborhoods subject to the segregation tax and therefore are unlikely to benefit from increasing property values relative to their household income level compared to owners in less diverse tracts.

A Closer Look at Type 3 Tracts: The Tale of Two Types of Suburban Melting Pots

Type 3 Tracts not only illustrate the implications of diversity on the strength of neighborhood property values, as discussed above, but also emphasize the role of in-migrating and immigrating people of color on MSAs' recent population trends and suburbanization patterns. These trends and patterns tend to differ between the Northeast and Midwest, on the one hand, and the South and West on the other.

Type 3 Tracts in general are most prevalent in those regions that are experiencing the largest population increases, namely the South and West. In all, 82 percent of Type 3 Tracts are in these two regions (see Table 3.15). In contrast, just 23 percent of Type 1 Tracts are in these two regions.

Table 3.15   Regional Breakdown of Type 1, 2, and 3 Tracts, 2005–2009

Region	Type 1 Tracts		Type 2 Tracts		Type 3 Tracts	
	Number	**Prop.**	**Number**	**Prop.**	**Number**	**Prop.**
Region 1 Northeast	2,335	40%	1,572	24%	290	9%
Region 2 Midwest	2,152	37%	1,311	20%	298	9%
Region 3 South	964	17%	2,344	35%	1,441	44%
Region 4 West	357	6%	1,424	21%	1,242	38%
Total	**5,808**		**6,651**		**3,271**	

Sources: 2005–2009 American Community Survey, The Brookings Institution, author.

Not only the prevalence of Type 3 Tracts but also the composition of their populations differs by region. According to Frey (2011a), "Hispanic suburbanization is making its largest impact in different parts of the country than black suburbanization" (10). This study, concurring with Frey (2011a), also found that Type 3 (Melting Pot) Tracts fell into two categories. First, non-Hispanic Blacks/African Americans are the largest proportion of people of color in Type 3 Tracts in MSAs in the Northeast, Midwest, and South (excluding Florida and Texas). Second, Latinos are the largest proportion of people of color in Type 3 Tracts in MSAs in the West, Florida, and Texas (see Figure 3.10).

At the census tract level, non-Hispanic Blacks/African Americans outnumber Latinos in 73 percent of all Type 3 Tracts in the Northeast, the Midwest, and the South (excluding Florida and Texas) and 79 percent of all moderate/high-poverty Type 3 Tracts in these states and regions (see Figure 3.11).

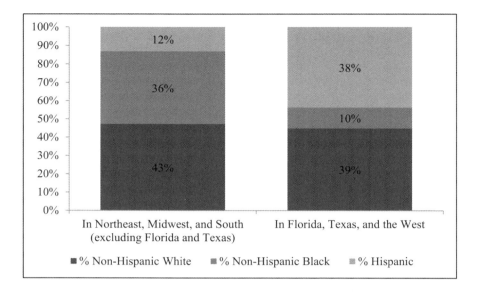

Figure 3.10   Racial and Ethnic Breakdown in Type 3 Tracts by Region, 2005–2009

Sources: 2005–2009 American Community Survey, The Brookings Institution, author.

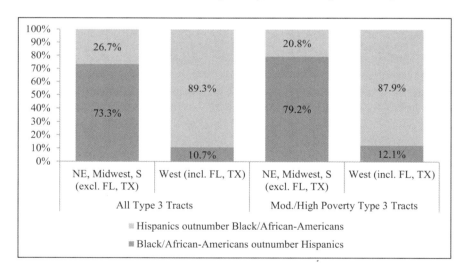

Figure 3.11   Predominant Racial and Ethnic groups in Type 3 Tracts by Region and Poverty Level, 2005–2009

Sources: 2005–2009 American Community Survey, The Brookings Institution, author.

In the West, as well as Florida and Texas, Latinos outnumber non-Hispanic Blacks/African Americans in 89 percent of all Type 3 Tracts and 88 percent of moderate/high-poverty Type 3 Tracts.

Interestingly, there were twice as many non-Hispanic Black/African American Type 3 Tracts in the Northeast, Midwest, and South (excluding Florida and Texas) compared to Latino Type 3 Tracts in the West, Florida, and Texas that lost residents between 1990 and 2005–2009: 33 percent versus 17 percent did so. (Thirty-five percent of these tracts in the Northeast and 62 percent of these tracts in the Midwest lost residents during this time.). Among Type 3 Tracts with moderate or high poverty rates, 40 percent of those with more non-Hispanic Blacks/African Americans than Latinos and located in the Northeast, Midwest, and South (excluding Florida and Texas) lost residents. (This was true of 49 percent of these tracts in the Northeast and 71 percent of them in the Midwest.). In contrast, this was the case with just 13 percent of moderate/high-poverty Type 3 Tracts in which Latinos outnumbered non-Hispanic Blacks/African Americans and that were located in the West as well as Florida and Texas.

These insights tell a tale of two types of suburban melting pots. On the one hand there are the largely Black/African American suburbs in most of the South, the Northeast, and the Midwest, many of which are losing population. These communities have long been and continue to be stymied by the legacies of residential segregation: the segregation tax, limited access to conventional mortgage financing, and unreasonably negative reputations (where, for example, popular perceptions of local crime rates far exceed actual crime rates). This reality is reflected in the ongoing decline in demand for housing illustrated by ongoing population declines, which, in turn, keeps home values stagnant and, in this way, creates the segregation tax imposed on these tracts. On the other hand are the growing, largely Latino Type 3 Tracts in MSAs in the West, Florida, and Texas, which were among the strongest housing markets during the house price bubble. These are census tracts in which 77 percent of housing units were built after 1970, or after the Fair Housing Act of 1968 officially outlawed discrimination in housing and lending. Rather than the challenges associated with decades of housing market discrimination, these melting pot suburbs continue to face the challenges brought on by the recent housing crisis. Like most places that boomed and busted, several melting pot suburbs have grappled with high foreclosure rates, property abandonment, and decimated property values (Chinni and Gimpel 2010).

Distinctions between Low Homeownership Tracts with Low versus Moderate or High Poverty Rates

The remaining suburban census tracts in the top 100 MSAs have lower homeownership rates (rates below 70 percent). As described earlier, some of these have strong single-family housing markets while some do not. Together, though, these low homeownership tracts account for 39 percent of suburban census tracts, and 67 percent of moderate/high-poverty suburban census tracts, in these MSAs. These tracts are also home to 56 percent of the suburban poor population. Yet just as melting pot suburban tracts split into two very distinct groups, the two types of low homeownership census tracts represent opposite ends of a spectrum: One (Type 4 Tracts) embodies the re-concentration of poor residents in weakening or already weak communities outside the urban cores; the other (Type 5 Tracts) shows the successful integration of affordable housing within stronger markets, (likely) offering poor residents better access to quality services and economic opportunity.

The Story behind Moderate/High Poverty in Type 4 Tracts: Poverty in Suburbs with Significant Rental Housing and Weak Housing Markets

Of all analyzed tract types, Type 4 suburban census tracts have the highest prevalence of moderate or high poverty rates: 84 percent of these tracts have a poverty rate of 10 percent or more. This proportion is more than double the share among all suburban census tracts (37 percent). One characteristic that tends to distinguish both low- and moderate/high-poverty Type 4 Tracts from other tract types are their relatively low overall homeownership rates, typically around 50 percent. In addition, households of color living in Type 4 Tracts have especially low levels of homeownership: just 38 percent of households of color in low-poverty Type 4 Tracts and 35 percent of households of color in moderate/high-poverty Type 4 Tracts own their homes.

These lower homeownership rates are at least partially explained by the housing stock in these census tracts. Type 4 Tracts tend to have a larger share of multifamily housing units, the vast majority of which are renter-occupied. Specifically in Type 4 Tracts, both those with moderate/high poverty levels and those with low poverty levels, 43 percent of all units are in multifamily structures.

Such low homeownership rates in Type 4 Tracts, however, are also at least partially explained by a weak demand for the single-family stock in these areas. In this way, Type 4 Tracts tell the story of the decline of the post-World War II suburbs. As Dreier, Mollenkopf, and Swanstrom (2001) have shown, suburban decline has "most affected not the oldest suburbs but those built between 1945 and 1970," primarily because the size of the typical single-family home in these communities is less than half the size of new homes built today (roughly 1,000 square feet versus close to 2,500 square feet) (42-43). This analysis found that Type 4 Tracts, compared to Type 1, 2, and 3 Tracts, typically have smaller owner-occupied housing units. Thirty-three percent of owner-occupied units in Type 4 Tracts have two or fewer bedrooms, compared to 23 percent in Type 5 Tracts and between 15 percent and 19 percent of owner-occupied units in high homeownership tracts. On the other hand, just 19 percent of owner-occupied units in Type 4 Tracts had at least four bedrooms, compared to 28 percent in Type 5 Tracts, 32 percent in Type 1 Tracts, 39 percent in Type 2 Tracts, and 36 percent in Type 3 Tracts (see Figure 3.12).

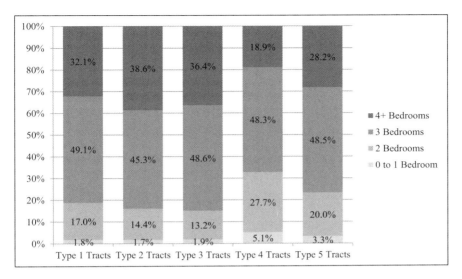

Figure 3.12   Number of Bedrooms in Owner-Occupied Housing Units by Tract Type, 2005–2009

Sources: 2005–2009 American Community Survey, The Brookings Institution, author.

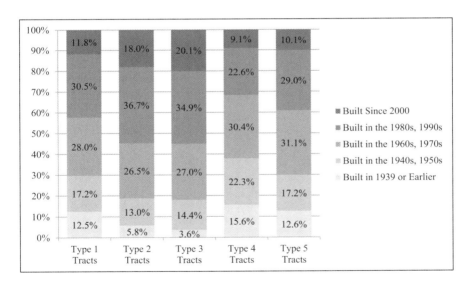

Figure 3.13   Age of Housing by Tract Type, 2005–2009

Sources: 2005–2009 American Community Survey, The Brookings Institution, author.

In regard to the median age of housing, in Type 4 suburban census tracts, 38 percent of units were built before 1960, the largest share of any tract type, and just 9 percent of all units have been added since 2000, the smallest share (see Figure 3.13).

By comparison, 30 percent of units in Type 1 and Type 5 Tracts were built prior to 1960; this was the case with just 19 percent of units in Type 2 Tracts and only 18 percent of units in Type 3 Tracts (see Figure 3.13).

There is substantial variation between Type 4 Tracts in terms of their age of housing in different regions of the country. In the Northeast and Midwest, home to most of the country's older industrial cities, over half of all units in Type 4 Tracts were built before 1960 (59 percent in the Midwest and 65 percent in the Northeast). The housing in southern and western Type 4 Tracts is more evenly split, with roughly one-third built prior to 1960, one-third built in the 1960s and 1970s, and one-third built since 1980 (see Table 3.16).

Table 3.16   Age of Housing in Type 4 Tracts by Region, 2005–2009

Census Region	Proportion of Units Built since 1980	Proportion of Units Built in the 1960s and 1970s	Proportion of Units Built before 1960
Region 1 Northeast	15.4%	19.4%	65.2%
Region 2 Midwest	16.3%	25.3%	58.5%
Region 3 South	39.6%	34.4%	26.0%
Region 4 West	35.6%	32.9%	31.5%

Sources: 2005–2009 American Community Survey, The Brookings Institution, author.

Regardless of the age of their housing stock, Type 4 census tracts typically represent a metropolitan area's weakest suburban areas—those with the lowest values, those having the hardest time keeping existing or attracting new homeowners, and those most frequently facing the challenge of higher poverty and vacancy rates. In stronger metropolitan areas with high-priced central cities (such as greater New York City, greater Boston, and greater San Francisco), Type 4 census tracts provide needed affordable housing opportunities. Yet even in these cases, property vacancy and abandonment and residents' low incomes call into question the ability of these tracts to ward off severe neighborhood decline.

The Story behind Moderate/High Poverty in Type 5 Tracts: Poverty in Suburbs with Significant Rental Housing and Strong Housing Markets

Last are those suburban census tracts with lower homeownership rates but with stronger single-family housing markets. Just 51 percent of these tracts have poverty rates above 10 percent. In other words, 49 percent of all Type 5 Tracts have low poverty rates, despite their prevalence of rental housing. In contrast, just 16 percent of Type 4 Tracts had low poverty levels while 49 percent had high poverty rates (i.e., 20 percent or more). As a result, the average poverty rate

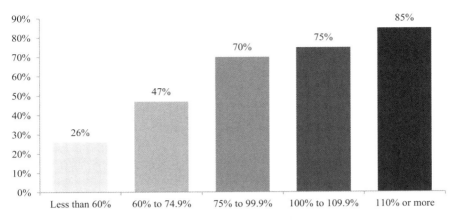

County Median Value as a Percent of the MSA Median Value

Figure 3.14   Percent of Counties with Higher Proportion of Type 5 than Type 4 Tracts, by Market Strength, 2005–2009

Sources: 2005–2009 American Community Survey, The Brookings Institution, author.

in Type 5 Tracts was roughly half the average for Type 4 Tracts: 11.7 percent versus 21.6 percent.

Possibly contributing to the success of the single-family market in these tracts is the fact that, in contrast to Type 4 Tracts, Type 5 Tracts typically have a slightly higher proportion of single-family, detached, and newer units. Far more significant in explaining the strength of Type 5 Tracts is the strength of their surrounding counties. Most Type 4 Tracts are in counties with median property values below their MSA's median; 11 percent are in counties with median property values equal to less than 75 percent of their MSA's median property value. Most Type 5 Tracts, in contrast, are in counties with median property values that exceed their MSA's median. Twenty-five percent of all Type 5 Tracts and even 19 percent of moderate/high-poverty Type 5 Tracts are in counties with median property values equal to 110 percent or more of their MSA's median.

Put another way, the economically stronger the county, the more likely it is to have a higher proportion of Type 5 Tracts than Type 4 Tracts. Just 26 percent of counties with median property values equal to less than 60 percent of their MSA's median have a higher proportion of Type 5 Tracts than Type 4 Tracts, while 85 percent of counties with median values equal to 110 percent or more of their MSA's median have a higher proportion of Type 5 Tracts than Type 4 Tracts (see Figure 3.14).

The ongoing strength of the single-family market in Type 5 Tracts in economically stronger counties—such as in Montgomery, Bucks, and Burlington[15]

---

15   Burlington County, New Jersey, is home to Mount Laurel, the defendant in a string of New Jersey Supreme Court decisions that deemed exclusionary zoning practices to be unconstitutional in the state and obligated all New Jersey municipalities to provide their

counties (surrounding Philadelphia), Lake County (north of Chicago), King County (including Seattle), and Clackamas County (south of Portland, Oregon)—illustrate how such areas can accommodate rental housing, even affordable rental housing, without destabilizing their single-family stock and, by doing so, provide low-income households with access to better services and more economic opportunity.

Conclusion

The discussion above has shown that suburban communities generally and moderate/high- poverty suburban communities in particular are not homogeneous. They include inner-ring suburbs and exurbs. They include places with population increases and others with population decreases. They include lily-White enclaves and melting pots. They include wide expanses of newly constructed single-family detached homes and urban centers with residential, commercial, and industrial land uses.

This analysis presents a typology of five types of suburban census tracts in the top 100 MSAs. The majority of these tracts have relatively high homeownership rates but differ in their degree of diversity. Even those with similar proportions of residents of color differ in important ways. Largely Black/African American suburban communities typically bear the unfair burden of decades of discriminatory practices and the larger market's undervaluing of their properties. Many of these communities were set up for failure from the start since, in many cases, local forces originally integrated what Sugrue (2011) dubs "secondhand suburbs": communities with deteriorating or older housing, depressed shopping districts, poorer services, fewer jobs, and shrinking tax bases. With or without this burden, non-Hispanic White homeowners and homebuyers tend to prefer units in predominantly non-Hispanic White neighborhoods and therefore choose to move out of, or to not move into, diversifying neighborhoods. Thus, median property values in most Black/African American communities remain low and stagnant.

In contrast, many of the diverse—and booming—suburbs in the South and West, often with larger Latino populations, are not hampered as much by this type of history. If anything, both their growth and their current diversity are signs of their strength, or their ability to provide quality housing and access to a wealth of (largely construction-oriented) jobs. But those days are history, at least for the foreseeable future, and the new reality in these communities, as in the Black/African American suburbs in the Northeast and Midwest, entails high numbers of foreclosures and abandoned and vacant properties.

Not only do these melting pot communities fly in the face of popular perceptions of suburbia as all-non-Hispanic White enclaves, so too do the significant portion

---

"fair share" of affordable housing. Follow-up studies of affordable housing projects in the community (Massey et al. 2013) found that they had no negative impacts on surrounding property values.

of suburban census tracts—39 percent of all suburban census tracts in the top 100 MSAs—with low homeownership rates and a high proportion of renters and multifamily housing. Of all tract types, those low homeownership tracts with weak single-family housing markets, often in the weakest MSAs or in an MSA's weaker counties, and home to smaller, post-World War II housing units, are overwhelmed by poverty. These weaker markets and their less attractive housing units act as regions' de facto suburban affordable housing strategies in much the same way that challenged neighborhoods and challenged housing units in central cities do. In many ways, these suburban communities are even less able to accommodate declining housing quality and increasing poverty than their urban counterparts, which have longer histories of intervening in the housing market and therefore have built up stronger networks (involving public, private, and nonprofit partners) to carry out such work.

Also turning perceptions of suburbia upside down and deflating the knee-jerk, NIMBY opposition to rental or affordable housing in suburbia are the census tracts that are successfully integrating such housing into communities with strong single-family housing markets. This is the case in 62 percent of low homeownership suburban census tracts where at least 70 percent of single-family units in these tracts are owner-occupied and values often rival those in other suburbs within the MSA. In strong counties, these places often present an opportunity for developing more affordable housing in the suburbs. In these locations, affordable housing is sustainable because tenants or low-income homebuyers will be better linked to economic opportunities and more likely to be residentially stable as a result. Affordable single-family and multifamily property values will be less likely to decline and therefore more likely to cover the costs associated with ongoing maintenance over the long term. Affordable housing will be less likely to have negative impacts on the values of nearby single-family housing or to undermine the favorable perceptions of these locations by the market. These locations offer a good opportunity for economic integration, something essential to the long-term success of metropolitan regions.

At the same time, the nature, scope, and scale of poverty in suburban communities is just as varied. In some cases, poverty is not influenced by in-migration but linked to declining household incomes of long-time owners as they switch from work-related incomes to retirement incomes or as they grapple with under- or unemployment. In some cases, poverty stems from the influx of new residents drawn to affordable housing opportunities. In some cases, poverty rates are modest; in others, they are high or extreme. The fact that suburbs, moderate/high-poverty suburbs, and the suburban poor come in so many shapes and sizes is another key lesson for policymakers looking to reinvigorate declining suburban housing markets or meet the various needs of poor residents.

As central cities have realized for decades, most of the consequences that suburbs must address stem from forces largely outside of their control and occurring far beyond their borders. Regional strength, for example, sets the stage for the inflows and outflows of people and the inflows and outflows of capital into the housing market. However, stakeholders and public officials are not helpless. There are countless ways for them to respond to regional trends and challenges. Understanding the type of suburban place and the type of suburban poverty they are working with can help policymakers tailor their responses to specific problems; the more tailored the response, the more likely it is to succeed.

References

Ahlbrandt, R.S. and Brophy, P.C. 1975. *Neighborhood Revitalization: Theory and Practice*. Lexington, MA: Heath.

Aitken, S. 1990. Local evaluations of neighborhood change. *Annals of the Association of American Geographers*, 80, 247–67.

Allard, S.W. and Roth, B. 2010. *Strained Suburbs: The Social Service Challenges of Rising Suburban Poverty*. Washington, DC: Brookings Institution.

Anacker, K.B. 2012. Shaky palaces? Analyzing property values and their appreciation rates in minority first suburbs. *International Journal of Urban and Regional Research*, 36, 791–816.

Anacker, K.B. 2010. Still Paying the race tax? Analyzing property values in homogeneous and mixed-race suburbs. *Journal of Urban Affairs*, 32, 55–77.

Anacker, K.B, and Morrow-Jones, H.A. 2011. Playing Both "Inside" and "Outside Games"? Evidence from Expert Interviews in Mature Suburbs in Ohio. *Urban Geography*, 32, 244–62.

Bajaj, B. Kingsley, G.T., and Pettit, K.L.S. 2005. *Business Patterns and Trends: National Summary*. Washington, DC: Urban Institute.

Berube, A. and Kneebone, E. 2011. *Parsing U.S. Poverty at the Metropolitan Level. Up Front Blog*. [Online]. Available at http://www.brookings.edu/opinions/2011/0922_metro_poverty_berube_kneebone.aspx [accessed 6 February 2012].

Bowman, M. 2008. *U.S. Commuting Statistical Analysis*. [Online]. Available at http://www.slideshare.net/marcus.bowman.slides/us-commuting-statistical-analysis [accessed: 3 February 2012].

Bradley, J. 2001. *Private Suburbs, Public Cities*. [Online: The American Prospect]. Available at http://prospect.org/article/private-suburbs-public-cities [accessed: 3 February 2012].

Brookings Institution. 2010. *State of Metropolitan America: On the Front Lines of Demographic Transformation* Washington, DC: Brookings Institution.

Chinni, D. and Gimpel, J. 2010. *Our Patchwork Nation: The Surprising Truth about the "Real" America*. New York, NY: Gotham Books.

Cohen, J.R. 2001. Abandoned housing: Exploring lessons from Baltimore. *Housing Policy Debate*, 12, 415–48.

Downs, A. 1981. *Neighborhoods and Urban Development*. Washington, DC: Brookings Institution.

Dreier, P., Mollenkopf, J. and Swanstrom, T. 2001. *Place Matters: Metropolitics for the Twenty-First Century*. Lawrence, KS: University Press of Kansas.

Frey, W.H. 2011a. *Melting Pot Cities and Suburbs: Racial and Ethnic Change in Metro America in the 2000s*. Washington, DC: Brookings Institution.

Frey, W.H. 2011b. *The New Metro Minority Map: Regional Shifts in Hispanics, Asians, and Blacks from Census 2010*. Washington, DC: Brookings Institution.

Frey, W.H. 2012. *The Demographic Lull Continues, Especially in Exurbia*. [Online]. Available at http://www.brookings.edu/blogs/up-front/posts/2012/04/06-census-exurbs-frey [accessed 1 May 2013].

Galster, G. 2009. *Do Neighborhoods Matter?* Washington, DC: Urban Institute.

Galster, G., Tatian, P., Santiago, A. Pettit, K, and Smith, R. 2003. *Why NOT in My Back Yard? The Neighborhood Impacts of Assisted Housing*. New Brunswick, NJ: Rutgers University/Center for Urban Policy Research Press.

Goetze, R. 1979. *Understanding Neighborhood Change: The Role of Expectations in Urban Revitalization*. Cambridge, MA: Ballinger Publishing Company.

Hobbs, F. and Stoops, N. 2002. *Demographic Trends in the 20th Century*. Washington, DC: U.S. Government Printing Office.

Jackson, K.T. 1985. *Crabgrass Frontier: The Suburbanization of the United States*. New York, NY: Oxford University Press.

Jones-Correa, M. 2006. Reshaping the American Dream: Immigrants, ethnic minorities, and the politics of the new suburbs, in *The New Suburban History*, edited by K. Kruse and T. Sugrue. Chicago, IL: The University of Chicago Press.

Kruse, K.M. and Sugrue, T.J. 2006. Introduction, in *The New Suburban History*, edited by K. Kruse and T. Sugrue. Chicago: The University of Chicago Press.

Lauria, M. 1998. A new model of neighborhood change: Reconsidering the role of White flight. *Housing Policy Debate,* 9, 395–424.

Leinberger, C.B. 2008. *The Next Slum?* [Online: Atlantic Magazine]. Available at http://www.theatlantic.com/magazine/archive/2008/03/the-next-slum/6653/ [accessed: 3 February 2012].

Logan, John R. and Stults, B.J. 2011. *The Persistence of Segregation in the Metropolis: New Findings from the 2010 Census*. [Online] Available at http://www.s4.brown.edu/us2010/Data/Report/report2.pdf [accessed: 28 February 2014].

Logan, J.R. and Zhang, C. 2010. Global neighborhoods: New pathways to diversity and separation. *American Journal of Sociology*, 115, 1069–1109.

Massey, D.S., Albright, L., Casciano, R., Derickson, E., and Kinsey, D.N. 2013. *Climbing Mount Laurel: The Struggle for Affordable Housing and Social Mobility in an American Suburb*. Princeton, NJ: Princeton University Press.

Massey, D.S., and Denton, N.A. 1993. *American Apartheid: Segregation and the Making of the Underclass*. Cambridge, MA: Harvard University Press.

Murphy, A. 2007. The suburban ghetto: The legacy of Herbert Gans in understanding the experience of poverty in recently impoverished American suburbs. *City & Community*, 6, 21–37.

Palen, J.J. 2005. *The Urban World*. New York, NY: McGraw Hill.

Rusk, D. 2001. *The "Segregation Tax": The Cost of Racial Segregation to Black Homeowners*. Washington, DC: Brookings Institution.

Short, K. 2011. *Supplemental Poverty Measure: 2010*. Washington, DC: U.S. Bureau of the Census.

Sugrue, T. 2011. A Dream Still Deferred. *The New York Times*, 26 March.

Suro, R., Wilson, J.H. and Singer, A. 2011. *Immigration and Poverty in America's Suburbs*. Washington, DC: Brookings Institution.

Teaford, J. 1990. *The Rough Road to Renaissance*. Baltimore, MD: Johns Hopkins University Press.

Temkin, K. 2000. Comment on John T. Metzger's "Planned Abandonment: The Neighborhood Life-Cycle Theory and National Urban Policy." *Housing Policy Debate*, 11, 55–60.

U.S. Bureau of the Census. 2005–2009 American Community Survey. Washington, DC: U.S. Bureau of the Census.

U.S. Bureau of the Census. 2000 Census. Washington, DC: U.S. Bureau of the Census.

U.S. Bureau of the Census. 1990 Census. Washington, DC: U.S. Bureau of the Census.

U.S. Bureau of the Census. N.d. Table 5: Homeownership Rates for the United States: 1968 to 2013 (in percent). Washington, DC: U.S. Bureau of the Census.

Weir, M. 2011. Creating justice for the poor in the new metropolis, in *Justice and the American Metropolis*, edited by C. Rile Hayward and T. Swanstrom. Minneapolis, MN: University of Minnesota Press.

SECTION II
Racial, Ethnic, and Nativist Change

Chapter 4

The Washington, DC Metropolitan Region—Traditional No More?

Carolyn Gallaher

This chapter analyzes the spatial distribution of key demographic data from the 2010 Census in the Washington Metropolitan Area.[1] In particular, Hanlon et al.'s (2006) call to rethink the Traditional Model of urban form is used as a benchmark for discussing these distributions. The goal in comparing the Washington Metropolitan Area to the Traditional Model, which is outlined and described below, is twofold—to identify key spatial patterns apparent in the 2010 data on the Washington Metro Area and to discuss what these trends suggest for future models.

Scholars have been modeling urban form and change for nearly 100 years. The first urban models were developed in the twenties and thirties (Park et al. 1925, Hoyt 1939). These models are often described as monocentric because they envision the central business district as the nucleus of economic activity in an urban area. After World War II polycentric models were developed to account for the appearance of multiple business centers within an urban area (Harris and Ullman 1945, Downs 1970, Anas, Arnott, and Small 1998). Some scholars even argue that urban areas like Los Angeles are so geographically expansive that polycentricity is no longer an adequate concept for describing the organization of economic activity (Gordon and Richardson 1996).

While monocentric and polycentric models of urban structure in the U.S. stem from different disciplines and time frames, they tend to hold two assumptions in common—that cities will expand and that higher-income residents tend to "move outward" with the growth (Anacker and Morrow-Jones 2008). This second assumption—that wealth concentrates on the edges of urban areas—is often amplified in popular and scholarly accounts of cities and has contributed to a persistent stereotype of inner cities as "places of danger, poverty and decay" and suburbs as "the ideal environment for healthy, wholesome, family living" (Hanlon

---

1   A Metropolitan Statistical Area is defined by the Office of Management and Budget as having "at least one urbanized area of 50,000 or more population, plus adjacent territory that has a high degree of social and economic integration with the core as measured by commuting ties" (OMB 2009). The formal name given to the Washington Metropolitan Area is: Washington-Arlington-Alexandria, DC-VA-MD-WV Metropolitan Statistical Area.

et al. 2006: 2130). Implicit in this stereotype is also a racial divide—people of color live in cities while non-Hispanic Whites live outside of them. Hanlon et al. (2006) call this abiding stereotype the Traditional Model.

To be fair, the city/suburban dichotomy did mirror reality inasmuch as many urban areas saw inner city decline and suburban boom during the 1970s and early 1980s. However, as Hanlon et al. (2006) note, the model has endured despite important changes in urban America over the past 40 years. In particular, the city/suburban dichotomy at the heart of the Traditional Model is collapsing (Holliday and Dwyer 2009, Hall and Lee 2010). By the late 1980s, for example, new immigrants to Los Angeles were bypassing traditional inner city areas for suburban locales instead (Estrada 1988). A similar pattern has been documented in Washington, DC (Center for Regional Analysis 2012). Many inner suburbs also find themselves fighting poverty and other social ills more commonly associated with inner cities (Puentes and Warren 2006, Kneebone, Nadeau, and Berube 2011). At the same time, formerly middle-class neighborhoods in close-in Brooklyn, New York, have become exclusive enclaves for the very wealthy (Lees 2003). In cities across the U.S. there are now concerted efforts to fight urban decline by attracting wealthier residents, such as young professionals and well-off retirees (Florida 2002). In Washington, DC this strategy has been dubbed "the adult strategy" (O'Cleireacain and Rivlin 2001).

Although scholars have examined the erosion of the city/suburban dichotomy in numerous metropolitan areas, the majority of metropolitan analyses have focused on the country's largest cities of New York, Los Angeles, and Chicago (Smith 1996, Lees 2003) or its shrinking industrial centers on the eastern seaboard and in the upper Midwest (Anacker and Morrow-Jones 2008, Vicino 2008). While there have been fewer studies of the Washington Metropolitan Area (see Gale 1987 for an important albeit outdated exception), there have also been few attempts to develop a model to capture the more recent patterns common across urban America as well as those that endure. To that end, this chapter explores the degree to which contemporary urban areas deviate from Hanlon et al.'s (2006) Traditional Model through a case analysis of the Washington Metropolitan Area. In so doing, this chapter hopes to proffer suggestions (with reference to the literature identifying changes in urban form) for the building blocks of a new urban model.

To make this assessment, this chapter uses 2010 and earlier Census data. In particular, this study analyzes four variables—proportion non-Hispanic White, proportion Black/African American, proportion Latino, and percent population 25–29 years of age. The first three variables were chosen to assess whether the Traditional Model's "White suburbs-/Black Cities" dichotomy still prevails in the Washington Metropolitan region. The age category was chosen because it is a variable not addressed in the Traditional Model but frequently associated with urban regeneration, and in particular "the adult strategy" in the literature (O'Cleireacain and Rivlin 2001, Florida 2002). Results suggest that the Washington Metropolitan Area deviates in important ways from the Traditional Model but also conforms to it important ways.

The remainder of this chapter is organized in the following manner. First, there will be a brief discussion of the chapter's case study—the Washington Metropolitan Area. Given that the principal city in the case study is a federal city, many readers may balk at using it as a case study for generalized urban change in America. To assuage these concerns, this chapter demonstrates how DC's urban fortunes have mirrored those of other U.S. cities despite its federal status. In the second section the basic assumptions that underpin what Hanlon et al. (2006) label the Traditional Model of the American city are outlined in order to establish a benchmark for assessing the degree to which DC approximates (or deviates from) it. The third section provides a brief overview of the data sources and analytic methods used here. In the remaining sections Census data (primarily from 2010) are examined to present a snapshot of the DC metropolitan region and assess its conformity to or deviation from the Traditional Model. The chapter concludes with a discussion of key patterns and what they say about the Traditional Model and future models. The potential future research questions raised by this snapshot are also discussed.

DC—Mean or Outlier in Urban America?

Although this chapter is about the Washington Metropolitan Area, the city at the center of it—Washington, DC—has a singular function in the country. As such, it bears considering whether the Washington Metropolitan Area is an appropriate case study for assessing changes in urban structure. It is argued here that DC is a useful case study not only because its trajectory is similar to those of other U.S. cities but because its growth and size/rank among U.S. cities warrants the same analytic attention given to large cities such as New York and Los Angeles.

Nevertheless, it is worth acknowledging the ways that DC is unique among American cities. First and foremost, DC is the nation's only federal district, and an entirely planned one at that. Unlike other American cities that developed organically in response to favorable physical and/or economic conditions, DC's location was chosen for idiosyncratic reasons.[2] Although the Constitution called for the establishment of a federal district, it did not specify a location. Northern states preferred a bustling (Northern) port to serve in the role. Southern states, by contrast, preferred a center of gravity closer to their coastal and Piedmont plantations. The ultimate location, straddling the Potomac River, was a compromise. Although it was carved from two slave-owning states, Maryland and Virginia,[3] Northern states acquiesced because Southern states agreed to allow the new

---

2   Although the District's location was not chosen for economic reasons, the Federal Government positively influenced economic conditions in the area over time. Today, for example, the city attracts private businesses interested in winning government contracts for defense and other activities.

3   In 1847 the portion of Virginia given to make the federal district was taken back in a formal declaration of retrocession by the Virginia General Assembly.

federal government to assume debts from the Revolutionary War, most of which were held by Northern states (Bowling 1991). In this regard, DC is comparable to other planned capital cities such as Belmopan, Canberra, or Brasilia. DC's federal status under the American constitution also makes it politically unique among American cities. Although the District is the seat of the federal government, its residents have limited political rights at the federal level. They may vote for a mayor and city council, but their elected officials to Congress are prohibited from casting votes on the floor of the Senate or House. Further, Congress has the power to circumvent city laws when it chooses, and it has used that power with regularity over the years (Jaffe and Sherwood 1994). City leaders complain that residents pay federal taxes and should have voting representatives in Congress as a result, but their efforts have been stymied by Republican and Democratic Congresses. In protest, the city began issuing license plates in 2000 with the phrase "taxation without representation" prominently displayed on them. Finally, the city's capital status also means that, unlike many other American cities, it never developed an industrial/manufacturing base. Its business is government, and as a result, it has been somewhat cushioned from the economic boom and bust cycles affecting other American cities, especially industrial ones.

Despite the singularity of Washington, DC, Gale (1987) observes that the post-World War II urban trajectory of DC mirrors those of other cities. Gale highlights three ways in particular. First, like other U.S. cities, Washington's urban landscape was scarred by rioting after the murder of Martin Luther King, Jr. in 1968. DC joined Chicago, Baltimore, Louisville, and Kansas City in dealing with the inner city destruction left by rioters. As in other riot-scarred cities, DC's non-Hispanic White and Black/African American middle-class residents also responded by decamping for the suburbs, leaving the poor, oftentimes of color, concentrated in the inner city. Like other cities, DC also experienced small-scale gentrification in close-in urban neighborhoods during the 1980s.

Although Gale was writing in the late 1980s, his finding—that Washington's urban patterns conform to those of other U.S. cities—continues to hold true. In the 1990s, for example, the District adopted the same sorts of neoliberal reforms other cities across the country did (Wyly and Hammel 2003). It cut social spending and instituted tax incentives to bring businesses and people back into the city. The city was also affected by the recent housing bubble, with house prices more than doubling between 1997 and 2007 (Tatian and Kingsley 2008). Like other metro areas, the Washington Metro Area also saw steep declines in mean house values—from nearly $500,000 in 2007 to just over $300,000 in 2009 (McClain 2010).[4] And, though the Washington Metropolitan Area's housing market has recovered faster than those in other metro areas, the data used in this chapter are from 2010, when the housing market was still subject to recessionary pressures.

---

4   Although the Washington Metro Area witnessed a drop in housing prices, its declines were not as sharp as many metro areas, particularly those in Florida, Arizona, and Nevada (McClain 2010).

In addition to having a similar trajectory, DC also presents a compelling case study because of its size. Once viewed as a sleepy backwater, the Washington Metropolitan Area is now the tenth largest metropolitan area in the country (U.S. Bureau of the Census 2011) and is part of the fourth largest combined statistical area (CSA)[5] in the country[6] (U.S. Bureau of the Census 2011). As such, examining the degree to which it deviates from or approximates extant city models and in what ways is surely an appropriate, even necessary exercise. A study of the Washington Metropolitan Area can also begin to fill an empirical void in the literature. Although numerous studies have been conducted on the cities that form the center of the country's major metropolitan areas, the same cannot be said of DC. Although there have been a variety of studies on the Washington Metro Area, most have been narrowly focused on debates about the National Mall (Benton-Short 2006, 2007), immigrant enclaves (Price et al. 2005, Price and Singer 2010), or iconic neighborhoods such as the U Street Corridor (Gillette 1995, Ruble 2010).

Unpacking the Traditional Model

In this chapter, Hanlon et al.'s (2006) Traditional Model is used as a benchmark for discussing change in terms of race, ethnicity, and a select age group in the Metropolitan Washington Area. Hanlon et al. (2006) argue that the Traditional Model is "a simple dichotomous model" (2006: 2129), which posits cities and suburbs as distinct and contrary places. In this regard the Traditional Model is not a formal model so much as an amalgam of assumptions held in common across multiple, often temporally disparate models (e.g., Park et al. 1925, Hoyt 1939, Harris and Ullman 1945). These assumptions are often applied to contemporary data with little regard for their current applicability.

Hanlon et al. (2006) argue that the Traditional Model distills a series of "crude dualisms" about the distribution of wealth, race and ethnicity, and land use across metropolitan areas today (2006: 2130). The first dualism, "rich suburbs—poor city" (2006: 2130), captures our traditional understanding of the distribution of income across space. In the concentric zone model, for example, the poorest residents tended to live in the so-called "zone of transition," an area surrounding the central business district (CBD) containing a mix of land uses, from light

---

5   According to the Office of Management and Budget (OMB), a Combined Statistical Area (CSA) can be created through various combinations of adjacent metropolitan and/ or micropolitan Statistical Areas. They "have social and economic ties as measured by commuting, but at lower levels than are found among counties within Metropolitan and Micropolitan Statistical Areas." They are best seen as "larger regions that reflect broader social and economic interactions, such as wholesaling, commodity distribution, and weekend recreation activities" (Office of Management and Budget 2009).

6   The formal name for this CSA is the Washington-Baltimore-Northern Virginia, DC-MD-VA-WV CSA.

industry and warehousing to flophouses and store-front churches (Park et al. 1925). As one moves away from the CBD in any direction, residents tend to be wealthier. Hoyt (1939) viewed the mixing of classes somewhat differently. He believed that the rich tended to concentrate along major thoroughfares leading out of the city, creating unidirectional corridors (rather than a concentric ring) of wealth. However, his model did not challenge the idea that the rich lived apart from the poor. Indeed, his model also placed the poor and working class near the CBD.

The second dualism, "White suburbs—Black Cities" (Hanlon et al. 2006: 2130), captured the "where" of racial segregation in the industrial era. It also draws heavily from the concentric zone (Park et al. 1925). In the rural South, Blacks had lived very close to Whites, first as slaves on plantations and later on the same or nearby fields as sharecroppers. Once the Great Migration began in the 1920s, nearly 3 million Blacks would move north into then-burgeoning industrial centers. When they arrived, they found their housing options limited to slum areas near the central business district. The same was true for immigrants arriving from Europe in the early 1900s. Most were also confined to the inner city slums, although they tended to live in enclaves rather than mix with Blacks or migrants from different countries.

The third dichotomy Hanlon et al. (2006) identify is between the sorts of land use that predominate in the city and suburb. In the Traditional Model industry is located in the city while housing is concentrated in the suburbs. This was not to suggest, of course, that no one lived in the city. Indeed, all of the major models observe that people of color, migrants (domestic and international), and the poor were clustered in inner cities. However, their housing choices were seen as circumscribed by their limited economic means and as such an exception to the rules governing housing construction and investment.

Before analyzing the degree to which demographic patterns in the Washington Metro Area deviate from the Traditional Model, it is important to state three caveats. First, all city models are generalizations and as such cannot mirror the reality of any one city so much as aggregate multiple city realities into a "mean" reality. The assessment here, then, examines how well DC approximates a "mean" rather than any specific city. Second, as noted above, it is useful to remember that the Traditional Model is itself an amalgam of multiple models (Park et al. 1925, Hoyt 1939, Harris and Ullman 1945). As a concept, it captures the assumptions that are held common across multiple models developed by different scholars at different times. What this means here is that metrics of comparison are quite broad. Finally, it bears mentioning that many American city models were developed over 50 years ago and made no pretense of describing or capturing cities of the future. The oldest and perhaps most well-known model, the concentric zone model, was developed in 1925 (Park et al. 1925). Polycentric models are relatively new by comparison, but their findings have not filtered up into the popular imagination of metro areas. Indeed, while Hanlon et al. (2006) do not distinguish between monocentric and polycentric models, it is clear from their discussion of the Traditional Model that most of the assumptions that drive it are quite old. However, it is not the goal of this chapter to make a straw man of the Traditional Model but rather to treat it as a baseline from which to measure how much one city deviates from it and in the process contribute to work designed to distill the key features/characteristics of demographic distribution in contemporary metro areas.

This sort of work, though descriptive, is an important first step in the process of reconceptualizing urban structure in the U.S. Indeed, as Taylor and Lang (2004) note, despite the plethora of studies documenting new patterns in urban American over the past 20 to 30 years, scholars have not yet developed a conceptual framework for placing them. This lacuna is evidenced by the fact that scholars cannot agree on what to call concepts once taken for granted. Taylor and Lang (2004) found 50 distinct terms to describe "new metropolitan form," and a context analysis suggests that many of the terms are not even describing the same thing. They conclude, "a degree of conceptual disintegration is to be expected, but this invention of concept after concept is hardly conducive to credible understanding of what is going on in and between our cities" (2004: 955).

In the following sections the DC metro area's conformity to the second dualism of Hanlon et al.'s (2006) Traditional Model is analyzed. In particular, this chapter will examine the degree to which the distribution of racial and ethnic groups across the Washington Metropolitan region fits the model's dichotomous assumption that people of color live inside the city and non-Hispanic Whites outside of it. It will also examine the degree to which the Washington Metropolitan region conforms to a feature often associated with urban regeneration—the residential clustering of young workers in the city. Examining the distribution of young workers will add to the assessment of the region's accordance with the Traditional Model by also gauging if it fits demographic patterns identified with new trends in urban form. Many scholars argue that urban regeneration depends on attracting the so-called creative class back to the city, and members of this class are (among other things) frequently young (Florida 2002, Malanga 2004). O'Cleireacain and Rivlin (2001) have made a similar argument in relation to DC, arguing that it may need to adopt an "adult strategy" to aid its revitalization. This strategy entails aggressively courting young workers and retirees to buy or rent in the city. These otherwise divergent populations tend to have greater disposable incomes and no dependent children and as such add to the tax base while taking little from it (in the way of public education and social services). Analyzing the distribution of young workers will be useful for determining whether an adult strategy is in play (whether purposively or not) in the inner core of the Washington Metro Area.

Data Sources, Presentation, and Analysis

The data used for this chapter come from Table DP-1—Profile of General Population and Housing Characteristics—in the 2010 Census. All data utilized here are from this table unless otherwise noted. Relevant race, ethnicity, and age data were selected from the table and used to create a smaller database, which was then imported into ArcGIS. In terms of race, three variables are analyzed: proportion Black/African American, proportion Latino[7] (any race), and proportion non-Hispanic White. The age variable is drawn from one Census five-year age increment—percent population 25–29 years of age.

In this chapter, descriptive measures are utilized to assess the case study's fit with the Traditional Model. In particular, mean, median, and standard deviations for each variable are reported, as well as general characteristics of overall distributions. In addition, geographic mean and standard distance measures are used to assess geographic patterns related to the variables above. The geographic mean (as defined by and calculated in ArcGIS) measures the geographic center of a set of spatially distributed features, such as a set of points (e.g., the addresses of fugitives) or polygons (e.g., census tracts).[8] In this chapter, geographic means are weighted relative to the numeric value being mapped at the census tract level (e.g., proportion Black/African American). This means that each central point for the metro area's census tracts is weighted to account for the variable being mapped. Standard distance measures are also weighted.

Data are visualized in three ways—frequency distribution histograms, choropleth maps, and overlay maps. While frequency distributions can be manipulated and are as such an imperfect data distribution measure, they are included here so readers can place the dataset being mapped into a statistical context. Also, the program-generated number of bins for each histogram is used to avoid inconsistent standards of categorization. The choropleth maps used in this contribution are classified into four categories, using a natural breaks classification scheme available in ArcMap. All categories are based on program-generated breaks to avoid the potentially inconsistent assignment of natural breaks by the author. Overlay maps are used to compare two or more variables meeting selected criteria.

When analyzing variables, the primary goal is to identify uneven or clustered elements of a distribution (e.g., tracts with percentages of a race, ethnicity, or age category well above the mean). In particular, tracts are identified as exhibiting clustering when the variable being mapped has a value greater than one positive standard deviation. Tracts with values greater than two standard deviations are identified as significantly clustered. Visual clustering is also identified in relation

---

7   Although the term "Latino" is used here for the purposes of consistency throughout this volume, data from the U.S. Bureau of the Census used in this chapter (Census Table DP-1) is categorized as "Hispanic or Latino."

8   One way to visualize a spatial mean is to think of a waiter carrying a tray with three glasses. If the glasses are evenly distributed on the tray, he will balance the tray by putting his hand under the middle of the tray. However, if the glasses are clustered on one side of the tray, he will balance the tray by moving his hand closer to the cluster of glasses. In this example, the glasses represent the spatial distribution of the variable being mapped, and the balancing point—i.e., where the waiter puts his hand—is akin to the spatial mean.

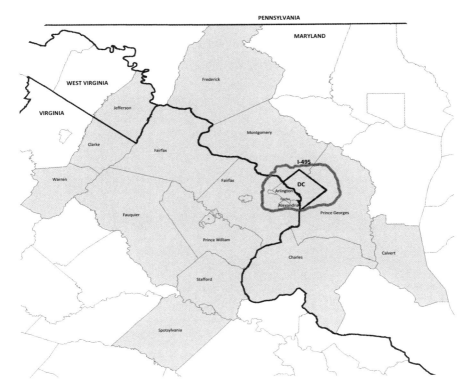

Figure 4.1   Washington, DC Metropolitan Area

Source: Author and Sophie Grumelard.

to geographic features, such as state and county boundaries, and transportation features, such as Interstate 495, the region's beltway road.

The Washington, DC Metropolitan Statistical Area

The Washington, DC metropolitan statistical area, the 10th largest in the country, contains a mix of geopolitical units. At the time of the 2010 Census the region included one federal district, 16 counties, and six independent cities spread over three states (see Figure 4.1).

In 2010 it was home to 5.58 million people, had a sex ratio[9] of .949, and a median age of 36.1 years (U.S. Bureau of the Census 2010). In terms of its age and sex distribution, the city is similar to the U.S. population as a whole. The region's sex ratio is slightly smaller than the country as a whole (.969 for the US), and its

___

9   A sex ratio measures the number of males for every 100 females in the population. A sex ratio of .949 means that there are 94.9 males for every 100 females.

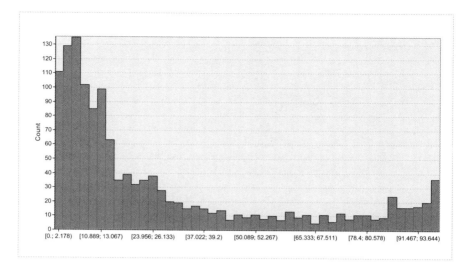

Figure 4.2   Frequency Distribution, Percent Black/African American, Washington, DC Metropolitan Area, 2010

Source: Author.

population is marginally younger—by 1.1 years (U.S. Bureau of the Census 2010). However, the racial and ethnic composition of the Washington Metropolitan Area varies quite substantially from the U.S. as a whole. Whereas 72.4 percent of the U.S. population is non-Hispanic White (U.S. Bureau of the Census 2010), only 54.8 percent of Washington Metropolitan Area residents are non-Hispanic White (U.S. Bureau of the Census 2010). And, while the U.S. population is only 12.6 percent Black/African American (U.S. Bureau of the Census 2010), the metro area's Black/African American residents constitute 25.8 percent of the area's total population (U.S. Bureau of the Census 2010). The region also has a larger Asian population—9.3 percent of the total population—than the U.S. as a whole—4.8 percent. However, the Latino proportion of the population is slightly smaller (13.8 percent) than the U.S. as a whole (16.3 percent).

Black/African American Population

The distribution of the Black/African American population in the Washington Metropolitan Area is highly uneven. The frequency distribution of the proportion of the population that is Black/African American by census tract demonstrates positive skew and bimodality (see Figure 4.2).

Not surprisingly, the mean and median figures for the metro area are quite varied—27.21 and 14 percent, respectively. The distribution's positive skew is evidenced by the large number of tracts in which the Black/African American

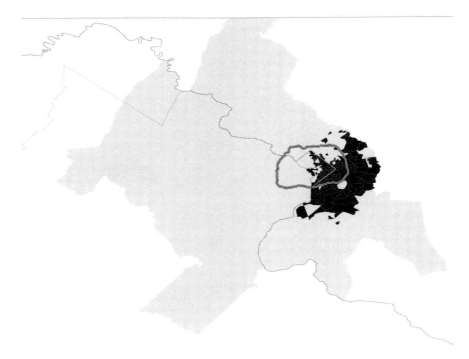

Figure 4.3   Census Tracts with Proportion Black/African Population Greater Than One Positive Standard Deviation from Mean, Washington, DC Metropolitan Area, 2010

Source: Author and Sophie Grumelard.

proportion of the population is higher than the mean. Indeed, of the 1,349 census tracts that make up the Washington Metropolitan region, 18.5 percent (250 tracts) have a percent Black/African American population that exceeds one positive standard deviation, and 8.9 percent (120 tracts) that exceed two positive standard deviations from the mean.[10] Recall that in a normal distribution only 15.8 percent of values lie outside one positive standard deviation from the mean and only 2.2 percent outside two positive standard deviations. Values outside two positive standard deviations are also considered statistically significant.

The Black/African American population is also spatially clustered. One hundred percent of tracts with a proportion of Blacks/African Americans greater than one positive standard deviation (250 tracts) are located within DC (94 tracts) and Maryland (156 tracts). These tracts form a compact cluster that extends from the eastern side of DC to the eastern boundary of the metropolitan area (see Figure 4.3).

---

10   One positive standard deviation includes tracts with a Black/African American proportion of the population greater than 56.3 percent. Tracts where the Black/African American population is greater than two standard deviations exceed 85.3 percent.

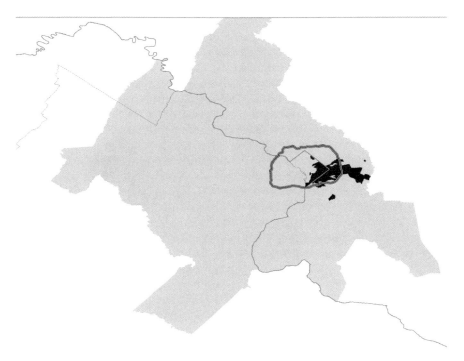

Figure 4.4   Census Tracts with Proportion Black/African American
Population Greater Than Two Positive Standard Deviations
from Mean, Washington, DC Metropolitan Area, 2010

Source: Author and Sophie Grumelard.

Indeed, nearly all of the tracts in Maryland (148 tracts) are located in just one county—Prince George's County. A similar pattern exists for tracts with values greater than two standard deviations. Of these tracts (120), half are in DC and half are in Maryland. Moreover, all the tracts in Maryland are also located in Prince George's County (see Figure 4.4). Despite this high degree of clustering, there is substantial income variation within Prince George's County's Black/African American population.

Other spatial statistics demonstrate clustering as well. The mean center of the Black/African American population is located just south of the National Mall, between the White House and the Capitol Building. The standard distance—approximately 36 miles—is compact in the context of the region as a whole (approximately 119 miles in its east-west expanse) and when compared to those of other racial and ethnic groups (see Figure 4.5).

Results suggest a number of interesting findings about the Washington Metropolitan Area's conformity to Hanlon et al.'s (2006) Traditional Model. The first is that the region's Black/African American population is no longer confined to the inner city, or even the city. In this regard, the metro region deviates

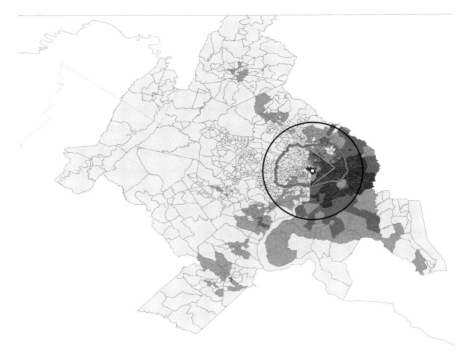

Figure 4.5   Weighted Spatial Mean and Standard Distance, Black/African American Proportion of the Population, Washington, DC Metropolitan Area, 2010

Source: Author and Sophie Grumelard.

substantially from the Traditional Model's depiction of the distribution of people of color in urban areas.

However, despite the dispersal of the Black/African American population away from the inner city, the data continues to show evidence of clustering, in some cases statistically significant clustering (i.e., values greater than two standard deviations). In the post-World War II era, the Black/African American population was clustered within the city, primarily on its eastern side. For many years, 16th Street, which runs north from the White House, was the unofficial dividing line between White and Black DC. After the Martin Luther King, Jr. riots, middle class suburbanization, which had already been underway (Jackson 1985), accelerated, and many Blacks/African Americans joined the exodus (Johnson 2002). The flow of Blacks/African Americans to the suburbs was not, however, evenly dispersed across the suburban landscape in the Washington Metropolitan Area. Rather, the great majority of Blacks/African Americans moved east into Prince George's County, which is today a majority Black/African American county.

Finally, while Black/African American suburbanization is advanced in terms of the proportion of the total population living in the suburbs, it has not eliminated

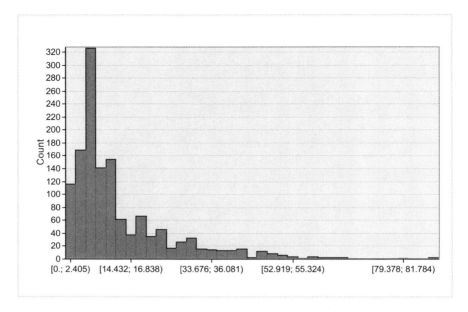

Figure 4.6   Frequency Distribution, Latino Proportion of the Population, Washington, DC Metropolitan Area, 2010

Source: Author.

Black/African American clustering inside DC. Indeed, 37.6 percent of metro region tracts with a Black/African American proportion of the population greater that one standard deviation are located in the city, and 50 percent of those with values greater than two standard deviations are as well. In both cases these tracts are clustered on the eastern side of the city in a compact area (see Figures 4.3 and 4.4).

The continued clustering of the region's Black/African American population suggests that while the city/suburban divide may no longer be *the* boundary between non-Hispanic Whites and Blacks/African Americans, a boundary clearly exists. That boundary, a north-south line just east of the city's main dividing line—16th Street—demonstrates that the city's Black/African American population is clustered on the metro area's eastern edge. In this regard, the Washington Metro region does not approximate the pattern found in other metro regions, such as Columbus, Ohio, where there is a "notable dispersal in all directions" for Asians, Latinos, and Blacks/African Americans (Brown and Chung 2008: 182).

Latino Population

The Latino population (of any race) comprises 13.8 percent of the Washington Metropolitan region's population. The frequency distribution of the Latino population (as a proportion of the total population) by census tract has a positive skew and a long tail (see Figure 4.6).

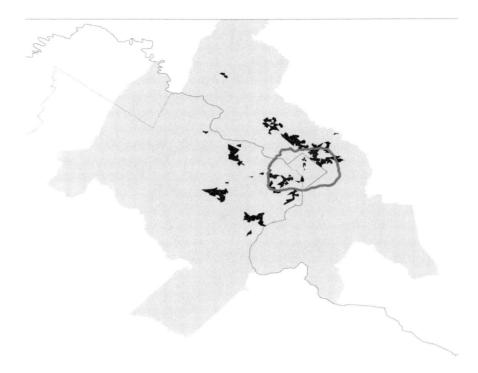

Figure 4.7   Census Tracts with Latino Proportion of the Population Greater Than One Positive Standard Deviation, Washington, DC Metropolitan Area, 2010

Source: Author and Sophie Grumelard.

However, the mean and median (12.3 percent and 8 percent, respectively) are not as divergent as they are for the Black/African American population (27.2 and 14 percent, respectively), suggesting a more clustered distribution. Indeed, the proportion of tracts with values beyond one positive standard deviation from the mean—13.9 percent (or 188 tracts)—is consistent with a normal distribution. The clustering is evident in the long tail, where 6.2 percent of census tracts (83 tracts) have a percent Latino population greater than two positive standard deviations from the mean.

The Latino population is also unevenly distributed across the metropolitan region. Unlike the Black/African American population, however, the Latino population has multiple, sizable clusters across the region. The majority of these clusters are suburban. Indeed, only 5.4 percent of tracts with Latino population greater than one positive standard deviation are located inside the District of Columbia. The remaining 94.7 percent of tracts (178 tracts) are split evenly between Virginia and Maryland (see Figure 4.7).

**Figure 4.8   Census Tracts with Latino Proportion of the Population
Greater Than Two Positive Standard Deviations, Washington,
DC Metropolitan Area, 2010**

Source: Author and Sophie Grumelard.

The pattern holds for tracts with values greater than two standard deviations. Only 2.4 percent of these tracts are located in DC (see Figure 4.8).

It is also notable that tracts with Latino clustering are found inside, outside, and straddling Interstate 495, the region's beltway road. The Beltway, a suburban loop road around the District, is often seen as the dividing line between older suburbs (usually built before 1950) and those built after rapid suburbanization got underway (Puentes and Warren 2006). The dispersed nature of Latino clusters is also evident in the calculations of the population's spatial mean and standard distance. The spatial mean, located in the Virginia suburbs roughly midway between the Beltway and the District's western boundary, has a standard distance of 38 miles—2 miles wider than the standard distance for the Black/African American population (see Figure 4.9).

Compared to the Traditional Model, Latino clustering is overwhelmingly suburban. As noted above, only 5.4 percent of tracts with notable clustering are located in DC. This finding is consistent with studies documenting the suburbanization of the Latino populations in other urban areas (Weeks et al.

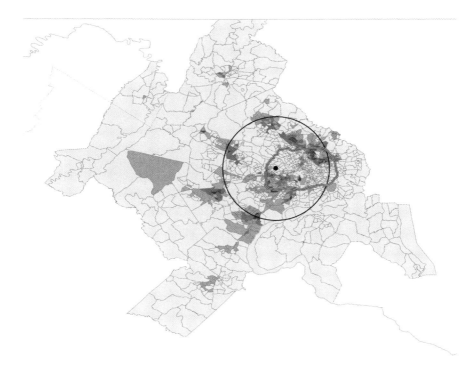

Figure 4.9   Weighted Spatial Mean and Standard Distance, Latino Proportion of the Population, Washington, DC Metropolitan Area, 2010

Source: Author and Sophie Grumelard.

2006–2007, Timberlake et al. 2011, Dawkins 2009). However, the extent of suburbanization in the Washington Metro Area is greater than it is in many other metropolitan areas. The country's three most populous cities—New York, Los Angeles, and Chicago—still had sizable concentrations of Latinos within their borders in 2010 (28.6, 48.5, and 28.9 percent, respectively). In DC, by contrast, the Latino proportion of the city's population was only 9.5 percent. This discrepancy is likely due to the fact that DC did not have a large Latino population during periods when people of color and immigrants tended to live in central city areas.[11] In 1990 the Latino proportion of the population was 5.4 percent while in New York, Los Angeles, and Chicago it was 27, 46.5 and 26 percent, respectively (U.S.

---

11   Suburban clustering in Maryland may be connected to the presence of the Seventh Day Adventist Church headquarters in eastern Montgomery County. The church has longstanding ties to Central America through its mission work and may have been an initial magnet for evangelical migrants coming to the metropolitan area in the 1980s. I would like to thank an anonymous reviewer for making this connection for me.

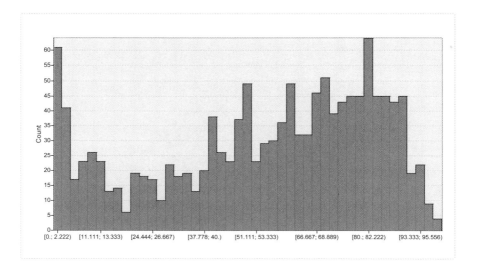

**Figure 4.10   Frequency Distribution, Non-Hispanic White Proportion of the
Population, Washington DC Metropolitan Area, 2010**

Source: Author.

Bureau of the Census 2000). What these figures suggest is that Latino clustering
in the suburbs is likely to be greater in places with relatively low proportions
of Latinos 20 years (or more) ago. Likewise, metropolitan areas with extant and
sizable Latino populations will likely have clusters both inside and outside city
limits. These findings also suggest that future urban models will have to account
for how differing settlement histories affect the distribution of Latinos across a
metro area.

A final observation concerns the dispersion of Latinos within the suburbs. In
the Washington Metro Area Latino clusters are found across suburban categorical
divides (e.g., inner and outer suburbs) rather than being concentrated in any one type
of suburb. There are Latino population clusters within, outside of, and straddling
the metro area's Beltway, which is a traditional marker for differentiating between
inner and outer suburbs. Finally, while the U.S. Bureau of the Census data on the
Latino population does not make a distinction between those born in the U.S. and
those who migrated here, the recent growth in the region's Latino population and
its definitively suburban character suggest that the Washington Metro Area may
mimic immigrant settlement patterns at the national level (Singer 2004).

Non-Hispanic White Population

Non-Hispanic Whites form a slim majority—54.8 percent—of the population
in the Washington Metro Area. The range of this proportion of the population is

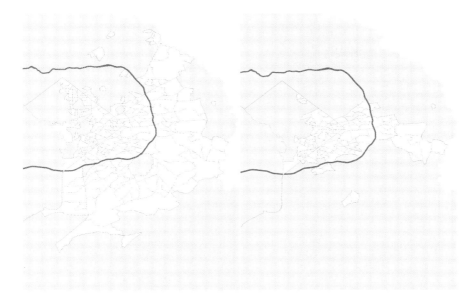

Figure 4.11   Census Tract Overlap of Non-Hispanic White and Black/ African American Population with Greater Than One and Two Positive Standard Deviations, Washington, DC Metropolitan Area, 2010

Note: Census tracts in white show overlap between the non-Hispanic White population less than one standard deviation and the Black/African American population greater than one standard deviation (left map) and a non-Hispanic White population less than 1.5 standard deviation and a Black/African American population greater than two standard deviations (right map).

Source: Author and Sophie Grumelard.

from 0 to 100 percent and the mean is 54.3 percent.[12] However, the median—60 percent—indicates that the population has a negative skew (see Figure 4.10).

That is, more than half of total tracts (56.2 percent) have a higher non-Hispanic White proportion than the mean. The frequency distribution also demonstrates bimodality on the negative tail (where the non-Hispanic White population would represent a minimal proportion of the population). Indeed, tracts with non-Hispanic White dispersal (i.e., those with a non-Hispanic White

---

12   This number and the previous one are similar but not identical because they are measuring two different things. The first number is the proportion of the population that is non-Hispanic White in the Washington Metropolitan Area while the second one is the mean of the proportion of the non-Hispanic White population for all tracts in the Washington Metropolitan Area.

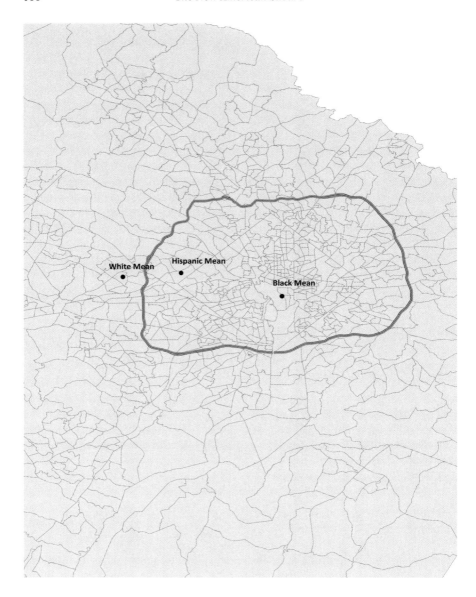

Figure 4.12   Spatial Means in Comparison

Source: Author and Sophie Grumelard.

proportion of the population less than one negative standard deviation) account for 20.6 percent (or 278) of all tracts, a proportion greater than found in a normal distribution. Eighty-three percent (232) of tracts with non-Hispanic White dispersal are also tracts in which the proportion of the Black/African American population is greater than one positive standard deviation from the mean. Likewise, 67.4 percent (or 120) tracts with a non-Hispanic White population less than negative 1.5 standard deviations[13] (178 tracts) are also tracts in which the proportion of the Black/African American population is greater than two positive standard deviations (see Figure 4.11).

In contrast, the overlap with the Latino population using the same criteria (i.e., tracts where the non-Hispanic White population is less than one or two standard deviations and the Latino proportion is greater than one or two standard deviations) is much smaller—14.8 and 0 percent, respectively. These results indicate that non-Hispanic Whites tend to take up a smaller proportion of the total population in tracts with concentrations of Blacks/African Americans than they do in tracts with concentrations of Latinos.

The non-Hispanic White population is also unevenly spread across the metropolitan area. At a macro level, the proportion of the non-Hispanic White population increases the further one moves westward from the District of Columbia.[14] Indeed, in comparison to the other spatial means provided here (Black/African American and Latino), the non-Hispanic White spatial mean is the furthest west and is the only mean located outside the region's Beltway, suggesting that the non-Hispanic White population is more suburban and, within the suburbs, more exurban (see Figure 4.12).

Indeed, of the 232 tracts that have a greater proportion than one positive standard deviation, only 8.2 percent (19 tracts) are located in DC, and only 32.8 percent are found inside the Beltway (see Figure 4.13).

However, it is also worth noting two important exceptions to the non-Hispanic White suburban pattern. The first is that of the three tracts that are 100 percent non-Hispanic White, two are inside the Beltway. The second is that many parts of the region with a large proportion of people of color had a rapid growth in the non-Hispanic White proportion of the population. In a recent analysis of demographic change by ZIP code, for example, Petrilli (2012) finds that three of the top 25 zip codes with the largest increase in the non-Hispanic White population in the United States are located in DC. These ZIP codes—20001, 20005, and 20010—are all located in rapidly gentrifying neighborhoods near downtown. Drawing on Petrilli, the author did a similar analysis here, albeit confined to DC and at the tract rather than zip code level. The results indicate that a large number of tracts have seen substantial growth in the proportion of the non-Hispanic White population over the past ten years. Figure 4.14 shows the top ten tracts in DC in terms of the percentage change between 2000 and 2010 in the non-Hispanic White proportion of the population.[15]

---

13   A negative 1.5 standard deviation was used here because a negative two standard deviations would be below zero.

14   A small cluster of counties in Charles County, located southeast of the District, is an exception.

15   Change in the non-Hispanic White proportion of the population is not a perfect measure. Some tracts had boundary changes, for example. Other tracts were merged, and still

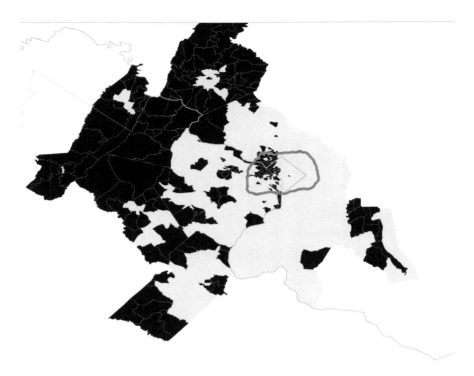

**Figure 4.13   Census Tracts with Non-Hispanic White Proportion of the
              Population Greater Than One Positive Standard Deviation,
              Washington, DC Metropolitan Area, 2010**

Source: Author and Sophie Grumelard.

Percent change in these tracts ranges from 28.3 percent to 56.5 percent. However, none of these tracts have a non-Hispanic White proportion of the population that demonstrates clustering because in all of them the proportion of the non-Hispanic White population was very low in 2000 (3.3 percent to 25.6 percent).

   The patterns discussed in this section suggest several aspects about DC's conformity to Hanlon et al.'s (2006) Traditional Model. The first is that the region is no longer shaped by a simple Black/African American/non-Hispanic White dichotomy as far as race is concerned. In the DC metro area only 67.4 percent of the population is Black/African American or non-Hispanic White. The remaining third is divided between numerous racial and ethnic groups. This conforms with studies that suggest that the U.S. will, by 2050, become a place in which no one racial or ethnic group comprises a majority of the population (Passel and Cohn 2008). The 2010 Census data suggests that DC is at the forefront of this sort of change given the slim majority the non-Hispanic White population currently holds.

---

others split. The tracts compared here only include tracts that existed in both 2000 and 2010.

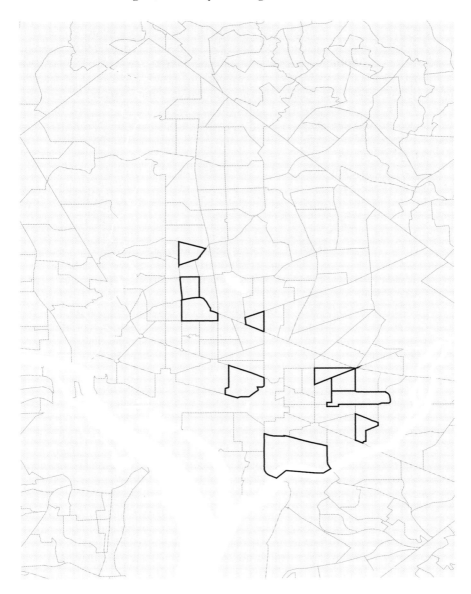

Figure 4.14   Top Ten Tracts with Greatest Positive Change in Proportion Non-Hispanic White Population, District of Columbia, 2010

Source: Author and Sophie Grumelard.

Nonetheless, the settlement of the District's non-Hispanic White population does bear some resemblance to the Traditional Model. Indeed, over 90 percent of tracts with evidence of non-Hispanic White clustering are located in the suburbs, indicating that non-Hispanic Whites continue to show a residential preference for suburban over urban areas. This may yet change if inner city tracts continue to witness an increased growth of non-Hispanic Whites, but it has not yet done so. Indeed, though the Black/African American population in DC recently fell below 50 percent for the first time in several decades, the non-Hispanic White proportion of the city is still quite low at just over 35 percent (Farmer 2012). The suburban diversity discussed frequently in the literature may be as much a function of the declining non-Hispanic White proportion of the population as an intentional form of mixing (Kneebone and Garr 2010). Sixty-seven percent of tracts with clustering are located outside the Beltway. This suggests that while city limit lines are no longer a racial dividing line, such lines continue to exist. Indeed, the tracts in which the non-Hispanic White population is dispersed (measured here as a non-Hispanic White proportion of the population less than one standard deviation) tend to overlap substantially with places where the Black/African American population is clustered. In short, the growth of the Latino population and other racial groups has complicated the simplistic non-Hispanic White suburban/Black/African American urban dichotomy outlined in the Traditional Model, but it has not erased its hold on the contemporary urban/metro landscape.

Young Workers

In this chapter young workers are defined based on the Census data category of 25 to 29 years of age. The U.S. Bureau of the Census collects data on age in five-year increments, and this category was chosen here for two reasons. The previous category (20–24 years of age) will likely include many college-age students who are not yet in the workforce or work part-time. Likewise, the next age category (30–34) is more likely to capture young people who have started families. In short, the 25 to 29 age category best approximates the notion of young workers employed by the adult strategy (the definition of young workers employed by the adult strategy excludes those with families because it is assumed that most will move to suburban locales to escape failing urban school systems). Thus, the term "young workers" will be used as shorthand for the 25 to 29 years olds.

In the metropolitan region 7.9 percent of the total population are young workers. By contrast, young workers only constitute 6.8 percent of the total U.S. population. The proportion of young workers in the metro population ranges from 0 to 36 percent, with a mean of 8.1 percent and a median of 7, suggesting a fairly narrow distribution (see Figure 4.15).

Indeed, the percentage of tracts falling outside one positive or negative standard deviation away from the mean is only 19 percent (in a normal distribution nearly

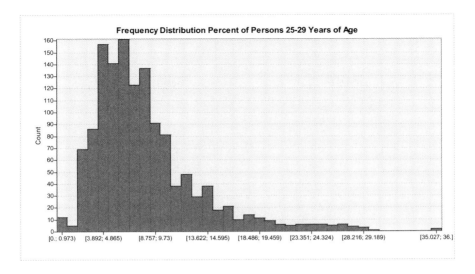

Figure 4.15   Frequency Distribution Proportion, Persons Age 25–29, Washington, DC Metropolitan Area, 2010

Source: Author.

30 percent of values would fall outside the standard deviation). However, the data does have a slight positive skew, which is exhibited by the fact that there are 12.7 percent of tracts outside one positive standard deviation and only 6.4 percent less than one negative standard deviation. The positive skew suggests that when the percentage of young workers falls outside the standard deviation, it is more likely to be on the high (clustered) rather than low (dispersed) end.

Some geographic clustering is also evident among young workers. Of the 171 tracts in which the percentage of persons age 25–29 is greater than one positive standard deviation, 50 percent (87) are located in Virginia (see Figure 4.16).

The remainder is split between DC (35 percent) and Maryland (15 percent). The relative dominance of Virginia as a site for young workers is also demonstrated by the fact that of the top ten tracts with the highest percentage of 25–29 year olds, eight are located in Virginia, two in DC, and none in Maryland or West Virginia. Geographic clustering of young workers is also evident in relation to the Beltway. Eighty-one percent of the tracts with clusters of young workers are located within (or contingent to) the Beltway (see Figure 4.8). By way of comparison, young worker clusters are not as compact as Black/African American clusters or as dispersed as those for Latinos. Clusters of young workers are distributed over a fairly wide area, with the Beltway serving as an outer limit for most of them. The decision to live within the Beltway may reflect the fact that young workers are less likely to own cars and as such choose to live near mass transit. This pattern is also evidenced by the location and extent, respectively, of the spatial mean and standard distance for young workers. The spatial mean for young workers lies in

**Figure 4.16   Young Worker Proportion of the Population Greater Than One
Standard Deviation, Washington, DC Metropolitan Area, 2010**

Source: Author and Sophie Grumelard.

between the Latino and Black/African American spatial means, albeit much closer
(westward) to the Latino mean (see Figure 4.17).

Is an "adult strategy," discussed above, shaping the metropolitan area's
distribution of young workers? Results suggest that while the "adult strategy"
is associated with DC, it may have also been adopted (or encouraged) in the
inner suburbs of Virginia, for example, Arlington and Alexandria, as an antidote
to growing poverty in so-called First Suburbs (Puentes and Warren 2006). It is
impossible, of course, to tell if suburban locales in Virginia have purposively
adopted such a strategy or whether other decisions made by planners, developers,
and others amount to a de facto (if accidental) adoption of it.

Conclusion

Although the data analyzed here are limited to four variables, results suggest that
this case study—the Washington Metro Area—departs in important ways from the
Traditional Model suggested by Hanlon et al. (2006). One of the most important

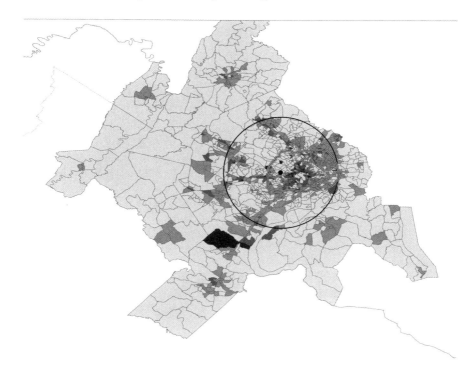

Figure 4.17 **Weighted Spatial Mean and Standard Distance, Young Worker Proportion of the Population, Washington, DC Metropolitan Area, 2010**

Source: Author and Sophie Grumelard.

ways that the DC metropolitan area diverges from the Traditional Model concerns the distribution of populations of color. Clusters of people who define themselves as Black/African Americans, for example, are now more likely to be located in suburban locales than inside city limits. The same is true for Latino population clusters, 95 percent of which are located in the suburbs. And, unlike the Black/African American clusters, Latino clusters are as likely to be in inner as outer suburbs. The distribution of the non-Hispanic White population also appears poised to defy expectations. The non-Hispanic White proportion of the population in many DC tracts grew very rapidly between 2000 and 2010.

However, there are also a number of characteristics that suggest that even though the distribution of racial and ethnic groups no longer conforms to the urban/suburban divide, there are still racial/ethnic dividing lines in place across the entire metropolitan area. The Black/African American population, for example, has suburbanized, but Blacks continue to cluster apart from non-Hispanic Whites. Indeed, 86.8 percent of Black suburban clusters are located in one single county in Maryland—Prince George's County. The concentration in one county suggests that the relevant lines denoting racial segregation are between counties rather than city and county. Likewise, while the non-Hispanic White population can be found across the region, it tends to cluster on the western side of the region. Again, residential segregation continues to exist, but instead of a city/suburb divide we now have an east/west divide. This divide is especially notable in that Black/African American clusters are associated with non-Hispanic White dispersal to a much greater extent than Latino clusters are. In short, the Washington Metropolitan Area is no longer primarily biracial, but many of the older patterns from that time (i.e., a region marked by informal segregation of non-Hispanic White and Black/African American populations) continue to persist in the landscape. What currently appears to be different today are the locations of the dividing lines between them.

In regard to the nontraditional variable—young workers—and its connection to future models of American urban areas, the findings here suggest consistency with the "adult strategy," which many cities have embarked on. There is some evidence that such a strategy may be in play in the region, even if only in ad hoc fashion. However, the results from the Washington Metropolitan region suggest that the "adult strategy" has been employed not only inside the District of Columbia but also within inner/first suburbs, such as Arlington and Alexandria, where public transportation options are plentiful. In this regard, beltways, as a marker between inner and outer suburbs, may be more important dividing lines than the city/suburban divide for locating young worker clusters.

The results presented above also raise as many questions as they answer. Three questions come especially to mind. The first concerns the growth of the proportion of non-Hispanic Whites inside city limits. In particular, it will be interesting to assess over time whether the pattern of rapid growth of the non-Hispanic White proportion of the population is an aberration, related to the property boom that encompassed much of the decade, or a more enduring trend. And, if growth in the proportion of non-Hispanic Whites inside city limits is an enduring pattern, it will be important to determine whether it occurs in tandem with White flight from suburban areas (or at least specific areas within them).

A second question concerns the impact of suburban Latinoization. In particular, it will be important to track whether Latinos continue to cluster in both inner and outer suburbs. It will also be important to track the evolution of these Latino suburbs to assess whether these suburbs become so-called "motors for the middle class" in the way that Prince George's County currently is for working-class African Americans in the Washington Metropolitan Area (DeRenzis and Rivlin 2007).[16] If Latino suburbs do function this way, their role may need to be highlighted in future metro models.

---

16   Although Prince George's County serves as a motor for the middle class it is worth noting that the county is the wealthiest Black/African American county in the country and has income averages on par with counties in which non-Hispanic Whites are a majority (Anacker et al. 2012).

A final question concerns the distribution of a variable not considered here—class. While the Traditional Model posited a steady increase in class positioning with distance from the central city, most scholars of urban form are more interested in the distribution of racial/ethnic groups than in class ones, which are much more difficult to conceptualize and operationalize. And, in some ways race and ethnicity are good proxies for class since groups of color are more likely to be working class or poor than non-Hispanic Whites. However, class stratification does not overlay perfectly with race and ethnicity or capture differences within races. For example, though the Black/African American population is concentrated in Prince George's County, the county itself has important class divisions within the Black/African American population, and these divisions play out geographically. Johnson (2002) notes that within the county working class and poor Blacks/African Americans have tended to live in neighborhoods inside the beltway while middle- and upper-class Blacks/African Americans live in areas outside of it.

Urban scholars still have much work to do to better identify and explain the macro level changes occurring across urban America. As they do so, the Washington Metropolitan Area can provide important insights on these processes. In particular, the Washington Metropolitan Area demonstrates that new and old patterns combine in interesting and sometimes confounding ways.

References

Anacker, K.B., Carr, J.H., and Pradhan, A. 2012. Analyzing foreclosures among high income Black/African American and Hispanic/Latino borrowers in Prince George's County, Maryland. *Housing and Society*, 29(1), 1–28.

Anacker, K.B. and Morrow-Jones, H.A. 2008. Mature suburbs, property values, and decline in the Midwest? The case of Cuyahoga County. *Housing Policy Debate,* 19, 519–49.

Anas, A., Arnott, R., and Small, K. 1998. Urban spatial structure. *Journal of Economic Literature,* 36(3), 1426–64.

Benton-Short, L. 2007. Bollards, barriers and bunkers: Securing the National Mall in Washington DC. *Society and Space,* 25(3), 424–46.

Benton-Short, L. 2006. Politics, public space and memorials: The brawl on the Mall. *Urban Geography,* 27(4), 297–329.

Bowling, K.R. 1991. *The Creation of Washington, D.C.: The Idea and Location of the American Capital.* Fairfax, VA: George Mason University Press.

Brown, L. and Chung, S. 2008. Market-led pluralism: Rethinking our understanding of racial/ethnic spatial patterning in U.S. Cities. *Annals of the Association of American Geographers,* 98(1), 180–212.

Center for Regional Analysis 2012. *Update from the American Community Survey: Foreign-Born Population in the Washington DC Metropolitan Area.* Arlington, VA: Center for Regional Analysis.

Dawkins, C. 2009. Exploring recent trends in immigrant suburbanization. *Cityscape: A Journal of Policy Development and Research,* 11(3), 81–98.

DeRenzis, B. and Rivlin, A. 2007. *A Pathway to the Middle Class: Migration and Demographic Change in Prince George's County.* Washington, DC: Brookings Institution.

Downs, A. 1970. *Urban Problems and Prospects*. Chicago, IL: Markham.

Estrada, L.F. 1988. *Hispanic Suburbanization in Los Angeles: Social Arrival and Barrio Formation*. Los Angeles, CA: Institute for Social Science Research.

Farmer, L. 2012. Blacks Lose Majority in the District. *The Washington Examiner*. 17 May.

Florida, R. 2002. *The Rise of the Creative Class: And How It's Transforming Work, Leisure, Community, and Everyday Life*. New York, NY: Basic Books.

Gale, D. 1987. *Washington, DC Inner-City Revitalization and Minority Suburbanization*. Philadelphia, PA: Temple University Press.

Gillette, H. 1995. *Between Justice and Beauty: Race, Planning, and the Failure of Urban Policy in Washington DC*. Philadelphia, PA: University of Pennsylvania Press.

Gordon, P. and Richardson, H. 1996. Beyond polycentricity: The dispersed metropolis, Los Angeles, 1970–1990. *Journal of the American Planning Association,* 62(3), 289–95.

Hanlon, B., Vicino, T., and Short, J.R. 2006. The new metropolitan reality in the U.S.: Rethinking the traditional model. *Urban Studies,* 43(12), 2129–43.

Hall, M. and Lee, B. 2010. How diverse are U.S. suburbs? *Urban Studies,* 47(1), 3–28.

Harris, C.D. and Ullman, E.L. 1945. The nature of cities. *Annals of the American Academy of Political and Social Science*, 242, 7–17.

Holliday, A. and Dwyer, R. 2009. Suburban neighborhood poverty in U.S. metropolitan areas in 2000. *City and Community*, 8(2), 155–76.

Hoyt, H. 1939. *The Structure and Growth of Residential Neighborhoods in American Cities*. Washington, DC: Federal Housing Administration.

Jackson, K. 1985. *Crabgrass Frontier: The Suburbanization of the United States*. New York: Oxford University Press.

Jaffe, H. and Sherwood, T. 1994. *Dream City: Race, Power, and the Decline of Washington, DC.* New York, NY: Simon and Schuster.

Johnson V. 2002. *Black Power in the Suburbs: The Myth or Reality of African-American Suburban Political Incorporation.* Albany, NY: State University of New York Press.

Kneebone, E. and Garr, E. 2010. *The Suburbanization of Poverty: Trends in Metropolitan America, 2000 to 2008.* Washington, DC: Brookings Institution.

Kneebone, E., Nadeau, C., and Berube, A. 2011. *The Re-Emergence of Concentrated Poverty: Metropolitan Trends in the 2000s.* Washington, DC: Brookings Institution.

Lees, L. 2003. Super-gentrification: The case of Brooklyn Heights, New York City. *Urban Studies*, 40(12), 2487–509.

Malanga, S. 2004. The curse of the Creative Class. *City Journal*, Winter, n.p.

McClain, J. 2010. *The Housing Market and Outlook*. Arlington, VA: Center for Regional Analysis.

O'Cleireacain C., and Rivlin A. 2001. *Envisioning a Future Washington*. Washington DC: Brookings Institution.

Office of Management and Budget. 2009. *OMB Bulletin No. 10–02*. Washington, DC: Office of Management and Budget.

Park, R., Burgess, E.W. and McKenzie, R.D. 1925. *The City*. Chicago, IL: University of Chicago Press.

Passel, J. and Cohn, D. 2008. *U.S. Population Projections: 2005–2050*. Washington DC: Pew Research Center.

Petrilli, M.J. 2012. The Fastest-Gentrifying Neighborhoods in the United States. [Online]. Available at: http://www.edexcellence.net/commentary/education-gadfly-daily/flypaper/2012/the-fastest-gentrifying-neighborhoods-in-the-united-states.html. [accessed 26 June 2012].

Price, M., Cheung, I., Friedman, S. and Singer, A. 2005. The world settles in: Washington, DC as an immigrant gateway. *Urban Geography*, 26(1), 61–83.

Puentes, R. and Warren, D. 2006. *One-Fifth of America: A Comprehensive Guide to America's First Suburbs*. Washington DC: Brookings Institution.

Ruble, B. 2010. *Washington's U Street: A Biography*. Baltimore, MD: Johns Hopkins University Press.

Singer, A. 2004. *The Rise of New Immigrant Gateways*. Washington DC: Brookings Institution.

Smith, N. 1996. *The New Urban Frontier: Gentrification and the Revanchist City*. New York, NY: Routledge.

Tatian, P. and Kingsley, G.T. 2008. Housing market update. *District of Columbia Housing Monitor*, Winter, 3–9.

Taylor P.J. and Lang R.E. 2004. The shock of the new: 100 concepts describing recent urban change. *Environment and Planning A*, 36(6), 951–8.

Timberlake, J., Howell, A. and Staight, A. 2011. Trends in the Suburbanization of Racial/Ethnic Groups in U.S. Metropolitan Areas, 1970–2000. *Urban Affairs Review* 47, 218–55.

U.S. Bureau of the Census. 2000. *The Hispanic Population*. Washington, DC: U.S. Bureau of the Census.

U.S. Bureau of the Census. 2010 Census. Washington, DC: U.S. Bureau of the Census.

U.S. Bureau of the Census. 2011. Annual Estimates of the Population of Metropolitan and Micropolitan Statistical Areas: April 1, 2010 to July 1, 2011. Washington, DC: U.S. Bureau of the Census.

Vicino, T. 2008. *Transforming Race and Class in Suburbia: Decline in Metropolitan Baltimore*. New York, NY: Palgrave Macmillan.

Weeks, G., Weeks, J. and Weeks, A. 2006–2007. Latino immigration in the U.S. South: "Carolatinos" and public policy in Charlotte, North Carolina. *Latino(a) Research Review*, 6(1–2), 50–71.

Wyly, E. and Hammel, D. 2003. *Mapping Neoliberal American Urbanism.* [Online]. Available at: http://www.geog.ubc.ca/~ewyly/research/neo.pdf. [accessed 27 June 2012].

Chapter 5

Local Immigration Legislation in Two Suburbs: An Examination of Immigration Policies in Farmers Branch, Texas, and Carpentersville, Illinois

Bernadette Hanlon and Thomas J. Vicino

Recently, there has been an escalation in the scholarly literature on the changing dynamics of migration and migration policy across the globe. Much of this work focuses on shifts in the geographic concentration of immigrants to nontraditional destinations (Jones 2008, Price and Benton-Short 2008, Singer, Hardwick, and Brettell 2008, Cavin 2013, Niedt 2013, Pastor 2013) and, in the context of the United States, on the proliferation of immigration policies at the state and local level (e.g., Varsanyi 2010b, Walker 2010, Vicino 2012). In recent decades, subnational governments have developed a variety of policies, planning rules, and programs to either incorporate migrants into their jurisdictions or, in some cases, inhibit the movement of migrant populations across local borders (Vicino 2012).

This devolution of immigration policy in the United States has occurred alongside an increase in the number and proportion of immigrants in the nation in recent decades, especially in the suburbs. Singer, Hardwick, and Brettell (2008) refer to emerging immigrant metropolitan areas where the foreign-born population has grown rapidly over the past 25 years. Immigration in these metropolitan areas tends to be mostly suburban rather than urban in nature (Hanlon, Short, and Vicino 2010). Suburbs are in many ways new immigrant gateway communities and, as such, they provide an ideal platform for unveiling local governmental responses to unaccustomed patterns of immigrant settlement.

In this chapter, we critically examine the policy responses implemented by two suburbs: Farmers Branch, outside Dallas in Texas, and Carpentersville, outside Chicago in Illinois. In the wake of the arrival of new immigrants in these suburbs, the local governments responded by formulating local immigration policies to limit the foreign-born population in their jurisdictions. We aim to demonstrate how and why Carpentersville and Farmers Branch took steps to curb undocumented immigration and regulate the local immigrant population by introducing exclusionary policies. Tables 5.1 and 5.2 show that both suburbs experienced growth of the immigrant population, changing the identity of

Table 5.1   Socioeconomic Characteristics of Farmers Branch, Texas, 1970–2005–2009

	1970	1970	1980	1980	1990	1990	2000	2000	2009	2009
	Number	Percent	Number	Percent	Number	Percent	Number	Percent	Number	Percent
Total Population	27,588	N/A	28,723	N/A	28,737	N/A	34,043	N/A	26,177	N/A
Foreign-Born Population	457	1.6%	1,573	5.4%	4,205	14.6%	9,385	27.5%	7,035	26.9%
Over 65 Population	712	2.6%	1,379	4.8%	2,459	8.6%	3,664	10.6%	3,401	12.9%
Non-Hispanic White	27,318	99.0%	26,706	92.9%	23,398	81.4%	25,946	76.2%	14,288	54.2%
Non-Hispanic Black	92	0.0%	386	1.3%	1,481	5.1%	1,584	4.7%	815	3.1%
Hispanic or Latino	1,427	5.2%	2,159	7.5%	5,697	19.8%	12,703	37.3%	12,091	45.8%
Average Household Income	$71,276	N/A	$69,583	N/A	$66,083	N/A	$78,815	N/A	$72,406	N/A
Per Capita Income	$20,178	N/A	$26,725	N/A	$27,574	N/A	$31,312	N/A	$27,258	N/A
Poverty	755	2.7%	1,355	4.8%	2,261	8.0%	2,369	7.0%	2,382	9.1%
Owner-Occupied Housing Units	5,949	78.6%	5,949	54.4%	6,286	56.1%	7,075	55.6%	6,278	66.8%
Renter-Occupied Housing Units	1,622	21.4%	4,549	41.6%	4,829	43.4%	5,614	44.2%	3,121	33.2%
Housing Units Built Pre-1970	N/A	N/A	N/A	N/A	N/A	N/A	N/A	N/A	6,046	61.6%
Manufacturing Employment	4,505	38.4%	5,821	33.8%	4,131	25.5%	3,846	21.7%	1,597	12.1%
Unemployment	281	2.3%	389	2.2%	992	5.8%	733	4.0%	1,184	8.2%

Source: Decennial U.S. Census of Housing and Population; American Community Survey (ACS) 2005–2009 (Data Release 2010). All figures are calculated as 2009 dollars.

Table 5.2   Socioeconomic Characteristics of Carpentersville, Illinois, 1970–2005–2009

	1970 Number	1970 Percent	1980 Number	1980 Percent	1990 Number	1990 Percent	2000 Number	2000 Percent	2009 Number	2009 Percent
Total Population	26,310	N/A	25,870	N/A	27,748	N/A	40,920	N/A	37,162	N/A
Foreign-Born Population	919	3.5%	1,545	5.9%	2,461	8.8%	8,961	22.0%	12,023	32.4%
Over 65 Population	648	2.4%	571	2.2%	1,464	5.2%	2,060	5.0%	1,725	4.6%
Non-Hispanic White	26,279	99.9%	24,939	96.3%	24,197	87.2%	30,819	75.3%	25,493	68.6%
Non-Hispanic Black	11	0.0%	125	0.0%	1,032	3.7%	2,051	5.0%	1,713	4.6%
Hispanic or Latino	1,078	4.0%	2,232	8.6%	3,823	13.8%	13,181	32.2%	17,576	47.3%
Average Household Income	$63,580	N/A	$59,127	N/A	$71,399	N/A	$78,786	N/A	$69,163	N/A
Per Capita Income	$15,340	N/A	$17,278	N/A	$22,189	N/A	$26,124	N/A	$21,267	N/A
Poverty	1,226	4.7%	1,681	7.0%	2,471	8.9%	3,198	7.8%	3,493	9.4%
Owner-Occupied Housing Units	5,231	82.3%	5,231	68.3%	6,338	75.6%	9,945	82.5%	9,062	83.0%
Renter-Occupied Housing Units	1,124	17.7%	1,782	23.3%	2,040	24.3%	2,102	17.4%	1,850	17.0%
Housing Units Built Pre-1970	N/A	N/A	N/A	N/A	N/A	N/A	N/A	N/A	5,991	48.3%
Manufacturing Employment	5,223	50.2%	5,900	48.6%	5,584	40.8%	5,552	29.9%	3,984	23.0%
Unemployment	286	2.7%	753	5.8%	910	6.2%	1,003	5.1%	1,381	5.4%

Source: Decennial U.S. Census of Housing and Population; American Community Survey (ACS) 2005–2009 (Data Release 2010). All figures are calculated as 2009 dollars.

these places as previously non-Hispanic White, moderate-income communities over three decades. In Farmers Branch, the foreign-born population increased from 1.6 percent to 26.9 percent of the total population between 1970 and 2005–2009. More than four out of every ten residents in Farmers Branch are Latino. A similar transformation occurred in Carpentersville. The foreign-born population grew there from 3.5 percent of the total population in 1970 to 32 percent in 2005–2009. Latinos composed one-half the population of Carpentersville by 2005–2009 (see Tables 5.1 and 5.2).

In the cases of Farmers Branch and Carpentersville, sociocultural and symbolic elements of suburbia heavily influenced reactions to local immigration and the power dynamics of local immigration policy creation. In this chapter, we argue that suburbs are socially constructed spaces where fervent ideas around safety, socioeconomic stability, homeownership, and immigrant assimilation exist, based on our two case studies. These characteristics helped the dominant group and power structure to mobilize support for the introduction of exclusionary immigration legislation. We argue that the suburban neoliberal traditions of decentralized governance and home rule encourage and enable mobilization around a perception or vision of these two suburbs that are in fact being challenged by the reality of their socioeconomic decline and demographic transformation.

We have two major objectives in this chapter. First, we examine evidence of immigration policy devolution in the U.S., utilizing two suburban case studies, and examine the recent literature that attempts to understand why local governments and suburbs in particular have become increasingly involved in developing policies aimed at controlling the immigrant population. Second, we explain how the formation of local immigration policy in Farmers Branch and Carpentersville occurred. To conduct our study, we analyzed census data, newspaper archives, maps, local laws, zoning, and newsletters. The major newspapers of record in each case were searched and examined for coverage of the Illegal Immigrant Reform Ordinance (IIRO) debate and socioeconomic decline. These data were organized by coding them according to date and theme. We also interviewed local government officials in both Carpentersville and Farmers Branch. Key informants were asked about their local histories in the community, their views on immigration and the IIRO debate, their views on the social and economic transformation of the community, policy recommendations, and future thoughts. A snowball strategy grew local contacts. Last, we engaged in participant observation during site visits. City council meetings, rallies, and elections were observed. As part of this discussion, we provide evidence of how the rise of neoliberalism as the dominant approach to political suburban governance has had a profound influence on local immigrant policy in the U.S. (Peck 2011), and how the changing nature of suburban demographics creates tension (Denton and Gibbons 2013).

In the following sections, we examine evidence of subnational immigration regulation in the United States and consider the literature that explains why the localization of immigration policy has occurred. We then examine immigration legislation in Farmers Branch and Carpentersville. Finally, we offer four defining characteristics of the political discourse around the formation of immigration policies in both suburbs. These include 1) suburbs as sites of successful home rule; 2) suburbs and assimilation; 3) suburbs and the single-family home; and 4) suburbs as sites of safety.

The Devolution of Immigration Policy

Since the 2000s, there has been a proliferation of subnational regulation designed to control the movement of immigrants in the U.S. For instance, in April 2010, Governor Jan Brewer of Arizona signed into law SB 1070, one of the toughest state policies on immigration control, allowing police to arrest immigrants who cannot prove that they are in the country legally (Arizona State Legislature 2010). One of the primary goals of the legislation is to identify, prosecute, and deport undocumented immigrants. By July 2010, the U.S. Department of Justice had filed a lawsuit, challenging the constitutionality of Arizona's immigration law. The federal lawsuit asked the U.S. District Court in Phoenix to uphold the federal government's plenary power over the formulation and enforcement of immigration and rule that Arizona's new law violates the supremacy clause of the U.S. Constitution. Upon filing the lawsuit, Attorney General Eric Holder stated, "Setting immigration policy and enforcing immigration laws is a national responsibility. Seeking to address the issue through a patchwork of state laws will only create more problems than it solves" (U.S. Department of Justice 2010). Ultimately, the U.S. Supreme Court was asked to review the constitutionality of Arizona's legislation. In June 2010, the Court delivered a split decision, upholding some and blocking other parts of the law, which dismissed provision of the law that criminalized undocumented immigrants for residing and seeking employment in Arizona. The most hotly debated provision requiring state law enforcement officers to determine the immigration status of people they arrest or suspect of being an undocumented immigrant was upheld (Arizona et al. Petitioners v. United States 2012).

Arizona is not alone in its tough stance on immigration. Other states have contemplated and developed their own versions of such legislation. Certainly, the Supreme Court decision on SB 1070 is likely to have implications far beyond Arizona. According to a study by the National Conference of State Legislatures (2011), Alabama, Georgia, Indiana, South Carolina, and Utah all enacted legislation similar to Arizona's law. But the federal government has filed complaints on immigrant enforcement legislation in three of these states—Alabama, South Carolina, and Utah—and class action lawsuits are pending, which question the constitutional grounds of Arizona's SB 1070. The trend shows that states are increasingly playing a role in the reform of immigration policy. But the debate over who has the power to enact this reform is far from settled.

States are not the only subnational battleground for immigration control. Small towns, suburbs, and cities across the United States have become increasingly active in the immigration debate, developing a host of both anti- and pro-immigration-related legislation. The Fair Immigration Reform Movement (2006) compiled a database of local government immigration-related legislation and found that a total of 135 anti-immigration measures have been introduced at the local jurisdictional level as of 2006. These include passing ordinances to fine landlords who rent to undocumented immigrants; enforcing housing code violations targeting overcrowding by immigrants; preventing establishments of day laboring sites; and ensuring immigration control by requiring local police officers to check the immigration status of detainees or, in some cases, local residents stopped for traffic violations.

Probably the most renowned local exclusionary immigration legislation is the one introduced by the community of Hazleton, Pennsylvania, in July 2006 (Varsanyi 2010a, 2010b). At that time, the city council in Hazleton passed the Illegal Immigration Relief Act (IIRA) by a vote of four-to-one. The ordinance had a number of elements aimed specifically at landlords, businesses, and social services that worked with undocumented immigrants. The ordinance sought to fine landlords $1,000 for each undocumented immigrant housed in his or her rental property; deny licenses to commercial entities that employed undocumented immigrants; and declare English the official language of Hazleton. Mayor Lou Barletta wore a bulletproof vest the day of the signing, stating at the time "[to] the illegal citizens, I would recommend they leave … what you see here tonight, really, is a city that wants to take back what America has given it" (NBC News 2006: n.p.).

In 2007, a federal judge struck down Hazleton's IIRA as an unconstitutional ordinance. The law has not been enforced since it passed the city council, and it is still in legal limbo as of this writing, in part because elements of Arizona's SB 1070 were struck down. Hazleton's IIRA inspired similar ordinances to be adopted across the country. As Lou Barletta stated back in 2006, "Hazleton has paved the way for other cities and states across the country to enact similar laws, so this is a great day for all of those cities and states, and for the people of Hazleton who had to endure criticism from those who opposed what we were trying to do because the federal government didn't want to do its job" (Fox News 2011: n.p.). The weighty elements of the narrative prior to passage of Hazleton's IIRA focused heavily on the notion of security. During the debate, local politicians and certain constituents in Hazleton were fixated on the undocumented immigrant as a perceived physical threat, hence Lou Barletta's bulletproof vest the day of signing, and an economic threat to a middle class way of life. Brettell and Nibbs (2011) demonstrate how exclusionary policies in Farmers Branch hung on the perceived threat to a middle-class identity. We suggest that the dynamics of immigration law formation in both Farmers Branch and Carpentersville are reliant on notions of what constitutes middle-class suburban living.

Unraveling the Localization of Immigration Policy

Much of the legal research examining the evolution of exclusionary policies at the state and local levels concludes that the federal government should maintain primary authority over the regulation of immigration (McKanders 2007, Harnett 2008). Many legal scholars and activists have been concerned that exclusionary policies violate the civil rights of immigrants and others. Many local ordinances have been found to violate due process rights of landlords and renters (Esbenshade 2007). On the other hand, some legal scholars suggest that local immigration policymaking may be a necessary step since, in many cases, local governments are required to enforce immigration law. Such requirements are viewed as unfunded mandates that undermine local control and self-government (Parlow 2007). Recent legal wrangling over local immigration regulation highlights the scalar tension in the policy arena of immigration reform (Varsanyi 2008a). Some in the legal community advocate that federal exclusivity in the arena of immigration ought to be reformulated, offering instead a functional account of subnational immigration regulation by suggesting that the federal–state–local dynamic should operate as an integrated system to manage contemporary immigration (Rodriguez 2007).

Noting the devolution of immigration reform, some scholars have argued that this trend began in earnest with the New Federalism model first introduced by President Reagan in the 1980s and then further amplified by new laws introduced in the mid-1990s, which limited noncitizens' access to welfare and medical programs (Varsanyi 2008b). These laws and strategies also included an expansion in the array of criminal offenses for which noncitizens could be deported. Local employers, service providers, and, in some cases, private citizens were encouraged to engage in enforcement of immigration law by neoliberal policies. For instance, the Immigration Reform and Control Act (IRCA) of 1986 introduced an employer sanctions program aimed at penalizing employers for hiring immigrants unauthorized to work, and as a result, employers became responsible for checking and maintaining immigration records of their employees (Ridgley 2008). This same act led to an increase in immigration raids in various cities, conducted at times with the help of municipal police and local officials (Ridgley 2008). The Illegal Immigration Reform and Immigrant Responsibility Act (IIRIRA) of 1996 allowed local police officers to receive training in immigration control from Immigration and Customs Enforcement (ICE) (Coleman 2007).

Welfare reform, the IIRIRA, and other federal-level policies passed the responsibility of immigrant service provision and enforcement of immigration control to states and local communities, thus engaging them in immigration legislation as a response to neoliberal federal policy. Various policymakers in state and local governments hold that the federal government did and continues to do little to discourage the entrance of large numbers of undocumented immigrants. At the same time, the federal government has minimized service provision for immigrants in local communities (Ellis 2006). The removal of state-centered welfare for new arrivals to the United States is an effect of the neoliberal framework that depletes the state's function as universal service provider. Under neoliberalism, the state's main role is to ensure the optimal functioning of the market and secure private property rights (Harvey 2007). Yet, the prominence of market efficiency over distribution and service provision does not mean minimization of government intervention. Rather, the role of the state has been reconstituted to also include new forms of social control, as demonstrated by recent engagement in the policing and regulation of immigrant communities (Peck and Tickell 2002).

This neoliberal shift and policy localization explains why some subnational governments introduce certain types of immigration policies. In one of the first quantitative studies of local immigration policy, Ramakrishnan and Wong (2010) found that political conservatism within a local community is typically coupled with the development of exclusionary policies. Republican-led city councils and voters are more likely to introduce policies aimed at curbing undocumented migration. According to Hopkins (2010), the sudden influx of immigrants and high immigrant concentration encourages stricter immigration control policies. Geographic patterns of immigration, as Wright and Ellis (2000) suggest, are inseparable from the politics of immigration reform.

The geographic nature of the politics of immigration is most succinctly analyzed in Walker and Leitner's (2011) study of immigration policies in 174 municipalities across the U.S. According to the authors, the South, above other regions of the country, is more likely to introduce anti-immigration policies. Similarly, suburbs, particularly outer suburbs, are more likely than cities to attempt to limit and control immigration within their jurisdictional boundaries. Explaining why the South has initiated exclusionary immigration policies, Walker and Leitner (2011) refer to Winders's (2007) work on the politics of immigration in southern communities, which demonstrates how the South's cultural history and past and present racial tension have powerfully influenced its communities and their reaction to recent immigration by a largely Latino population. In many respects, immigrants are seen as a threat to the Southern way of life. As Winders (2007: 934) states, "Protecting state resources from 'illegal immigrants' in Georgia and Mississippi, for instance, becomes protecting 'southern hospitality' and ways of life, avoiding a language of race by embracing a discourse of culture." Similarly, Walker and Leitner (2011) suggest that exclusionary policies in a suburban context are the result of the notion that suburbia reflects the realization of the American Dream of upward mobility and success restricted to a non-Hispanic White middle class. Anti-immigration policies among U.S. suburbs are, for Walker and Leitner (2011: 165), the "continuation of [an] exclusive white imaginary." The white imaginary melds with the transformative powers of neoliberalism to enable particular reactions to immigration within a period of socioeconomic decline in both the suburbs of Carpentersville and Farmers Branch. The rise of suburban poverty (Kneebone and Berube 2013) is creating tension in suburbs where large-scale demographic shifts occur.

Immigration Legislation Formation in Farmers Branch and Carpentersville

In this section, we first describe the different immigration policies in our analyzed suburbs. The local governments of Farmers Branch and Carpentersville reacted to a rapid increase in their immigrant populations since 1980 by introducing a series of measures designed to take local control of immigration policy. In the summer and fall of 2006 politicians and residents of Farmers Branch debated the merits of an Illegal Immigrant Reform Ordinance (IIRO) for their inner-ring suburban community of Dallas. Former City Councilman Tim O'Hare led the initiative, arguing that undocumented immigration created problems in the community. Thus, Farmers Branch supported a comprehensive ordinance with the following measures: authorize local police to enforce federal immigration laws; prohibit landlords from renting to undocumented immigrants; prohibit the employment of undocumented immigrants; and declare English as the official language. On November 13, 2006, the city council passed and later amended several ordinances to implement an IIRO. Months later, the residents of Farmers Branch voted for the IIRO by referendum. It passed by over a two-to-one margin.

In the fall of 2006, Paul Humpfer and Judy Sigwalt, trustees of the Village of Carpentersville, introduced an IIRO to confront what they believed to be problems related to the growth of undocumented immigrants in their suburb. Humpfer, Sigwalt, and supporters of Carpentersville's IIRO argued that the social and economic problems stemming from undocumented immigration included, among other issues, the overcrowding of housing, the lack of jobs, and the loss of community investment. The IIRO aimed to deal with these issues by making it a crime for a landlord to rent to or a business to hire an undocumented immigrant. This legislation also established English as the official language of the suburb.

As traditional postwar suburbs in the process of marked socioeconomic change, the discourse on immigration reform in Farmers Branch and Carpentersville was largely framed around the suburban sociocultural and symbolic elements. The first defining characteristic of this suburban discourse is the notion of suburbs as sites of successful home rule. During this period of neoliberalism, governance of immigration in the two suburbs of Farmers Branch and Carpentersville is formulated in particular ways because of the emerging reality of suburban fiscal stress and socioeconomic decline.

Suburbs and Successful Home Rule

In a series of well-publicized appearances, Trustee Paul Humpfer, proponent of the IIRO in Carpentersville, complained about the burden that undocumented immigrants posed on the level, quality, and cost of educational and health services in the suburb. He complained that schools were overcrowded because of increasing immigration, and he stated that if 1,300 students were undocumented immigrants, the suburb would take on an additional $10 million in education expenses. Humpfer stated that local public hospitals were bustling with people seeking basic health care. Referring to undocumented immigrants, he regularly stated, "$372,000 was written off the village's coffers because collection agencies could not find these people [i.e., undocumented immigrants]" (Larrisa Chinwah, personal communication, 7 May 2009). For Humpfer and his supporters, "these people" were seen as a burden to the suburb and did not deserve the public services that other residents enjoyed because they did not pay local taxes.

Characterization of the effects of non-taxpaying, undocumented immigrants held particular sway with increasing visibility of a declining suburban infrastructure. Residents responded to the trustee's comments. "I was raised in Carpentersville. My old neighborhood is now at least half Mexican. ... The issue is that rooms are rented out. ... The landlord does not pay taxes on these tenants while costs are driven up in the schools and the extra load is on [Carpentersville]" (Free Republic Blog 2006a: n.p.). Humpfer and other supporters argued that undocumented immigrants did not deserve public services such as schools and hospitals because they broke the law and did not pay taxes. Only law-abiding citizens deserved such public services. He summed it up: "This is unfair to our residents, to be forced to shoulder the burden of scofflaws" (Free Republic Blog 2006b: n.p.). In Farmers Branch, the quality of public services, such as police protection, trash collection, schools, and hospitals, were said to have diminished as the demands from the incoming immigrant population increased. As in Carpentersville, the political actors argued that the new population of immigrants placed more frequent demands on these services to deal with increasingly more severe problems.

Both Carpentersville and Farmers Branch experienced stagnation and decline over the past few decades, which added to the fiscal stress of both local economies. As independent political units that employ the powers of the state, Farmers Branch and Carpentersville worried about maintaining the neoliberal tradition of successful home rule in light of increasing fiscal stress caused by an aging infrastructure and socioeconomic decline. Decentralized suburban governance has traditionally enabled exclusion of and succession by particular groups (Burns 1994; Beauregard 2006). In times of fiscal stress, the exclusionary immigrant policies of Farmers Branch and Carpentersville were framed in ways that appealed to residents concerned about the demise of successful self-governance. Advocates of exclusionary immigration policies effectively framed undocumented immigrants as a fiscal threat to suburban self-governance and stability. In their minds, an undeserving population of undocumented immigrants weighing down a fiscally stressed regime undermines suburban governance.

As Coleman (2008: 10) has demonstrated, undocumented immigrants are often perceived as "dangerous" because of so-called "fraudulent entitlements collection, job market crowding, and use of public schooling and medical facilities." As frontier spaces of neoliberalism and hyper-individuality, the postwar suburbs of Farmers Branch and Carpentersville proved particularly adept at painting undocumented immigrants as an undeserving burden on public services, especially as the reality of decline and fiscal capacity threatened the solidity and success of suburban self-governance.

Suburbs and Assimilation

The traditional immigrant story in the United States is one where new arrivals join friends and family, live in clustered neighborhoods in the city, and gradually, with increasing contact with the new culture and customs, lose connections with their home country, create new social ties, adopt the language and ways of the receiving nation, disperse, and achieve the dream of success and homeownership in the suburbs (Anacker 2013). Suburban space is imagined in ways that assumes immigrants living there will have already assimilated into American society when in fact some immigrants are bypassing cities and moving directly into suburbs.

The notion of suburbs as sites for those immigrants who have already assimilated and who are therefore ready to achieve the American Dream of suburban living was an important element in the political debate around the development of immigration policy in both suburbs. Ordinance 2892, Farmers Branch's anti-immigration initiative, was a comprehensive local law that declared English as the official language of the suburb. Carpentersville's IIRO introduced a similar clause. Suburbanites and their local politicians identified immigrants' use of a foreign language—namely Spanish—as a problem in their communities. One resident asserted, "I grew up there and it saddens me to see what it [Farmers Branch] has become. I am tired of hearing Spanish in the streets and trying to figure out if someone understands what I'm saying" (Anonymous 2006: n.p.). Another resident reflected that, "I can still remember going to high school with Hispanic kids, but back then, they were more like us … not like today's foolish kids" (Anonymous 2006: n.p.). Language and symbols were used as weapons to define community identity, which provided powerful messages and conveyed meaning about who was welcome in the suburb.

Flags were prominently displayed in Carpentersville's neighborhoods during the time of the immigration debate, and flags emerged as dividing lines. To show support for the IIRO policy proposal, residents flew the American flag on their houses or in their yards. To show opposition to the IIRO, other residents flew the Mexican flag. The flags came to symbolize many things. For suburbanites, the American flag symbolized freedom, security, patriotism, and ultimately the American Dream. Residents said that it demonstrated the struggles of their previous relatives who immigrated to the United States, worked hard, learned English, and only then progressed to suburban living, fully assimilating to suburban society. Trustee Sigwalt, initiator and ardent supporter of Carpentersville's IIRO, regularly asked residents, "Are you tired of seeing the Mexican flag flown above our flag"? She stated, "You have Americans giving up on their own country" (Kotlowitz 2007). Sigwalt oftentimes carried photographs with her that showed the desecration of the American flag. A Carpentersville resident's comments highlight the symbolic nature of the flag: "Once here legally, immigrants should strive to Americanize themselves. Not fly their homeland's flag. They left that third world cesspool. Time to forget it" (Anonymous 2006: n.p.).

Said (1994), in his critique of western Americans' cultural and political perceptions of the East, developed his understanding of territorial distinctions by stressing how familiar spaces are created both physically and mentally as "ours." In a similar way, the U.S. suburbs are perceived as belonging to those who are middle-class Americans. In a study of the southern suburbs, Nagel (2013: 636) found that privileged, white suburban residents accept only nonwhite neighbors who adhere to middle-class values; they are the ones who "have earned the right to live the American suburban dream." In the context of the familiar American immigrant story, suburbs only belong to those that have fully assimilated, embraced American society, and reached the success necessary to achieve the suburban dream. In our examination of the rhetoric and concern voiced by residents and politicians in the immigration debate around legislation in Farmers Branch and Carpentersville, we found that certain immigrants were deemed not yet ready to live in suburbia. These immigrants had not yet become fully Americanized or assimilated to American society and so, as such, they were not yet welcome in suburbia, the traditional home of the immigrant success story.

Suburbs and the Single-Family Home

Politicians and supporters of exclusion immigration policy stressed the sanctity of the suburban single-family home. Farmers Branch and Carpentersville both introduced ordinances that included provisions to fine landlords if they knowingly rented to undocumented immigrants. These provisions were introduced in light of the imbalance of some vacant yet other overcrowded single-family houses and the transformation of owner-occupied single-family housing into rental properties. In the debate about immigration reform, vacant yet overcrowded and ill-maintained housing were defined as problems associated with undocumented immigrants. One resident in Carpentersville complained, "I'm tired of seeing homes with tall grass and broken windows." Another stated, "There are too many overcrowded and vacant houses in Carpentersville." Trustee Humpfer of Carpentersville commented, "Some homes are so overcrowded, people are living in garages." These issues became problems caused by undocumented immigrants. Trustee Sigwalt echoed a frequent sentiment that "too many illegals don't take care of their homes." One resident observed, "Every day I see illegals that urinate in their front lawns. It's disgusting."[1]

In Farmers Branch similar public statements echoed the perceived relationship between housing decline and undocumented immigrants. Scattered trash, loud noises at night, lack of parking, overcrowding, and lack of maintenance were among the chief complaints. Homeowners worried about the value of their homes. One resident stated concern for so-called Latino color preferences by suggesting that, "When you paint your house some fluorescent or garish color scheme, you

---

1   These comments were collected from anonymous personal interviews May 1 to 9, 2009 in Carpentersville, Illinois.

negatively affect my home value" (Sandoval 2007: 27). Overcrowding was also described as problem because of immigration. "A single-family home is for a single family, not a hotel for six or seven individuals" (Anonymous 2006: n.p.).

The immigration debate included numerous concerns about the housing stock in Farmers Branch and Carpentersville. Many political actors and residents alike blamed housing problems on undocumented immigrants. Residents and politicians in both Farmers Branch and Carpentersville displayed anger and frustration about the perceived threat of undocumented immigration to the sanctuary of the suburban home and the sanctity of suburban homeownership, which was once so much a part of the postwar suburban experience.

Suburbs as Sites of Safety

The importance of suburbs as safe places was a large part of the political debate around immigration. In the mid-2000s, a series of widely reported crimes became crucial to framing undocumented immigrants as criminal and dangerous, a threat to suburban safety. Stories included a drunk driver who rear-ended a car into a minivan, which killed a mother of three. A resident was struck and killed in a crosswalk, allegedly by an undocumented immigrant who fled the scene of the crime. The owner of a local diner and his family were kidnapped and held at gunpoint for ransom. There were stories about organized gang activity by immigrant groups that politicians, the media, and others repeatedly told to suburban residents. Carpentersville residents first became aware of gangs when numerous properties were defaced with graffiti by competing gangs of undocumented residents. Then, residents were shocked to learn about coordinated raids by Carpentersville police, Illinois state police, and the FBI. The story that emerged was that the Latin Kings gang allegedly had been recruiting undocumented immigrants and dealing cocaine in Carpentersville. For many residents, the memory of Carpentersville as a safe place faded and was replaced by stories about crime and its perceived connection to undocumented immigrants.

Similar attention to violent and criminal activities shaped the public discourse in Farmers Branch. Residents began to worry about violent crime after learning about the shooting and killing of a police officer in Houston, Texas. Juan Leonardo Quintero, an undocumented immigrant, shot and killed Officer Rodney Johnson when he was arrested after a routine traffic stop. In a nationally televised interview, Houston's Police Chief Harold Hurtt indicted the federal government's failure of protecting the nation's borders. Hurtt asserted, "The subject [Quintero] was deported [in 2004], and yet he came back, so if the government [had] fulfilled their responsibility of protecting the border we would probably not be standing here today" (Von Fremd 2006). Farmers Branch politicians, the media, and concerned residents repeatedly reiterated this story to make the case that undocumented immigration was a safety issue. Residents verbalized their yearning for the era when Farmers Branch was once a quiet suburb of Dallas.

Conclusion

Subnational governments in the U.S. have become increasingly involved in immigration reform. This descaling of immigration legislation is characteristic of the age of neoliberalism (Varsanyi 2008a). As new sites of immigration, suburbs that construct immigration legislation tend to introduce exclusionary policies designed to curb undocumented immigration and control immigrant communities (Walker and Leitner 2011). In this chapter, we examined exclusionary immigration policies in two postwar suburbs, Farmers Branch and Carpentersville. These suburbs successfully introduced ordinances to restrict undocumented immigration into their jurisdictions. Their ordinances appealed to notions of suburban assimilation, home rule, safety, and homeownership, and these notions dominated the discourse. During a period of socioeconomic distress and demographic transformation in both suburbs, appeals to these suburban ideals were numerous. Indeed, such classic characteristics of suburbia held sway. Conjuring nostalgia for an imagined suburbia of prosperity and homogeneity, the principal elements of the discourse on immigration framed the undocumented immigrant as a specific threat to a certain way of life. Within the context of metropolitan governance splintering, a preponderance for suburban self-rule, and a time of socioeconomic decline in a neoliberal age, both suburbs successfully framed undocumented immigration as a process that undermines self-governance and reliance, threatens suburban safety, destabilizes the suburban home, and negates the suburbs as sites for the assimilated and for those who have achieved the American Dream.

The development of exclusionary policies in suburbs such as Farmers Branch and Carpentersville has a number of potential consequences. First, exclusionary policies are only one type of response to increased immigration. Some jurisdictions, mostly central cities, are inclined to seek the integration of immigrants into their communities. As Walker and Leitner (2011) suggest, this leads to a variegated metropolitan landscape of immigration policy. But this variegation goes even beyond the metropolitan region to include what Varsanyi (2008a: 892) refers to as "the rise to bizarre geographies of contradictory scalar priorities" where immigration is potentially supported at the state level while it is discouraged at a local level within the same state. What are the consequences of this variation in immigration policy for the metropolitan United States? It is possible that anti-immigrant measures will contribute to the out-movement of immigrants from jurisdictions like Farmers Branch and Carpentersville into more welcoming cities and suburbs. It is also likely that other jurisdictions will continue to attract immigrants while still others will see the numbers of immigrants dwindle in their communities. With different policy responses to immigration, we will continue to witness an even more ethnically and racially segregated metropolis and nation. In consequence, the question of who has a right to the suburb becomes an important question for residents and policymakers of suburbia (Carpio, Irazábal, and Pulido 2011).

Second, suburbs in decline, such as Farmers Branch and Carpentersville, potentially need immigrants to help revitalize their local economies and businesses. Without foreign-born in-migration, the chances are that both Farmers Branch and Carpentersville would have over time experienced population loss to the outer suburbs. As a reaction to exclusionary immigration policies, such suburbs could in the future lose residents who disagree with the community's position on the local control of immigration. Additional research on the potential impacts of local immigration policy in postwar declining suburbs is needed, especially in light of the descaling of immigration reform policies.

References

Anacker, K.B. 2013. Immigrating, assimilating, cashing in? Analyzing property values in suburbs of immigrant gateways. *Housing Studies*, 28, 720–45.

Anonymous. 2006. Letter to the editor. *Dallas Morning News*, 24 August.

Arizona State Legislature. 2010. *Support Our Law Enforcement and Safe Neighborhoods Act*. 49th Legislature. 2nd Regular Session.

Arizona et al. Petitioners v. United States, 641 F. 3d 339 (No. 11–182).

Beauregard, R.A. 2006. *When America Became Suburban*. Minneapolis, MN: University of Minnesota Press.

Brettell, C.B. and Nibbs, F.G. 2011. Immigrant suburban settlement and the "threat" to middle class status and identity: The case of Farmers Branch, Texas. *International Migration*, 49, 1–30.

Burns, N. 1994. *The Formation of American Local Governments: Private Values in Public Institutions*. Oxford: Oxford University Press.

Carpio, G., Irazábal, C., and Pulido, L. 2011. Right to the suburb? Rethinking Lefebvre and immigrant activism. *Journal of Urban Affairs,* 33, 185–208.

Cavin, A. 2013. Fringe politics: Suburban expansion and the Mexican American struggle for Alviso, California, in *Social Justice in Diverse Suburbs*, edited by C. Niedt. Philadelphia, PA: Temple University Press.

Chinwah, L. Personal communication. 7 May 2009.

Coleman, M. 2008. Between public policy and foreign policy: U.S. immigration law reform and the undocumented migrant. *Urban Geography*, 29, 4–28.

Coleman, M. 2007. Immigration geopolitics beyond the Mexico–US border. *Antipode*, 39, 54–76.

Denton, N.A. and Gibbons, J.R. 2013. Twenty-first-century suburban demography: Increasing diversity yet lingering exclusion, in *Social Justice in Diverse Suburbs*, edited by C. Niedt. Philadelphia, PA: Temple University Press.

Ellis, M. 2006. Unsettling immigrant geographies: U.S. immigration and the politics of scale. *Tijdschrift voor Economische en Sociale Geografie*, 97, 49–58.

Esbenshade, J.L. 2007. *Division and Dislocation: Regulating Immigration through Local Housing Ordinances*. Washington, DC: American Immigration Policy Center.

Fair Immigration Reform Movement. 2006. *Database of Recent Local Ordinances on Immigration*. [Online]. Available at http://www.fairimmigration.org/learn/ immigration-reform-andimmigrants/local-level/ [accessed 20 February 2014].

Free Republic Blog. 2006a. *Kristi*. [Online]. Available at http://www.freerepublic. com [accessed February 20, 2014].

Free Republic Blog. 2006b. *10 questions for Carpentersville Trustee Paul Humpfer*. [Online]. Available at http://www.freerepublic.com [accessed February 20, 2014].

Fox News. 2011. Supreme Court Tells Court to Reconsider Hazleton Immigration Regulations. 6 June.

Hanlon, B., Short, J.R., and Vicino, T.J. 2010. *Cities and Suburbs: New Metropolitan Realities in the U.S.* New York, NY: Routledge.

Harnett, H.M. 2008. State and local anti-immigrant initiatives: Can they withstand legal scrutiny? *Widener Law Journal*, 17, 365–82.

Harvey, D. 2007. *A Brief History of Neoliberalism*. Oxford: Oxford University Press.

Hopkins, D.J. 2010. Politicized places: Explaining where and when immigrants provoke local opposition. *American Political Science Review*, 104(01), 40–60.

Jones, R.C. 2008. *Immigrants Outside Megalopolis: Ethnic Transformation in the Heartland*. Lanham, MD: Rowman and Littlefield.

Kneebone, E. and Berube, A. 2013. *Confronting Suburban Poverty in America*. Washington, DC: Brookings Institution.

Kotlowitz, A. 2007. Our Town. *The New York Times*, 5 August.

McKanders, K.M. 2007. Welcome to Hazleton! "Illegal" immigrants beware: Local immigration ordinances and what the federal government must do about it. *Loyola University Chicago Law Journal*, 39, 1–49.

Nagel, C.R. 2013. Reconfiguring belonging in the suburban U.S. south: Diversity, "merit" and the persistence of white privilege. *International Journal of Urban and Regional Research*, 37, 618–40.

National Conference of State Legislatures. 2011. Immigration-Related Laws and Resolutions in the States. [Online]. Available at http://www.ncsl.org/issues-research/immig/state-immigration-laws-january-to-june-2011.aspx [accessed: 20 February 2014].

NBC News. 2006. PA City Passes Law against Illegal Immigrants. *Associated Press*, July 13.

Niedt, C. 2013. Introduction, in *Social Justice in Diverse Suburbs*, edited by C. Niedt. Philadelphia, PA: Temple University Press.

Parlow, M. 2007. Localist's case for decentralizing immigration policy. *Denver University Law Review*, 84, 1061–73.

Pastor, M. 2013. Maywood, not Mayberry: Latinos and suburbia in Los Angeles County, in *Social Justice in Diverse Suburbs*, edited by C. Niedt. Philadelphia, PA: Temple University Press.

Peck, J. 2011. Neoliberal suburbanism: Frontier space. *Urban Geography*, 32, 884–919.

Peck, J. and Tickell, A. 2002. Neoliberalizing space. *Antipode*, 34, 380–404.

Price, M. and Benton-Short, L. 2008. *Migrants to the Metropolis: The Rise of Immigrant Gateway Cities*. Syracuse, NY: Syracuse University Press.

Ramakrishnan, S.K. and Wong, T. 2010. Partisanship, not Spanish: Explaining municipal ordinances affecting undocumented immigrants, in *Taking Local Control: Immigration Policy Activism in US Cities and States*, edited by M. Varsanyi. Palo Alto, CA: Stanford University Press.

Ridgley, J. 2008. Cities of refuge: Immigration enforcement, police, and the insurgent genealogies of citizenship in U.S. sanctuary cities. *Urban Geography*, 29, 53–77.

Rodriguez, C. 2007. The significance of the local in immigration regulation. *New York Public Law and Legal Theory Working Papers*. Paper 75.

Said, E.W. 1994. *Orientalism*. New York, NY: Vintage Books.

Sandoval, S. 2007. Grocer Rumor Raises Racial Tensions in FB. *Dallas Morning News*, 27 March.

Singer, A., Hardwick, S.W., and Brettell, C.B. 2008. *Twenty-First Century Gateways: Immigrant Incorporation in Suburban America*. Washington, DC: Brookings Institution.

U.S. Department of Justice. 2010. Citing Conflict with Federal Law, Department of Justice Challenges Arizona's Immigration Law. [Online]. Available at http://www.justice.gov/opa/pr/2010/July/10-opa-776.html [accessed: 20 February 2014].

Von Fremd, M. 2006. *Cop Killing Sparks Immigration Debate*. [Online: ABC News]. Available at http://abcnews.go.com/GMA/story?id=2487004#.Txs-92PUOPA [accessed: 20 February 2014].

Varsanyi, M. 2010a. Neoliberalism and nativism: Local anti-immigrant policy activism and emerging politics of scale. *International Journal of Urban and Regional Research*, 35, 295–311.

Varsanyi, M. 2010b. *Taking Local Control: Immigration Policy Activism in U.S. Cities and States*. Palo Alto, CA: Stanford University Press.

Varsanyi, M. 2008a. Rescaling the 'alien,' rescaling personhood: Neoliberalism, immigration, and the state. *Annals of the Association of American Geographers*, 98, 877–96.

Varsanyi, M. 2008b. Immigration policing through the backdoor: City ordinances, the 'right to the city' and the exclusion of undocumented day laborers. *Urban Geography*, 29, 29–52.

Vicino, T.J. 2012. *Suburban Crossroads: The Fight to Control Local Immigration Policy*. Lanham, MA: Rowman and Littlefield.

Walker, K. 2010. *The Geographies of Local Immigration Policies*. Ph.D. dissertation. University of Minnesota.

Walker, K.E. and Leitner, H. 2011. The variegated landscape of local immigration policies in the United States. *Urban Geography*, 32, 156–78.

Winders, J. 2007. Bringing back the (b)order: Post-9/11 politics of immigration, borders, and belonging in the contemporary U.S. south. *Antipode*, 39, 920–42.

Wright, R. and Ellis, M. 2000. Race, region and the territorial politics of immigration in the U.S. *International Journal of Population Geography*, 6, 197–211.

SECTION III
Suburban Decline—or Not?

Chapter 6

Beyond Sprawl: Social Sustainability and Reinvestment in the Baltimore Suburbs

Bernadette Hanlon

In the current discourse on environmental and social sustainability, suburbs are typically described as mere roadblocks to the development of a more sustainable metropolis (Hildebrand 1999). The discourse suggests that to be more sustainable, suburbs must become more city-like and be redeveloped in ways that make them more dense and compact (Elkin, McLaren and Hillman 1991). The focus is on retrofitting suburbia physically in ways that improve their environmental sustainability. In this chapter, I argue that this sustainability turn in the debate about suburbia is, in fact, likely to produce a less socially sustainable metropolis and that reinvestment in the suburbs is occurring in ways that are in fact increasing social inequity within the metropolis more broadly.

My focus in this chapter is on reinvestment in the suburbs of Baltimore, centering on single-family residential redevelopment, particularly among inner suburbs. Inner suburbs are those suburbs built before 1970 and closest to the traditional central city core (Hanlon 2009). These suburbs are increasingly becoming new sites for reinvestment, and how they redevelop will be central to the social sustainability of metropolitan regions. Inner suburban redevelopment has a tremendous impact on regional social configurations, impacting social sustainability.

To begin this chapter, I discuss the concept of sustainability, considering this topic in the context of suburbs. Next, I will examine the recent focus on suburban redevelopment and analyze recent work related to the topic area. I then discuss my analysis of suburban redevelopment in the Baltimore region and end this chapter with a warning about the importance of studying redevelopment in ways that consider its impact on the creation of a socially sustainable suburbia.

Sustainability and the Suburban Context

In recent decades there have been a tremendous number of articles and books on the topic of sustainability (e.g., Edwards 2005, Fitzgerald 2010). Yet, sustainability remains a rather elusive and tricky concept. It can mean different things to different people and, at the moment, it is popular with just about everyone. As Swyngedouw (2007: 20) declared some time back, "Greenpeace is in favor, George Bush Jr. and

Sr. are, the World Bank and its chairman (a prime warmonger on Iraq) are, the Pope is, my son Arno is, the rubber trappers in the Brazilian Amazon forest are, Bill Gates is, the labor unions are." With such wide auspicious champions, it is no surprise that sustainability can be interpreted and employed in very different ways (Whitehead 2007). It is very much a contested concept (Giddings, Hopwood, and O'Brien 2002), with different political ideologies voicing different opinions on both what sustainability is and what it means for the way we live.

Suburbs, especially those on the exurban fringe, have long been criticized for their negative impacts on environmental sustainability (Johnson 2001). Environmental problems resulting from sprawling development include increased air pollution; higher energy consumption; loss of open space, farmland, and species habitat; and shifts in patterns of local and regional species diversity. Suburbs are therefore central to the development of a sustainable metropolitan agenda, and yet individually suburbs have thus far been behind cities in developing public sector plans, policies, or ways of living that move toward environmental sustainability (Dierwechter 2010). There are few suburban sustainability plans, although there has been a recent focus at the federal level on the development of regional sustainability plans of which suburbs are necessary contributors as manifest in action by the United States Housing and Urban Development's (HUD) Office of Sustainable Housing and Communities. In recent years, HUD's Office of Sustainable Housing and Communities has offered a number of planning grants at the neighborhood, county, and regional levels. For instance, in 2011 the suburb of Oak Park, as part of a coalition of suburban communities in Cook County, Illinois, outside Chicago, received $2.9 million to revisit outdated zoning and infrastructure plans to, in part, encourage more transit-oriented development and increase the amount of affordable housing in these suburbs.

Many of the relevant policy-related actions aimed at improving suburban sustainability fall under the rubric of smart growth, a set of growth management strategies that, in part, focuses on the redevelopment of older areas of metropolitan area rather than the continuation of new development on the suburban fringe (Frece 2009). Of particular importance in smart growth planning are inner suburbs, those older suburbs built in between the city core and the exurban fringe. As I demonstrate later in this chapter, smart growth policy is highly relevant in the context of the Baltimore region. The inner suburbs of Baltimore are increasingly becoming places ripe for redevelopment because of smart growth initiatives.

For a variety of reasons a number of central cities have turned their attention toward the topic of sustainability. Concern, particularly over climate change, water quality, and quality of life, has encouraged local policy makers to develop plans aimed at creating more sustainable urban centers (Portney 2005). In general, cities have focused on reducing their carbon footprint, managing green space, and, especially in the context of the U.K. and U.S., encouraging neighborhood revitalization. Portney and Berry (2010) found that cities most committed to pursuing sustainability tend to be more participatory places with respect to signing petitions, participating in demonstrations, belonging to local reform groups, and joining neighborhood associations. Cities with greater civic capacity and engagement tend to pursue sustainability policies. The move toward sustainability can signify civic concern.

More cynically, however, cities also pursue ecological policies and climate action plans because they are compatible with their efforts to be competitive economically, part of a so-called "sustainability fix" or "green turn" in the urban entrepreneurial politics of many cities of the 1980s (While et al. 2004). The principles of sustainability are positioned within a contemporary sociopolitical context where the focus is on market-based solutions and private sector investment in land development planning. Sustainability can be a way to repackage development planning to present a "green façade" in the face of "business as usual exploitation of people and resources" (Sneddon 2000: 522). For instance, the desire for regeneration in the city in the name of sustainability has led to the promotion of gentrification and the subsequent displacement of poorer residents in city neighborhoods (Bunce 2009). This is also the case with suburban redevelopment, where the needs of poorer suburbanites are at times neglected in the push for more sustainable design as well as by the investment of private capital in residential development. The "green turn" in public sector planning can, at times, mean the neglect of issues of social equity and social justice, which are central to the sustainability debate. There are three so-called prongs to sustainability: environment, economy, and society; and yet it is this last prong concerning social sustainability that is often ignored. It is important to keep in mind the potential negative impacts of increasing centrality and inner suburban retrofitting on social sustainability in the metropolis more broadly. In the following sections, I argue that the merits for reinvesting in inner suburbs for environmental sustainability should not be overstated and certainly should be done in ways that lead to more equity in suburbia and the metropolitan region.

The Focus on Suburban Redevelopment

Over the past 40 years or more, U.S. suburbia has been marked by large-scale demographic, social, and economic shifts. On the one hand, outward expansion into undeveloped areas has continued in the form of suburban sprawl, albeit tempered somewhat by housing market stress in recent years. On the other hand, there is now a significant body of research on the problems of suburban decline and poverty, with a particular focus on older and denser suburbs (Lucy and Phillips 2000, Hanlon 2009, Kneebone and Berube 2013). A newly emerging arena of suburban study considers the processes of suburban reinvestment and redevelopment. There is a growing discourse that suggests we are now witnessing a sprawl slowdown, stressing the need for suburban redevelopment over continuing development (Nelson 2009).

Much of this has occurred since the recent economic downturn and financial crisis that revealed serious vulnerability in the global capitalist economy

(Immergluck 2009). The crisis has had an enormous impact on housing markets across cities and suburbs of many national economies (Crump et al. 2008). In the metropolitan U.S., the impact of this crisis was manifested by a tremendous increase in housing foreclosures, a decline in house prices, and an unprecedented slowdown in new housing construction that had ripple effects throughout the U.S. economy (Joint Center for Housing Studies 2012). Many households became burdened with mortgages bigger than the value of their homes as real estate prices plummeted, and foreclosure still remains a serious problem for many families (Immergluck and Smith 2006). Foreclosures have always been a problem for low-income neighborhoods of color, but the problem worsened with the house price crash (Anacker and Carr 2011). During this time, suburbs were certainly not immune, and the mainstream press and politicians began to comment when foreclosures began to affect non-Hispanic White middle class suburbanites in mid-2007 (Harvey 2012).

According to Lucy (2010), repossessions of foreclosed residences in April 2010 occurred at a higher rate in one or more outer suburban counties than in central cities in 23 of 34 large metropolitan areas. Foreclosures in many poorer communities were largely the result of predatory lending practices or "reverse redlining." Foreclosures in outer suburbs occurred where there was overbuilding and excess speculation among large-scale developers, creating clusters of vacant and abandoned homes far out on the metropolitan fringes, especially in states like Florida, Nevada, California, and Arizona (Hollander 2011). This over-speculation and the housing market slump marked the beginnings of a new urban form: the abandoned exurb (Hanlon 2013). For the first time in two decades, the annual population growth rate of cities and their adjacent suburbs surpassed that of the exurbs (Heavens 2012). Between 2010 and 2012, the population in cities and older suburbs increased annually by 0.8 percent, compared to only 0.4 percent in the exurbs (Heavens 2012).

Some argue that the prospect of abandonment in fringe areas of the U.S. metropolis has been made worse by changing demographics. According to Lucy (2010), the number of households in the 30- to 45-year-old age group has declined by 3.4 million since 2000. This decrease has reduced demand for large suburban houses found on the exurban fringe. He suggests that the reason for this decrease is more a change in household age and structure than the effects of the recent economic and credit crisis that negatively impacted new housing construction. The changing age demographic lowers the need for the typical McMansion-style home in the outer suburbs, a reality that results in the sluggishness of outward sprawl and a complementary resurgence in metropolitan centrality.

Some suggest the sprawl slowdown is not merely a blip in what has until now been a continuous outward movement. It is likely to persist. Nelson (2009) suggests a new urbanity of the U.S. metropolis and notes how during the so-called baby boom period between 1946 and 1964 about half of American households were raising children, yet that by 2030 only about a quarter of households will be parents. Also, by 2030 about 19 percent of the population will be over 65 years old.

Older households and households without children will be looking for something different than the typical suburban home and the suburban lifestyle. Instead, they will demand a more urban way of life and will want accessible neighborhoods with urban amenities, such as restaurants and shopping, and more mixed housing choices. The discourse that is emerging stresses that new and future demographic shifts, including the projected dearth of traditional married couples with children, will force the need to retrofit the suburbs (Nelson 2009). In the future, suburbs will need to be redesigned in ways that cater to older people as well as singles and childless couples. So, how will these suburbs be redesigned?

Suburban Retrofit and Redesign

Architects and urban designers have examined ways in which suburbs are being redesigned and how, in their minds, suburbs need to be redesigned to be more like cities (Dunham-Jones and Williamson 2011). This work has examined the redevelopment of dead malls and the retrofitting of large suburban spaces to include more dense residential development. Much of this work falls under the rubric of New Urbanism, an urban design movement that promotes the development of more walkable, mixed-use, and neo-traditional neighborhoods.

Probably the most active researchers in this context are architects Ellen Dunham-Jones and June Williamson. In their recent book, *Retrofitting Suburbia*, Dunham-Jones and Williamson (2011) document and analyze examples of suburban redevelopment, particularly the redevelopment of vacant big box stores, dead malls, underutilized commercial strips, outdated office parks, and aging apartment complexes in various suburbs across North America. They have collected hundreds of examples of suburban retrofitting throughout the United States, identifying 460 cases thus far (Williamson 2013).

In their work, Dunham-Jones and Williamson (2011) categorized the different types of suburban retrofitting they found. The first of these types include what they refer to as *reinhabitation*, the adaptive reuse of older retail sites often into such public use facilities as libraries and government offices. The second is *redevelopment*, typically a large-scale transformation from a single-use development to a more mixed-use configuration. The third strategy is *regreening*, with the introduction of small green spaces, parks, and other ecologically beneficial sites and civic spaces. Regreening is taking place mostly as a result of reusing commercial space in more sustainable ways. Dunham-Jones and Williamson (2011) provide different examples of these three strategies. Some of these retrofits were initiated by developers, others by local governments, and in some cases what were once private parcels have been redesigned and now house public institutions such as libraries, government offices, and so on.

Architects and urban designers have been involved in a number of design competitions to identify new ways to retrofit and redesign more traditional suburbs. Examples include *Reburbia*, a competition partly sponsored by *Dwell* magazine, and *Foreclosed: Rehousing the American Dream*, an exhibit at the Museum of Modern Art in New York. Recently, Williamson (2013) published another book, *Designing Suburban Futures*, based on an exhibit and competition among urban designers and architectures to retrofit Long Island, outside of New York and home to the classic postwar suburb of Levittown. Williamson (2013) examines results from the design competition, *Build a Better Burb*. Sponsored by the Long Island Index, a project funded by the Rauch Foundation, the competition offered a variety of potential redevelopment projects. One design entry advocates the complete rezoning of Long Island to recreate a network of densely populated diverse centers; another focuses on the renowned suburb of Levittown, advocating infill development and the expansion of housing choices to include multigenerational development to attract young people while catering to seniors; others consider, for instance, such options as retrofitting shopping centers with dense housing, urban agriculture, and the development of a transit system from suburban centers to outlying suburbs. Densification is an important aspect of the redesign agenda, and some projects offer suggestions on how to adapt suburbs in a time of climate change.

Dealing with the problem of climate change has made the need for more sustainable suburban design more urgent. Of importance in this regard is addressing the rise in greenhouse gases (Boden, Marland, and Andres 2010). According to the EPA, greenhouse gas emissions that are caused by human activities increased by 14 percent from 1990 to 2008 in the United States. The largest source of greenhouse gas emissions is related to electricity generation, followed closely by transportation. From 1990 to 2008, transportation-related CO_2 emissions increased by 20 percent, with a small decrease of 6 percent between 2007 and 2008, largely because of the recession and the increased price in gasoline during 2008.

Glaeser and Kahn (2010) examined differences in CO_2 emissions between cities and suburbs across the U.S. They estimated the difference between what that average household would emit in CO_2 upon settling in the central city compared to the suburbs of the 48 metropolitan areas in their study. In almost every metro area, they found that CO_2 emissions were significantly lower for people in central cities than for suburbanites. Among the different metropolitan areas, New York had the most significant gap in emissions for cities versus suburbs. The study found that the average New York City resident emits 4,462 pounds less transportation-related carbon dioxide than the average New York suburbanite annually. Differences in CO_2 emissions from heating and electricity were similarly large. In some cases, it is not that the cities were particularly sustainable but that their less-dense, driving-intensive suburbs were far less "green." According to Glaeser and Kahn (2010), the characteristics of more compact development in cities contributed to their lower CO_2 emissions. If suburbs could be redeveloped in ways that make them more compact they could become more sustainable.

There has been some controversy over the relationship between compact development and sustainability. In the U.K context, Echenique et al. (2012) found that while different urban forms (i.e., compact development, sprawl, edge expansion, and new towns) have different sustainability outcomes, no one urban form is superior. Ewing and Cervero (2010) reviewed a large body of work on the effects of the urban form on travel behavior. In their meta-analysis of travel and the built environment, they found that population and job densities do not appear to be the primary determinants of the number of vehicle miles traveled. Rather, other factors such as destination accessibility, defined as ease of access to trip attractions, distance to downtown, and design metrics such as intersection density and street connectivity are the determinants. One of the more interesting findings from their analysis is that any development in a central location is likely to generate less driving than "the best designed, compact, mixed use development in a remote location" (Ewing and Cervero 2010: 276).

New Urbanism emphasizes the design of urban and suburban space, stressing a return to more traditional forms of development that encourage mixed uses, pedestrian activity, and social contact among community members. New Urbanist forms of development have long been criticized for being built in sites and places where residents are still reliant on the automobile. These communities may look like town centers, they appear walkable, and they have the village façade but often behind the scenes of these neo-traditional forms of development are large parking lots full of cars (Hall 2000). Thus, it is not only design that matters, it is also location and connectivity. Suburbs, even if well designed, may still encourage driving, especially if they are not close and connected to regional attractions and employment. Density is only one characteristic to contend with if we want to address the problem of climate change and urge environmental sustainability in the suburbs.

But more importantly, largely missing from the literature on suburban retrofitting are the effects this form of reinvestment has on populations living in the suburbs. The environmental benefits may exist, but what are the impacts on people? For example, in the older suburb of Essex, outside Baltimore city, there has been much decline (Hanlon and Vicino 2007). As this decline occurred, many of Essex's old garden apartments that housed manufacturing workers during the 1940s and 1950s became publically subsidized housing for low-income residents. In efforts to revitalize Essex in the early 2000s, the local county government razed a number of these complexes, displacing tenants. Built in their place were neo-traditional town center-style developments. For instance, in 2002 the 1,140-unit Riverdale Village complex was demolished and eventually replaced with the Waterview Town Center, a $45 million project featuring 175 single-family housing units, linked with sidewalks and bikeways to the 96,000-square-foot commercial center that includes a supermarket, a bank, and other retailers. In another similar project in Essex, a postwar apartment complex was replaced with a new $60 million development of 262 new housing units with 86 single-family homes and 176 condominiums, a swimming pool, restaurant, and private marina. In both projects, the revitalization efforts aimed to take advantage of the waterfront location. Built with a vague notion that they included "affordable housing" units, the property values of these waterfront developments soared during the housing market boom.

There was a great deal of tension around waterfront redevelopment both in Baltimore City and the surrounding industrial suburbs. At issue in Essex and neighboring suburb Middle River was the 2000 Senate Bill 509, a measure allowing condemnation and seizure via eminent domain of older apartment complexes and waterfront properties in Baltimore County, the jurisdiction where Essex is located. Some properties were seized and sold to private developers, and in these cases low-income residents in older apartment complexes, homeowners with modest incomes, and small businesses along the waterfront were displaced by high-end residential development, restaurants, and private marinas.

Suburban redevelopment, advocated as part of a retrofit strategy, can lead to displacement. The discussion above presented a case study of this phenomenon. More cases need to be studied to identify the extent of this type of suburban gentrification. Largely missing from any significant analysis of suburban retrofitting are planning theorists, political scientists, economists, sociologists, geographers, or others in the field of social science research. There is a lack of any critical analysis of the idea of suburban retrofitting and encouraging the redesign of suburbia for purposes of sustainability.

McMansion Infill

Suburban retrofitting is one type of suburban redevelopment. Another type is the reinvestment in single-family residential development in the form of McMansion infill or mansionization or overexpansion of the housing stock. This is taking place in many older suburbs, as recently discussed by Charles (2013). She examined the tearing down and rebuilding of single-family houses in Chicago's suburbs and found that properties that are smaller, with lower floor-to-area ratios and lower property values relative to the region, are more likely to be redeveloped. She also found that redevelopment is less likely to occur in neighborhoods with high proportions of Black and Latino residents and in high-performing school districts.

Earlier work on the "teardown and rebuild" process also focused on Chicago. Dye and McMillen (2007) examined housing demolition and redevelopment in the Chicago suburbs to find that many of the teardowns were small, older homes close to public transportation and traditional village centers. Like Charles (2013), Dye and McMillen determined that suburban redevelopment occurred among older suburbs in Chicago. Charles (2013) suggests that this form of suburban redevelopment leads to gentrification because low- to moderate-income families can no longer afford to live in inner-ring suburban neighborhoods where reinvestment is significant.

Figure 6.1 provides an image of what McMansion infill or mansionization can look like. In some cases, older homes are not demolished and rebuilt but rather amended and expanded. This expansion creates problems in certain communities as property owners living next door to expanded homes complain

Figure 6.1   Example of Mansionization in Baltimore County, Maryland

Source: Author.

about the increase in building height or the increase in the footprint. Thus, local planning departments and planners have intervened to develop regulations to control the mansionization process in certain communities. According to a recent study of the mansionization process, two-thirds of jurisdictions within 50 large regions reported some form of McMansion infill, and some have implemented regulations to control the phenomenon (Nasar et al. 2007). The most common regulatory code used is a limit on building height as a way to control oversized houses. However, suburban officials also have mixed feelings about this way of regulation. Although McMansion infill can negatively impact the character of a neighborhood, local governments recognize the potential benefits in the form of increased property values and, thus, increased tax revenue.

As suburbs are redeveloped, whether in a piecemeal fashion as in the case of mansionization or in a much more dramatic way visualized and examined as suburban retrofitting on a larger scale, there is the potential that this redevelopment can lead to increased property values and the displacement of low-income suburban households. In the remaining sections of this chapter, I describe the extent of reinvestment in single-family residences in the Baltimore suburbs, demonstrating the role that policy and the market play in the residential redevelopment process.

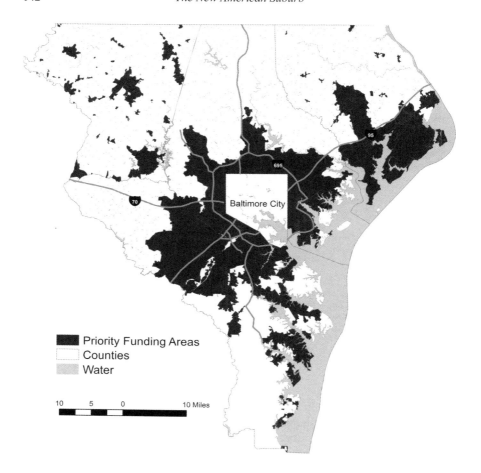

Figure 6.2   Priority Funding Areas in the Baltimore Region

Source: Author, based on data from MdProperty View purchased from the Maryland
Department of Planning.

Analysis of Residential Redevelopment in the Baltimore Suburbs

Previous research notes that decline has occurred in some older suburbs in
the Baltimore region (Hanlon and Vicino 2007), particularly among older
manufacturing suburbs that have witnessed increasing unemployment and a
growth in underutilized industrial properties. Have these older suburbs experienced
residential redevelopment in recent times? Are there signs of reinvestment in
these suburbs? Many of the older suburbs in the region are located in Baltimore
County, right outside of the city of Baltimore. Baltimore County has initiated
community conservation policies since the 1990s (Vicino 2008), designating
certain neighborhoods and districts in the county to receive public funding for

redevelopment. Is there evidence to indicate that this public source of reinvestment is initiating private reinvestment to take place in older suburbs? What is the role of statewide policy initiatives?

Many consider Maryland as the poster child for smart growth, passing the nationally and internationally recognized Neighborhood Conservation and Smart Growth Act in 1997. An important element of the smart growth initiative in Maryland is the Priority Funding Area (PFA) program (Frece 2009). The state provides funding to local jurisdictions for infrastructure such as public sewer expansion, roads, and schools only if development takes place inside PFAs (see Figure 6.2).

This type of funding is aimed at providing incentives for local governments in the state to target growth inside rather than outside these designated growth areas. In short, the PFA program stresses the need to increase density and redevelop existing communities rather than continue development out on the metropolitan fringe. There has been much research to determine if Maryland's PFA program has been successful at limiting new development in the exurbs. Hanlon, Howland, and McGuire (2012) suggest that at least in the fast-growing exurban county of Frederick, Maryland, the PFA program has not been completely effective in this regard. Others have similarly found that development is still occurring outside PFAs (Lewis, Knaap, and Sohn 2009), and yet few if any researchers have examined the relationship between residential redevelopment and smart growth initiatives.

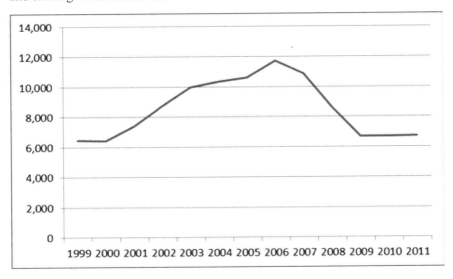

Figure 6.3   Number of Permits Issued for Single-Family Residential Redevelopment in the Baltimore Suburbs, 1999 to 2011

Source: Author, based on Building Permit Data purchased from the Baltimore Metropolitan Council.

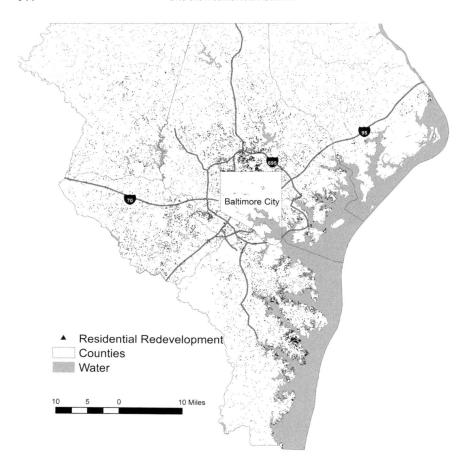

**Figure 6.4   Location of Single-Family Residential Redevelopment Permits
Issued in the Baltimore Suburbs, 1999 to 2011**

Source: Author, based on Building Permit Data purchased from the Baltimore
Metropolitan Council.

The effects of smart policy and housing market dynamics suggest that private
reinvestment in residential development may not be evenly distributed across
different suburbs in the Baltimore region. To examine this further, I assembled a
dataset using permit data to identify suburban residential property redevelopment
from 1999 to 2011. I had permit data available only for these years. Owners
and developers must obtain a permit from the local jurisdiction for any new
construction but also for any demolition and any additions, amendments, and
repair of residential and other properties. This permit information is tracked by
each jurisdiction in the Baltimore region but also compiled at the regional level by
the Baltimore Metropolitan Council (BMC). I purchased the permit data from the

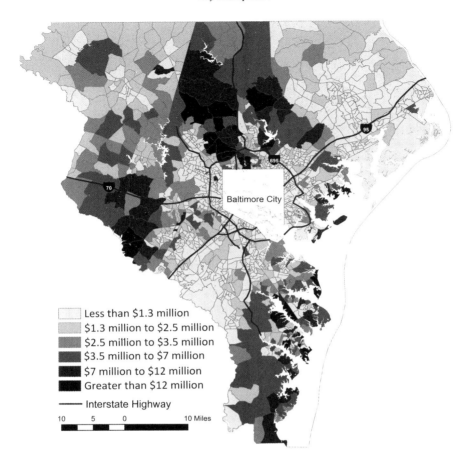

Figure 6.5   Dollar Amount for Single-Family Residential Development in the Baltimore Suburbs by Census Block Group, 1999 to 2011

Source: Author, based on Building Permit Data purchased from the Baltimore Metropolitan Council and TIGER/Line files from the U.S. Bureau of the Census.

BMC and extracted from their dataset permit information for residential property redevelopment in the Baltimore suburbs, mapping the data for those permits whose investment was greater than $50,000 (see Figure 6.4). The permit data includes the dollar amount the expected redevelopment will cost, and while there is no guarantee that the redevelopment actually took place, it is highly likely it did once the permit was issued. For my analysis I focus on the dollar amount issued for redevelopment permits for residential properties between 1999 and 2011.

During these years, a total of 81,412 single-family residential properties in the Baltimore suburbs were redeveloped (i.e. they were either demolished and rebuilt or underwent extensive repairs and expansion). As Figure 6.3 suggests, most of this residential redevelopment peaked in 2006 and, with the housing market crash, permits issued for redevelopment purposes began to plummet to a low of 4,663 in 2009, although they began rising slowly again in 2009. In terms of dollars, an estimated $3.7 billion worth of permits were issued for residential redevelopment in the suburbs from 1999 to 2011, again peaking in 2006, decreasing after 2006, and rising slightly since 2009. About 1–2 percent of all single-family houses in the Baltimore suburbs were redeveloped each year between 1999 and 2011. While the proportion of single-family houses that was redeveloped is small, the dollar amount of reinvestment from 1999 to 2011 was substantial.

Figure 6.4 illustrates the location of permits for redevelopment in the Baltimore suburbs. As this map suggests, residential redevelopment occurred between 1999 and 2011 throughout the suburbs, although there are definite signs of spatial clustering of redevelopment permits in areas along the water, north of Baltimore City and inside the 695 Beltway, and southwest into Howard County. An important question to consider is not only the number of permits issued but also the dollar amount for the investments of these permits. Figure 6.5 shows the total dollar amount for permits by census block group. As this map demonstrates, the northern part of Baltimore County experienced large sums for residential redevelopment, as did parts of Howard County and areas along the waterfront in Anne Arundel County.

I further analyzed residential redevelopment by conducting a stepwise regression to understand and identify the predictors of this type of redevelopment for 1,269 suburban neighborhoods of Baltimore for the years 1999 to 2011. This analysis was performed using a dataset that included the aforementioned permit data, tax assessment information on individual single-family residential parcels from the Maryland State Department of Assessments and Taxation, policy-related information, and data from the U.S. Bureau of the Census. All these data were aggregated to the census block group. The dependent variable in the regression model is the dollar amount for a permit for redevelopment of each single-family residence, aggregated to the census block group. Table 6.1 provides the results of this analysis. As these results suggest, nine variables are significant at the 5 percent level, predicting single-family residential reinvestment. Let me consider them in turn.

First, according to the model results, the value of residential land is positive and significant. For every dollar increase in the average assessed value of residential land, the amount spent on redevelopment is expected to increase by a relative small amount of $12. The assessed value of the residential structure is predicted to have a similar effect ($15). As land values increase, we expect to see redevelopment of structures on this land to occur.

The total dollar amount for investment also increases as the lot size increases. This is an intuitive finding since larger lot sizes allow for the expansion of residential structures. The coefficient is positive and significant. For every acre increase in the lot size of a residential parcel, the amount spent on residential redevelopment would increase by $950,518 at a census block group scale. Also, like

Table 6.1 Coefficient Results from Stepwise Regression. Dependent Variable: Total Dollar Amount for Redevelopment Permits Issued by Census Block Group

	Unstandardized Coefficients		Standardized Coefficients		Sig.	VIF
	B	Std. Error	Beta	t		
(Constant)	113,182,500.0	11,311,140.0		10.006	0	
Average assessed value of the land	12.3	1.4	0.291	8.681	0	2.463
Average assessed value of residential property	15.0	2.0	0.289	7.405	0	3.327
Average lot size in acres	950,518.0	131,540.0	0.219	7.226	0	2
Average year residential properties were built	-60,021.0	5,804.0	-0.269	-10.341	0	1.483
Percent of vacant housing	14,526,336.0	2,762,954.0	0.134	5.258	0	1.433
Number of parcels inside 1,000 feet of waterfront	3,150.0	532.0	0.152	5.921	0	1.444
Percent of households with Income greater than $200,000	3,153,815.0	1,203,312.0	0.093	2.621	0.009	2.777
Percent of Black/African American population	876,767.0	411,954.0	0.052	2.128	0.034	1.293
Number of parcels in PFA	2,047.0	354.0	0.167	5.777	0	1.835

Source: Author

in the studies of residential redevelopment in Chicago (Charles 2013), as housing ages, reinvestment increases. The results of my stepwise regression suggest that a one-year increase in the age of housing leads to about a $60,000 decrease in investment in redevelopment. This is an intuitive finding, as housing needs to be repaired over time. Also, as the proportion of vacant housing hypothetically grows within a suburban census block group, so do the reinvestment dollars for residential redevelopment (indeed, about $14.5 million), and the coefficient is significant at the 5 percent level. Redevelopment of vacant houses is typically easier than redevelopment of occupied housing.

Location close to the waterfront is also relevant. As the number of residences located inside a 1,000-foot buffer of the waterfront increases, so too does the dollar amount spent on residential redevelopment ($3,150), as the waterfront is a desirable location. In the above discussion about waterfront redevelopment in Essex, the large-scale retrofitting of apartment complexes and business is coupled by more piecemeal redevelopment of individual single-family houses.

The amount spent on residential redevelopment in the suburbs increases as the percentage of households with incomes greater than $200,000 increases. Again, this finding is expected, as high-income households use their disposable income to reinvest in housing structures. For every 1 percent increase in the percentage of households earning more than $200,000 in income in the census block group, the amount of residential redevelopment increases by $3.1 million. An unexpected result is the proportion of Black residents. As the percentage of Black residents increases, redevelopment also increases. This is opposite to the effect Charles (2013) found in her study of single-family residential redevelopment in the suburbs of Chicago. In the case of Baltimore, there are a number of middle-class black suburbs north of the city that experienced redevelopment in the past ten years or so. The variable related to the percentage of Latinos in each census block group was included in the stepwise regression but was not significant and therefore not included in the final results.

In the context of Maryland smart growth, findings from this analysis suggest that more dollars are likely to be spent on residential redevelopment inside Priority Funding Areas (PFA), as expected. As the number of single-family houses located inside the PFA increases, so does reinvestment. To conclude, reinvestment in residential redevelopment is affected by a number of important factors related to household income, the percentage of Black residents, age and the value of housing, lot size, and housing vacancy status. Another important predictor relates to the Priority Funding Area policy implemented at the state level.

Recognizing some of the predictors of single-family housing redevelopment is one step in this research. Next steps in this work are to examine the effects of reinvestment on the social status of suburbs. In the Baltimore context, as high-income households move into certain suburbs (i.e., those close to the waterfront, inside PFAs, and with small houses but significant lot sizes), there is the potential for reinvestment in ways that will change the social configuration of these places.

Concluding Remarks

The recent discourse on suburban redevelopment is taking place within the context of changing demographics, the New Urbanist call for redesigning metropolitan neighborhoods and places, and the policy push for more centrality and density to improve environmental sustainability. Suburban retrofitting is happening across the nation. Yet, there is a need for more analyses on the impacts of suburban redevelopment on social sustainability and the social configuration of metropolitan regions. This chapter is a step in that direction, examining the recent literature on suburban retrofitting and redevelopment and providing an analysis of single-family residential reinvestment among the Baltimore suburbs.

Dealing with the problem of climate change, the effects of the recent global financial crisis, the needs of a changing demographic, and our future energy needs within the U.S. metropolis are important as we consider ways to move beyond sprawl and toward environmental sustainability (Davis 2003, Newman, Beatley, and Boyer 2009, Atkinson 2010). It is likely that inner suburbs close to urban centers will become more desirable with changing demographics, new modes of transportation, the need for different types of housing, and the desire for densification and new designs. Suburbs cannot be ignored in the efforts to create a much more sustainable metropolis. Yet, in the move to redevelop inner suburbs, it is important to remember how redevelopment can negatively impact low-income households, which has happened in many gentrifying areas of the city. We ought not make the same mistake with suburbs.

References

Anacker, K.B. and Carr, J.H. 2011. Analyzing determinants of foreclosure among high-income African American and Hispanic borrowers in the Washington, DC metropolitan area. *International Journal of Housing Policy*, 11(2), 195–220.

Atkinson, A. 2010. Where do we stand? Progress in acknowledging and confronting climate change and 'peak oil.' *City*, 14(3), 314–22.

Boden, T.A., Marland, G., and Andres, R.J. 2010. *Global, Regional, and National Fossil-Fuel CO₂ Emissions*. Oak Ridge, TN: Carbon Dioxide Information Analysis Center, Oak Ridge National Laboratory, and U.S. Department of Energy.

Bunce, S. 2009. Developing sustainability: Sustainability policy and gentrification on Toronto's waterfront. *Local Environment*, 14(7), 651–67.

Charles, S.L. 2013. Understanding the determinants of single-family residential redevelopment in the inner-ring suburbs of Chicago. *Urban Studies*, 50(8), 1505–22.

Crump, J., Newman, K., Belsky, E.S., Ashton, P., Kaplan, D.H., Hammel, D.J, and Wyly, E. 2008. Cities destroyed (again) for cash: Forum on the U.S. foreclosure crisis. *Urban Geography*, 29(8), 745–84.

Davis, G. 2003. Meeting future energy needs. *The Bridge*. National Academies Press, summer.

Dierwechter, Y. 2010. Metropolitan geographies of U.S. climate action: Cities, suburbs, and the local divide in global responsibilities. *Journal of Environmental Policy and Planning*, 12(1), 59–82.

Dunham-Jones, E. and Williamson, J. 2011. *Retrofitting Suburbia*. Hoboken, NJ: Wiley.

Dye, R.F. and McMillen, D.P. 2007. Teardowns and land values in the Chicago metropolitan area. *Journal of Urban Economics*, 61(1), 45–63.

Echenique, M.H., Hargreaves, A.J., Mitchell, G, and Namdeo, A. 2012. Growing cities sustainably: Does urban form really matter? *Journal of the American Planning Association*, 78(2), 121–37.

Edwards, A.R. 2005. *The Sustainability Revolution: Portrait of a Paradigm Shift*. Gabriola Island, Canada: New Society Publishers.

Elkin, T., McLaren, D, and Hillman, M. 1991. *Reviving the City: Towards Sustainable Urban Development*. London: Friends of the Earth.

Ewing, R, and Cervero, R. 2010. Travel and the built environment: A meta-analysis. *Journal of the American Planning Association*, 76(3), 265–94.

Fitzgerald, J. 2010. *Emerald Cities: Urban Sustainability and Economic Development*. Oxford: Oxford University Press.

Frece, J. 2009. *Sprawl and Politics: The Inside Story of Smart Growth in Maryland*. Albany, NY: SUNY Press.

Giddings, B., Hopwood, B, and O'Brien, G. 2002. Environment, economy and society: Fitting them together into sustainable development. *Sustainable Development*, 10(4), 187–96.

Glaeser, E.L, and Kahn, M.E. 2010. The greenness of cities: Carbon dioxide emissions and urban development. *Journal of Urban Economics*, 67(3), 404–18.

Hall, P. 2000. Urban renaissance/New Urbanism: Two sides of the same coin? *Journal of the American Planning Association*, 66(4), 359–60.

Hanlon, B. 2013. Suburban challenges, in *Cities of North America: Contemporary Challenges in U.S. and Canadian Cities*, edited by L. Benton-Short. Lanham, MA: Rowan and Littlefield.

Hanlon, B. 2009. *Once the American Dream: Inner-ring Suburbs in the Metropolitan United States*. Philadelphia, PA: Temple University Press.

Hanlon, B., Howland, M, and McGuire, M.P. 2012. Hotspots for growth: Does Maryland's Priority Funding Area Program reduce sprawl? *Journal of the American Planning Association*, 78(3), 256–68.

Hanlon, B, and Vicino, T.J. 2007. The fate of inner suburbs: evidence from metropolitan Baltimore. *Urban Geography*, 28(3), 249–75.

Harvey, D. 2012. *Rebel Cities: From the Right to the City to the Urban Revolution*. New York, NY: Verso Books.

Heavens, A. 2012. *Census: Cities, not Exurbs, Have Been Growing*. [Online]. Available at http://articles.philly.com/2012–04–06/news/31300447_1_census-data-housing-boom-fels-institute [accessed 5 December 5, 2013].

Hildebrand, F. (ed.) 1999. *Designing the City: Towards a More Sustainable Urban Form*. London: E & FN Spon.

Hollander, J.B. 2011. *Sunburnt Cities: The Great Recession, Depopulation and Urban Planning in the American Sunbelt*. New York, NY: Routledge.

Immergluck, D. 2009. *Foreclosed: High-Risk Lending, Deregulation, and the Undermining of America's Mortgage Market*. Ithaca, NY: Cornell University Press.

Immergluck, D, and Smith, G. 2006. The external costs of foreclosure: The impact of single-family mortgage foreclosures on property values. *Housing Policy Debate*, 17(1), 57–79.

Joint Center for Housing Studies. 2012. *The State of the Nation's Housing 2012*. Cambridge, MA: Harvard University.

Johnson, M.P. 2001. Environmental impacts of urban sprawl: A survey of the literature and proposed research agenda. *Environment and Planning A*, 33(4), 717–35.

Kneebone, E. and Berube, A. 2013. *Confronting Suburban Poverty in America*. Washington DC: Brookings Institution.

Lewis, R., Knaap, G.J, and Sohn, J. 2009. Managing growth with priority funding areas: A good idea whose time has yet to come. *Journal of the American Planning Association*, 75(4), 457–78.

Lucy, W.H. 2010. *Foreclosing the Dream: How America's Housing Crisis is Changing Our Cities and Suburbs*. Chicago, IL: Planners Press.

Lucy, W.H. and Phillips, D.L. 2000. *Confronting Suburban Decline*. Washington, DC: Island Press.

Maryland Department of Planning. 2010. *MdProperty View*. Annapolis, MD: Maryland Department of Planning.

Nasar, J.L., Evans-Cowley, J.S. and Mantero, V. 2007. McMansions: The extent and regulation of super-sized houses. *Journal of Urban Design*, 12(3), 339–58.

Nelson, A.C. 2009. The new urbanity: The rise of a new America. *The Annals of the American Academy of Political and Social Science*, 626(1), 192–208.

Newman, P., Beatley, T, and Boyer, H. 2009. *Resilient Cities: Responding to Peak Oil and Climate Change*. Washington, DC: Island Press.

Portney, K. 2005. Civic engagement and sustainable cities in the United States. *Public Administration Review*, 65(5), 579–91.

Portney, K.E, and Berry, J.M. 2010. Participation and the pursuit of sustainability in U.S. cities. *Urban Affairs Review*, 46(1), 119–39.

Sneddon, C.S. 2000. 'Sustainability' in ecological economics, ecology and livelihoods: A review. *Progress in Human Geography*, 24(4), 521–49.

Swyngedouw, E. 2007. Impossible/Undesirable sustainability and the post-political condition, in *The Sustainable Development Paradox*, edited by J. R. Krueger and D. Gibbs. New York, NY: Guilford Press.

Vicino, T.J. 2008. The quest to confront suburban decline political realities and lessons. *Urban Affairs Review*, 43(4), 553–81.

While, A., Jonas, A.E., and Gibbs, D. 2004. The environment and the entrepreneurial city: Searching for the urban 'sustainability fix' in Manchester and Leeds. *International Journal of Urban and Regional Research*, 28(3), 549–69.

Whitehead, M. 2007. *Spaces of Sustainability: Geographical Perspectives on the Sustainable Society*. New York, NY: Routledge.

Williamson, J. 2013. *Designing Suburban Futures: New Models from Build a Better Burb*. Washington, DC: Island Press.

Chapter 7

Metropolitan Growth Patterns and Inner-Ring Suburban Decline: A Longitudinal Analysis of the 100 Largest U.S. Metropolitan Areas

Sugie Lee, Nancey Green Leigh and Andrew McMillan

In the past several decades, U.S. metropolitan areas have experienced rapid decentralization patterns as population and employment shifted from central cities to the suburbs. This outward migration of typically middle- and upper-income households led to an acceleration of mostly uncontrolled suburban development. The loss of middle- and high-earning households played a crucial role in the decline of central cities and inner-ring suburbs. Many urban scholars and policymakers have already documented the negative consequences of uncontrolled suburban development. These include increased traffic congestion, decreased air quality, accelerated land consumption, reduced open space, and greater socioeconomic disparity (Newman and Kenworthy 1989, Bullard, Johnson and Torres 1999, Ewing, Pendall and Chen 2002). Concern for these negative impacts led to the creation of the smart growth movement and an attendant focus on regional growth management policies, which include the reuse of existing resources and the redirection of population, jobs, and investment from the suburban fringe back into urbanized areas. Previous studies found a positive relationship between metropolitan regions with growth management policies and central-city revitalization (Dawkins and Nelson 2003, Nelson et al. 2004). But few studies have considered the impact of growth management policies on inner-ring suburban communities, which have often experienced patterns of decline similar to central cities. This study examines patterns of inner-ring suburban change of the 100 largest U.S. metropolitan areas, focusing on metropolitan growth patterns and urban containment policies.

Intra-Metropolitan Spatial Differentiation and Inner-Ring Suburbs

Many researchers have documented the transformation of the metropolitan structure during the past several decades (Garreau 1991, Giuliano and Small 1991, Gordon and Richardson 1996, Lee 2011). Prior to World War II, the dominant model of metropolitan spatial structure was monocentric, consisting of the central city and its surrounding suburbs (see Diagram A in Figure 7.1 below). This

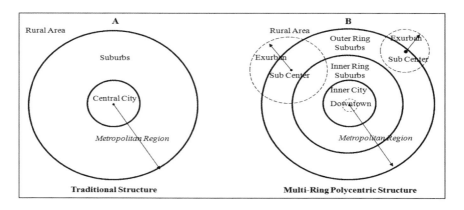

**Figure 7.1   Transformation of the Metropolitan Spatial Structure and
               Inner-Ring Suburbs**

Source: Leigh and Lee (2004: 16).

monocentric form reflects a metropolitan region where the primary employment
and residential centers are clustered in and around the central city. In the pre-World
War II era, most citizens relied on public transportation, such as electric streetcars
and trolleys. The streetcar and trolley networks ran primarily through the central
city and adjacent suburbs, which kept residents and employment concentrated
around the central city. After World War II, the increased availability of private
automobiles and the development of the Interstate Highway System spurred a
dispersal of population and employment that rapidly transformed the traditional
metropolitan spatial model from a monocentric form into a multi-ring polycentric
form (see Diagram B in Figure 7.1 above).

   Diagram B shows the intra-metropolitan spatial differentiation within a
metropolitan region and makes distinctions between the inner city, the inner-ring
suburbs, and the outer-ring suburbs. This presents a more accurate depiction of
the contemporary metropolitan spatial structure, as both the central city and its
surrounding suburbs have grown more heterogeneous. As intra-metropolitan
spatial differentiation progresses, many scholars have grown interested in the
decline of the suburbs that constitute the inner ring of these metropolitan areas
(Orfield 1997, Lucy and Phillips 2000, Hudnut 2003, Leigh and Lee 2004, 2005,
Short, Hanlon and Vicino 2007, Anacker and Morrow-Jones 2008, Hanlon
2008a, Vicino 2008a). These studies found that inner-ring suburbs are more
likely than their outer-ring counterparts to show trajectories of decline similar to
those experienced in central cities. Characteristics of decline include increased
concentrations of poverty, housing deterioration, disinvestment, and an exodus of
middle- and upper-income households. For example, Orfield (1997) observed a
gradual expansion of poverty from the central city to adjacent inner-ring suburban
communities in the Minneapolis and St. Paul metropolitan region. Stegman

and Turner (1996) described the expansion of high-poverty areas into adjacent suburban communities:

> The distress and decline of high-poverty areas do not remain confined to the central city but gradually spread out to affect suburban areas as well. Older suburbs—and even some "edge cities"—increasingly find themselves in competition with newer areas of development that can attract more affluent families, retail centers, and jobs (Stegman and Turner 1996: 159–60).

Somewhat recent literature has also contested the long-perceived homogeneity of suburbs and has found that suburbs vary vastly in their social, economic, racial, and ethnic construction (Orfield 2002, Mikelbank 2004), and that inner-ring suburbs are no different (Hanlon 2009). Inner-ring suburbs have experienced significant spatial, social, racial, and ethnic shifts in recent decades (Vicino 2008b, Mikelbank 2011). Katz et al. (2010) found that new immigration patterns have changed the racial and ethnic composition of the suburbs in the Philadelphia metropolitan areas and that an influx of immigrants moderated the population loss within the region's inner-ring suburbs. Inner-ring suburban poverty may manifest itself differently than central city poverty. Cooke (2010) examined poverty trends in inner-ring suburbs from 1989 to 2005 using the Panel Study of Income Dynamics. He found that inner-ring suburban poverty increased nationally from 1989 to 1997. Yet from 1997 to 2005, poverty declined and then stabilized to 1989 levels. His research posits that patterns of inner-ring suburban poverty are more closely related to economic conditions than the migration of central city residents into inner-ring suburbs. Notably, Holliday and Dwyer (2009) found that suburban poverty is more diverse than the traditional models of central city poverty. Some metropolitan areas experience poverty concentrated in the inner-ring suburbs, others experience poverty concentrated in newer suburbs, and yet others experience a mix of both.

Currently, there are no federal or state policies that explicitly address inner-ring suburban decline (Hanlon 2008b). Vicino (2008a) studied Baltimore County's efforts to confront suburban decline, noting that barriers to implementing policy at local and regional levels include the lack of political will, regional political fragmentation, and a narrow tax base. Alliances between regional inner-ring suburban governments have formed with the goal of overcoming these barriers. Keating and Bier (2008) assessed the impact of the Northeast Ohio First Suburbs Consortium, an interest group for the inner-ring suburbs surrounding Cleveland. They note that while the group failed to influence state and national anti-sprawl policies, cooperation among the inner-ring suburbs led to several successful local revitalization programs. Through three case studies of inner-ring suburbs in Ohio, Anacker and Morrow-Jones (2011) found that these communities focus on and implement revitalization programs based on their current policies or funding situations.

Metropolitan Growth Policies and Inner-Ring Suburban Decline

A few recent studies focused on the relationship between metropolitan growth patterns and inner-ring suburban decline (Skaburskis and Moos 2008, Wilson and Song 2009, Kim and Morrow-Jones 2011, Lee 2011). Skaburskis and Moos (2008) examined metropolitan growth patterns in the Montreal, Toronto, and Vancouver areas with regard to property values. They found shifts in wealth away from the older, inner suburban ring and towards the inner city and newer suburbs. In a case study of Columbus, Ohio, Kim and Morrow-Jones (2010) found that when households move from older suburbs to newer, outer suburbs, they often claim the desire for newer housing as their primary motivation. They suggest that new development or redevelopment of old homes may draw middle- and upper-income households back into the inner-ring suburbs. Wilson and Song (2009) examined new residential development in two metropolitan regions with vastly different growth policies. They found that development in Portland, a region with strong growth management policies, was likely to occur in the inner- and middle-ring suburbs. In contrast, new development in Charlotte, a region with no growth management policies, was more likely to occur on the urban periphery.

While much research has highlighted the decline of inner-ring suburbs in U.S. metropolitan areas, no prior studies have directly examined the impact of metropolitan growth patterns and growth policies on inner-ring suburban decline. Notably, a few studies examined the impact of regional growth policies, such as urban containment, on central-city revitalization (Dawkins and Nelson 2003, Nelson et al. 2004). Those studies found positive associations between urban containment and central-city revitalization. Recently, Lee (2011) examined the relationship between metropolitan growth patterns and socioeconomic disparity among the inner city, inner-ring suburbs, and outer-ring suburbs for six metropolitan regions. He found an observable positive association between compact development policies and relatively lower levels of intra-metropolitan socioeconomic disparity and polarization.

Figure 7.2 below illustrates the theoretical foundation for the relationship between metropolitan growth patterns and inner-ring suburban decline. Diagram A (Sprawl Model) in Figure 7.2 shows the disadvantages inner-ring suburbs face relative to downtown and outer-ring suburbs in regions with uncontrolled sprawl. Sprawl attracts employment and middle- and upper-income households from the inner city and inner-ring suburbs to outer-ring suburban communities. The back-to-the-city trend may benefit downtown and certain areas of the inner city, but it skips the inner-ring suburbs. In contrast, Diagram B (Compact Model) shows the results of urban containment policies that restrict sprawl, thereby redirecting development and investment into urbanized areas. Downtown and inner city areas will benefit from urban containment policies, as these areas offer greater accessibility to urban employment centers. But the community-revitalizing benefits of development and investment may skip inner-ring suburban communities. In short, inner-ring suburbs do not experience the

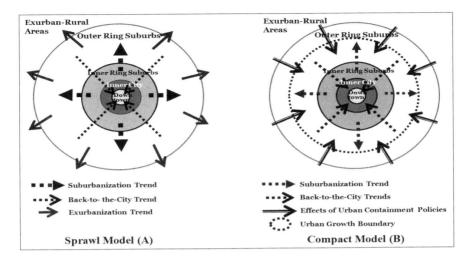

Figure 7.2   Metropolitan Growth Patterns and Inner-Ring Suburban Decline

Source: Lee (2011: 992). Reprinted with permission.

benefits of either metropolitan growth model, which makes them more likely to experience decline than the inner city and outer-ring suburbs.

This research examines the impact of metropolitan growth patterns and policies on inner-ring suburban decline. In particular, this study focuses on the 100 largest metropolitan areas and examines whether metropolitan areas with growth management policies, such as urban containment, have an observable association with lower levels of inner-ring suburban decline than metropolitan areas with no growth management policies.

Case Study and Methodology

This study examines the 100 largest U.S. metropolitan statistical areas (Core Based Statistical Areas (CBSAs)) based on population from the 2000 United States Census. CBSAs are geographical areas that have an urban center with a population of at least 10,000 and have adjacent counties socioeconomically connected to the urban center by commuting patterns. The intra-metropolitan sub-areas within these CBSAs are inner cities, inner-ring suburbs, and outer-ring suburbs classified based on Census tract-based housing density information for a specific time period.[1]

It is important to note that the definition of inner-ring suburbs differs slightly among scholars. Lee and Leigh (2005) summarized the confusing array of terms

---

1   For more information on the method of this classification see Lee and Leigh (2004, 2007).

for inner-ring suburbs, which include older suburbs, first-ring suburbs, and inner suburbs. For the sake of clarity, they defined inner-ring suburbs as "the post–World War II suburbs constructed between 1950 and 1969 for which the primary mode of transportation access has been the automobile" (Lee and Leigh 2005: 333). Their definition of inner-ring suburbs focuses on the post-World War II suburbs that are located between inner cities and outer-ring suburbs.

The inner city, inner-ring suburbs, and outer-ring suburbs are categorized using tract-based housing stock information from the decennial census. This study defines inner-ring suburbs as suburban neighborhoods that have a dominant housing stock built between 1950 and 1970. Areas identified as the inner city have a dominant housing stock built before 1950, and outer-ring suburbs have a dominant housing stock built after 1970. In addition to the classification of the dominant housing stock built during a designated time period, this study uses the Spatial Analyst method in ArcGIS 10.0 to apply housing density contour lines that identify continuous boundaries for each sub-area. The threshold of housing density contour lines for each era (pre-1950, between 1950 and 1970, and after 1970) is slightly different across metropolitan areas. Most metropolitan areas show 600–800 units per square mile for areas with a primarily pre-1950 housing stock and 300–400 units per square mile for areas with a housing stock built between 1950 and 1970. The remaining areas beyond the inner-ring suburbs, defined as outer-ring suburbs, have a dominant housing stock built after 1970.

This study uses descriptive statistical analysis with cross-sectional and longitudinal databases. The data sources are from the 1970, 1980, 1990, and 2000 U.S. Census and the 2005–2009 American Community Survey (ACS). The unit of analysis is the CBSA and its corresponding aggregated tract-level census information. The geography is the 100 largest CBSAs. The key variables for this analysis of metropolitan growth policies and inner-ring suburban decline are per capita income (PCI), the poverty rate, the proportion of the population of color, and the proportion of college graduates.

This study also uses the urban containment catalog developed by Nelson and Dawkins (2003) and Wassmer (2006). This catalog categorizes each metropolitan area by urban containment type and the strength of its urban containment policies. Table 7.1 below shows that 34 of the 100 largest CBSAs have regional or local urban containment policies. Twelve of those CBSAs have implemented an urban growth boundary and are thus characterized as having strong containment policies. The remaining 66 CBSAs have no urban growth boundaries, urban services areas, or urban limit lines.

In addition to the urban containment catalog for metropolitan areas, this study uses a metropolitan sprawl index to measure the actual level of urban sprawl for the 100 largest CBSAs. Although previous literature has provided a few sprawl indices (Fulton et al. 2001, Galster et al. 2001, Lopez and Hynes 2003, Ewing, Pendal, and Chen 2002), this study applies a sprawl index using the method developed by Lopez and Hynes (2003). As Galster et al. (2001) point out, urban sprawl has multidimensional aspects, of which residential density is only one of

Table 7.1   100 Largest CBSAs by Urban Containment Policy Type

Urban Containment		Strong Containment		Weak Containment	
		Accommodate	Restrict	Accommodate	Restrict
		Future Growth	**Future Growth**	**Future Growth**	**Future Growth**
Regional	15	12	1	7	1
Local	19	8	4	8	4
Subtotal	34	20	5	15	5
None	66	–	–	–	–
Total	**100**	–	–	–	–

Note: Some metropolitan areas have mixed policies of strong containment and weak containment.

Sources: Nelson and Dawkins (2003) and Wassmer (2006).

the key dimensions. Lopez and Hynes' method focuses on residential density and decentralization to measure sprawl index. The sprawl index is calculated as follows for

* high-density tracts (greater than 3,500 persons per square mile)
* low-density tracts[2] (between 3,500 and 200 persons per square mile):

$$SI_i = ((L\%_i - H\%_i)/100 + 1)*50$$

Where:

SI_i = *sprawl index for a metropolitan area$_i$*,
$H\%_i$ = *percentage of total population in high-density census tract$_i$*,
$L\%_i$ = *percentage of total population in low-density census tract$_i$.*

The sprawl index ranges from 0 (lowest sprawl) to 100 (highest sprawl). While Lopez and Hynes' (2003) index is sensitive to metropolitan population size, their method has a strong advantage in measuring sprawl for the type of cross-sectional and longitudinal analysis used in this study, which uses tract-based population data from the 1970–2000 Census and the 2005–2009 ACS.

---

2   Lopez and Hynes (2003) defined census tracts with fewer than 200 persons per square mile as rural tracts.

Table 7.2   Average Relative Per Capita Income (PCI) and Relative PCI Change of the 100 Largest CBSAs by Sub-area (1970–2007)

	Relative PCI (%)					Change Difference (%)			
	1970	1980	1990	2000	2007	1970–1980	1980–1990	1990–2000	2000–2007
Inner Cities	96.5	90.7	83.1	83.9	86.9	-5.8	-7.6	0.7	3.1
Inner-Ring Suburbs	108.8	108.3	104.3	97.7	93.7	-0.5	-4	-6.6	-3.9
Outer-Ring Suburbs	95.8	99.7	104.8	107.1	107.2	3.9	5.1	2.3	0.1
Average (100 CBSAs)	100	100	100	100	100	–	–	–	–

Source: Authors.

Table 7.3   Poverty Rate for the 100 Largest CBSAs by Sub-area (1970–2007)

	Poverty Rate (%)					Change Difference (%)			
	1970	1980	1990	2000	2007	1970–1980	1980–1990	1990–2000	2000–2007
Inner Cities	17.7	19.3	22.7	22	22.9	1.6	3.3	-0.7	0.9
Inner-Ring Suburbs	9.1	9.7	11.5	12.6	14.8	0.6	1.8	1.2	2.2
Outer-Ring Suburbs	11	9	9	8.2	9.2	-2	0	-0.7	1.0
Average (100 CBSAs)	12.2	11.4	12.1	11.5	12.5	-0.8	0.7	-0.6	1.0

Source: Authors.

Analysis and Findings

This study analyzes intra-metropolitan sub-areas using four primary variables—the per capita income (PCI), the poverty rate, the proportion of the population of color, and the proportion of college graduates—for the 100 largest CBSAs from 1970 to 2007. Since the raw values of PCI are not directly comparable across

Figure 7.3   Trends of Relative Per Capita Income (PCI for the 100 largest CBSAs by Sub-area (1970–2007

Source: Authors.

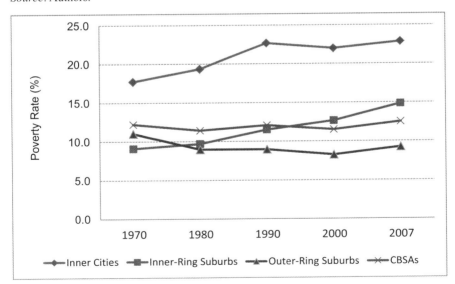

Figure 7.4   Poverty Rate for the 100 Largest CBSAs by Sub-area (1970–2007)

Source: Authors.

Table 7.4   Proportion of Population of Color for the 100 Largest CBSAs by Sub-area (1970–2007)

	Rate Population of Color (%)					Change Difference (%)			
	1970	**1980**	**1990**	**2000**	**2007**	**1970– 1980**	**1980– 1990**	**1990– 2000**	**2000– 2007**
Inner Cities	26.5	31.7	36.1	42.2	42.1	5.2	4.4	6.1	-0.1
Inner-Ring Suburb	13.2	17.7	22.2	30.3	34.2	4.5	4.5	8.1	3.8
Outer-Ring Suburbs	11.7	11.7	13.4	17.2	20.1	0	1.7	3.8	2.8
All 100 CBSAs	17.1	18.5	20.5	25.1	27.2	1.4	2	4.6	2.1

Source: Authors.

metropolitan areas and time periods, the PCIs were converted into the relative PCI of the average of the 100 largest CBSAs.

Table 7.2 shows the average relative PCI for each sub-area from 1970 to 2007. The relative PCI of the inner city declined dramatically from 1980 to 1990 and showed a small, gradual increase from 1990 to 2007. In contrast, inner-ring suburban areas showed a relatively higher than average PCI by 1990, but those areas experienced substantial decline in the 1990s (−6.64 percentage points) and 2000s (−3.93 percentage points). In comparison to the inner city and inner-ring suburbs, the relative PCI of outer-ring suburbs showed significant increases by 1990 and steady increases from 2000 to 2007.

Figure 7.3 illustrates the trend of the relative PCI from 1970 to 2007 for the 100 largest CBSAs by sub-area. The relative PCI indicates a continuous income decline of inner-ring suburbs with a particularly fast decline in the 1990s and 2000s. It also indicates a widening income disparity between inner-ring suburbs and outer-ring suburbs. As shown in Figure 7.3, the widening gap between inner-ring suburbs and outer-ring suburbs has been substantial and increasingly divergent since 1990. In contrast, the inner city showed a gradual increase after dramatic decline from 1970 to 1990.

Table 7.3 shows the poverty rate and the change in the poverty rate by sub-area from 1970 to 2007. The average poverty rate for all 100 CBSAs was 11.5 percent in 2000, although there were substantial differences within each sub-area. Table 7.3 also shows that the poverty rate of inner-ring suburbs increased dramatically from 1970 (9.1 percent) to 2007 (14.8 percent). In contrast, the poverty rate of outer-ring suburbs has remained relatively low and stable at under 10 percent since 1970. Lastly, the inner city's poverty rate shows dramatic increases from 1970

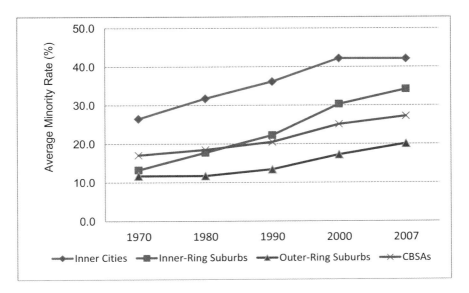

Figure 7.5   Proportion of Population of Color for the 100 Largest CBSAs by Sub-area (1970–2007)

Source: Authors.

(17.7 percent) to 1990 (22.7 percent) and a slight increase in 2007. The poverty rate in the inner city was still relatively higher than other sub-areas.

Figure 7.4 illustrates the change of the poverty rate by sub-area and the poverty difference among sub-areas from 1970 to 2007. The poverty rate difference between the inner city and other sub-areas was still substantially high and consistent over time. The graph also shows that the poverty rate difference between inner-ring suburbs and outer-ring suburbs increased dramatically after 1980. This trend indicates that inner-ring suburbs experienced substantial increases in the poverty rate compared to outer-ring suburbs from 1980 to 2007.

Table 7.4 and Figure 7.5 above show the proportion of the population of color and its change by sub-area for the 100 largest CBSAs from 1970 to 2007. The overall population of color in the 100 largest CBSAs increased by more than 10 percentage points from 1970 (17.1 percent) to 2007 (27.2 percent), with a substantial increase occurring in the 1990s. Inner cities remained the primary location for people of color, with a proportion of 42.1 percent in 2007. However, the inner city's population of color was stable in the 2000s after having experienced continuous increases from 1970 to 2000. This phenomenon might be associated with the back-to-the-city movement of middle class non-Hispanic White households.

Inner-ring suburbs experienced continuous and substantial increases in the proportion of the population of color from 1970 (13.2 percent) to 2007 (34.2 percent). Compared to other sub-areas, the increase in the proportion of the population of color was highest in the inner-ring suburbs after the 1970s. Outer-

Table 7.5   Proportion of College Graduates for the 100 Largest CSBAs by Sub-area (1970–2007)

	College Graduate Rate (%) and Its Relative Percent (%) to the Average of 100 CBSAs					Change Percentage Point (%)			
	1970	1980	1990	2000	2007	1970–1980	1980–1990	1990–2000	2000–2007
Inner Cities:									
• College Graduate Rate	11.0	16.9	21.1	25.1	29.2	5.9	4.2	4.0	4.1
• College Graduate Rate Relative to CBSA Average	91.2	96.7	98.8	98.0	101.5	5.5	2.0	-0.8	3.5
Inner-Ring Suburbs:									
• College Graduate Rate	14.7	19.4	22.5	25.1	27.1	4.7	3.1	2.5	2.0
• College Graduate Rate Relative to CBSA Average	121.9	111.0	105.5	97.9	94.2	-10.9	-5.4	-7.6	-3.7
Outer-Ring Suburbs:									
• College Graduate Rate	11.3	17.4	21.7	26.9	30.1	6.1	4.3	5.2	3.2
• College Graduate Rate Relative to CBSA Average	94.3	99.8	101.8	105.0	104.8	5.5	2.0	3.2	-0.2
Totals:									
• Average College Graduate Rate (100 CBSAs)	12.0	17.5	21.4	25.6	28.8	5.4	3.9	4.3	3.1
• College Graduate Rate Relative to Average (100 CBSAs)	100.0	100.0	100.0	100.0	100.0	–	–	–	–

Source: Authors.

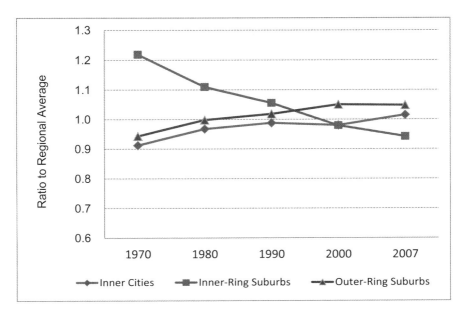

Figure 7.6   Ratio of the Proportion of College Graduates to the Average for the 100 Largest CBSAs by Sub-area (1970–2007)

Source: Authors.

ring suburbs have experienced a more gradual increase in the proportion of the population of color since 1990.

Table 7.5 shows that the proportion of college graduates improved substantially from 1970 (12.0 percent) to 2007 (28.8 percent) in the 100 largest CBSAs. All sub-areas experienced substantial increases in the proportion of college graduates over time. However, if we apply a relative measure of educational attainment by sub-area, the percentage of college graduates of inner-ring suburbs relative to the average of all sub-areas within the largest 100 CBSAs showed substantial declines. In 1970, the proportion of college graduates in inner-ring suburbs was 121.9 percent, indicating that inner-ring suburbs had a higher proportion of college graduates. By 2007, the proportion of college graduates in inner-ring suburbs had fallen to 94.2 percent, indicating that inner-ring suburbs had a lower proportion of college graduates. In contrast, inner city and outer-ring suburbs showed gradual increases in the proportion of college graduates from 1970 to 2007.

Figure 7.6 below confirms that inner-ring suburbs experienced a dramatic decline in the proportion of college graduates from 1970 to 2007. The proportion of college graduates in inner-ring suburbs was the highest of the three sub-areas before 1990. However, this proportion was lowest after 2000. In contrast, inner cities experienced a 3.5 percent growth in the proportion of college graduates during the 2000s, which indicates that the inner city plays a role in attracting highly educated human capital. The continuous decline of the relative proportion

Table 7.6   ANOVA Mean Difference Test for the 100 Largest CBSAs by Metropolitan Growth Policy

Variables	Sub-area	Mean Difference (Urban Containment–Non-Containment)				
		1970	1980	1990	2000	2007
Per Capita	Inner Cities	140.6	448.7*	1,245.50*	2,654.00**	4,857.20**
Income	Inner-Ring Suburbs	32.9	-2.1	485.7	606.4	1,382.60
	Outer-Ring Suburbs	-36.3	289.7	1,004.20	1,384.40	1,931.90
	All 100 CBSAs	59.9	305.6	1,081.50*	1,658.50*	2,499.00*
Poverty	Inner Cities	0.49	-0.8	-1.72	-1.22	-2.83*
Rate (%)	Inner-Ring Suburbs	0.39	0.37	0.02	0.58	-2.87
	Outer-Ring Suburbs	1.3	-0.03	-1.1	-0.46	-0.75
	All 100 CBSAs	0.35	-0.63	-1.53	-0.99	-1.46
Population	Inner Cities	-0.92	-2.04	-2.38	-3.21	-4.48
of	Inner-Ring Suburbs	0.13	-0.31	0.36	1.83	2.25
Color (%)	Outer-Ring Suburbs	2.8	1.43	1.52	2.89	3.84
	All 100 CBSAs	-0.06	-1.11	-0.91	0.05	0.73
College	Inner Cities	1.75	3.66*	4.38*	5.75**	6.99**
Graduates	Inner-Ring Suburbs	1.57*	1.61	1.5	1.44	1.56
(%)	Outer-Ring Suburbs	0.94	1.18	1.54	2.06	2.15
	All 100 CBSAs	1.6*	2.03*	2.24*	2.8*	3*

Note: *statistically significant at α=0.05; **statistically significant at α=0.01.
Source: Authors.

of college graduates in the inner-ring suburbs might be associated with increases in the population of color and the poverty rate.

Overall, descriptive analyses for the four variables indicate that inner-ring suburbs have experienced a decline in per capita income, an increase in the poverty rate, an increase in the proportion of the population of color, and a decline in the relative proportion of college graduates from 1970 to 2007.

This study hypothesizes that urban containment policy or the level of urban sprawl plays a role in the decline of inner-ring suburban communities. Consistent with classifications defined in previous studies (Nelson and Dawkins 2003, Wassmer 2006), this study identified 34 metropolitan areas with urban containment policies and 66 areas with non-containment policies (100 total).

Table 7.6 shows the Analysis of Variance (ANOVA) mean difference test between metropolitan areas with urban containment policies and metropolitan areas with non-containment policies for PCI, the poverty rate, the proportion of the population of color, and the proportion of the college graduates. The PCI of metropolitan areas with urban containment policies is higher than in areas without urban containment policies, and the mean differences are statistically significant for 1990, 2000, and 2007. The same finding applies to inner cities for all years except 1970. This indicates that inner cities located in CBSAs with urban containment policies are more likely to have a higher per capita income than inner cities located in CBSAs without urban containment policies. However, comparing the PCI in inner-ring suburbs with and without urban containment and the PCI in outer-ring suburbs with and without urban containment does not show any statistically significant differences. This indicates that urban containment policies may have an impact on inner cities but not on other sub-areas in terms of the PCI.

In terms of the poverty rate, Table 7.6 above does not show a statistically significant relationship between urban containment policies and the poverty rate in any year for all CBSAs, for the inner-ring suburbs, or for the outer-ring suburbs. However, the mean difference for inner cities in 2007 is statistically significant at 2.83 percent, which indicates that metropolitan areas with urban containment policies have significantly lower poverty rates in the inner cities than metropolitan areas without urban containment policies.

In terms of the proportion of the population of color, Table 7.6 does not show a statistically significant mean difference for the CBSAs or for any sub-area in any year. In terms of the proportion of college graduates, Table 7.6 shows significant differences for the CBSAs for every year, for the inner cities in all analyzed years except 1970, and for the inner-ring suburbs in 1970.

Table 7.7 lists descriptive statistics of the sprawl index for the 100 largest CBSAs from 1970 to 2007. As indicated above, the sprawl index ranges from 0 (lowest sprawl) to 100 (highest sprawl). For all CBSAs, the average sprawl index value increased from 44.9 in 1970 to 55.5 in 2007. After 1990, the average sprawl index values for CBSAs with urban containment policies are slightly lower than CBSAs with non-containment regions. In 2007, the average sprawl index for CBSAs with non-containment policies was 3.6 points higher than CBSAs

Table 7.7   Sprawl Index by Containment Type for the 100 Largest CBSAs (1970–2007)

Year	Containment Type	Number of CBSAs	Mean	Std. Dev.	Min	Max
1970	Containment	33	46.9	17.0	19.3	76.7
	Non-Containment	66	43.9	14.0	11.8	77.6
	All	99	44.9	15.0	11.8	77.6
1980	Containment	34	50.3	17.2	16.0	83.8
	Non-Containment	66	50.1	14.9	11.5	82.3
	All	100	50.2	15.7	11.5	83.8
1990	Containment	34	50.4	18.6	15.0	83.0
	Non-Containment	66	52.5	16.3	10.4	83.1
	All	100	51.7	17.0	10.4	83.1
2000	Containment	34	51.4	19.7	15.1	86.4
	Non-Containment	66	54.3	16.7	10.0	86.5
	All	100	53.3	17.8	10.0	86.5
2007	Containment	34	53.1	20.5	14.5	87.2
	Non-Containment	66	56.7	16.4	10.3	87.4
	All	100	55.5	17.9	10.3	87.4

Source: Authors.

with urban containment policies, although the differences are not statistically significant according to ANOVA analyses (not shown here).

Figure 7.7 utilizes scatterplots, comparing the sprawl index with the PCI for inner-ring suburban areas from 1980 to 2007. The overall patterns show negative associations between the two variables. While the negative relationship between the sprawl index and the PCI was very strong in 1980, indicating low sprawl and a high income for some communities and high sprawl and low incomes for others, it weakened over time. Based on visual examination, the graphs also show that metropolitan areas with urban containment policies, indicated by solid circles in Figure 7.7, were not substantially different from metropolitan areas without urban containment policies, indicated by hollow circles.

Figure 7.8 shows the relationship between the sprawl index and the poverty rate in inner-ring suburbs for 1980, 1990, 2000, and 2007. The graphs show a positive association between the sprawl index and the inner-ring suburban poverty rate, indicating low sprawl and low poverty for some communities and high sprawl and high poverty for others. However, that linear relationship has weakened over time, changing from a clustered pattern in 1980 to a more dispersed pattern in 2007. Interestingly, the inner-ring suburban areas between the sprawl index values

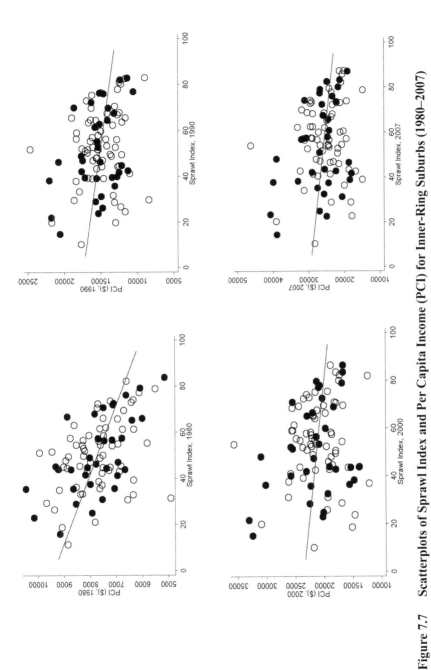

Figure 7.7   Scatterplots of Sprawl Index and Per Capita Income (PCI) for Inner-Ring Suburbs (1980–2007)

Note: Solid circles on the graphs are CBSAs with urban containment policies. Hollow circles are CBSAs without urban containment policies.

Source: Authors.

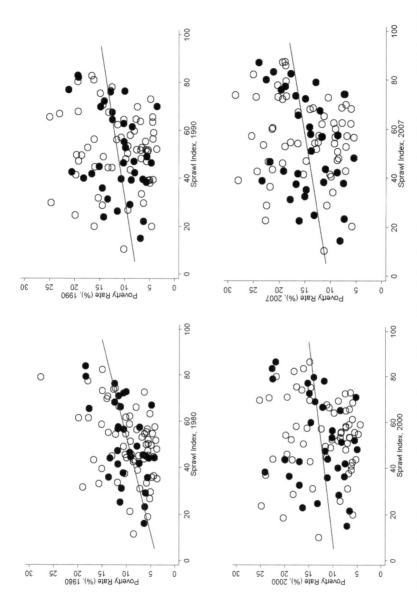

Figure 7.8   Scatterplots Comparing Sprawl Index and Inner-Ring Suburban Poverty for the 100 Largest CBSAs (1980–2007)

Note: Solid circles on the graphs are CBSAs with urban containment policies. Hollow circles are CBSAs without urban containment policies.

Source: Authors.

of 40 and 100 on all graphs cluster to form an upward-sloping curvilinear pattern. This curvilinear pattern increases sharply between the approximate values of 60 and 100, indicating that the highest-sprawl metropolitan areas have a strong positive association with inner-ring suburban decline in terms of poverty. The metropolitan areas with urban containment policies, indicated by solid dots, display no discernible pattern in terms of the sprawl index, indicating that urban containment policies do not necessarily guarantee a lower sprawl index or a lower poverty rate in inner-ring suburbs.

Conclusion and Policy Implications

This study examined the general pattern of inner-ring suburban change and the impact of metropolitan growth patterns and policies on inner-ring suburban decline for the 100 largest U.S. metropolitan areas, using longitudinal data from the 1970, 1980, 1990, 2000 Census and the 2005–2009 ACS.

Results show that inner-ring suburbs experienced observable symptoms of decline in terms of per capita income, poverty rate, the proportion of the population of color, and proportion of college graduates. In addition, the relationship between the sprawl index and inner-ring suburban decline showed interesting results. This study found a negative relationship between the sprawl index and per capita income in inner-ring suburbs. In other words, metropolitan areas with greater levels of sprawl tended to have inner-ring suburbs with relatively lower per-capita incomes (and vice versa), but that negative relationship weakened from 1980 to 2007. In addition, the relationship between the sprawl index and the poverty rate in inner-ring suburbs was a U-shaped curve. Inner-ring poverty gradually decreased as the sprawl index increased up to an approximate threshold of 60. Beyond 60, inner-ring suburban poverty levels began to increase sharply and showed strong positive associations between sprawl index levels of 60 and 100.

However, this study was unable to confirm the impact of urban containment policies on the level of inner-ring suburban decline, as the ANOVA analysis showed no statistical significance for the relationship. This finding indicates that urban containment policies may not necessarily guarantee a lower level of decline for inner-ring suburbs. While urban growth boundaries may control further decentralization within metropolitan areas, development and investment are redirected towards downtown or outer-ring suburban areas and skip inner-ring suburban communities. In addition, metropolitan areas with urban containment policies may not necessarily show the compact development patterns that adequately control sprawl.

This study concludes that inner-ring suburban decline in terms of per capita income and poverty is associated with the metropolitan growth patterns illustrated by the sprawl index. However, metropolitan areas with urban containment policies do not show relatively lower rates of inner-ring suburban decline in terms of per capita income, the poverty rate, and the proportion of college graduates than metropolitan areas with no urban containment policies. Inner-ring suburban decline presents itself as a universal issue among metropolitan areas regardless of regional initiatives such as urban containment policies. The findings of this study indicate the need for strategic initiatives that encourage revitalization in inner-ring suburban areas. Examples of these policies include regional tax-sharing programs, such as those in the Minneapolis-St. Paul region (Orfield 2002), and public-private advocacy organizations, such as the First Suburbs Consortium in Northeast Ohio (Keating and Bier 2008). In addition, coalitions between central cities and inner-ring suburbs can benefit both areas by advocating as a single voice to state and federal legislators for revitalization funds (Lee and Leigh 2005). Inner-ring suburbs offer many benefits that make them desirable places to live and work, such as extensive existing infrastructure and proximity to downtown. But without attention from planners and policymakers, the continued economic decline of inner-ring suburbs will hinder smart growth goals and create barriers to regional prosperity.

References

Anacker, K.B. and Morrow-Jones, H.A. 2011. Playing both "inside" and "outside" games"? Evidence from expert interviews in mature suburbs in Ohio. *Urban Geography*, 32(2), 244–62.
Anacker, K.B. and Morrow-Jones, H.A. 2008. Mature suburbs, property values, and decline in the Midwest? The case of Cuyahoga County. *Housing Policy Debate*, 19(3), 519–52.
Bullard, R.D., Johnson, G.S. and Torres, A.O. 1999. *Sprawl Atlanta: Social Equity Dimensions of Uneven Growth and Development*. Atlanta, GA: Clark Atlanta University.
Cooke, T.J. 2010. Residential mobility of the poor and the growth of poverty in inner-ring suburbs. *Urban Geography*, 31(2), 179–93.
Dawkins, C. and Nelson, A.C. 2003. State growth management programs and central-city revitalization. *Journal of the American Planning Association*, 69(4), 381–96.
Ewing, R., Pendall, R. and Chen, D. 2002. *Measuring Sprawl and its Impact*. Washington, DC: Smart Growth America.
Fulton, W., Pendall, R., Nguyen, M. and Harrison, A. 2001. *Who Sprawls Most: How Growth Patterns Differ across the United States*. Washington, DC: Brookings Institution.
Galster, G., Hanson, R., Ratcliffe, M.R., Wolman, H., Coleman S. and Freihage, J. 2001. Wrestling sprawl to the ground: Defining and measuring an elusive concept. *Housing Policy Debate*, 12(4), 681–717.
Garreau, J. 1991. *Edge City: Life on the New Frontier*. New York, NY: Doubleday.
Giuliano, G. and Small, K. 1991. Subcenters in the Los Angeles region. *Regional Science & Urban Economics*, 21(2), 163–82.

Gordon, P. and Richardson, H.W. 1996. Beyond polycentricity: The dispersed metropolis, Los Angeles, 1970–1990. *Journal of the American Planning Association*, 62(3), 289–95.

Hanlon, B. 2008a. The decline of older, inner suburbs in metropolitan America. *Housing Policy Debate*, 19(3), 423–56.

Hanlon, B. 2008b. Fixing inner-ring suburbs: A policy retrospective. *International Journal of Neighbourhood Renewal*, 1(3), 1–30.

Hanlon, B. 2009. A typology of inner-ring suburbs: class, race, and ethnicity in U.S. suburbs. *City & Community*, 8(3), 221–46.

Holliday, A.L., and Dwyer, R.E. 2009. Suburban neighborhood poverty in U.S. metropolitan areas in 2000. *City & Community*, 8(2), 155–76.

Hudnut, W.H. 2003. *Halfway to Everywhere: A Portrait of America's First-Tier Suburbs*. Washington, DC: Urban Land Institute.

Katz, M.B., Creighton, D.J., Amsterdam, D. and Chowkwanyun, M. 2010. Immigration and the new metropolitan geography. *Journal of Urban Affairs*, 32(5), 523–47.

Keating, W.D. and Bier, T. 2008. Greater Cleveland's First Suburbs Consortium: Fighting sprawl and suburban decline. *Housing Policy Debate*, 19(3), 457–77.

Kim, M.J. and Morrow-Jones, H.A. 2011. Intrametropolitan residential mobility and older inner suburbs: A case study of the Greater Columbus, Ohio, metropolitan area. *Housing Policy Debate*, 21(3), 133–64.

Lee, S. 2011. Metropolitan Growth Patterns and Socio-Economic Disparity in Six U.S. Metropolitan Areas 1970–2000. *International Journal of Urban and Regional Research*, 35(5), 988–1011.

Lee, S. and Leigh, N. 2005. The role of inner ring suburbs in metropolitan smart growth strategies. *Journal of Planning Literature*, 19(3), 330–46.

Lee, S. and Leigh, N. 2007. Intrametropolitan spatial differentiation and decline of inner-ring suburbs: A comparison of four U.S. metropolitan areas. *Journal of Planning Education and Research*, 27(2), 146–64.

Leigh, N. and Lee, S. 2004. Philadelphia's space in between: Inner ring suburb evolution. *Opolis: An International Journal of Suburban and Metropolitan Studies*, 1(1), 13–32.

Lopez, R. and Hynes, H.P. 2003. Sprawl in the 1990s: Measurement, distribution, and trends. *Urban Affairs Review*, 38(3), 325–55.

Lucy, W. and Phillips, D. 2000. *Confronting Suburban Decline: Strategic Planning for Metropolitan Renewal.* Washington, DC: Island Press.

Mikelbank B. 2011 Neighborhood déjà vu: Classification in metropolitan Cleveland, 1970–2000. *Urban Geography*, 32(3), 317–33.

Mikelbank, B. 2004. A typology of U.S. suburban places. *Housing Policy Debate*, 15(4), 935–64.

Nelson, A.C., Burby, R.J., Feser, E., Dawkins, C.J., Malizia, E.E. and Quercia, R. 2004. Urban containment and central-city revitalization. *Journal of the American Planning Association*, 70(4), 411–25.

Newman, P. and Kenworthy, J. 1989. Gasoline consumption and cities: A comparison of U.S. cities with a global survey. *Journal of the American Planning Association*, 55(1), 24–37.

Orfield, M. 2002. *American Metropolitics: The New Suburban Reality*. Washington, DC: Brookings Institution.

Orfield, M. 1997. *Metropolitics: A Regional Agenda for Community Stability*. Washington, DC: Brookings Institution.

Skaburskis, A. and Moos, M. 2008. The redistribution of residential property values in Montreal, Toronto, and Vancouver: Examining neoclassical and Marxist views on changing investment patterns. *Environment and Planning A*, 40(4), 905–27.

Short, J.R., Hanlon, B.F. and Vicino, T.J. 2007. The decline of inner suburbs: The new suburban gothic in the United States. *Geography Compass*, 1(3), 641–56.

Stegman, M.A. and Turner, M.A. 1996. The future of urban America in the global economy. *Journal of the American Planning Association*, 62(2), 157–64.

Vicino, T.J. 2008a. The quest to confront suburban decline. *Urban Affairs Review*, 43(4), 553–81.

Vicino, T.J. 2008b. The spatial transformation of first-tier suburbs, 1970 to 2000: The case of metropolitan Baltimore. *Housing Policy Debate*, 19(3), 479–518.

Wassmer, R.W. 2006. The influence of local urban containment policies and statewide growth management on the size of United States urban areas. *Journal of Regional Science*, 46(1), 25–65.

Wilson, B. and Song, Y. 2009. Comparing apples with apples: How different are recent residential development patterns in Portland and Charlotte? *Journal of Urbanism*, 2(1), 51–74.

SECTION IV
Suburban Foreclosures

Chapter 8

Responses to Foreclosure and Abandonment in Cleveland's Inner Suburbs: Three Case Studies

W. Dennis Keating

Introduction

For several years, much of metropolitan America has been engulfed in a foreclosure crisis that was initially triggered by risky subprime lending and real estate speculation that contributed to the financial crisis that shook the economy in 2008 and more recently by homeowners unable to meet their obligations because of job losses and financial problems related to a severe recession and weak economic recovery, along with trigger events such as medical expenses, divorce, or the death of a spouse, among others. It is estimated that several million homeowners may eventually lose their homes, and with a glut of unsold vacant and abandoned homes, many homeowners have seen sharp declines in the value of their homes (Center for Responsible Lending 2011). Those most affected, about one-fifth of homeowners, find themselves underwater (i.e., the amount due on their mortgage loan(s) exceeds the current market value of their house). The Sunbelt states of Arizona, California, Florida, and Nevada have seen the highest number of foreclosures. The city of Las Vegas, Nevada, has been the hardest hit major city in the United States. Before that, older Rustbelt cities like Baltimore, Buffalo, Cleveland, Detroit, and Philadelphia saw foreclosures and abandonment rise dramatically, devastating entire neighborhoods.

In response, the federal government provided assistance, first for homeowner counseling through HUD-funded agencies. It also has had differing approaches attempting to convince mortgage lenders to voluntarily modify delinquent mortgages in default and in danger of foreclosure so that hard-pressed homeowners can still afford to stay in their homes. These programs, including the Obama administration's Home Affordable Modification Program (HAMP), have not been notably successful to date in reaching their goals. In addition, in the 2008 Housing and Economic Recovery Act (HERA), the Neighborhood Stabilization Program (NSP) was created to provide short term aid to localities, aimed at demolition of blighted abandoned housing, renovation of foreclosed housing that can be saved, and new housing construction (Mallach 2009). Despite three rounds of NSP funding, this federal aid has fallen far short of the need in those localities hardest hit. Cities like Cleveland, with many thousands of abandoned houses that have become nuisance properties, cannot afford to fund the demolitions or renovations to either tear down or renovate all of these properties. They have either had to give priority to the most badly blighted buildings or have targeted some areas with the hope that they can serve as models for containing blight and beginning the rebuilding process (or both).

Within the past several years, this wave of foreclosures and abandonment has spread to the suburbs, especially the older, inner suburbs. Alarmed suburban mayors in Cleveland's suburbs called for the county to act (Hexter and Coulton 2010). Cuyahoga County responded by overhauling the legal foreclosure process and increasing funding to the courts to eliminate a longstanding backlog of foreclosure cases. And in August 2005, it launched a Foreclosure Prevention Initiative, which has provided funding to several counseling agencies to help homeowners facing foreclosure (Hexter and Schnoke 2009). In 2008, the total number of all foreclosure filings (mortgage and tax) in suburban Cuyahoga County exceeded those in the city of Cleveland for the first time: 7,695 versus 7,114 (NEO CANDO 2011). For most of these suburbs, the scale of this phenomenon has far exceeded the normal number of foreclosures. The number of vacant homes and the length of time that they lay vacant in these suburbs has also far exceeded what has been the norm in the past. This chapter will describe and analyze the experience of three older suburbs of Cleveland, Ohio, including their responses: Cleveland Heights, Shaker Heights, and South Euclid. Their responses can be compared to the experience and response to the same crisis at a much greater magnitude in the larger central city of Cleveland.

Cleveland

Cleveland, without a housing bubble inflating prices and spurring speculation comparable to cities like Las Vegas in the Sunbelt states, nevertheless began to experience rising rates of foreclosures. Between 1995 and 2007, the rate of foreclosures in Cuyahoga County quadrupled, with most foreclosures taking place in the central city of Cleveland. In 2007, there were 7,848 foreclosure filings in Cleveland. In each of the following two years, there were just over 7,000 foreclosure filings. In 2010, the number dropped to just under 6,000 (NEO CANDO 2011). In 2000, the U.S. Bureau of the Census found over 25,000 vacant housing units (out of 216,000 units, thus 11.57 percent); by 2010, this had increased to about 40,000 housing units (out of 208,000 units, thus 19.23 percent). While part of this increase reflects the city's loss of about 81,000 residents (from 478,000 to 397,000) during this decade, it also reflects the increase in vacant and abandoned houses resulting from the foreclosure crisis. The city has had to greatly increase demolitions of nuisance structures, but it cannot afford to eliminate all of the thousands of these abandoned structures due to limited resources. It has had to rely primarily upon federal NSP grants over the past few years to pay for demolitions. While these demolitions are scattered throughout the city, the city has concentrated some demolitions in six targeted neighborhood sites that comprise the Opportunity Homes redevelopment projects sponsored by Neighborhood Progress, Inc. (NPI) in partnership with six community development corporations (CDCs) and the Cleveland Housing Network (CHN).

Over more than a decade, the city and its Housing Court, CDCs and intermediaries, and other public and nonprofit organizations have developed a variety of responses to foreclosures and abandonment. These have included legislation, litigation, homeowner counseling, and the rebuilding of affected neighborhoods with the assistance of the NSP funding (Hexter and Coulton 2010). In 2009, a newly created Cuyahoga County land bank began to assist both the city and surrounding suburbs in dealing with blighted, nuisance properties (Keating and Lind 2012). Cleveland's Slavic Village neighborhood gained notoriety as one of the hardest hit urban areas in the United States despite the best efforts of its longtime CDC Slavic Village Development (SVD), as reported in *The New York Times* (Kotlowitz 2009). Working with local intermediaries CHN and NPI, SVD and other CDCs have been involved in neighborhood rebuilding efforts for several years (Keating and Lind 2012). There are differing possible outcomes of the reuse of the growing amount of vacant land in Cleveland due to the demolition of foreclosed, abandoned housing, including planned shrinkage (Keating 2010).

Cuyahoga County Suburbs

In comparison to a major city like Cleveland, suburbs are not always as well equipped to deal with a crisis like that presented by a greatly increased number of foreclosures. They do not have community development, housing, and planning departments on the same scale as large central cities, if they have them at all. They do not have specialized courts and judges dealing with housing problems. What they do have are building and housing inspectors and planners, often more concerned with new housing when they were growing as opposed to declining. The latter trend has characterized many older inner suburbs, including the three case study suburbs that are the subject of this chapter. All have seen not only declines in population but also a rise in the number and percentage of lower-income residents, including those living in poverty (Hanlon 2010). With this decline and losses of higher-income residents and businesses in competition with the newer exurbs, these suburbs do not have the financial resources to adequately address a crisis on this scale. This is especially true of bedroom suburbs like the three discussed examples, which do not have major commercial or industrial tax bases other than shopping malls, strip retail districts, and offices. Heavily dependent upon property taxes to finance services, including their public schools, they can ill afford to see large numbers of tax-delinquent properties vacant for long periods. These three case studies offer examples of how older, inner suburbs in greater Cleveland are coping with this problem.

Cleveland Heights

Cleveland Heights is one of the older eastern suburbs of Cleveland, incorporated as a city in 1921 (Keating 1994, Morton 2002, Hanlon 2010). It borders the University Circle area of Cleveland, which features two major hospitals, Case Western Reserve University, and many cultural institutions (including the Cleveland Art Museum and the Cleveland Orchestra's symphony hall). Its adjacent suburbs are East Cleveland (now the poorest suburb in Cuyahoga County), Shaker Heights (discussed below), South Euclid (also discussed below), and University Heights (with which it shares a school district). Once a streetcar suburb, Cleveland Heights has a variety of housing, from mansions to starter homes and clusters of rental housing. It has a shopping center, around which are located City Hall and other services, and several strip retail districts.

In the 1970s, a previously almost all non-Hispanic White Cleveland Heights underwent racial change (following massive White flight in East Cleveland), which it mostly successfully managed. It adopted a policy of promoting racial integration and diversity (Keating 1994). In 2010 its non-Hispanic White population was just under 50 percent, compared to a Black/African American population of 42.5 percent. Overall, its population has continued to decline, losing 7.7 percent in the previous decade, from about 50,000 in 2000 to just over 46,000 in 2010. Its population had peaked in 1970 at just over 60,000. In competition with other eastern suburbs, Cleveland Heights has promoted itself as a center of the arts, conveniently located close to University Circle and other amenities and encompassing a variety of housing.

In 1996, Cleveland Heights was instrumental in forming the First Suburbs Consortium (FSC), along with Shaker Heights and Lakewood (and now having 17 inner suburbs as members). FSC has advocated changes in state policy more favorable to the older, inner suburbs and has promoted demonstration projects and cooperative arrangements among their member cities (Bier and Keating 2008). Its FSC Development Council has sponsored a special fund to deal with vacant properties in response to their increase in the inner suburbs.

As part of its pro-integration policy, Cleveland Heights has long had a strict housing code enforcement program aimed at maintenance of existing housing (including pre-sale inspections requiring that necessary repairs be made or the cost escrowed before property transfers and periodic exterior inspections. Given the age of much of its housing, this was considered crucial to preventing any decline in housing values (and to prevent any claims that a decline was related to racial change).

Beginning in 2003, the city began to see a sharp rise in bank foreclosures. In the previous year there had been only 44 vacant residential properties that required nuisance abatement (board-ups, grass cutting, etc.) by the city. In cases of the most blighted properties, the city made necessary repairs and filed liens to attempt to recover its costs. As the foreclosure rate grew in Cleveland, Cuyahoga County, and the United States, so too did it in Cleveland Heights. In 2006, there were 486 residential foreclosures. The number has increased every year since then, with 563 foreclosures in 2010, about 2.5 percent of its housing stock, and 2,005 cumulatively over the five-year period of 2006–2010. By 2008, there were 455 residential properties in the city that were listed as nuisance properties, with the city spending close to a total of $100,000 on them (Bushinski 2009). In 2000, the U.S. Bureau of the Census found 21,798 housing units in the city with 885 vacant, a housing vacancy rate of 4.06 percent. This is slightly below what is considered a normal rate (5 percent). In 2010, out of a slightly increased total residential housing stock of 22,465 units, 2,508 units were vacant, an increased housing vacancy rate of 11.16 percent and almost a tripling of the housing vacancy rate a decade earlier. While part of this increase was no doubt attributable to the reduced population over the decade, a significant part of this vacant stock was attributable to foreclosures. With the national and regional economic recession and the glut of housing on the market (including foreclosed units), much of this housing was not being sold, even at greatly reduced prices. The latest (spring 2011) available estimate by the city's housing inspection service department of vacant properties in the city is approximately 1,500, about 6.67 percent. Of these, about 300 are Real Estate Owned (REO) (i.e., bank-owned) properties. The city identified 30 nuisance properties to either be condemned and demolished or repaired by the city.

Unlike many suburbs, Cleveland Heights has had an active housing department in addition to its housing inspection service. However, the city's financial resources are limited (and in 2008 voters rejected a proposed increase in the city's income tax, which would have been the first since 1979). In 2011, it faced even more difficult financial challenges when Ohio's newly elected governor and legislature, facing a huge deficit, made major cuts in state aid to localities and repealed the estate tax (shared with localities), as well as a likely major cut in the funding of the federal Community Development Block Grant (CDBG) program (Cleveland Heights has been an entitlement city since its inception in 1974). Therefore, dealing with vacant, foreclosed, and nuisance properties that have grown tremendously in numbers is beyond the city's available financial means.

In 2007, Cleveland Heights instituted a program to encourage homeownership on a street with an increasing number of poorly maintained, absentee-owned properties. Using its federal CDBG funds, it bought three two-family houses and intended to convert them into condominiums. This targeted program is intended to stabilize part of this street in the neighborhood. They are now nearing completion but as single-family renovations (Betz 2011).

In 2009, Cleveland Heights benefitted from the NSP1 program through the state of Ohio's Affordable Rental Housing Initiative, receiving $2.352 million. In accordance with the program's guidelines, Cleveland Heights planned to demolish 12 blighted homes and renovate another 12 to be sold to eligible homebuyers in four residential NSP1 target areas. As of May 2011, it had demolished 14 nuisance properties and renovated 12 properties. Eight of the latter were HUD-foreclosed properties sold to the city for $1. Five of the renovated properties have been sold with two other sales pending (Betz 2011). Using federal HOME funds, the city provides down payment grants up to $10,000 to eligible single-family homebuyers (forgiven after ten years). For a family of four, the gross income limit is $50,250. Cleveland Heights will apply to Cuyahoga County for an NSP3 grant ($250,000 maximum).

Renovation of vacant, deteriorated homes is also being done by the Home Repair Resource Center (HRRC) (www.hrrc-ch.org), a nonprofit organization in Cleveland Heights, through its Home in the Heights program. HRRC was founded in 1971 to assist homeowners in Cleveland Heights. It provides homeowner education and foreclosure prevention counseling. HRRC has purchased and renovated three neglected properties with its own borrowed funds, with the first two sold and the third nearing completion (Betz 2010).

Obviously, the efforts of the city, using federal funds, and HRRC in purchasing vacant, foreclosed problem properties and either renovating or demolishing them have only dealt with a small number compared to the greatly increased number requiring attention. Using the NSP-required targeting requirement, the city has attempted to address properties that either threaten to destabilize particular streets or whose renovation and sale can contribute to increasing housing values in those neighborhoods. This strategy resembles that used by cities like Cleveland. Unlike Cleveland, Cleveland Heights does not have active CDCs, although some neighborhoods do have block clubs. However, HRRC plays a valuable role in the city's efforts to maintain its aging housing stock, an important component of its effort to retain residents and attract newcomers.

Shaker Heights

Shaker Heights gained is renowned as a planned suburb. Like its neighbor Cleveland Heights (and earlier in the 1950s and 1960s), it went from a racially segregated, non-Hispanic White, upper class suburb to a model of racial diversity (Keating 1994). Also like Cleveland Heights, its housing stock is a mix of mansions, more modest owner-occupied single-family homes (and condominiums), and concentrations of rental housing. And, like Cleveland Heights, it has strict code enforcement and inspection standards (including point-of-sale) to maintain the quality of its aging housing stock. As a bedroom community, its retail and office tax base is limited. Its property tax rate (supporting its excellent public schools) is the highest in Ohio (with the Cleveland Heights tax rate being second highest). Its declining population totaled 28,448 in 2010 compared to 29,405 in 2000. Its population is significantly more affluent generally than that in the other two case study suburbs. In 2009, the median household income of Shaker Heights residents was $80,420, compared to $55,013 in South Euclid and $49,056 in Cleveland Heights (U.S. Bureau of the Census 2009).

Of its 13,318 housing units in 2010, 1,478 were vacant, a rate of 11.10 percent, which was almost double what it was in 2000 (6 percent). Over the period 2006–

2010, 914 housing units were foreclosed. The peak annual number was 257 in 2008. In 2006, the city's Fair Housing Review Board commissioned the study "Understanding Foreclosure Trends in Shaker Heights, Ohio" (Duda and Apgar 2007). It found an increasing number of foreclosures from 2000 (49) to 2005 (125), with the highest rates in four southwest neighborhoods bordering Cleveland with higher rates of subprime refinancing and FHA and VA loans (Eckholm 2007). These neighborhoods had higher rates of Black/African American residents than other neighborhoods in Shaker Heights.

Prior to 2008, demolitions of nuisance properties were a rarity. Instead, the city would make necessary repairs and impose liens for its costs. The city had a revolving fund to deal with nuisance abatement in partnership with the Cuyahoga County Treasurer. In 2008, the city demolished 13 houses it had acquired and one other at a total cost of $178,000. In 2009, this more than doubled to 33 houses at a total cost of $479,000, with almost 40 percent coming from the city's own funds, 42 percent from HUD NSP1 funds through Cuyahoga County, and 9 percent from the First Suburbs Consortium (FSC). In 2010, the city only demolished four properties (at a total cost of $85,000, 47 percent from its funds and 53 percent from the FSC grant).

Generally, the city has not itself renovated deteriorated housing (with one exception in the Winslow Road historical district). It has transferred three city-owned properties to private rehabbers, two with NSP2 funds. Its Shaker Renovator program invites developers to consider rehabilitating Shaker Heights homes.

An innovative response to post-demolition vacant lots is a proposed orchard near a community garden, using NSP1 funds, in the Lomond neighborhood (Jewell 2010). Another reuse of vacant lots has been a neighborhood playground. Shaker Heights has a city housing infill and vacant lot program, which began in 2001, with 53 lots currently available for development of new housing or side lots. In July 2011, for example, it sold three vacant lots for one dollar each to a local developer for the development of single-family homes subsidized through the County's NSP1 funding (Jewell 2011).

What distinguishes Shaker Heights from the other two suburbs is its decision and ability to use its own nuisance abatement funds to pay for demolitions and its policy of not itself usually renovating deteriorated houses that it acquires.

South Euclid

South Euclid is a bedroom community bordering Cleveland Heights to the east. Much of its housing stock (9,607 units in 2010) consists of owner-occupied starter homes, many of which are post-World War II ranch homes and bungalows. From a peak population of over 29,000 in 1970, its population has consistently declined to a total of 22,295 in 2010. From a low housing vacancy rate of only 3 percent in 2000 in its stock of 9,854 units, it had more than doubled to 7.22 percent (694 units) by 2010. Foreclosures have steadily risen from 230 in 2006 (2.33 percent) to 339 in 2010 (3.52 percent) and cumulatively are 1,166 over this five-year period. This led the city in 2008 to hire a housing manager to deal with the growing problem of vacant and foreclosed residential properties. She estimates that there are currently 600 to 700 vacant housing units and an increasing number of foreclosed homes that were previously owner-occupied now being rented by absentee landlords. There is a concentration of vacant units around the city's border with Cleveland Heights.

Before this period, nuisance abatement rarely resulted in demolitions. Since 2009, the city (and the county's land bank) has demolished 21 houses and expects to double that figure in the near future. The city has completed four renovated units and there are four others to be renovated by private developers. Renovated units are part of the city's Green Neighborhoods Initiative to undertake gut rehabs to bungalows to meet LEED for homes standards. A new green LEED-certified house has been built. Other than some modest funds from the County to abate nuisances, the city has little funding of its own to engage in these activities. It has financed these to date through the HUD NSP1 funds it obtained from the County ($800,000) and an additional $300,000 from the First Suburbs Development Council's Vacant and Abandoned Property Fund, which was funded by the Cuyahoga Department of Development.

The city's strategy has been to demolish the worst nuisance properties. Unless it obtains additional NSP funds in the future, it may not be able to continue demolitions. Two vacant lots post-demolition have been converted into community gardens, with a third in development. They are maintained by the gardeners.

The city has attempted to maintain housing code standards. The exteriors of owner-occupied homes are inspected every five years and the exteriors and interiors of rental units are inspected very three years. In 2007, the city adopted a point-of-sale ordinance requiring repairs before property transfers, but resident opposition led to its repeal before its implementation. In March 2010, the city adopted an ordinance requiring the owners of vacant properties to register them at an annual fee of $200. After inspection, owners must make any code violation repairs or put 100 percent of the cost of repairs in escrow (Livingston 2010). To date, about 200 vacant units have been inspected. Block clubs have assisted the city in identifying deteriorated and vacant housing units. In an effort to prevent more foreclosures, and with the help of Northeast Ohio Community and Neighborhood Data for Organizing (NEOCANDO) data, the city has mailed notices to approximately 700 at-risk homeowners in the hope that they would seek counseling through Empowering and Strengthening Ohio's People (ESOP). Its impact is unknown as of this writing.

With most homeowners of relatively modest means and the city itself having little funding to address the persistent problems of dealing with deteriorated foreclosed, vacant units, the city has only been able to directly address a small number of these vacant units. However, it is hoped that its vacant unit registration ordinance will succeed in preventing their further deterioration.

Conclusion

As these three case studies indicate, inner suburbs have undertaken similar responses to the foreclosure and abandonment crisis such as targeted demolition of blighted houses and reuse of vacant lots including infill housing and also adopted different policies such as the South Euclid policy requiring registration of vacant homes. All lack adequate resources to address the problem, even with the addition of federal NSP funding through Cuyahoga County and the state of Ohio. These responses differ from those of a large city like Cleveland mainly in scale. Similar to Cleveland, with the expected end of federal NSP funding, these suburbs will be left with unprecedented numbers of vacant and abandoned homes, many so blighted as to require demolition. As Cleveland has long experienced, declining population and a housing market that has not recovered will negatively impact certain neighborhoods, especially those in which lower-income residents predominate. It may also trigger more conversions of owner-occupied housing into rental housing, which suburbs have previously resisted. Another ripple effect will be the loss of property taxes from these vacant homes to the public schools, which face significant cuts in state funding with the end of federal stimulus funding for education.

References

Betz, L. 2010. HRRC Set to Renovate Third Vacant CH Home. *Sun Press*, 20 May.

Betz, L. 2011. Cleveland Hts. Set to Sell Three Renovated Homes. *Sun Press*, 12 May.

Bier, T. and Keating, W.D. 2008. Greater Cleveland's First Suburbs Consortium: Fighting sprawl and suburban decline. *Housing Policy Debate*, 19(3), 457–77.

Bushinski, K. 2009. City of Cleveland Heights Battles Foreclosure Burdens. *Heights Observer*, 1 September.

Center for Responsible Lending. 2011. More Costly Foreclosures. 26 September.

Duda, M. and Apgar, W.C. 2007. *Understanding Mortgage Foreclosure Trends in Shaker Heights, Ohio*. Cambridge: Joint Center on Housing Studies.

Eckholm, E. 2007. Foreclosures Force Suburbs to Fight Blight. *The New York Times*. 23 March.

Hanlon, B. 2010. *Once the American Dream: Inner-Ring Suburbs of the Metropolitan United States*. Philadelphia, PA: Temple University Press.

Hexter, K. and Coulton, C. 2010. *Facing the Foreclosure Crisis in Greater Cleveland: What Happened and How Communities are Responding*. Cleveland, OH: Federal Reserve Bank of Cleveland.

Hexter, K.W. and Schnoke, M. 2009. *Responding to Foreclosures in Cuyahoga County: Evaluation Report, Program Year Three*. Cleveland, CA: Cleveland State University.

Jewell, T. 2010. Shaker Allows Three New Infill Houses. *Sun Press*, 7 July.

Jewell, T. 2011. Neglected Home Turned into Orchard. *Sun Press*, 15 September.

Keating, W.D. 2010. Redevelopment of vacant land in the blighted neighbourhoods of Cleveland, Ohio, resulting from the housing foreclosure crisis. *Journal of Urban Regeneration and Renewal*, 4(1), 39–52.

Keating, W.D. 1994. *The Suburban Racial Dilemma: Housing and Neighborhoods.* Philadelphia, PA: Temple University Press.

Keating, W.D. and Lind, K. 2012. Responding to the Mortgage Crisis: Three Cleveland Examples. *The Urban Lawyer.* 44(1), 1–35.

Kotlowitz, A. 2009. All Boarded Up. *New York Times Magazine*, 8 March.

Livingston, S. 2010. South Euclid Finds a Tool to Combat Blight of Abandoned and Neglected Property. *The Plain Dealer*, 29 March.

Mallach, A. 2009. *Stabilizing Communities: A Federal Response to the Secondary Impacts of the Foreclosure Crisis.* Washington, DC: Brookings Institution.

Morton, M.J. 2002. *Cleveland Heights: The Making of an Urban Suburb.* Mount Pleasant, SC: Arcadia Publishing.

NEO CANDO. 2011. *Cuyahoga County Foreclosure Filings: 2006–2010.* Cleveland, OH: Northeast Ohio Community and Neighborhood Data for Organizing.

U.S. Bureau of the Census. 2005–2009 American Community Survey. Washington, DC: U.S. Bureau of the Census.

U.S. Bureau of the Census. 2010 Census. Washington, DC: U.S. Bureau of the Census.

Chapter 9

Punctuated Equilibrium: Community Responses to Neoliberalism in Three Suburban Communities in Baltimore County, Maryland

Gregory Smithsimon

For decades, neighborhood racial transition from White to Black/African American has been characterized as blockbusting, accompanied by expectations of rapid, dramatic declines in property values, income, and public services. My research on Randallstown, a Black/African American suburban community that grew around the Liberty Road commercial corridor in Baltimore County, Maryland, indicates that since the early 1970s, racial transition in this community has followed a pattern different than blockbusting. That pattern is produced by two opposing forces. The first is the civil rights movement, in which Black/African American activists, residents, and allied institutions broke the color line and gained entry for Blacks/African Americans into previously segregated suburbs where residents sought to create secure, stable communities. The second force is neoliberalism,[1] the political and economic policy that has defined capitalism in the U.S. and abroad since the 1970s. Neoliberalism has been characterized by governance through crisis (Klein 2007).

The outcome of these two forces is not the "precipitous decline" (Seligman 2005: 220) characteristic of incidents of blockbusting, but a process, borrowing the term from Gould and Eldredge (1977), who famously sought to develop an alternative to the evolutionary model of gradualism. In this study, punctuated equilibrium is used to replace notions of inevitable, constant change with a model of long periods of stability interrupted by moments of crisis. In such a scenario, not only may a neighborhood remain stable for long periods, but decline is not inevitable. Rather, decline is only one possible outcome of periodic crisis.

In this study, I am applying the concept of punctuated equilibrium to Liberty Road, which has experienced decades of remarkable stability—as measured, for instance, in median property values and median household incomes. However, the underlying contradictions between the collective demands of civil rights and

---

1   Note that "neoliberalism" has little to do with the term "liberal" as it is used in the U.S. nowadays.

the individualized prescriptions of neoliberalism can erupt in periodic crises that disrupt that equilibrium. The house price decline that lasted from mid-2006 until recently and the Great Recession that occurred from December 2007 to June 2009 are examples of two such crises.

In this chapter I analyze 40 years of data from the U.S. Bureau of the Census to compare three suburban areas in Baltimore County, Maryland—one Black/ African American (Liberty Road), one non-Hispanic White (Bel Air Road), and one racially mixed, that is, Black/African American and non-Hispanic White (Reisterstown Road).[2] More specifically, I examine how changes in racial composition among the three communities do not necessarily lead to the decline in median property values predicted by conventional understandings of residential racial transition. This comparative, longitudinal study in the three suburban communities, based on data analyses and ethnographic work, demonstrates the subtle threats that have developed to neighborhood stability and the agency people exercise in a dedicated effort to mitigate these threats and maintain neighborhood stability, particularly in a Black/African American suburban community. These efforts, however, have been in opposition to systemic neoliberal pressures that threaten neighborhoods' stability. The sharpest such threat has been the wave of foreclosures that started in early 2007, following the bursting of the house price bubble in the summer of 2006. This chapter concludes with accounts by activists who work with homeowners facing foreclosure. The accounts describe the sources and scope of the housing crisis that threatens to disrupt those decades of stability.

As the housing crisis is still unfolding, it is too early to tell what the long-term effects of the bursting of that bubble will be on African American communities (Carr, Anacker and Mulcahy 2011, Anacker and Carr 2012, Carr and Anacker 2012, Carr, Anacker and Hernandez 2013). Nevertheless, this chapter's analyses indicate that neoliberalism's individual-level approaches are ill-suited to resolving the ongoing quest of people of color for quality housing and stable communities.

Studying Black/African American Suburban Communities in Baltimore County

While urban sociologists have studied low-income, urban Black/African American communities for decades (Liebow 1967, Stack 1974, Venkatesh 2000), they have looked more rarely at middle-income communities (Haynes 2001, Lacy 2007). However, nowadays more than half of all racial and ethnic groups residing in the 100 largest metropolitan areas live in suburbs (Frey 2010). Since 2007 I have been studying Randallstown, a predominantly Black/African

---

    2   For the 1970–2010 Census data the Longitudinal Tract Database compiled by Logan, Xu and Stults (2014) was used.

American unincorporated, census designated place outside of Baltimore, Maryland, that developed along Liberty Road. I have conducted ethnographic observations and over 40 interviews, primarily with active members of the Black/African American community, such as neighborhood activists, elected officials, county National Association for the Advancement of Colored People (NAACP) officials, and ministers, as well as realtors, teachers, and planners. A smaller number of the interviews have been with non-Hispanic Whites who work and live in and around Randallstown. In this chapter, I make use of Census data to compare three suburban areas: Liberty Road (primarily Black/African American Liberty Road, which is the primary corridor through Randallstown, and two areas elsewhere in the county); Bel Air Road (primarily non-Hispanic White), and Reisterstown Road (currently predominantly non-Hispanic White but transitioning due to a growing number and proportion of Black/African American residents). Through this comparison I gain an understanding of how house price decline and the Great Recession affect Black/African American and non-Hispanic White suburban communities differently.

The three areas are defined using a combination of census and county-level boundaries. In Baltimore County, suburban communities typically cluster around commercial roads that radiate out from the center city. Suburbanization in Baltimore County has a technical outer boundary called the Urban-Rural Demarcation Line, beyond which public water and sewer pipes are generally not provided, preventing construction of large-scale exurban housing developments and restricting sprawl (Niedt 2007).[3] For this study, three commercial roads were selected: Liberty Road, Bel Air Road, and Reisterstown Road, based on their similarities in terms of their age and style of the housing stock, median household incomes, geographical size, commercial arteries, distance to Baltimore City, and other features. The three areas studied in this chapter are made up of all the census tracts adjacent to each of the three commercial streets, from the city line to the Urban-Rural Demarcation Line. The location of the three suburban routes and the adjacent census tracts are displayed in Figure 9.1.

The three study communities are analyzed in terms of household median property values and median household income. While they were all predominantly non-Hispanic White in the 1950s, their racial composition has diverged significantly since the 1970s, so comparisons among the three compare the impact of changes in the racial composition on suburban communities.

Research on these three areas demonstrated considerable difference between recent events and traditional model of blockbusting. The differences result in large

---

3   The Urban-Rural Demarcation Line, called the URDL, was a zoning innovation pioneered by Baltimore County to contain sprawl. The county resists installing water and sewer pipes beyond the URDL, so developers concentrate development-density houses in the Southern half of the county. Homes can be built at lower densities using septic tank sewage systems, but the line effectively demarcates suburb from rural; in the case of the three communities studied here, there is limited suburban development beyond the URDL.

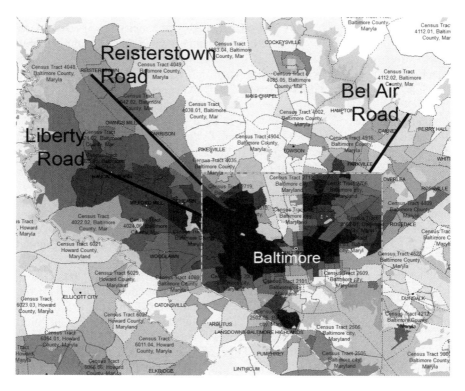

**Figure 9.1   Locations of Liberty Road, Bel Air Road, and Reisterstown
Road in Baltimore County, Maryland**

Source: SocialExplorer.com

part from the influence of civil rights activism and neoliberalism. Before examining
how median property values and median household incomes changed during
racial transition in different parts of Baltimore County, it is worth understanding
the blockbusting model, and the role of civil rights activism and neoliberalism in
residential racial transition.

Blockbusting

Formal definitions of blockbusting specify that it is catalyzed by those real estate
brokers who seed fear among Whites and sell homes to Blacks/African Americans
at inflated prices. "Blockbusting is a practice in which a real estate agent attempts
to move a nonwhite, usually Black family, into an all white neighborhood for
the purpose of exploiting white fears of impending racial turnover and property
devaluation to buy up other property on the block at depressed prices" (Gotham
2002: 25; see also Satter 2009 for a particularly detailed account of the practice
in Chicago). Courts have used similar definitions (Barrick Realty, Inc. v. City

of Gary [491 F.2d 161] 1974). The decrease in property values leads many non-Hispanic White homeowners to expect that a residential racial transition from non-Hispanic White to Black/African American will lead to "precipitous decline" (Seligman 2005: 220).

Blockbusting typified the process of racial transition in Baltimore as late as the 1950s. Orser (1994) details the process of blockbusting and residents' efforts to stop blockbusters. Ethnographic fieldwork for this study found an elderly White Randallstown resident who described the rapidity of blockbusting. She told the story of a friend who played cards in a group. One week, they played as normal. The next time they gathered, everyone in the group had sold their homes.

But while accounts of blockbusting have dominated our understanding of residential racial transition (Rieder 1985, Gotham 2002, Kefalas 2003), it is not clear that they should. First, although earlier work identified a range of different patterns of racial transition, blockbusting has been adopted as the single model of such change (Taeuber and Taeuber 1969). Second, in popular and academic usage, blockbusting has spread beyond its technical definition and refers not strictly to incidents where realtors sow fear and reap profits, but simply to the process of non-Hispanic White-to-Black/African American racial transition (Rieder 1985, Seligman 2005). As a result, blockbusting became a slur rather than a description, such that realtors who opposed segregation and showed homes to people, regardless of race, were regularly branded "blockbusters" (Satter 2009). Third, as Woldoff argues, it is time for researchers to "update and extend the white flight narrative" (Woldoff 2011: 3). Even in communities like the one she studies in the Philadelphia area, where racial transition occurs rapidly, there is more to the story than the dispersal of non-Hispanic Whites and the arrival of Blacks/African Americans. Such a revision is even more necessary in cases such as Baltimore County, where racial transition happened much more slowly—over a period of 30 years—and was less the result of non-Hispanic White realtors seeking to profit than of Black/African American residents and activists trying to breech the barrier of segregation to gain access to suburban homes and amenities on an equal basis with Whites. The term "blockbusting" obscures that important story.

One expectation that has become central to the narrative of blockbusting is that residential transition from White to Black/African American will bring swift, inevitable, and dramatic decline in median property values, median household incomes, and a host of other social indicators. In the 40 years since Blacks/African Americans first moved into Randallstown, this suburb, however, has not followed that trajectory. In this chapter I argue and provide evidence that Randallstown's stability and crises were largely the product of local civil rights activism and neoliberal policies, respectively.

Civil Rights Activism

Until the early 1970s, the color line in Baltimore County was impenetrable. For example, Herbert Lindsay, a sociologist who had taken a job at a historically Black/African American university in Baltimore, tried to rent an apartment in a suburban Baltimore County community but was told that he should look elsewhere and was given the name of a predominantly Black/African American apartment complex in another county. Likewise, after Louis Diggs tried to buy property on a traditionally non-Hispanic White block in the county, the windows of his car were shot out and a cross was burned on his church's lawn. In 1972, the county executive issued an executive order requiring that any real estate broker who sold to a Black/African American buyer had to report his actions to the police. A Civil Rights Commission representative scoffed at the executive's claim that this was to protect homebuyers from racial violence, responding that the purpose was to "clearly intimidate rather than help the potential black buyer in the county" (Pietila 2010: 235).

But despite experiences like these, local activists were determined to open up the county to Black/African American home seekers. Groups like Baltimore Neighborhoods seized on the opportunity provided by passage of the Fair Housing Act of 1968 and began sending testers to ferret out discriminatory treatment. Activists involved in the war on poverty and the NAACP (which soon had two chapters in the county, in addition to the national headquarters in Baltimore City) were involved in similar drives to open up houses and apartments in the suburbs to Black/African American home seekers. In one of the most unexpected components of the civil rights campaign, the Social Security Administration (SSA) headquarters were relocated from Baltimore City to Baltimore County, and it happened to be run by Robert Ball, a non-Hispanic White liberal who was involved in open-housing organizations. With the encouragement of his colleague John Michener, a Quaker and long-time open housing activist, the SSA became actively involved in the search for housing near its suburban headquarters for its significant number of Black/African American employees. Employees participated in fair housing organizations, the SSA supplied material support to those organizations, and when realtors refused to share home listings with prospective Black/African American buyers, the SSA was able to obtain a machine that printed the multiple listings and installed it in its own headquarters to supply listings to employees on a nondiscriminatory basis.

Collectively, these activists, with the help of other supporters, were able to break the hold of segregation in Baltimore County. After a decade, Baltimore County's Black/African American population had grown by 178 percent—over 34,500 people—from 19,416 in 1970 to 53,955 in 1980, while the non-Hispanic White population held steady near 590,000. Desegregation was a significant but partial success. Even in 2010, the vast majority of the 209,738 Blacks/African Americans in the county lived in the vicinity of Liberty Road, which runs not far from the headquarters of the SSA.

Neoliberalism

At the same time that civil rights activism was reshaping Baltimore County, a new political-economic order was reshaping the region, the nation, and the world. The economic shocks of the 1970s, including falling rates of profit, stagflation, and rising oil prices, disrupted the American postwar economic order of high union wages in exchange for high productivity (Shepard and Smithsimon 2011). Corporations responded with a series of historic changes to the business-labor accord, which were eventually understood to constitute a new economic ideology called neoliberalism.

As described by Harvey and others, neoliberalism was an effort by corporate elites to reassert power and consisted of several components (Harvey 2005). First and foremost, it sought to reverse the postwar conditions of high incomes and benefits, seeking instead to lower incomes by insisting on conciliatory contracts, by breaking unions in industrialized nations and by rewriting tariff and trade regulations to encourage and even subsidize the relocation of production facilities to foreign countries with lower labor costs (and often with dictatorial governments that would prevent unionized demands for raises) (Stein 2010). As a result, plants closed in the U.S. and moved overseas, working-class incomes in the U.S. fell, and U.S. unionization rates declined precipitously. Secondly, neoliberalism entailed selective efforts towards government deregulation. Elites and their corporations pushed for cuts to welfare, unemployment, and health benefits, both to reduce taxes and costs to themselves. Thus, people had fewer choices but to work for lower incomes, sometimes taking on several jobs. Environmental regulations, along with health and safety standards, were opposed or weakened by the elites who argued that they constrained business and increased costs. Regulations on banking and lending were weakened. Trade agreements, such as the North American Free Trade Agreement (NAFTA), the General Agreement on Tariffs and Trade (GATT), and others, which facilitated production in low-cost countries, were also pursued in the name of deregulation.

But while neoliberalism has those strategic and ideological components, Harvey (2005) argues that it is best understood not as an abstract ideology but class warfare.[4] Also, he argues that neoliberalism has not been successful on its own terms: it was supposed to reverse the economic declines of the 1970s and restart economic growth. However, neoliberalism's "actual record in stimulating economic growth is dismal"; globally, growth rates have been lower in the neoliberal era than they were even in the crisis decade of the 1970s (Harvey 2005: 151). Instead, neoliberalism's main accomplishment has not been to create more wealth but to create conditions of widespread powerlessness in order to redistribute the existing wealth upward. As a result, Harvey concludes that neoliberalism is

---

4   For instance, the commitment to deregulation or the free market has been highly selective. In recent years, neoliberals have told bankrupt homeowners not to expect bailouts, but bankrupt banks still received them.

class warfare: an assault by elites on the middle-class, the working-class, and the poor in the U.S. and around the world.

Theorists such as Harvey who have convincingly articulated the class dimension of neoliberalism have not yet adequately explored the racial dimension of neoliberalism, which is crucial in the U.S. case. The policy changes required to implement neoliberalism were accomplished in the U.S. through what Oliver and Shapiro, in writing about gaps between Black and White wealth, call the "racialization of state policy" (Oliver and Shapiro 2006: 225). For instance, cuts to welfare were accomplished by painting welfare recipients as Black/African Americans who are members of the "undeserving poor" (Katz 1989). Higher levels of unemployment afflicted Black/African American than other communities, and lenders operating in an underregulated mortgage market preyed on Black/African American homebuyers. Beyond the realm of employment, social policy, and the economy, some theorists have argued that the move toward mass incarceration, which has disproportionately affected Blacks/African Americans, is a component of the neoliberal state (Wacquant 2010). As Goldberg has written, "race is a key structuring technology ... of neoliberalism" (Goldberg 2009: 338).

The effects of neoliberalism have been significant. First, incomes for most Americans except those at the top of the income scale have fallen in the U.S. since the 1970s (Pew Research 2012). Second, the relative security that union-influenced jobs and benefits provide—the security of lifetime employment, raises with seniority, and a solid retirement—have been put in peril with the diminishing influence of unions and the resultant deterioration of incomes, benefits, and job security. Beyond the workplace, in the past decade the mortgage market that had been underregulated in classic neoliberal fashion played havoc with home values and mortgages, first inflating and then deflating property values in many communities while often increasing costs to borrowers and profits to lenders. Third, progressive or liberal efforts to mitigate the damage of these trends were impaired by the widespread adoption of the neoliberal belief in individual responsibility, which has been used to argue against collective safety net benefits and other social programs and as a bludgeon to collectivist social movements for greater equality (Harvey 2005). Linked to the call for individual-level approaches to collective social problems is the successful neoliberal promotion of small government as a populist counterargument to government intervention in the market or public sector mitigation of free market social harm (Harvey 2006, Wacquant 2010, Krippner 2011).

Thus, at the same moment that local civil rights activists were breaking into the White enclaves of suburban Baltimore County to secure a foothold for Black/African American families, neoliberalism was reconfiguring the economic foundation upon which such middle-class lives had been built. The new Black/African American residents preserved their community, ensuring that it did not suffer the decline of earlier neighborhoods in the era of blockbusting. In seeking to maintain their neighborhoods—which to residents meant keeping homes maintained to preserve home values, retaining middle-class residents with solidly middle-class incomes, and obtaining the level of public services the area had known when it was predominantly White residents were unintentionally confronting the key areas in which neoliberalism posed challenges for many communities, and in none more acutely than Black/African American ones.

Comparing Liberty Road, Bel Air Road, and Reisterstown Road

Baltimore City is mostly surrounded by Baltimore County, the latter containing many unincorporated census designated places (Vicino 2008). Baltimore County is a particularly useful place to conduct comparative analyses between predominantly Black/African American and White suburban communities. Baltimore County's Black/African American suburban communities are similar to suburbs found outside Chicago, Atlanta, and Washington, DC, among many others, in that they include high proportions of Blacks/African Americans, in addition to Prince George's County, which is primarily Black/African American. Other metropolitan areas are less well suited to studying Black/African American suburbs, for example, Philadelphia and Boston have noticeably few suburbs with a high proportion of Blacks/African Americans.

Another reason for studying Baltimore County is that suburbanization in this county occurred at a relatively even pace across the county. Baltimore's suburban communities developed along commercial routes that radiated out from Baltimore City. This radial growth pattern of suburban communities developing out into farmland resulted in several communities that are very similar in terms of median property values and median household income, but each varies from the other in terms of racial composition after the 1970s.

In 1970, Liberty Road was the largest of the three study areas, with a population of about 42,000, reflecting a slightly earlier and more rapid suburbanization along the Liberty Road corridor, followed by Reisterstown Road, with a population of about 34,000, and Bel Air Road, with a population of 23,000. By 2010, the three suburban areas were closer in population, with 59,000 in Liberty Road, 58,000 in Reisterstown Road, and 54,000 in Bel Air Road.

In 1970, Baltimore County, as well as the three study areas were predominantly non-Hispanic White. The entire county was only 3.1 percent Black/African American. The few people of color lived in historic Black/African American neighborhoods that were rural in character, many of which have documented histories that predate emancipation.

Over the next 40 years, from 1970 to 2010, however, the three study areas diverged, most notably by race rather than by median property values and median household incomes. According to the 2006–2010 American Community Survey (ACS), Bel Air Road had changed the least in terms of the proportion of Blacks/African Americans; only 13 percent of its residents were Black/African American in 2010 (up from 1.10 percent in 1970). Liberty Road had become 83 percent Black/African American by that year (up from 5.46 percent in 1970). Nearby

Reisterstown Road was in the middle, at 30 percent Black/African American in 2010 (up from 3.79 percent in 1970). Liberty Road's racial transition had begun soon after 1970 but had progressed slowly. Reisterstown Road's number of Blacks/ African Americans increased after Liberty Road's transition had started and experienced a similarly gradual increase. Neither Liberty Road nor Reisterstown exhibited the overnight transition that blockbusting is typically associated with and that was described above; instead, racial transition took 30 years.

In 2000, the Black/African American suburban communities around Randallstown had a higher median household income ($53,753) than Baltimore County ($50,667), Maryland ($52,868), or the United States ($41,994). The median household income in tracts that surround Randallstown in 2000 ranged from about $30,000 to about $70,000, however.

Because the three study communities are similar in terms of median property values and median household income but dissimilar in terms of racial composition, we can examine the difference that race makes for these three suburban study communities and identify how much neoliberalism's detrimental effects are disproportionately borne by Blacks/African Americans. Descriptive analyses of ACS 2006–2010 data and examination of community-level activism through interviews show that residents have used a variety of tactics to maintain their community's status, but the growth of modest but meaningful racial gaps in median household incomes and median property values in the three study communities indicate the limits of such strategies.

Analyzing Select Aspects of Neoliberalism: Median Property Values and Median Household Incomes

Median Property Values

Most homeowners are typically concerned with preserving the value of their homes, and Liberty Road residents are no exception. They have gone to great lengths to preserve property values, defying the fear of declining property values typically posed by accounts of blockbusting.

Table 9.1 shows the degree of similarity in the shifts in median property values in the three study communities from 1970 to 2010 (all values provided in 2010 dollars). From a common starting point around $20,000 in 1970, median property values increased and decreased roughly in tandem through the inflationary 1970s, the bearish 1990s, and the bullish 2000s until the house price bubble burst in 2006.[5] Despite the increase in its African American racial proportion, property values in Liberty Road kept pace with the other two study communities.

---

5   The five-year sample time period of the ACS is problematic, particularly in trying to measure the effect of the house price bubble and the subsequent house price crash. Comparing median property value graphs of the house price bubble, it appears that prices

Table 9.1   Median Property Values of Single-Family Owner-Occupied Homes in Liberty Road, Bel Air Road, and Reisterstown Road, 1970 to 2006–2010 (in 2010 Dollars)

	1970	1980	1990	2000	2006 to 2010 (ACS)
Liberty Road	$114,041	$154,320	$152,966	$148,051	$244,651
Bel Air Road	$100,405	$152,048	$169,990	$153,825	$268,509
Reisterstown Road	$117,039	$164,833	$188,171	$162,963	$267,217

Source: Longitudinal Tract Data Base, Logan, Xu, and Stults (2014).

However, on closer inspection important differences emerge. Liberty Road's median property values fell between 1980 and 2000 from $154,320 to $148,051, different from the increases the other two study communities experienced. Liberty Road, which had become predominantly Black/African American by 1990, lost ground, slipping from a middle spot in 1970 to the lowest median property value of the three study communities in 1990, where it has remained since.

Median Household Incomes

The racial transition of a neighborhood from primarily non-Hispanic White to Black/African American is often associated with declining median household incomes (Anderson 1990). In her nuanced study of West Philadelphia, Woldoff (2011) found that incomes often decline not because of the arrival of the first generation of Black/African American "pioneers" but because of the subsequent second generation, who are less financially secure and have greater difficulty paying for their homes.

Comparing inflation-adjusted median household incomes by race within the three study communities, one can conclude that Blacks/African Americans moving to Liberty Road were anything but poor. Table 9.2 below illustrates that Blacks/African Americans in Liberty Road had the highest median household incomes of any group in 1980 and 1990.

Consistent with Waldoff's hypothesis of a "second wave," however, median household incomes of Blacks/African Americans in Liberty Road fell after 1990. By 2006–2010, they had lost 12 percent of their median household incomes compared to 1990, although the incomes of Blacks/African Americans in Liberty Road did not fall nearly as much as the incomes of non-Hispanic White residents

---

in the ACS 2006–2010 survey represent values near but not at the top of the bubble. The utilized median property value is self-assessed by the homeowner, so the assessment might be higher than the present market value.

Table 9.2   Median Household Incomes in Liberty Road, Bel Air Road, and Reisterstown Road, 1970 to 2006–2010 (inflation-adjusted)

	1970	1980	1990	2000	2006–2010
Liberty Road	$71,194	$60,388	$64,904	$62,123	$60,098
Bel Air Road	$63,583	$60,689	$66,610	$65,724	$68,086
Reisterstown Road	$62,642	$52,650	$63,941	$64,221	$59,149

Source: Longitudinal Tract Data Base, Logan, Xu, and Stults (2014).

in this community, which declined by 17 percent. The latter decrease can be attributed to the increasing proportion of retirees in the community.

In the same period, median household incomes in Reisterstown Road, the study community that had a Black/African population of 10 percent in 1980, 21 percent in 2000, and 30 percent in 2006–2010, were increasing for both non-Hispanic Whites and Black/African Americans from 1980 to 2000. However, this growth was reversed in 2006–2010, when the median household income for non-Hispanic Whites was $61,907, below the level they had been in 1980 ($63,854), and the median household incomes for Blacks/African Americans was $56,040, slightly below the Black median household income in 2000.

In sum, these changes can be attributed to many factors, including long-term stagnant or declining incomes and increased unemployment and underemployment rates for Blacks/African Americans; in-movers with lower incomes than the established residents; and an increase in the number and proportion of retirees.

Homeowners' Strategies in Liberty Road to Maintain the Status of Their Community

Many White residents were familiar with blockbusting and the expectation that racial transition from a primarily non-Hispanic White to a primarily Black/African American community would decrease property values. Residents in Liberty Road sought to maintain the status of their neighborhoods through a variety of methods, some of which sought to slow residents who might try to sell and move out and others of which sought to aim at high standards of maintenance and services in the community.

For example, Emily Wolfson, 86, was a leading activist in her community for years. White and Jewish, Wolfson grew up in Brooklyn, and when she moved to Baltimore City in 1941 as an adult, she had no patience for the degree to which she found the Jewish community to be "ghettoized." Though her own social circle was Jewish, she felt uncomfortable in a setting whose extreme segregation was a contrast to her childhood in diverse New York City.

In 1958 she moved from her primarily Jewish neighborhood in Baltimore City to Liberty Road, choosing a new, more religiously diverse non-Hispanic White community that eventually became largely Jewish as well. A dozen years after she had moved to Randallstown, civil rights activists fractured the segregationists' stranglehold on the county, and Blacks/African Americans began to move into new suburban communities, though most Blacks/African Americans moved into housing developments along commercial corridors around Liberty Road.

In contrast to the rapid racial changes she had seen elsewhere, when the first Black/African American resident moved into Wolfson's new neighborhood in 1958, residents took action to prevent White flight while allowing racial change. First, residents organized to prevent non-Hispanic Whites from fleeing in fear. Wolfson described how they did so:

> Wolfson: There were enough people I think that made a real effort to calm it down. Why did the women go door to door and say, "Oh, Mr. Mackey [an early African American resident] is moving in. Isn't that wonderful? Let's really be nice to him."

> Q: Did they actually do that?

> Wolfson: Yes, yes. Two Jewish ladies. Both of them well educated, both of them understood what was going on. They didn't want trouble in their neighborhoods, they wanted everybody to live peacefully. And they stayed in their neighborhoods.

Wolfson credits the community's organization—the work of people like those "two Jewish ladies"—for stopping White fear selling. One important goal was to prevent a "precipitous decline" (Seligman 2005: 220) in home values, which would have furthered accelerated panic selling. With non-Hispanic Whites not moving out *en masse* and telling others not to, property values and the incomes needed to buy them have remained constant. Other residents tried to oppose blockbusting by promoting bans on for sale signs (which, if they proliferated, might increase the desire to sell).

By Emily Wolfson's account, residents moved out "when it was appropriate"— when they retired, for instance. Some did leave sooner, but their numbers were small, and racial transition happened more slowly than it had in other neighborhoods. According to Wolfson, Liberty Road residents soon recognized that racial transition was a reality. Thus, surburban communities in the Baltimore area that became African American then organized to make sure that maintenance of their community did not decline at any stage of racial change and that neighborly tolerance remained steady.

Knowing that communities of color are at risk of declining property values, residents in Liberty Road have also been particularly vigilant about protecting their community's property values by aiming at high standards of maintenance and services. Ella White Campbell, one of the interviewed residents in my field work and president of her local homeowner's association, epitomized the commitment of homeowners to maintaining the community's property values and demonstrated how suburbanites of color make use of suburban institutions, such as neighborhood associations and rigid suburban zoning enforcement. From 1970 to 2000 the racial composition of Campbell's neighborhood in Randallstown shifted slowly from primarily non-Hispanic White to primarily Black/African American. According to Campbell, a neighborhood activist since before she moved to Randallstown in 1986, most non-Hispanic White residents typically stayed until it was time to retire or move out of the region.

We spoke in the kitchen of the split-level ranch house she and her husband had lived in for 21 years. Outside was the motor home they used for family trips, taking her children, and now grandchildren, to see historic and natural sites around the country. She sat straight in her chair. Speaking in precise, carefully chosen words, she explained how her community association had played a central role in stabilizing the neighborhood.

In earlier interviews, several community members described their approaches to the task of maintaining the status, appearance, and reputation of their communities after racial transition, but none so vividly and effectively as Ella White Campbell. Campbell has been a respected and influential institution in her community. She had been president of her neighborhood improvement association since she moved to the community, when she began organizing against a neighboring hospital's medical waste incinerator. Campbell has been able to turn out 300 people for a meeting within 24 hours, and politicians accorded the homeowners' group, made up of little more than 100 households, the respect of a much larger institution. The association's cohesion and Campbell's power as a community organizer proved to be key ingredients in residents' ability to maintain the status and appearance of their neighborhood.

Campbell explained how the vigilance of the improvement association prevented neighborhood decline. "We have a reputation: we do not play. We mean business," she said. The strategy of Campbell and the association was to aggressively enforce community standards, association rules, and county regulations. "We tell the neighbors [what] our standard is, if there's a complaint, and it reaches the … association, [we have] a three strike process." Campbell described how the association acted politely but quickly and rapidly escalated their actions to force homeowners to maintain their property. If a resident did not mow and rake the lawn, brought trash cans out to the curb too long before trash pickup, or failed to maintain their home in a serious way, the association noticed the violation of local rules and took action. "On the first strike you're going to get a call from either me or one of the officers." Then came the second strike. "If things don't change, then you get a visit from two or three of the officers. And we repeat the complaint, okay? But before that visit takes place you get a letter in the mail from the organization detailing the fact that we have contacted you on whatever date it was, this problem has not been rectified, so we'll be paying you a visit to find out if you need our help in rectifying it." According to Campbell, the association did not hesitate to compel compliance. "If that doesn't work, the third strike you're out because we will report you to the county. In other words, we will find the legal source of the violation and we'll see to it you're penalized, so it's one, two, three. Three strikes you're out. And we stick to that rigidly."

The county government appears especially responsive to problems in Campbell's neighborhood, and this is likely in large part a result of Campbell. When a neighbor is not maintaining their house to community standards, she is confident that the county and the association can "find" a code violation encompassing the offense. Campbell vividly illustrated her group's particular ability to convince the county to act in their interests:

> So you don't drive around this community and see high grass. In fact there's only one house in which you might see that, and that's because we had the house condemned. Down the street. And we are trying to force the owner to sell it, because of poor maintenance and the fact that the owner kept putting undesirable tenants in the house. So we went to war with him, with the owner. And got the county to condemn the house, and took the owner to court, so that the owner *can't* rent it out. And we're on the county to force the owner to sell the house. But that's the kind of thing we do.

In the suburban context, Campbell's story of getting a home condemned is stunning. Unlike severely disinvested neighborhoods in Baltimore City, where abandonment and condemnation left blocks of boarded up buildings, in suburban communities like this one more homes are condemned to enlarge floodplains than for inadequate maintenance. Nor was the building abandoned; it was condemned while the owner was still actively seeking to rent it because he had run afoul of the local homeowners' association.

The condemnation illustrated how maintenance and behavior were regulated by the homeowners' association. As Campbell made clear, residents wanted the house condemned not only because of inadequate maintenance but because of the "undesirable" tenants. Similarly, her fellow residents, who "advocate being nosy neighbors," enforced an association-established curfew for children and became involved with other households when there were significant problems in the home. In these ways, homeowners used the association to regulate, restrict, and sanction the behavior of their fellow neighbors. They did so for fear that to be any more permissive would set into motion a cycle of neighborhood economic and social decline. In sum, residents of color used suburban institutions such as homeowners' associations and strict zoning codes to demand high standards of property maintenance, hoping to maintain property values as well. Such a strategy can have effects, but it has limits. For all but one of the survey years, Campbell's neighborhood remained above the median property value of Liberty Road but lost ground to Bel Air and Reisterstown Road.

In sum, since Liberty Road became a predominantly African American community in the 1980s, residents like Ella White Campbell and Emily Wolfson have worked to maintain the community's status. While they worked on local issues, macro-level factors have also threatened the community. The recent foreclosure crisis may be the most serious threat Randallstown has yet faced, discussed below.

Institutional Strategies to Maintain Communities during the Foreclosure Crisis

In the Baltimore metropolitan area, as in the rest of the country, foreclosure rates have been higher in Black/African American neighborhoods than in non-Hispanic White ones. Lenders originated a higher proportion of high-cost or subprime loans in Black/African American neighborhoods than in others (Rugh and Massey 2010). Interviews at nonprofit foreclosure counseling organizations in the Baltimore area illustrate how foreclosure had become a serious problem in Black/African American communities like Liberty Road, how the problem was and was not framed in neoliberal terms, and what Black/African American communities were doing to address the crisis.

I visited and interviewed directors or counselors in three nonprofit organizations. The first, We Are Family, is a community-service nonprofit organization founded by Union Bethel AME Church, the oldest African American church in Liberty Road. The second was the Maryland Housing Counselor Network in Baltimore County. The third was the 70-year-old nonprofit organization Citizens Planning and Housing Association (CPHA), which serves the Baltimore metropolitan area.

Since the start of the foreclosure crisis, nonprofit organizations have scrambled to provide much needed services in different ways. We Are Family added foreclosure counseling provided by former mortgage lenders who became foreclosure counselors to its menu of services. Also, venerable community groups that had worked on neighborhood preservation increasingly focused on foreclosures.

Joyce Coleman, an interviewed African American foreclosure specialist at the Housing Counselors Network, was in a unique position to understand how the foreclosure crisis had come into being and why it was concentrated in African American communities.[6] For 15 years, she had worked in the mortgage industry as a mortgage originator for lenders in Baltimore and North Carolina that specialized in subprime mortgages.

When the supply of capital for mortgages dried up, she could no longer continue selling mortgages and switched sides. She heard about a position of a housing counselor, which felt, she said, like "a natural transition." Sitting in a

---

6   Although the counselor gave permission to use her real name, a pseudonym is used here.

windowless office upstairs from a sleepy shopping mall in a deindustrialized non-Hispanic White working-class area on the east side of the county, she reflected on her new job. She knew many people who had switched from lending to mortgage counseling; though the money was not as good, it provided a paycheck. She said that she enjoyed the work she was doing but was still looking for ways to restart her career in real estate.

Though Coleman denied that she had sold risky mortgages or had added hidden fees to increase her profits, she had been an enthusiastic proponent of home ownership. In North Carolina, Coleman had hosted a radio program called "Possess the Land," borrowing its name from a passage in the Bible's first book of Joshua. It was a call-in show on a Christian radio station, and Coleman interwove Biblical imagery and housing advice. She would tell her listeners, "don't be afraid, you may have obstacles, you may have giants in the land, but you can conquer these giants. And I'm going to help you. We will get your credit ready. If you need money for down payment we will help you to possess your piece of the land." Twice a week, she told callers about finance options, no-money-down mortgages, and grants for down payments.

The goal was to get buyers into a house. Coleman would give customers an adjustable rate mortgage (ARM). Assuming their credit score improved after two or three years, when the interest rate would reset to a higher rate, she would explain, they could refinance at a lower rate. Coleman said she did not expect what actually happened, that is, that most of her borrowers had a decrease in their credit score. "I would coach them through that year: 'keep your mortgage paid.' But then what would happen after the two years [after the interest rates reset]—I don't know why I just didn't think [about] this—after two years, you go back to the people, their credit is worse than what it was before! And so they couldn't refinance to get into the prime rate." Coleman conveyed surprise at this outcome. With the hindsight of the mortgage collapse that revealed the peril of such lending, it may seem difficult to believe that people, from homebuyers to lenders to investors, believed that these loans could be repaid. But at the time Coleman's employer, along with television commentators, enthusiastic economists, and many others, insisted that the housing market's upward momentum would have no end. Perhaps she failed to carefully consider the overly optimistic claims of the company that had trained and employed her. Or she may have found it easier to conduct her job by adopting unquestioning optimism rather than applying critical skepticism that might have endangered her job. Others in the industry adopted a brutal cynicism about their actions. Whether Coleman could foresee or was willfully unaware of the consequences of the mortgages she gave to customers with scarred credit, the consequences were the same.

Coleman did also have first-hand knowledge of other lenders' tactics for targeting homeowners for subprime second mortgages. First, mortgage lenders would obtain mailing lists of people with 30 percent home equity and credit scores between 500 or 600 points. One lender would send out 10,000 mailers every month, offering a tempting "bogus" low interest rate on a second mortgage, specifying that the rate was only available to people with a credit score of 700. When the customers called, they were told that they did not qualify for the advertised low interest rate mortgage because of their credit score—but that an alternative, higher priced, loan was available.

Coleman explained how she was taught to sell such second mortgages, despite the higher interest rate. She would tell borrowers, "'You don't qualify for that rate, but you can get this rate. ... You will be able to have $10,000 cash in a month.' And people hear that, and they're like, 'Oh wow! I can get $10,000? Great! I can pay off all my bills.' And that's how they taught us to sell: sell the benefits, don't worry about the interest rate. Don't worry about the loan amount, sell the benefits." She would tell prospective clients, "Your payments are going to be reduced—I don't even know how that's going to happen—you're going to save 100 bucks a month."

According to Coleman, "lenders, especially up here in Maryland, when they would send out mailers they would target African American people." She went on, "I worked in some places and [have] seen some things that just turned my head, like I can't believe you guys are charging so much for a client. And they would target minorities. ... The mailers would target minority people." Lenders were looking for people with equity, debt, and poor credit. Subprime lenders did not want to deal with "A paper," that is, mortgages for people with high credit scores. Such people would "nickel and dime you, they're going to shop around, they're going to look for options, they're not going to be hung on your every word. That is why some loan officers stay away from those types of people. But I actually enjoyed that [i.e., working with people with a high credit score]. ... That was a good type of loan that we had. ... I did okay doing that."

Counselors at We Are Family agreed that predatory lending targeted people of color. "It's also targeted by community ... . I mean, you target neighborhoods by race. People don't want to say that." From their perspective, steering borrowers towards unaffordable homes and mortgages began with realtors and continued through several layers of the home-buying industry.

By 2006 or 2007, the market in North Carolina changed, and Joyce Coleman was no longer able to sell products to callers on her radio show. "The banking industry changed and, it was about mid-like 2006 beginning of 2007. And I remember because I [had been] able to get people into products where they didn't have to put a lot of money down. And those banks that would come to our office that were able to help people just closed down, and they were gone. So the clientele that I had I wasn't able to service as much anymore. Couldn't get them mortgages."

Coleman knew that lenders were targeting people with debt and equity. "Those are the people that are going to need to refinance, because those are the people that have a bunch of credit card bills that they can't pay." But she was not in a position to identify why lenders targeted African Americans to find those kinds of customers. Community groups that had worked in these communities had seen more of the causes of financial stress.

We Are Family had already been providing emergency community services—they were known as a place to go when renters were at risk of eviction or having their utilities turned off. I first sat down to talk to leaders of the organization after the ribbon cutting for their new offices. Located in a single-story business park, the new space gave We Are Family room for the wide range of community services they conducted. Beyond the reception desk was a glass wall revealing a large meeting area. Further back was a neatly arranged, garage-like space used for the group's food pantry, where residents could pick up bags of food based on scheduled appointments rather than wait in lines. In offices on either side of the meeting room, counselors helped people with emergency assistance for heat and electricity, among other necessities. Once a month, the group also held first-time homebuyer classes, even while it helped other homeowners facing foreclosure.

At the grand opening in 2011, Reverend Charles Sembly, pastor of the church that had founded We Are Family, introduced me to the director, Reverend Linda Mouzon. We sat down at a large table with her, Adrienne Jones, a state delegate and member of the church, and staff of We Are Family.

While Joyce Coleman could only speculate as to why African Americans were targeted in the search for distressed homeowners, We Are Family's broader experience with community assistance gave the members concrete experience with the factors that put people, disproportionately Blacks/African Americans, in situations of financial distress. Rather than articulate what made people attractive targets for subprime mortgages, they listed these features in explaining how people ended up at risk of foreclosure. First, Blacks/African Americans as a group have been traditionally less economically secure. "Last hired, first fired," said Mouzon, citing a Black/African American adage regarding employment insecurity. In addition, many people who sought the group's assistance were older workers who had been laid off and had not been able to find a job that paid what they had made before. Other people worked in financial or technology companies and had been laid off in bust cycles. While many had found new jobs, they had lower salaries and were having trouble making ends meet and paying bills. Other members of the group highlighted the role of predatory lending. "A lot of people bought a bag of goods that wasn't there." While some clients were seniors, "most of them are families."

Other clients had faced crises in their lives.[7] "We'll hear about somebody who died," explained Mouzon, recalling clients who explained their financial stress by saying, "I had to plan for a funeral." An unexpected medical bill could push people into debt they were unable to get out of. While such events could befall anyone, interviews with Blacks/African Americans, Latinos, and non-Hispanic Whites indicated that the first two groups were much more likely to experience such crises and acute downward economic mobility than non-Hispanic Whites.

---

7   This insight is consistent with the author's previous findings on financial experiences of Blacks/African Americans, who are more likely to experience dramatic reversals of their financial situation. Such events could be said to constitute punctuated equilibrium at a personal level.

Mel Freeman, director of CPHA, which added considerable amounts of housing counseling to its portfolio of client services in the years after the housing bubble had burst, gave a similar assessment of the causes of financial distress for homeowners, calling it "the four Ds," which included death, disability, divorce, and debt. Blacks/African Americans are more likely to face financial difficulties and were targeted by lenders for subprime loan products. In addition, some of the interviewed foreclosure experts suggested that lenders had exploited their status and relationships with clients. Freeman noted that maps that displayed foreclosures had shown that the same brokers and lenders appeared multiple times on the same block. He attributed this to neighbors' tendency to talk to each other and recommend a broker or lender. But Coleman suggested a different explanation. "I think that African Americans are 'relational,' and I think that if we found somebody we liked, we trusted them. You know, you have a nice face, you look like, you're a Caucasian, you're a nice guy, I can trust you, you're not going to steer me wrong." Consistent with this thesis, some research has suggested that while non-Hispanic Whites are more likely to obtain loans from banks, Blacks/African Americans are more likely to obtain loans from people they already know in their communities. Social networks could be exploited to obtain more business from people who were not shopping around (Iwarere and Williams 2003, Reid 2011).

Such an explanation for the concentration of subprime mortgages among African Americans can skirt close to a reductionist, culturalist syllogism. But Coleman elaborated in a way that suggested a different explanation. The problem was whom to trust: according to her, African Americans "will go to this loan officer they feel comfortable with and go back next year and refinance next year with them again. It's like their financial person, [even though] this guy is just after what you can get out of them." White homebuyers might have less attachment to an individual and feel confident shopping around because they believe that they could trust reputable institutions, such as mainstream banks. But African Americans have had less positive experiences with institutions respected by most non-Hispanic Whites (such as the police, the judicial system, the labor market, and mainstream banks themselves). With experiences that augur against trusting even mainstream institutions, they must seek out individuals to trust, with less weight given to institutions than non-Hispanic Whites typically give, since even venerated institutions regularly have histories of discriminatory treatment. Personal relationships create stronger ties and obligations and reduce the ease with which someone can cut ties and shop around. In the end, everyone must put their trust somewhere. As Coleman explained, the attitude of buyers she worked with toward lenders was, "It's like a professional in your life. They are the expert in mortgages—I'm not the expert, I don't know anything about this stuff, so there's no way you can go out there and rip me off, because you're licensed, you have a legitimate office."

Public policies that address the foreclosure crisis have been inadequate so far. While some national and state programs have been implemented, all three interviewed organizations pointed to state programs that had been useful until, as the leaders of We Are Family explained, "the money dried up."

In some respects, the neoliberal philosophy of individual responsibility has hampered the development of programs to sufficiently address the foreclosure crisis. Some counselors would chastise a hypothetical homebuyer for using their house "like an ATM" from which equity could be irresponsibly withdrawn, even while their specific stories were of clients who needed money to pay legitimate debts. Others criticized homebuyers, concluding that "the issue is you really can't afford the home anyway." That criticism ignored counselors' intimate familiarity with the chain of manipulations from realtor to lender that led people into houses whose prices had been inflated. Blaming individuals also bypassed counselors' knowledge that the people who were buying homes they could not afford were concentrated in Black/African American neighborhoods.

In a related vein, many interviewees considered homebuyer education, particularly in the form of first-time homebuyer programs, as the key to reduce the number of borrowers who were victimized. While such an approach seems unobjectionable, other researchers have noted the way that education-based remedies relocate the source of predatory lending from a widespread social structural to an individual-level issue.[8] Such neoliberal explanations and solutions, among others, have hindered addressing the foreclosure crisis at the local and national level. Also, foreclosure reflects the racialization of neoliberalism. First, the damage of neoliberalism's financialization, speculation, and deregulation targeted and affected Blacks/African Americans more than non-Hispanic Whites. Then, there was inadequate political motivation to provide adequate solutions to problems that disproportionately affected African Americans.

Thus, people in communities hard-hit by foreclosure have been left to assemble ad-hoc responses out of the irregular programs they have found. While all three interviewed organizations made use of federal or state programs when they were available, others in the community have sought to do more. For example, Congressman Elijah Cummings has regularly organized events for borrowers facing foreclosure. The Congressman has used his influence to demand attendance from representatives of the major lenders so that borrowers could sit down face to face with representatives of the lenders and try to resolve their problems. All three interviewed nonprofit organizations have given this approach high praise. It is not coincidental that Cummings is African American, as were all of the housing counselors with whom I spoke.

---

8   The distinction between social "issues" and individual "troubles" is based on C. Wright Mills. Regarding education as a solution that individualized social problems, Arthur (2011) states that "to the extent that [a financial education program] mystifies and depoliticizes the social relations of production and the capitalist economy by individualizing socially-related risk (and treating it as a technical rather than political problem), [such education] aids in disempowering the citizen, delegitimizes collective risk solutions and unjustly holds the individual consumers responsible for economic risks they cannot manage" (32).

Patterns of Punctuated Equilibrium

Black/African American suburbs outside Baltimore have defied the patterns that most racially transitioning neighborhoods in Baltimore and elsewhere have followed. They did not follow the pattern of "precipitous decline" (Seligman 2005: 220). Instead, residents and activists sought and worked to maintain stability while the deregulated, neoliberal market sowed the seeds of crisis. The outcome of the conflict between these two opposing interests is best described as one of punctuated equilibrium.

Over the past four decades, when Blacks/African Americans have maintained the status in Black/African American suburban communities in Baltimore County, residents have been remarkably successful at altering the traditional story of racial transition from non-Hispanic White to Black/African American that often results in a decrease of median property values and median household incomes, among other factors. Blacks/African Americans have used the strategies and the momentum of the civil rights movement to desegregate parts of Baltimore County. For example, Emily Wolfson challenged White flight to maintain her neighborhood's demographic. Ella White-Campbell used the prerogative of homeowners to ensure that property values in her community remained stable. The analysis of Census data shows that these communities were successful.

However, there are inherent contradictions in this process. Maintaining property values while household incomes gradually decline was partly dependent on easy access to mortgages (Rajan 2010). However, the foreclosure crisis, the lending freeze, and the silent housing affordability crisis have made maintaining property values more challenging. Blacks/African Americans are typically less able than non-Hispanic Whites to muster political support for effective political responses to crises that disproportionately affect Black/African American communities. Congressman Cumming's approach, discussed above, is an exception to this pattern.

Punctuated equilibrium is produced not only by the threats a neighborhood faces but also by the mitigating influence of residents and other actors. The force of the events that punctuated the area's relative equilibrium appears unprecedented in suburbs. The ultimate outcome of the foreclosure crisis will depend not only on responses at the national and state level but on the response of residents and community activists.

References

Anacker, K.B., Carr, J.H. and Pradhan, A. 2012. Analyzing foreclosures among high-income Black/African American and Hispanic/Latino borrowers in Prince George's County, Maryland. *Housing and Society* 39(1), 1–28.

Anderson, E. 1990. *Streetwise: Race, Class and Change in an Urban Community.* Chicago, IL: University of Chicago Press.

Arthur, C. 2011. *Financial Literacy: Neoliberalism, the Consumer and the Citizen.* MA Thesis. Department of Theory and Policy Studies. Ontario Institute for Studies in Education of the University of Toronto.

Barrick Realty, Inc. v. City of Gary, Indiana, 491 F.2d 161 (7th Cir 1974).

Carr, J.H., Anacker, K.B. and Hernandez, I. 2013. *The State of the U.S. Economy and Homeownership for African Americans.* Lanham, MD: National Association of Real Estate Brokers (NAREB).

Carr, J.H. and Anacker, K.B. 2012. *Long-Term Social Impacts and Financial Costs of Foreclosure on Families and Communities of Color: A Review of the Literature.* Washington, DC: National Community Reinvestment Coalition.

Carr, J.H., Anacker, K.B. and Mulcahy, M.L. 2011. *The Foreclosure Crisis and Its Impact on Communities of Color: Research and Solutions.* Washington, DC: National Community Reinvestment Coalition.

Frey, W.H. 2010. Race and ethnicity, in *State of Metropolitan America.* Washington, DC: Brookings Institution.

Goldberg, D.T. 2009. *The Threat of Race: Reflections on Racial Neoliberalism.* Malden, MA: Wiley-Blackwell.

Gotham, K.F. 2002. *Race, Real Estate and Uneven Development: The Kansas City Experience, 1900–2000.* Albany, NY: State University of New York Press.

Gould, S.J. and Eldredge, N. 1977. Punctuated equilibria: The tempo and mode of evolution reconsidered. *Paleontology* 3(2), 115–51.

Harvey, D. 2005. *A Brief History of Neoliberalism.* New York, NY: Oxford University Press.

Harvey, D. 2006. Neo-liberalism as creative destruction. *Geografiska Annaler: Series B, Human Geography*, 88(2), 145–58.

Haynes, B.D. 2001. *Red Lines, Black Spaces: The Politics of Race and Space in a Black Middle-Class Suburb.* New Haven, CT: Yale University Press.

Iwarere, L.J. and Williams, J.E. 2003. The effect of income, ethnicity/race and institutional factors on mortgage borrower behavior, *Journal of Real Estate Research*, 25(4), 509–28.

Katz, M.B. 1989. *The Undeserving Poor: From the War on Poverty to the War on Welfare.* New York, NY: Pantheon.

Kefalas, M. 2003. *Working-Class Heroes: Protecting Home, Community, and Nation in a Chicago Neighborhood.* Berkeley, CA: University of California Press.

Klein, N. 2007. *The Shock Doctrine: The Rise of Disaster Capitalism.* New York, NY: Picador.

Krippner, G. 2011. *Capitalizing on Crisis: The Political Origins of the Rise of Finance.* Cambridge, MA: Harvard University Press.

Lacy, K.R. 2007. *Blue Chip Black: Race, Class, and Status in the New Black Middle Class.* Berkeley, CA: University of California Press.

Liebow, E. 1967. *Tally's Corner.* Boston, MA: Little, Brown.

Logan, J.R., Xu, Z. and Stults, B. 2014. Interpolating US decennial Census tract data from as early as 1970 to 2010: A longitudinal tract database. *Professional Geographer*, 66(3), 412–20.

Niedt, C.W. 2007. *The Politics of Prosperity and Crisis in an Industrial Suburb: Dundalk, Maryland, 1920–2005*. Ph.D. dissertation. University of California, Berkeley.

Oliver, M.L. and Shapiro, T.M. 2006. *Black Wealth/White Wealth: A New Perspective on Racial Inequality*. New York, NY: Routledge.

Orser, W.E. 1994. *Blockbusting in Baltimore: The Edmondson Village Story*. Lexington, KY: University Press of Kentucky.

Pew Research. 2012. *Fewer, Poorer, Gloomier: The Lost Decade of the Middle Class*. Washington, DC: Pew Research Center.

Pietila, A. 2010. *Not in My Neighborhood: How Bigotry Shaped a Great American City*. Chicago, IL: Ivan R. Dee/Rowman & Littlefield.

Rajan, R.G. 2010. *Fault Lines: How Hidden Fractures Still Threaten the World Economy*. Princeton, NY: Princeton University Press.

Reid, C. 2011. *Addressing the Disparate Impact of Foreclosures on Communities of Color*. Northern California Grantmakers. http://www.ncg.org.

Rieder, J. 1985 *Canarsie: The Jews and Italians of Brooklyn Against Liberalism*. Cambridge, MA: Harvard Press.

Rugh, J.S. and Massey, D.S. 2010. Racial segregation and the American foreclosure crisis. *American Sociological Review*, 75(5), 629–51.

Satter, B. 2009. *Family Properties: How the Struggle Over Race and Real Estate Transformed Chicago and Urban America*. New York, NY: Metropolitan Books.

Seligman, A.I. 2005. *Block by Block: Neighborhoods and Public Policy on Chicago's West Side*. Chicago, IL: University of Chicago Press.

Shepard, B. and Smithsimon, G. 2011. *The Beach beneath the Streets: Contesting New York City's Public Spaces*. Albany, NY: State University of New York Press.

Stack, C. 1974. *All Our Kin.* New York, NY: Harper/Colophon Books.

Stein, J. 2010. *Pivotal Decade: How the United States Traded Factories for Finance in the Seventies*. New Haven, CT: Yale University Press.

Taeuber, K. and Taeuber, A. 1969. *Negroes in Cities: Residential Segregation and Neighborhood Change*. New York, NY: Atheneum.

Venkatesh, S. 2000. *American Project: The Rise and Fall of a Modern Ghetto*. Cambridge, MA: Harvard University Press.

Vicino, T.J. 2008. *Transforming Race and Class in Suburbia: Decline in Metropolitan Baltimore*. New York, NY: Palgrave Macmillan.

Wacquant, L. 2010. Crafting the Neoliberal state: Workfare, prisonfare, and social insecurity. *Sociological Forum*, 25(5), 197–220.

Woldoff, R. 2011. *White Flight/Black Flight: The Dynamics of Racial Change in an American Neighborhood*. Ithaca, NY: Cornell University Press.

SECTION V
Suburban Policy

Chapter 10

Revitalizing Distressed Older Suburbs: Case Studies in Alabama, Michigan, Ohio, and Pennsylvania

Kathryn W. Hexter, Edward W. (Ned) Hill, Benjamin Y. Clark, Brian A. Mikelbank and Charles Post

Cities and their regions are dynamic, continuously evolving places. American suburbs are a relatively new phenomenon in the history of places of urban settlement, although some are more than 100 years old. As some of the earliest suburbs, especially those of older Northeastern and Midwestern cities, enter their second centuries, they are experiencing dynamics more typically associated with central cities.

The release of the 2010 Census and American Community Survey (ACS) data, along with earlier Census data, offers a snapshot of America's older suburbs and allows for the identification of demographic and socioeconomic trends. The numbers are useful in a variety of ways, including determining federal and state funding levels for needed programs. But the numbers do not tell the whole story. The authors undertook a study (Hexter et al. 2011) to supplement the Census information with a deeper understanding of the underlying forces shaping these older, distressed suburbs, many of which are losing population to newer suburbs and, with that, facing the possibility of losing formula-based federal funds. This chapter is based on that study.

The study addressed three sets of research questions: first, where are these distressed, older suburbs and what are their demographic, socioeconomic, and fiscal characteristics? Based on our analysis, 168 suburbs and small cities were identified as most distressed, and four suburbs were selected for case studies. These suburbs received in-depth analysis, including site visits and interviews, to provide sufficient context in which to identify best practices and unmet needs.

Second, what policies and strategies work? A literature review of research on older suburbs was conducted to help us identify national, state, local, and foundation programs and strategies that have worked in these suburbs and to understand what made the programs successful.

Third, what is possible? What needs to be invented? Based on lessons from the case studies and the new and growing body of literature on older, distressed suburbs, we identified common public policy, social, and economic issues faced by severely distressed suburbs. This analysis points to how well current programs are working in these suburbs and suggests some federal policy options to address unmet needs.

Case studies were conducted in four distressed suburbs of older, large industrial cities: East Cleveland, Ohio; Inkster, Michigan; Chester, Pennsylvania; and Prichard, Alabama. These places once were thriving communities but are now characterized by high rates of poverty, foreclosure, unemployment, and population loss; limited tax bases; underfunded or failing schools; and inadequate public services. Other types of suburbs likely face many of these issues as well. The methodology developed for this analysis could be applied to identify other types of older suburbs for comparative analyses.

The fine-grained case study analysis can provide useful information in considering various federal policy responses that might be used to help position distressed suburbs to thrive in the next century. Understanding what works and what does not work in these four places can inform federal policy responses to better position distressed suburbs to meet the challenges of the future.

Literature Review: Suburban Typologies

There is a growing body of literature on suburbia in general and on older, inner-ring or first suburbs in particular. Much of this literature paints a broad brush picture of the various types of suburbs, distinguishes suburbs from central cities, makes the case for suburbs to form coalitions, and calls for tailored state and federal policy recommendations. The vast majority of authors call for more research to better understand the context of these challenges faced by the different types of suburban places before reforming current policies (Puentes and Orfield 2002, Puentes and Warren 2006, Hanlon 2010).

Surprisingly, there is very little research on programs and policies that are actually working on the ground in distressed inner-ring suburbs to improve either the quality of life of residents or the managerial and service delivery capacities of these governmental units. Much of the extant research focuses on distressed neighborhoods of central cities (Hill and Nowak 2002, Bright 2003, Fox 2008). Some of the strategies employed in central cities may be applicable to older suburbs, but further exploration is needed to see what works. Our research focuses on older suburbs of formerly industrial cities that are experiencing extreme levels of social distress and that have very little capacity to respond.

Previous research has identified suburban typologies, as we will discuss below (Puentes and Orfield 2002, Mikelbank 2004, Puentes and Warren 2006, Hanlon 2010). Mikelbank (2004) created a typology of all U.S. suburban places consisting of 3,567 non-central city, metropolitan, incorporated places with a minimum population of 2,500, based on a hierarchical cluster analysis. His research identified similarities and differences among the nation's suburban municipalities, classified each of them based on that information, and substantively explained the groupings. More than two-thirds of the people covered in Mikelbank's (2004) research reside in a suburb that does not match traditional perceptions of suburban America. He gathered data for these places along three dimensions: population and place, based on the 2000 U.S. Census, and the economy and government, based on the 1997 Economic Census. He found ten clusters that were then subjected to discriminant analysis to better understand the underlying data structure of each cluster.

About half (50.9 percent) of the 3,567 suburbs analyzed by Mikelbank (2004) appear to fit into the stereotypical view of suburbs: non-Hispanic White bedroom communities that are prospering but aging. They have little or below-average employment and little in the way of family structure or racial and ethnic diversity. Yet, even within this category, there is variation. They account for only 31.9 percent of the population covered by the study. The remaining suburbs, however, account for just under half of all suburbs (49.1 percent) and are home to 68.1 percent of suburbanites in Mikelbank's study. They vary in terms of race and ethnicity, family structure, and employment composition and levels. Like central cities, many are actually victims of sprawl. Their challenges are multidimensional.

Working stability suburbs have large populations and high numbers of business establishments and employment bases, many of which are in manufacturing. While similar to manufacturing suburbs in economic structure, the presence of other "healthy" characteristics separates them into a distinct cluster.

From Mikelbank's (2004) 10-cluster solution, five clusters containing 1,056 suburbs appeared to be relevant for our analysis of distressed older suburbs:

- Manufacturing-black suburbs (179)
- Manufacturing-struggling suburbs (828)
- Working diversity-south/western suburbs (85)
- Working diversity-central suburbs (203)
- Suburban success-working stability suburbs (457)

Another example of a suburban typology is provided by Orfield (2002), who grouped 4,600 municipalities in 25 metropolitan areas according to their fiscal condition. He identified six classifications for suburban fiscal condition, that is, revenue capacity versus expenditure needs, and founds that 8 percent of the total population of the 25 largest metropolitan areas was living in suburbs that were very stressed, poor, and almost totally segregated with very low revenue capacity and very high expenditure needs. Forty percent of the population in Orfield's study lived in suburbs with revenue capacity ranging from low to very low and expenditure needs ranging from high to very high.

Hanlon (2010) focuses on inner-ring suburbs, defined as those places located contiguous with or adjacent to a central city and where more than half of housing was built before 1969. Her typology described different types of inner-ring suburbs (wealthy, elite, ethnic, middle class, declining, and in-crisis). She examined inner-ring suburbs in the 100 most-populated urban areas in the United States and compares them to their newer outer suburban counterparts. Her work focuses on regional variations and inner-ring suburbs in decline.

Using a national sample, Hanlon found that two-thirds of suburbs in crisis were inner-ring suburbs. While she found extreme cases of increased poverty among inner-ring suburbs in all regions of the country, the Midwest and the South had the highest proportion of inner-ring suburbs in crisis. Many of these were once home to manufacturing workers and were industrial in nature. Hanlon also found that "suburbs with high levels of poverty tended to be suburbs with high concentrations of minorities. In particular, these suburbs, more likely inner-ring than outer ring, became poorer over time" (Hanlon 2010: 153). In many of these suburbs, racial transition occurred from 1980 to 2000.

Hanlon's (2010) examination suggests that the forces shaping inner-ring suburbs include housing market dynamics, demographics, labor-market restructuring, and metropolitan fragmentation. For example, she found that housing age is important. Almost half the housing stock in declining inner-ring suburbs was built between 1950 and 1969, typically called postwar housing. Yet, almost one in three houses in advancing or relatively strong inner-ring suburbs were built before 1939. Older housing possesses a certain cachet, while postwar housing is becoming functionally and architecturally obsolete. Hanlon concluded that some suburbs resemble poor inner-city neighborhoods and suggested the need to look beyond traditional notions of cities and suburbs and recognize that decline is not urban or suburban, but metropolitan. New theories of metropolitan growth, decline, and transformation are needed along with new tools and strategies to improve these suburbs.

Puentes and Orfield (2002) and Puentes and Warren (2006) also used a national framework for their work on first suburbs (although Puentes and Orfield (2002) focused on the Northeast and the Midwest). The methodologies used county-level data and divide counties with first suburbs into first suburbs, primary cities, and newer suburbs. They used the term "first suburbs" to define places just outside central cities that were part of metropolitan America before 1950.

Puentes and Warren (2006) found that first suburbs were home to 52.4 million people in 2000, 18.6 percent of the population, including 29 percent of the foreign born. First suburbs now have more foreign-born residents (9.0 million) than their primary cities (8.6 million). First suburbs have largely retained their position as home to some of the most highly educated and wealthy residents; they also have the highest shares of residents with white-collar jobs and the highest house values.

Yet, even these places face challenges including a declining population, greater disparities between races and ethnicities in education and income, growing rates of poverty, and stagnant incomes. While the number of high-poverty neighborhoods is dropping sharply in urban areas, it is increasing at an alarming rate in the first suburbs. Three-quarters of the first suburbs saw an increase in the percentage of their census tracts with at least a 20 percent poverty rate from 1970 to 2000.

Like Hanlon (2010), Puentes and Warren's (2006) analysis is regional. Yet, first suburbs may be hampered in developing a common policy agenda by their own heterogeneity. Regional differences abound. Puentes and Warren concluded that first suburbs in the Northeast and Midwest are almost exclusively slow- or no-growth places with a high proportion of non-Hispanic Whites, especially in Ohio, Pennsylvania, and upstate New York, while their counterparts in the Sun Belt and Western states have been growing in recent decades. Suburban populations in the Northeast and Midwest are older and live in smaller households than those of the Sun Belt. The aging population brings challenges in housing, transportation, and health care. Further, the increasing foreign-born population needs to be economically and socially integrated.

These typologies are useful in illustrating the diversity among suburbs and contribute to understanding that different types of suburbs have different characteristics and different needs. It places into context our focus on severely distressed, older suburbs of post-manufacturing cities, which is a small subset of all suburbs.

Data and Methods

This study focuses on suburbs that once were thriving but are now severely distressed and have limited capacity to respond to increasing needs. Three indicators were used to analyze how distressed each suburb is: the poverty rate, the unemployment rate, and the foreclosure rate.[1]

To identify these suburbs, the authors started with a database of all cities and villages in the United States with populations of at least 2,500 in 2000, excluding small central cities that were part of larger metropolitan areas, resulting in a total of 4,066 suburbs. Next, *m*-scores were calculated for these suburbs. *M*-scores are similar to *z*-scores, which quantitatively measure a data point's deviation from the population mean, divided by the standard deviation of the distribution. The higher the value for *z*, the farther the value is from the mean of the distribution.

In the case of the variables of interest in this study, namely poverty, unemployment, and foreclosure rates, the larger the value of *z*, the more distressed the suburb is. However, using the *z*-score, our distributions of poverty, unemployment, and foreclosure rates are skewed to the right. Thus, the mean is susceptible to these outliers, making the mean higher than the median value. Also, the standard deviation will be large relative to the mean, since it is influenced by outliers as well.

Adjustments were made to deal with such skewed data. We measure the deviation of one suburb from the mean of the entire population of suburbs. More specifically, instead of transforming the data based on the mean, our transformation

---

1 Poverty and unemployment data for 2000 were extracted from place-level data sets available at the Minnesota Population Center: National Historical Geographic Information System, at http://www.nhgis.org. Foreclosure data for 2007 through June 2008 were extracted from the HUD User site at http://www.huduser.org/portal/datasets/nsp_foreclosure_data.html. Data were downloaded separately for each state.

is based on the median, based on Hill, Wolman, and Brennan (1998) and Furdell, Wolman, and Hill (2005). In the case of this particular transformation, the median is not susceptible to the magnitude of extreme outliers. The alternative transformation is called an m-score. A major advantage of the m-score is that the information generated by an outlier is retained in relation to the true center of the distribution without biasing the measure of other components in the formula. The m-score has the advantage of being interpreted in a manner similar to the z-score, that is, in terms of the number of standard deviations from the center of the distribution. In the case of the z-score, the center is the mean. For the m-score, the center is the median.

For the purposes of this study, "most distressed" suburbs were those having m-score values above 1.5 for each of the three indicators of distress: poverty rate, unemployment rate, and foreclosure rate.

Using an m-score threshold of 1.5 yielded 168 suburbs, or 4.13 percent, as most distressed from the initial pool of 4,066 suburbs. These 168 suburbs represented a total population of 4.1 million in 2000, which is 6 percent of the total suburban population of 68.3 million in our subset of 4,066 suburbs.

The contexts in which these suburbs operate are varied, depending on such factors as the age of the suburb, its economic and demographic history, and other variables. To better understand the different suburban contexts, the authors grouped the 168 most-distressed suburbs by population and economic trends. Table 10.1 below illustrates the six different types of places. Regional economic trends were measured using m-score values for inflation-adjusted percentage change in gross domestic product (GDP) per capita from 1980 to 2009[2] for the core-based statistical area (CBSA) in which the suburb is located. The top row contains grouped suburbs where the regional economy grew at a rate that was above the overall median rate of growth ("fast-growth suburbs"), whereas the bottom row contains grouped suburbs where the regional economy grew at a rate that was below the overall median rate of growth, or where the regional economy declined ("slow-growth suburbs").

Population trends from 1980 to 2000 were measured in terms of absolute population loss, slow population growth (below the median rate, i.e., a negative m-score), and fast population growth (above the median rate, i.e., a positive m-score), displayed in the columns of Table 10.1.[3]

One would expect that most-distressed suburbs in regions with fast-growth economies might show some benefits from the regional growth—a rising tide lifting all boats. Conversely, most-distressed suburbs in regions with slow-growth economies might face additional challenges.

---

2   Data taken from Moody's Economy.com for 1980 and 2009 and from the 1980, 1990, and 2000 U.S. Censuses. The 2009 GDP was used to capture any impact from the recession.

3   Data taken from 1980 to 2000 U.S. Censuses.

Table 10.1   Most-Distressed Suburbs Classification by Per Capita GDP and Total Population Change

	Population Change, 1980–2000		
	Absolute Population Loss	**Population Growth but Below the Median (Negative *M*-score)**	**Population Growth Above the Median (Positive *M*-score)**
M-score for Inflation- + adjusted % Change in GDP per capita, 1980–2009	*Bucket 4* (N=40) (Pop=875,757)	*Bucket 5* (N=7) (Pop=305,860)	*Bucket 6* (N=6) (Pop=111,531)
−	*Bucket 1* (N=26) (Pop=339,509)	*Bucket 2* (N=13) (Pop=258,598)	*Bucket 3* (N=76) (Pop=2,182,583)
	Total N=168, Total Population=4,073,838		

Source: Hexter et al. (2011).

Of the six groupings, by far the largest number of suburbs (76, or about 45 percent) was in Group 3. These suburbs are in four states: California (58), Texas (8), Arizona (3), and Florida (7). Each of these suburbs is likely growing because of immigration but is located in a region experiencing below-median growth in per capita GDP. The second largest number of suburbs fell into Group 4, which represents suburbs in fast-growth economic regions but with absolute losses in population.

We were most interested in a small subset of distressed suburbs, those with majority (i.e., more than 50 percent) non-Hispanic White populations and an older housing stock (i.e., median year housing built was pre-1968). This further narrowed our pool of potential study subjects to 65 suburbs. We decided to further narrow our focus to those most-distressed suburbs that had lost population from 1980 to 2000, which limited the selection to groups 1 and 4. The four case study suburbs were selected from those most-distressed suburbs that had a proportion of residents of color higher than 50 percent, had a pre-1968 housing stock, and had lost population from 1980 to 2000.

Research Question 1: Selecting Case Study Suburbs

In consultation with the project partners (the Urban Institute, the U.S. Department of Housing and Urban Development, Office of Policy Development and Research, and the Brookings Institute), we selected two suburbs from regions with slow-growing economies, where one was a direct entitlement[4] community of the U.S.

---

4   Under the U.S. Department of Housing and Urban Development Community Development Block Grant Entitlement Communities Grants, eligible grantees are as follows:
*   principal cities of Metropolitan Statistical Areas (MSAs);
*   other metropolitan cities with populations of at least 50,000; and

Department of Housing and Urban Development and one was not, and two suburbs from regions with fast-growing economies, where one was a direct entitlement community and one was not.

Cities in slow-growing economic regions (Group 1):

- East Cleveland, Ohio (U.S. Department of Housing and Urban Development [HUD] direct entitlement grantee)
- Inkster, Michigan (nonentitlement grantee)

Cities in fast-growing economic regions (Group 4):

- Chester, Pennsylvania (HUD direct entitlement grantee)
- Prichard, Alabama (nonentitlement grantee)

These are distressed suburbs, predominantly of color, of older, large industrial cities, some of which have special designations as direct entitlement cities. Special designation entitles these municipalities to receive Community Development Block Grant and Home Investment Partnerships (HOME) monies directly, without meeting the more typical 50,000-population cutoff for this designation. It is the result of the so-called Stokes Amendment, sponsored by the Congressional Black Caucus and Ohio Rep. Louis Stokes in the late 1980s. This designation was made to address the challenges faced by these places.[5]

Demographic and Socioeconomic Characteristics of Case Study Suburbs

We used the Neighborhood Change Database (NCDB), 1970–2000,[6] to conduct a background data analysis for each of the four case study suburbs and to compare each suburb with the other suburbs in its cell of Table 10.1. The NCDB provides data from the 1970 through the 2000 Censuses at the census tract level that are

---

- qualified urban counties with populations of at least 200,000 (excluding the population of entitled cities) (HUD.GOV website).

Other cities, including East Cleveland and Chester, were designated grantees as a result of a statutory amendment sponsored by the Congressional Black Caucus (CBC) in the late 1980s. This designation provided Community Development Block Grant (CDBG) and HOME monies directly to a handful of majority-minority cities, even though their populations fell below the 50,000 cutoff noted above.

5   According to information provided by the HUD Office of Policy Development and Research, 264 cities with populations below 50,000 were designated direct entitlement cities in 2010.

6   Author calculations, based on the Neighborhood Change Database (Peter Tatian, Census CD Neighborhood Change Database 1970–2000 Tract Data Users' Guide, Long Form Release [Washington, DC: The Urban Institute, 2003]. Retrieved December 9, 2010, from http://www.geolytics.com/pdf/NCDB-LF-Data-Users-Guide.pdf).

standardized, that is, comparable. Census tract data were aggregated to municipal boundaries and then reported for each case study city and summarized for each group. Acknowledging potential aggregation issues going from the census tract geography to the municipal geography, we think that these aggregated data are still useful for broader context and comparison.

Group 1. East Cleveland, Ohio, and Inkster, Michigan

All 26 suburbs in this group experienced an absolute population loss between 1980 and 2000 and were in regions that had slow economic growth (i.e., negative *m*-scores based on inflation-adjusted percentage change in GDP per capita between 1980 and 2009).

Both East Cleveland and Inkster have larger populations than the average within this group, but both have been losing population consistently since 1970. The rate of population loss is roughly on par with the group as a whole—slightly faster in East Cleveland, slightly slower in Inkster.

Taken together, the average racial composition for all 26 suburbs in this group is roughly 80 percent Black/African American and 20 percent non-Hispanic White. East Cleveland and Inkster differ substantially from this profile. East Cleveland is 94 percent Black/African American (an increase higher than 60 percent since 1970) and 5 percent non-Hispanic White (a nearly 90 percent decrease since 1970). In 2000, less than 1 percent of East Cleveland's population was Latino.

Inkster, on the other hand, was 26 percent non-Hispanic White in 2000 (a decrease larger than 50 percent from 1970 to 2000) and 69 percent Black/African American (an increase higher than 55 percent from 1970 to 2000). Inkster's Latino population was roughly 2 percent. The remainder of the population belonged to other races.

While none of the 26 suburbs differ considerably on the percentage of population who are elderly or children (within 3–4 percent of the group averages of 11 and 30 percent, respectively), their rates of change differ from each other and from the average. For the suburbs in Group 1, the elderly population has increased 14 percent since 1970; in East Cleveland, it increased 24 percent, and in Inkster, it increased 117 percent. Since 1970, the average percentage of the population age 18 and under for this group has decreased 15 percent, but it decreased only 3 percent in East Cleveland and 28 percent in Inkster. Inkster is clearly gaining elderly and losing youth residents at much greater rates than East Cleveland and the group average.

The case study suburbs also differ from the other suburbs in Group 1 on the shares of all households with children that are headed by females. The average for the 26 suburbs is 60 percent, whereas the comparable percentages for East Cleveland and Inkster are 65 percent and 50 percent, respectively. The percentages are increasing faster than the average in both cases.

The 26 suburbs in Group 1 had an average poverty rate of 31 percent and an average elderly poverty rate of 20 percent. The average percentage of households receiving public assistance is 25 percent. East Cleveland's poverty and elderly poverty rates are slightly (within 4 percent) above this average for the group. Inkster's poverty rate is lower than the average rate for the group. Inkster has a 20 percent poverty rate and 13 percent elderly poverty rate. Somewhat surprisingly, both suburbs have lower percentages of households receiving public assistance than the average in Group 1, with Inkster at 17 percent and East Cleveland at 22 percent. The rates in both suburbs, however, have grown dramatically since 1970.

Inkster has a lower unemployment rate than the average of Group 1 (10 percent versus 14 percent), and its rate has grown more slowly than the group's average since 1970 (67 percent versus 88 percent). The opposite is true for East Cleveland. Its unemployment rate, 15 percent, has grown 208 percent since 1970.

Inkster has a higher percentage of owner-occupied homes (54 percent) than Group 1 on average (40 percent) or East Cleveland (30 percent). These percentages, however, might have changed dramatically since the beginning of the housing crisis.

Group 4. Chester, Pennsylvania, and Prichard, Alabama

All 40 suburbs in Group 4 experienced absolute population loss, similar to Group 1, but were located in regions with fast economic growth (i.e., positive *m*-scores for inflation-adjusted percentage change in GDP per capita from 1980 to 2009). Chester, with a population of 36,854 in 2000, and Prichard, at 28,050, both have a population larger than the average population for the suburbs in this group. The rate of population decline from 1980 to 2000 is similar to the average in this group (30 percent): 35 percent in Chester and 29 percent in Prichard. However, since the average population of the other suburbs in this group is much smaller than Chester or Prichard, the rates of population decline, while similar, actually mean much larger absolute population losses for the case study sites.

Chester and Prichard are similar in terms of diversity of their populations to the other suburbs in their group. In 2000, Chester was 19 percent non-Hispanic White and Prichard was 18 percent non-Hispanic White, while the average proportion was 19 percent. Chester's Black/African American population was 77 percent, Prichard's was 81 percent, and the average of Group 4 was 80 percent Black/African American. Chester's Black/African American population increased 71 percent between 1970 and 2000 (the average of Group 4 is 71 percent), while Prichard's increased 55 percent. Both suburbs are losing non-Hispanic White population at rates very near the mean of 64 percent.

The average percentage of Latino residents in this group is low, at 1.4 percent. Prichard's population is less than 1 percent Latino, while Chester's population is 5.4 percent Latino. Both case study sites have larger increases from 1970 to 2000 than the average, though: 200 percent for Prichard and nearly 300 percent for Chester, versus the average of 131 percent. In absolute numbers, however, these percentages still translate to very small Latino populations in 2000: 187 in Prichard and 2,003 in Chester.

Both case study suburbs have shares of elderly residents and youth similar to the shares in Group 4, with less than 1 percent differences from the mean on either variable for either suburb. The change in the elderly population in both cities, however, differs from the group average. Since 1970, the average increase in the percentage of elderly for the group has been 26 percent. In Chester it was only 14 percent, while in Prichard it was 59 percent.

In Chester, the share of population age 18 and under decreased from 1970 to 2000 by 13 percent, a rate very close to the group average. The share in Prichard decreased 23 percent.

The share of households with children that are headed by females is similar to the group average in both suburbs. But, between 1970 and 2000, the proportion of female-headed families grew substantially by an average of 156 percent for all 40 suburbs in this group, including Prichard; it grew more slowly in Chester, at 122 percent.

While Chester's poverty rate of 27 percent is about the average of Group 4, Prichard's poverty rate is higher than the group average, at 34 percent. Additionally, elderly poverty is greater than average (17 percent) in both Chester (22 percent) and Prichard (25 percent). The share of households receiving public assistance is slightly below the average in both cases, while the growth in this percentage in both cities was well below the average of 147 percent in Group 4: Chester's grew by 49 percent and Prichard's by 68 percent.

In Chester, unemployment is roughly two percent higher than the average. Unemployment in Chester grew faster than the group average (222 percent versus 155 percent). In Prichard, unemployment and its growth are comparable to the averages for the group as a whole. The homeownership rate in Chester is less than the group average (41 percent versus 48 percent), but the rate in Prichard is greater than average, at 53 percent. Similar to the point made above, these percentages, however, might have changed dramatically since the beginning of the housing crisis.

Fiscal Characteristics of Case Study Suburbs

We also analyzed the finances of each of these suburbs and find that Chester, East Cleveland, Inkster, and Prichard face financial challenges common to many aging inner-ring suburbs. These challenges are compounded by histories of mismanagement in East Cleveland, Chester, and Prichard. The city manager form of government in Inkster seems to have somewhat insulated this community from management issues.

Governments use a particular accounting style that separates the type of activities into separate ledgers or funds. There are two broad types of funds relevant for our analysis: governmental and proprietary funds. Governmental funds include a range of specific funds that tend to encompass all general government operations—this might include public safety, human resources, finance, management, and parks and recreation, for example. The General Fund is the largest of the governmental

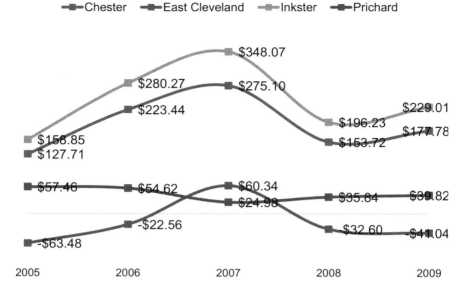

**Figure 10.1   General Fund Balance per Capita for Case Study Cities,
2005–09 (2011 Dollars)**

Source: Hexter et al. (2011)

funds and typically includes all but a few of.the activities generally considered government operations.

The second broad type of fund is proprietary funds. These are distinct from governmental funds in that they account for a government's business-like activities— the services for which fees are collected to cover the cost of operations. These might include water and sewer, transit systems, golf courses, and convention centers.

The General Fund balance per capita is a barometer of the available financial resources in a government, while the common size ratio can be used to measure the size of governmental activities. The latter measure includes the General Fund and other governmental funds but excludes enterprise funds and proprietary funds such as water and sewer and trash facilities in case municipalities run these as business-like activities, which not all governments do.[7]

The General Fund balance per capita measures a different aspect than the common size ratio by more closely examining how much cash or liquid assets the municipality has on hand at that given point in time—but it does not control for the size of the government, rather it controls for the population size. Figure 10.1

---

7 Government Finance Officers Association (GFOA), "Best Practice: Appropriate Level of Unrestricted Fund Balance in the General Fund (2002 and 2009) (BUDGET and CAAFR)" (Chicago: GFOA, 2009). http://www.gfoa.org/downloads/ AppropriateLevelUnrestrictedFundBalanceGeneralFund_BestPractice.pdf.

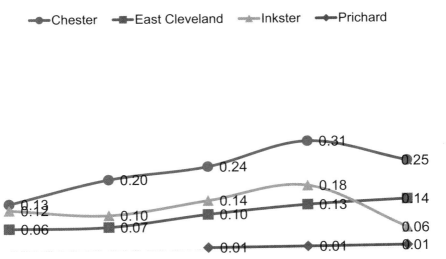

2005   2006   2007   2008   2009

**Figure 10.2   Common Size Ratio for All Governmental Funds, Case Study
                Sites, 2005–09**

Source: Hexter et al. (2011).

above demonstrates that Chester and Inkster are in better financial shape than East
Cleveland and Prichard, which have unsustainable financial situations. The latter
two are near or below zero dollars General Fund balance per resident, an indicator
that these two municipalities are at or near financial insolvency. Prichard's numbers
are actually much worse than reported because the city stopped paying pension
benefits to its retirees in 2009 and only recently restarted those payments. Both
cities require significant overhauls of their operations. Prichard recently filed for
bankruptcy, but the court denied the filing. The State of Ohio Auditor, David Yost,
issued a "Declaration of Fiscal Caution" for the city of East Cleveland on January
5, 2012.[8] This declaration gives the State of Ohio much more control over how the
city is financed and managed and is another strong indicator that East Cleveland's
financial condition is unsustainable.

   A frequent method for comparing organizations or governments is to use the
common size ratio. This ratio is useful to study the comparative sizes of similarly
sized organizations' financial structures. Here, the common size ratio, which

---

   8   http://www.auditor.state.oh.us/auditsearch/Reports/2012/City_of_East_Cleveland_
Fiscal_Caution_Declaration.pdf

measures the amount of available cash relative to total assets, was used to compare the four suburbs.

The larger the common size ratio, the more cash is on hand relative to total assets. A smaller common size ratio could indicate that the government is underfunded. As Figure 10.2 above illustrates, the governments of the four suburbs have differing common size ratios. These differences could stem from a desire for a more limited government or from being vastly underfunded. It also illustrates the trends in the size of governmental funds for each. The declines of the common size ratios of both Chester and Inkster are likely linked to the broader decline in the U.S. economy since 2007. What can be taken away from the movement in the common size ratio is that some governments, Prichard for example, are woefully and consistently underfunded, while others, like Chester and Inkster, are demonstrating how progress towards financial stability can be devastated during an economic downturn.

A closer look at the financial statements of the four suburbs reveals that Prichard has very little available cash, particularly compared with its total assets. Inkster has a much smaller collection of assets in its governmental funds than Prichard, but it has nearly twice as much available cash as Prichard. This means that Prichard will likely have more assets (e.g., vehicles, buildings, and infrastructure) to maintain and pay for over time but very little cash to pay for them. Meanwhile, Inkster has a smaller array of assets to maintain but sufficient cash to cover those expenses.

While there is not one single tool that can provide an assessment of financial condition, taken together it is clear that none of these municipalities is in good financial condition, even if some are in better shape than others. East Cleveland and Prichard have the most systemic financial and budgetary problems. Three of the four municipalities are in or have been in some form of fiscal emergency in the past decade; only Inkster has thus far avoided such a status.

Unfunded long-term liabilities, such as pensions and other post-employment benefits (OPEB), are a concern for all four study sites and will be their biggest long-term challenge to surviving as distinct political entities. Chester has an unfunded OPEB liability of $114 million and an unfunded pension liability of about $27 million. To put these dollar amounts in context, Chester's General Fund operating budget for FY2011 was $41.6 million, about 36 percent of the OPEB obligation and about 154 percent of the pension liability. East Cleveland has an unfunded liability payable to the state pension system of about $1.4 million per year for the next 25 years. East Cleveland's FY2009 budget was nearly $20 million—with the pension liability totaling about 7 percent of its annual General Fund budget, and this does not include the additional pension liability it would incur each year. Inkster's pension system is more than adequately funded, but it has an unfunded OPEB liability of $27.8 million. Its General Fund budget appropriation for FY2010/11 was nearly $19 million, or about equal to the OPEB liability. And Prichard has an estimated $17 million unfunded pension liability, but this estimate was generated in 2003 and has not been updated. It is possible that the amount of the unfunded pension liability is now much larger. The FY2009 expenditures for Prichard were $11.1 million or about 65 percent of its known unfunded liability.

Research Question 2: Lessons from the Four Case Study Suburbs

"I truly hope this [study] will help small cities"
— Hilliard Hampton II, mayor of Inkster

Members of the research team made site visits and conducted interviews with public officials and other key stakeholders in all four case study suburbs. The detailed case studies offer a window into the dynamic forces that have shaped and are shaping these four suburbs. They illustrate how each city is dealing with challenges on the ground. Below we will discuss select topics, such as (a) race, ethnicity, and context, (b) housing and community development, (c) concentrated poverty, (d) lack of trust, (e) anchor institutions, (f) education, (g) local government capacity, (h) regional collaboration, and (i) state programs. At the end of most subsections we discuss what works and what does not work.

Race and Context

The current context in which the four suburbs operate is, to some extent, a legacy of the racial prejudice and institutional discrimination based on race and ethnicity, for example, in housing, employment, and politics, which characterized many American cities before the civil rights movement. Just as the Civil Rights Act ended segregation and opened up housing and employment opportunities for people of color in the 1960s and 1970s, American manufacturing began its decline.

These forces combined to bring about rapid racial and ethnic change in all four case study cities. All lost total population at a fairly alarming rate between 1970 and 2000, the same period in which they underwent racial and ethnic transition. Only Chester's population loss began to slow between 2000 and 2010. All four suburbs have high poverty rates along with high unemployment rates and high economic segregation. None of the four case study sites is benefiting from immigration.

Although the dynamics of White flight played out slightly differently in each suburb, all faced challenges. We found stories of "land grabs," formally called annexations, by neighboring cities (Inkster and Prichard), blockbusting (East Cleveland), and segregation in housing (East Cleveland, Chester, Inkster, Prichard) and workplaces (Chester, Prichard, Inkster). East Cleveland experienced what Keating calls the classic "invasion and succession" story of integration (Keating 1994: 77). Inkster was the community where Henry Ford's Black auto workers lived, and Chester's segregated shipyards were the subject of intense national debate about employment opportunity versus discrimination. Both Inkster and Prichard experienced "land grabs"—Inkster by neighboring Dearborn Heights and

Prichard by Mobile—resulting in significant losses of tax base. In the 1940s and 1950s Inkster residents were asked to vote on incorporation as a city several times, but they voted it down. A portion of what was then the Village of Inkster separated into northern and southern Dearborn Heights, formerly Dearborn Township. To become a city, Dearborn Heights needed a contiguous land mass and took a small strip of Inkster's land to connect the two parts of the township. Years later Inkster sued, and Dearborn Heights was ordered to compensate Inkster for the land taken. The Dearborn Heights "land grab" motivated Inkster residents to vote to incorporate as a city in 1964 to prevent future losses.

The annexation of the Plateau area of Prichard by Mobile in the early 1970s was a defining and, some say, racially motivated incident in Prichard's recent history. Adjacent to Mobile Bay, Plateau was predominantly Black/African American, and some attribute the annexation to an effort by non-Hispanic White political leaders to reduce the number of Black/African American voters in Prichard and retain non-Hispanic White control of city politics.

These suburbs were clearly affected by race relations in the United States. How strongly race continues to influence development these days is less clear, however. Some people we interviewed see current problems more as class discrimination, while others see racial discrimination continuing to play a role.

Housing and Community Development

One of the questions for this study was how city officials view the importance of the direct entitlement designation by HUD. Officials from the two direct entitlement cities (East Cleveland and Chester) are very clear about its importance. They see it as a much-needed source of funds that can be used for code enforcement, demolition, foreclosure prevention, public safety, street repair and street lighting, redevelopment, public services, public works, and other expenditures. The predictability of the funds makes longer-term budget planning possible.

The two nonentitlement cities (Prichard and Inkster) do not enjoy the same level of predictability and have a lower level of funding. They are competing with other cities to receive block grant and HOME monies through their county governments, which administer the funds. City officials in Inkster and Prichard stated that "they use our poverty and don't give us the money" and "Our voice is not heard." These comments illustrate their frustration. The Community Development Block Grant (CDBG) program formula gives more money to areas of high poverty. The perception is that the high poverty rates in these municipalities raise the poverty rate in the county in which they are located. Although the county receives monies from HUD, it is very difficult for the municipalities to lobby the counties for enough block grant and HOME monies to meet their needs.

In 2010, East Cleveland was allocated about $1.1 million in block grant and $500,000 in HOME funds. East Cleveland also received $1.68 million in Neighborhood Stabilization Program (NSP) funds. In 2010, Chester's allocation was $1.5 million in block grant and $470,000 in HOME monies. Compared to 2009, these monies represent a 16.2 percent reduction in block grant funding and a 12.5 percent reduction in HOME funding. In 2010, Chester received $586,000 in NSP funds. In contrast, in 2010, Inkster received $350,000 in block grant funds and $40,000 in other federal housing funds. The same year, Prichard received about $300,000 of these funds through Mobile County. Despite these monies, all cities have insufficient funds to meet necessary capital outlays.

The four suburbs have varying capacities to administer their block grant money effectively. Chester and Prichard administer their funds through quasigovernmental authorities,[9] which seem to provide a higher level of fiscal and management capacity. While both East Cleveland and Chester are entitlement cities, they have sometimes mismanaged their block grant dollars, offering two contrasting examples of how to address this problem, as described below.

From the late 1980s to 2004, East Cleveland had difficulty effectively managing its block grant and HOME allocations. Its community development director in the late 1980s, who later served seven years as mayor (1997–2004), was convicted on federal charges of racketeering and corruption in 2004 and sentenced to nine years in prison. Despite specific recommendations by the state auditor (Petro 2002) when the city was in fiscal emergency (from 1988 to 2006) to institute tighter spending controls in the Department of Community Development and Building Services, East Cleveland continued business as usual. The Department continued to experience high staff turnover, low salaries, and, in some cases, corruption and incompetence. When Mayor Gary Norton took office in 2010, one of his first acts was to assign his chief of staff to run the department. She was able to effect some changes, and, for the first time in 10 years, the city was able to spend its block grant money on time. In early 2011, the city was able to attract and hire an experienced community development director.

The Chester Housing Authority (CHA) had a history of mismanagement and corruption that led to HUD designating it a "troubled" authority in 1991. CHA has been operating under court receivership since 1994 as a result of a lawsuit brought by public housing residents asserting "constructive abandonment." Residents claimed that the units were in such disrepair that they were uninhabitable.

Inkster's housing authority, like the housing authorities in the other cities, has worked to modernize and renovate public housing units. East Cleveland, like all cities in Cuyahoga County, is served by the Cuyahoga Metropolitan Housing Authority (CMHA); it does not have its own housing authority. Also, officials in all four case study cities feel that they have more than their fair share of affordable housing and need some market-rate housing to attract higher-income residents in the future.

9　Chester's Economic Development Authority and Prichard's Housing Authority.

What Policies and Strategies Work?

In the case of Chester, its Economic Development Authority (CEDA), a quasigovernmental authority, has been the vehicle for delivering community, economic, and housing development services in this community since 1995. CEDA was established to reorganize economic and community development within Chester after HUD froze the city's CDBG funds for five years due to mismanagement. Creating CEDA enabled Chester to implement effective management practices and to retain consistent long-term leadership that is somewhat insulated from city politics while still under city control. CEDA has a separate board appointed by the mayor and city council.

In the case of Prichard, the Housing Authority has become the de facto redevelopment authority and community development agency for this community. It is in a stronger financial position than the city for two reasons: its pension fund is separate from the city's, and, in addition to block grant and other HUD funds, it has created several income streams from its homeownership and housing development programs. Most recently, the Housing Authority applied for and received $20 million in Program for Revitalization of Severely Distressed Public Housing (HOPE VI) funds and $20 million in NSP2 funds to create a land bank and build 75 units for homeowners and 50 units for renters. More specifically, the NSP2 dollars will be used to develop 30 rental properties in the highly distressed Alabama Village area and 20 new rental properties in other distressed census tracts. The Prichard Housing Authority uses a consultant who is experienced in writing successful HUD proposals to obtain needed funds.

Concentrated Poverty

The new, growing body of research about older, distressed suburbs has identified a number of issues, especially concentrated poverty (Kneebone and Garr 2010). Each of the four case study suburbs has experienced several factors that contribute to the concentration of poverty, for example, (a) increasing poverty over decades, (b) one or more forms of physical, social, racial, or ethnic forms of isolation from the larger economy and community, or (c) significant demographic and socioeconomic changes resulting from the formation of single-parent households, the aging of the population, or low educational attainment, among other factors (Berube, Erickson, and Reid 2008).[10]

In addition, there is the question of how extensively HUD policies contribute to concentrating poverty by targeting affordable housing dollars and programs to underserved, low-income neighborhoods. Chester, for example, would like to be able to use HUD funds to attract middle- and upper-income households to the city.

---

10   None of our four case study cities experienced immigration in significant numbers. We intentionally did not look at cities with large immigrant populations.

Berube et al. (2008) suggest that relatively strong regional economic growth is not enough to lift these places out of poverty. This is true for Prichard and, to some extent, Chester, the two case study suburbs that are located in the Mobile and Philadelphia regions, respectively. While these regions have relatively strong economic growth, Prichard and Chester have not experienced the same level of economic benefits from this growth as their more prosperous primary cities, especially in regard to access to jobs for residents.

All four case study suburbs are isolated in terms of many aspects: economically, socially, perceptually, politically, and physically. In regard to the latter aspect, the four case study sites are isolated; even though people may drive through these communities every day, they rarely have an occasion to drive to them. Also, many residents are isolated from regional economic opportunities. Prichard, for example, has not yet had many successes, despite recent collaborative efforts around economic development starting in the early to mid-2000s. In an effort to embrace a more regional approach and to attract new development to increase the city's tax base, the mayor recently entered into a partnership with the neighboring municipality of Saraland, Mobile County, and the state of Alabama to attract a speedway on land with good freeway access in the largely undeveloped northern part of the city. He was lauded for taking the noisy motor sports park that other communities did not want. In December 2006, Prichard was selected as the site of the Alabama Motorsports Park, a Dale Earnhardt Jr. speedway and theme park. However, the economic downturn in the late 2000s put these plans on hold, the options on the land expired, and Saraland has repealed the 2 percent tax credit for its part of the property. Nevertheless, Prichard officials are still hopeful that the park, or some other use, will go forward on the site.

What Policies and Strategies Work?

Chester has begun to capture some growth through its riverfront economic development. For example, Chester used Pennsylvania's Keystone Opportunity Zone (KOZ) legislation, passed in 1998 and offering 15-year, 100 percent property tax abatement and other incentives, to attract developers for three new developments along its riverfront. The Wharf at Rivertown office building opened in 2006, Harrah's Chester Casino & Racetrack opened in 2007, and PPL Park, a Major League Soccer stadium that is home to the Philadelphia Union soccer club, opened in 2010. The KOZ, combined with strong local leadership, the advantage of location, and transportation investments, was key to launching this central piece of Chester's economic development strategy.

Additional state investment in predevelopment, infrastructure (i.e., two new Interstate 95 highway ramps leading to the waterfront development site), and environmental cleanup helped move these projects forward. The two new on/off-ramps connecting I-95 to the Chester waterfront were fully operational by summer 2011. The state has also invested in upgrading Pennsylvania Route 291, which runs along the waterfront. Chester's former mayor Dominic Pileggi is now State

Senate majority leader, which gives the city a strong voice at the state level. The new jobs created by Harrah's and the Wharf office building represent a 40 percent increase in private-sector jobs in the city and a significant diversification of the city's economy. A small percentage of these jobs were taken by Chester residents (David Scioccetti, personal communication, February 16, 2011).

These development projects are regional draws, attracting people to the city and bringing much-needed revenue to the city government. Although the KOZ provides a 15-year property tax abatement, Chester is able to collect income tax from the casino now. The agreement between the city and Harrah's guarantees the city $10 million minimum a year from the casino, about 25 percent of Chester's budget. In 2014, the casino and racetrack will start paying property tax.

While having a redevelopment or economic development authority does not guarantee that distressed cities will successfully address the problems associated with concentrated poverty, such a structure can be effective, provided cities can demonstrate that they can be trusted to follow through on commitments.

These two examples also point to the importance of organizational capacity, together with the staff experience and expertise required to sustain economic development efforts. CEDA played a key role in Chester's riverfront development, and the organization's long-time, experienced staff was able to sustain efforts on several complicated deals. Perhaps if Prichard had a similar economic development authority, its efforts to attract the motor sports park would have been more effective.

Lack of Trust

The four case study suburbs have faced varying types of governance challenges that include historical instances of corruption and mismanagement, redistributive politics, high turnover among city professional staff due to poor working environments and low wages, ineffective state and federal political representation, and a fragmented local government system combined with a lack of effective mechanisms that could foster joint public/private/nonprofit decision making.

Instances or periods of mismanagement or corruption at any level, such as the city, the school board, or the housing authority, can create a lingering atmosphere of distrust that can have long-term effects, making it difficult to carry out basic city functions. In such situations, city residents can lose trust in their government, city employees can lose the ability to perform their jobs effectively, potential partners can lose trust in the city, the city can lose its seat or its voice at the table, and potential developers can shy away.

Internally, city employees work for comparatively low pay in environments in which their ability to perform their job duties is limited by a lack of resources and hampered by mismanagement. To be effective in such an environment, a worker must either have a strong personal commitment to helping the city or be insulated from city politics through an authority or some other quasigovernmental entity.

Also, residents, anchor institutions, and other city stakeholders can lose trust in the government in these kinds of environments.

Externally, other cities and higher levels of government such as counties or states, as well as private investors and developers, are wary of collaborating or working with these cities. It becomes difficult for city leaders to have a seat at the table where decisions are made; if they have a seat, it becomes difficult for them to have an effective voice.

The current elected and appointed leaders of each of the four case study suburbs are committed to creating environments of integrity and trust. The importance of this goal cannot be overstated. They recognize that this process is slow and happens one demonstrated success at a time, for example, with Inkster's new state social services building; Chester's casino, soccer stadium, and office building; East Cleveland's new Huron Community Health Center; and Prichard's recent agreement on its pension fund. However, until outsiders' perceptions about these cities change, their ability to work with potential developers, undertake collaborative ventures, or engage in collaborative decision making with neighboring cities is severely limited. This may be one of the most critical issues in addressing the challenges of concentrated poverty, since it sets the context for most types of interventions, particularly as community development policies and programs increasingly require broad public-private partnerships and resident participation.

In regions with declining economies, competition for any new development is fierce. If cities cannot respond in a timely and professional manner to development opportunities, they will lose out to cities that can. Cities need to demonstrate that they are reliable partners and responsible stewards of public, philanthropic, and private funds or those funds will stop flowing.

What Policies and Strategies Work?

Inkster has demonstrated that it is a reliable development partner. In 2008, Michigan issued a bid for a new social services building in Inkster. The site selected was an old car dealership and a brownfield, located in a Tax Increment Finance Authority (TIFA) zone, a prime location in the city's long-dormant downtown area. The state selected a developer, Ronald Boji, to work with the city on the project. At the time, Boji was unfamiliar with Inkster but had a great deal of experience working for the state. When he began to work with the city, the city manager was changing, and the project had a rocky start. Once a new city manager was hired, things began to move more smoothly. From a developer's perspective, it was important that the city followed through and fulfilled commitments in a timely manner. Boji commented that his experience working with Inkster was positive, in part because Inkster had a sense of urgency not present in other cities (Ronald Boji, personal communication, February 15, 2011).

Inkster saw the office building as a catalyst for new development along its main street, Michigan Avenue. The entire development included a new Wayne

County district office of the Michigan Department of Human Services, the YWCA of Western Wayne County headquarters, and a new justice center for the Inkster Police Department and the 22nd District Court. The city strongly encouraged the developer to include a retail center of 10,000 square feet. The result is a new 32,000-square-foot, $25 million, LEED-certified human services building that opened in December 2010.

Boji thinks that there will eventually be a market for retail if the city can move the "hourly hotels" (Ronald Boji, personal communication, February 15, 2011). Once the new justice center opens, these hotels may voluntarily move. It is hoped that the new building will catalyze additional development in Inkster.

Anchor Institutions

Berube et al. (2008) note that unique histories and locational advantages such as proximity to anchor institutions and high-growth sectors can form the basis of a recovery strategy. All four cities have important locational advantages, including freeway access, parks and green space, access to transit, and, in the cases of Chester and East Cleveland, anchor institutions. However, to take advantage of these assets, city leaders must create atmospheres of trust. The most-distressed suburbs must change the context in which these assets are valued. In short, they must change how they operate.

For example, East Cleveland's greatest potential asset is its proximity to the anchor institutions in University Circle, a major employment center in the region for "eds and meds" and home to the region's two largest health systems, the Cleveland Clinic and University Hospitals, as well as Case Western Reserve University and Cleveland's major museums and cultural institutions. However, University Circle sits just across the border in the city of Cleveland, and East Cleveland has not been able to capture any spinoff investment from the tremendous investment taking place there. More than $3 billion in projects are planned or under way from downtown east to the Cleveland border, none of it crossing over into East Cleveland.

However, East Cleveland is trying to change that and to capitalize on its location. It is spending $750,000 of NSP dollars on acquisition, renovation, and resale of prime residential property in a targeted investment area that runs along Euclid Avenue and will be anchored by the new health center and the Louis Stokes Rapid Station of the Greater Cleveland Regional Transit Authority (RTA). The station is the end point of the RTA's $200 million bus rapid transit line connecting East Cleveland, through University Circle, to downtown Cleveland.

Developers have expressed an interest in East Cleveland because of its proximity to University Circle, but the city would have to offer huge subsidies to overcome multiple barriers including high crime rates, low levels of city services, fiscal mismanagement, and a general perception of city government as dysfunctional. The new mayor and his staff are working hard to change this perception and become known as a city that can make things happen. The city recently was awarded an opportunity to demonstrate that change is underway. In September 2011, a developer and University Circle, Inc., a Community Service Corporation serving University Circle, broke ground on a 20-unit townhouse project in East Cleveland. The $5 million development is just across the border from University Circle and is the first new housing built in East Cleveland in decades. The 20 apartments are heavily subsidized, with East Cleveland, Cuyahoga County, and the Cuyahoga County Land Bank contributing funds (McFee 2011).

The two largest anchors in East Cleveland are the Cleveland Clinic's Huron Road Hospital and General Electric. The Cleveland Clinic is investing $25 million to build the Huron Community Health Center in front of the Huron Hospital, which the Clinic plans to close and demolish, so the city will lose that anchor. General Electric is beginning to work more closely with the city and has entered into some small partnership projects under the leadership of Mayor Norton.

Case Western created the East Cleveland Partnership to work with the city on a number of community development and social service projects. While the partnership has some successful projects and relationships are being strengthened, it has not yet resulted in any economic development.

What Policies and Strategies Work?

The new spirit of collaboration between the public and private sectors in Chester involves the city and two of its largest employers and anchors. From the city's perspective, Crozer-Chester Medical Center and Widener University are assets and are being embraced. The anchors now see their futures as intertwined with that of the city, and they are demonstrating this by building physical connections such as a hotel and small commercial development instead of barriers. The positive impact of Widener and Crozer-Chester is evident in the northeastern section of the city. Crozer-Chester and Widener also partnered to open a satellite Chester police station near the institutions.

Widener and Crozer-Chester are also involved in economic development in Chester through the Institute for Economic Development, Inc. (IED), a private, nonprofit consortium that advocates to "enhance the city's economic, social and cultural climates while serving as a catalyst for future development." (Institute for Economic Development 2010). Through the IED, the two anchors partnered, along with the city of Chester, the Reinvestment Fund, Delaware County, and Teres Holdings LLC, on two development projects in northeast Chester. One is University Crossings, a residential and commercial development that includes a small, green Best Western hotel, the first hotel built in Chester in 35 years. The second is University Technology Park, a technology corridor between the Widener main campus and the Crozer-Chester Medical Center. The project is supported by the city of Chester, the Benjamin Franklin Technology Center, and the Economic Development Administration of the U.S. Department of Commerce.

Education

Inkster, Chester, and East Cleveland schools face the challenges of declining tax bases, fiscal mismanagement, low educational performance among students, and providing safe environments in which students can learn. All three cities have been or are still in fiscal emergency. Prichard is part of the Mobile County School District, which has not experienced the same level of problems as the other two cities, although the county district's graduation rate is about 50 percent. Interestingly, both Chester and Inkster had contracts with Edison Schools, a for-profit manager of public schools that was publicly traded on the NASDAQ from 2001 to 2005. The hope was that Edison Schools would turn the districts around, but in both cases the arrangements ended badly, and the contracts were not renewed.

The Chester Upland School District (CUSD) has also had no shortage of challenges, and it has ranked at or near the bottom of Pennsylvania's 501 school districts for more than two decades. In the 2009–10 school year, its graduation rate was 44 percent (Pennsylvania Department of Education 2011).

Charter schools provide an option for Chester parents, but, apart from the small Widener Partnership Charter School in Chester, it is not clear that they offer a much higher level of education. As long as their school districts continue to underperform, the cities will have difficulty attracting families.

What Strategies and Policies Work?

Historically, Inkster had a highly regarded school district. However, school quality began to deteriorate in the 1980s. By 1999, the district had a $1.4 million deficit (Schnaiberg 1999). In 2000, Inkster entered into a five-year contract with Edison Schools to forestall a rumored state takeover. However, the school board was not satisfied with how Edison was managing the schools and by 2002 was in a dispute with the company.

From 2002 to 2005, the district was placed under the oversight of a state emergency financial manager (EFM), who was given authority over all fiscal matters, supplanting the school board. Under the EFM, the district budget was balanced and a fund balance surplus was achieved for three consecutive years, after seven consecutive years of fund balance deficits. In addition, test scores on the Michigan Education Assessment Program increased significantly. The schools also met adequate yearly progress standards under the No Child Left Behind Act for two consecutive years, after having never complied with these standards.

Nevertheless, the Edison Schools contract was not renewed in 2005, and the Inkster Public School District is now back in the hands of the elected school board. Enrollment has increased from 1,400 in 2003 to 3,200 in 2010. Inkster now attracts students from Detroit who are looking for better schools, but it still faces mounting debt, reportedly close to $10 million.

Local Government Capacity

All four case study sites have had fiscal challenges. East Cleveland and Prichard are at or near fiscal insolvency. Chester, East Cleveland, and Prichard are or have been in some form of fiscal emergency in the past decade. In their analysis of policies to help distressed cities uncover their competitive advantages, Hill and Nowak (2002) explored the relationship between local management issues and fiscal insolvency. Their work is instructive for understanding some options available to strengthen the position of distressed suburbs as they look to the future. The following two quotes reflect Hill and Nowak's assessment of the problem. First, "distressed cities have histories of redistributive politics, including the use of public-sector operations and contracts as jobs machines, which are deeply entrenched. Moreover, distressed cities have operating bureaucracies whose personnel and strategies reflect decades of decline and low expectations about performance" (267). Second, "when probed, what appears to be corruption in public service is really the end result of incompetence, mismanagement, and a regulatory system that does not function" (268).

Hill and Nowak point out that distressed central cities have outdated tax structures, broken political cultures, uncompetitive staffing levels, vacant and abandoned land, and inappropriate arrays and mixes of public services.

Although Hill and Nowak are looking at central cities in their study, these characteristics of distress are evident in all four suburbs in our study. Hill and Nowak suggest a range of strategies to address these issues. First, they suggest that a well-functioning public-sector bureaucracy is necessary to reconnect distressed cities to their regional economies and provide the seedbed for development and opportunity. Further, they argue that meaningful administrative reform depends on making new arrangements with public-sector unions.

The four case study suburbs illustrate Hill's and Nowak's point that when cities cannot offer competitive wages and potential municipal employees do not see a career track because of political instability, they experience high staff turnover. However, all the suburbs except Prichard have unionized employees, and while the suburbs could point to instances where union rules were barriers to reorganizing specific functions, this did not emerge from the expert interviews and site visits as a high-priority issue.

Hill and Nowak (2002) also look at the importance of leadership in forming the social capital of a city. Whether leadership comes from foundations, nonprofit development organizations, or elite leadership in politics and the private sector, it sets the norms for a city. This returns us to the issue of integrity and trust, discussed above. All four mayors interviewed noted that effective leaders who can demonstrate integrity are needed to keep moving forward on the long-term civic agenda.

Meaningful reform for cities facing fiscal insolvency, according to Hill and Nowak, requires bringing in outside agents and possibly the state through a fiscal emergency commission. They argue that bringing in outside agents enables local politicians to shift the blame for necessary, painful restructuring to those agents. Reforms may need to include restructuring state and local taxes or new political leadership. For example, a new, dynamic, competent mayor can attract talented staff and make a great difference in attitudes, performance, and perceptions about the city. The problem is that he or she often does not have either the financial resources or the institutional flexibility to hire enough people to turn around the performance of the city. Thus, the mayor and any new staff can often only work at the margin of reform (Hill and Nowak 2002).

Moreover, Hill and Nowak (2002) point to some other options that have worked in larger cities. New mayors seeking reform have successfully used management improvement task forces to review city operations with an eye to staffing levels and competence. States can step in with loaned executives. Other reforms could include the creation of an entity such as a city or countywide land bank to address land assembly issues. These strategies might work in distressed suburbs as well.

The rate and magnitude of economic change, especially during the most recent recession, have made things worse for many suburbs. Our four case study suburbs have been hit harder than others that have more diversity in income and employment among their residents. In their current configurations, the case study sites have very little ability to respond to economic downturns. Their physical forms match outdated economic and social conditions. The jobs that provided most of their residents with working- or middle-class lifestyles no longer exist. The businesses that provided the property and income tax (where applicable) revenue are gone. While neighborhoods in each city have some high-quality, well-kempt housing, much of their older housing stock, especially workforce housing, is old and obsolete. White flight has turned to green flight as residents looking to move up are moving out.

Chester and East Cleveland have had state-appointed emergency fiscal managers with varying degrees of success. There is a question as to how far these managers can go, especially in restructuring city contracts. In Pennsylvania, for example, Act 47, Pennsylvania's Financially Distressed Communities Act, provides that a recovery plan be prepared by a state-appointed recovery coordinator in consultation with the city executive, legislature, and other stakeholders and adopted as a city ordinance. The mayor and the council continue to run the municipality while the coordinator ensures recovery plan implementation and helps build capacity for a return to independent governance.

The Act also gives the city the capacity to raise additional revenue through an income tax of up to three percent on city residents and up to two percent on nonresidents. The Chester mayor credits Act 47 with helping the city create a much-needed capital budget in 2010.

In 2006, Fairmount Capital Advisors Inc., Chester's recovery coordinator, reported that despite making some progress, Chester has remained a distressed community, with operating deficits in nine of the past ten years (Fairmount Capital Advisors 2006). Fairmount's five-year plan noted that improvements in the police department, fire department, and economic development had helped but stated that the city faced an extremely challenging situation. It projected continued deficits unless corrective measures were implemented and gaming revenues from the new Harrah's Chester Casino & Racetrack were realized as anticipated and spent wisely, in which case the city could have operating surpluses and new resources that would enable it to reduce tax rates and emerge from Act 47 status. While Chester has balanced its budget for the past three years, it has remained under Act 47.

What Policies and Strategies Work?

While state intervention has helped some cities in cases of fiscal emergency, it does not seem to have helped East Cleveland. In Chester, the impact of state intervention remains to be seen. The city continues to be in fiscal emergency, but it is beginning to bring its finances in order, mostly because of the casino revenue, as evidenced by the city's first capital budget enacted in 2011. The limits of state intervention are being tested in Michigan, where an interesting scenario is playing out. Michigan has granted more control to state-appointed emergency managers to undo, in some cases, provisions of union contracts. But Michigan residents have recently filed suit, claiming that the law violates the state constitution (Davey 2011).

Chester is rebuilding a public-private leadership group, the IED, discussed above, and is capitalizing on a new culture of collaboration and trust that enables it to tap leaders from anchor institutions and the private and nonprofit sectors to move the civic agenda forward. But to be effective, the relationship of trust and mutual benefit being built (and in some cases rebuilt) must be sustained.

The city manager form of government seems to serve Inkster well fiscally. Despite its shrinking tax base, lower amounts of revenue sharing from the state, and declining taxable property values, the city's finances have been managed well and, to date, services have not been cut and staff layoffs have been minimal. The state of Michigan rates the financial capacity of all cities using a fiscal indicator score,[11] which includes several factors. Based on 2009 data, Inkster rates 3 on a scale from 1 to 10, with 1 being the best rating. This puts Inkster at the midpoint among Wayne County cities. This is an accomplishment, considering the general finances of most cities in Michigan are weak. Inkster officials are proud of being able to provide a high level of fire and police services—"some of the best around," according to the mayor—as the city's police department prepares to apply to the Commission on Accreditation for Law Enforcement Agencies Inc., a process that takes up to three years to complete. Water and sewer service are provided regionally, under an agreement made in 1953. Garbage collection is contracted out.

---

11   See http://www.munetrix.com. The Southeast Michigan Council of Governments notes that the fiscal indicator score should be viewed as a coarse estimate. Although the Michigan fiscal indicator scoring system has come under much criticism, healthy communities tend to have low scores, and distressed communities tend to have high scores.

The city, through its TIFA, recently purchased a small building, refurbished it into a new city hall, and is building a new justice center. Recently, Inkster has forged a new, aggressive policy of going after grant funding. The city hired a state lobbyist to assist it in Lansing, and the city council is considering the same proactive attitude to assist the city in Washington, DC.

Regional Collaboration

Regional collaboration is an option that is under serious consideration and discussion in these cities as city leaders seek out new models of governance. Public officials in both East Cleveland and Prichard have questioned whether their cities can continue to function independently. At a Cleveland State University public forum on regional prosperity on January 27, 2011, the mayor of East Cleveland said, "One day there might not be a city of East Cleveland as we know it. There might not be a city of Cleveland as we know it. There might be a city of Cuyahoga [the county in which these two cities are located]." Similarly, a September 22, 2010, article in the *Mobile Press-Register* (Pickett 2010) described a plan championed by Prichard City Councilwoman Earline Martin-Harris to dissolve city government for 30 years, with voters living within the current city boundaries deciding whether to re-form it in 2040.

What Policies and Strategies Work?

Regional collaboration is high on the civic agenda for all communities in northeastern Ohio as they seek to realize greater efficiencies and save money in an environment of declining fiscal resources. Perhaps more than others, East Cleveland's leaders see opportunity in reaching out to regional partners to deliver city services. Despite the well-documented political barriers to regional collaboration, East Cleveland has entered into service agreements with other entities. One example is the 2008 agreement for the city of Cleveland to take over East Cleveland's water department. In another example, East Cleveland leaders are working with neighboring communities and the Northeast Ohio Regional Sewer District to reopen discussions about developing a watershed planning project.

Mayor Norton is openly seeking regional solutions for city services such as fire services, police services, and garbage collection. He recently reached an agreement that provides for the county engineer to take over maintenance and repair of the city's sanitary sewers. He is also pursuing the purchase of firefighting and garbage collection services from the city of Cleveland.

East Cleveland has entered into a memorandum of understanding with the newly formed Cuyahoga County Land Reutilization Corporation, informally known as the Cuyahoga County land bank. This agreement will provide East Cleveland with a credible system to improve its housing stock and infrastructure and to create the right opportunities and atmosphere for economic development. The land bank could be a boon for East Cleveland and other inner-ring suburbs struggling with surplus, vacant, and largely abandoned property (Douglas Shelby, personal communication, October 10, 2010).

State Programs

Chester and Inkster offer good examples of how distressed cities can benefit from state incentive programs, federal and state infrastructure investments, and other state programs designed to attract development to underserved areas. State programs to assist cities facing fiscal emergency have also helped East Cleveland and Chester put their finances in order and avoid bankruptcy, albeit with varying levels of success. As noted above, Michigan, Ohio, and Pennsylvania all have programs to step in with emergency financial managers when cities' or school districts' finances reach a crisis point. Inkster has not needed this type of state assistance, and Alabama does not have any programs that could assist cities like Prichard.

Michigan has several state programs available for distressed cities. For example, Michigan's fiscal receivership program for distressed cities was used by Hamtramck, a city in Wayne County. It was in receivership from 2000 to 2007, during which an emergency financial manager ran the city. The city is now trying to declare bankruptcy, which it sees as the most viable way forward. Hamtramck is in a dispute with Detroit, which completely surrounds it, over shared tax revenue from the General Motors Company Poletown plant. However, Michigan law makes it extremely difficult for cities to enter bankruptcy. Instead, the state offered the city loans, which as of December 2010, Hamtramck had not accepted (Alden 2010).

Michigan also has the Cities of Promise initiative for the eight poorest cities in the state: Benton Harbor, Detroit, Flint, Hamtramck, Highland Park, Muskegon Heights, Pontiac, and Saginaw. Created in 2006 and led by the Michigan State Housing Development Authority, the program applies resources and the expertise of statewide partners to restore the cities' neighborhoods and districts. It provides an action team for each city that can help cut through red tape to take advantage of state and federal grants.

Another program that can help cities in distress is the Redevelopment Ready Communities program run through the Michigan Suburbs Alliance, which also streamlines government assistance to foster development in 11 of Michigan's distressed suburbs.

Ohio has some similar programs available for distressed cities, but in recent years East Cleveland has not been in a position to take advantage of any economic development tools available through the state. It is hoped that with its new mayor and a new community development director experienced at working with state programs, this will change.

Prichard's state and local leaders have realistic goals and recognize the difficulties of overcoming perceptions, especially in a Republican-dominated state that provides very little assistance to cities. City leaders hope that this might change with the newly elected state legislator, Napoleon Bracy Jr., a former Prichard City Council member. There is widespread agreement that Prichard will never have the capacity to turn itself around unless the state and county governments help.

However, the tools offered by Alabama are limited. Prichard cannot adopt an income tax. Thus, it is completely reliant on property and sales taxes. It is designated by the state as foreign trade zone and an enterprise zone but so far has not been able to capitalize on these designations. It also has the ability to use tax increment financing.

What Policies and Strategies Work?

Pennsylvania has a wide range of programs available for redevelopment of distressed cities, such as Act 47, the Keystone Opportunity Zones, and support for transportation infrastructure. Chester has taken advantage of these tools to begin rebuilding its tax base and diversifying the city's economic base. The state has also invested in Chester; for example, it located a new prison there in 1997, a move that created 397 jobs. These state tools and investment have played key roles as the city begins to turn around.

Inkster has taken advantage of several development tools and programs offered by the state of Michigan. To spur development, it has created a Downtown Development Authority (DDA) in the past ten years along with its TIFA, designed to prevent unemployment and urban deterioration and promote economic growth. Inkster's TIFA is governed by a nine-member board appointed by the mayor and confirmed by the city council.

Research Question 3: Recommendations and Conclusions

Regionalize, Repurpose, Restructure

Even if these four case study suburbs, and others like them across the country, did everything right and implemented a whole host of cost-saving measures, they would still be in precarious fiscal situations. On March 10, 2011, NPR's "Planet Money" ran a story called "A Failing City Calls in the Finance Doctor" about Reading, Pennsylvania, a small city that recently requested assistance through Pennsylvania's Act 47. The story concludes:

> Reading, like a lot of places, has real long-term problems. Problems that even if you stopped painting the lines completely, even if you cashed every check correctly, stopped borrowing from the sewer fund, those problems would still be there. … It'll put the city on better footing. But it still may not be a cure (Kestenbaum and Joffe-Walt 2011: n.p.).

Fiscally distressed cities need to rethink their basic functions to find effective ways to change how they work and to capitalize on their physical assets and the personal commitments of their leadership. This may mean that some of them will no longer exist as cities in the same form they do today. Other governance options that should be considered include regional service delivery, regional government, annexation, dissolution, and repurposing.

The Federal Role in Most-Distressed Suburbs

Officials in all four analyzed suburbs have suggestions to make HUD programs more effective. Every city has requested greater flexibility to spend HUD dollars in ways that meet its most pressing needs and support economic development projects. Other suggestion were as follows:

- Prichard housing officials suggest that larger entitlement cities be required to help smaller, nonentitlement communities. Housing officials would also like more flexible regulations, accompanied by stronger performance measures. Other suggestions are to create and fund a national housing trust fund to benefit communities like Prichard and to revise the allocation formula for tax credits to provide an incentive for nonprofit developers to leverage the tax credits.
- Inkster city officials would like Inkster to become an entitlement community.
- The Southeast Michigan Council of Governments (SEMCOG) has submitted policy recommendations to HUD that would assist large and small communities in the Midwest, recognizing the particular hardships and economic devastation experienced by states like Michigan and allowing for maximum flexibility of programs such as CDBG. Specific recommendations that would also assist smaller communities like Inkster include more flexibility in using block grant money for economic development projects to help restart local economic improvements. SEMCOG recommends that HUD redefine its policy on aging to improve the stability of neighborhoods and housing stock while providing more opportunities for aging in place.
- Chester city officials view the retention and attraction of a strong middle class as their biggest challenge. They believe they have more than their fair share of their region's affordable housing and feel strongly that HUD programs contribute to this, encouraging the development of affordable housing in already low- and moderate-income areas. The barriers to attracting a critical mass of middle-class residents are very high, and Chester officials recognize that they cannot do this on their own. The Delaware Valley Regional Planning agency is undertaking an analysis to try to remedy this, including designing a region-wide fair share housing program. Chester officials have suggested that HUD conduct a demonstration program in Chester to test new program options that would enable them to attract

higher-income households, which in turn would deconcentrate poverty. One specific suggestion is to revisit fair-market rents. Another is to develop strategies that help people move up, not out.
• East Cleveland officials say they would like to see more flexibility in HUD programs so more money can be used for demolition.

Implementing these recommendations would improve how programs operate and would probably marginally improve the ability of the most-distressed suburbs to provide basic services for their 4.1 million residents who live in the 168 distressed suburbs under potential study consideration, discussed at the beginning of this chapter. But none of these distressed suburbs will significantly change the economic trajectory sufficiently to ensure that these places remain viable entities that are able to serve their residents into the future. To accomplish significant structural change, these distressed suburbs need capacity building. The federal government has a somewhat limited role in this regard because cities are creatures of the state, established and empowered by state governments. However, it is an area in which the federal government is beginning to invest resources through technical assistance, fellowships, and other programs for cities.

The federal government could bring in highly trained contractors or loaned executives from the private industry or the federal or state governments to work with local leaders and citizens for extended periods on structural change to help cities develop road maps for restructuring. The most-distressed suburbs and small cities cannot continue business as usual, and states cannot afford to have them continue business as usual. Their basic options are to regionalize, repurpose, or restructure—or some combination of the three.

The federal role in building the capacity of the most-distressed suburbs could include these five activities:

• Partnering with states on behalf of distressed suburbs to provide additional block grant dollars, loan guarantees, and debt reduction that can be used as incentives for cities that meet "good government" criteria. This money could be targeted to initiatives that will increase the cities' tax bases and regionalize or restructure services, beginning with public safety. This could include, for example, ensuring that adequate and ongoing public safety will be provided in any federally supported development project.
• Providing technical assistance to suburbs and small cities on municipal management practices. Before distressed suburbs can discuss partnerships or agreements with other city or county governments, they need to get their own houses in order.
• Developing model legislation for states on reasonable ways to restructure city operations and finances.
• Protecting the federal government's historic investment in these communities.
• Creating cross-agency partnerships—for example, with public health

providers or the U.S. Environmental Protection Agency—that provide leverage points and opportunities for federal/state/local funds.

Every suburb and small city has assets. The goal is to give cities the tools to enhance the value of those assets and ensure that the benefits accrue back to them and their residents in the long term.

References

Alden, W. 2010. Hamtramck's Budget Nightmare: Michigan Town Left with Nothing Else to Cut. *Huffington Post*, 15 December.

Berube, A., Erickson, D. and Reid, C. 2008. Learning from concentrated poverty: A synthesis of themes from the case studies, in *The Enduring Challenge of Concentrated Poverty in America*, edited by D. Erickson et al. Richmond, VA: Federal Reserve System and Brookings Institution.

Boji, R. Personal communication. 15 February 2011.

Bright, E. 2003. *Reviving America's Forgotten Neighborhoods: An Investigation of Inner-City Revitalization Efforts*. New York, NY: Routledge.

Davey, M. 2011. Michigan Residents Sue over Law on Emergency Management of Struggling Cities. *New York Times*, 23 June.

Fairmount Capital Advisors, Inc. 2006. *City of Chester Five-Year Financial Plan, Act 47 Recovery Plan*. City of Chester.

Fox, R. 2008. *To be Strong Again: Renewing the Promise in Smaller Industrial Cities*. Oakland, CA: PolicyLink.

Furdell, K., Wolman, H, and Hill, E.W. 2005. Did central cities come back? Which ones, how far, and why? *Journal of Urban Affairs*, 27(3), 283–305.

Hanlon, B. 2010. *Once the American Dream: Inner-Ring Suburbs of the Metropolitan United States*. Philadelphia, PA: Temple University Press.

Hexter, K.W., Hill, E.W., Mikelbank, B.A., Clark, B.Y, and Post, C. 2011. *Revitalizing Distressed Older Suburbs*. Washington, DC: Urban Institute.

Hill, E. and Nowak, J. 2002. Policies to uncover the competitive advantages of America's distressed cities, in *Urban Competitiveness, Policy for Dynamic Cities*, edited by I. Begg. Bristol: Policy Press.

Hill, E.W., Wolman, H.L, and Brennan, J. 1998. What is a central city in the United States? Applying a statistical technique for developing taxonomies. *Urban Studies*, 35(11), 1935–69.

Institute for Economic Development. 2010. Brochure. City: Institute for Economic Development, Chester, Pennsylvania.

Keating, W.D. 1994. *The Suburban Racial Dilemma: Housing and Neighborhoods*. Philadelphia, PA: Temple University Press.

Kestenbaum, D. and Joffe-Walt, C. 2011. A Failing City Calls in the Finance Doctor. *National Public Radio: Planet Money*. 10 March.

Kneebone, E. and Garr, E. 2010. *The Suburbanization of Poverty: Trends in Metropolitan America, 2000 to 2008*. Washington, DC: Brookings Institution.

McFee, M.J. 2011. University Circle Sees Residential Potential in East Cleveland; City, County Backing $5 Million Project. *The Plain Dealer,* 13 September.

Mikelbank, B. 2004. A typology of U.S. suburban places. *Housing Policy Debate*, 15(4), 935–64.

Orfield, M. 2002. *American Metropolitics: The New Suburban Reality.* Washington, DC: Brookings Institution.

Pennsylvania Department of Education. 2011. *Preliminary 2009–10 Four-Year Cohort Graduation Rate. Revised 12 April 2011.* [Online]. Available at: http://www.education.state.pa.us [accessed: 20 May 2012].

Petro, J. 2002. *City of East Cleveland Performance Audit, Executive Summary.* Columbus, OH: Auditor of the State of Ohio.

Pickett, Rhoda A. 2010. Prichard Councilwoman Pushes Plan to Dissolve City, *Mobile Press-Register*, 22 September 22.

Furdell, K., Wolman, H, and Hill, E.W. 2005. Did central cities come back? Which ones, how far, and why? *Journal of Urban Affairs*, 27(3), 283–305.

Puentes, R. and Orfield, M. 2002. *Valuing America's First Suburbs: A Policy Agenda for Older Suburbs in the Midwest*. Washington, DC: Brookings Institution.

Puentes, R. and Warren, D. 2006. *One-Fifth of America: A Comprehensive Guide to America's First Suburbs*. Washington, DC: Brookings Institution.

Schnaiberg, L. 1999. Facing an uncertain future under choice. *Education Week*, 19(5), 1.

Scioccetti, D. Personal communication. 16 February 2011.

Shelby, D. Personal communication. 10 October 2010.

Chapter 11

The Response of the Nonprofit Safety Net to Rising Suburban Poverty

Benjamin J. Roth and Scott W. Allard

Introduction

America's suburban communities have been racially and economically diverse since their emergence and growth in the twentieth century (Farley 1964, Logan and Schneider 1981, Wiese 1999, Pitti 2003) but historically have not experienced high rates of concentrated poverty present in many central city areas. Research on poverty in the twentieth century, therefore, has tended to focus on the loss of well-paying jobs, flight of middle-class residents, increase in crime rates, and greater race and class segregation in urban areas (Wilson 1987, Danziger and Gottschalk 1993, Massey and Denton 1993, Gottschalk and Danziger 2005). In the past decade, however, the geography of poverty has decidedly shifted to many suburbs. Across the largest U.S. metropolitan areas in 1999 there was, on average, an even balance of poor people in suburbs and central cities, but by 2005 the number of poor people living in the suburbs of these metropolitan areas surpassed the number of poor in their companion central cities by over 1 million (Berube and Kneebone 2006). The number of suburban poor has continued to grow nearly five times faster than the number of central city poor from 2005 to 2009. Central city residents are still more likely to be poor than their suburban counterparts, but as of 2009, 1.6 million more poor people lived in suburbs (13.7 million) than in central cities (12.1 million) of the largest metropolitan areas in the U.S. (Kneebone 2010, Kneebone and Garr 2010b).

Rising poverty in suburban communities has created heightened demand for safety net assistance. Programs in place to assist low-income households in suburbs, as in cities and rural areas, include several cash assistance, in-kind assistance, and social service programs. The most common cash or in-kind public assistance programs are the Temporary Assistance for Needy Families (TANF) welfare cash assistance program, the Supplemental Nutrition Assistance Program (SNAP, formerly the Food Stamp Program), Unemployment Insurance (UI), the Earned Income Tax Credit (EITC), and the refundable portion of the Child Tax Credit (CTC). In total, these five programs provided about \$230 billion in assistance to low-income Americans in 2009 (U.S. House of Representatives, House Committee on Ways and Means 2004, Simms 2008, Isaacs, Vericker, Macomber and Kent 2009, Kneebone 2009, Center on Budget and Policy Priorities 2010, Tax Policy

Center, Urban Institute and Brookings Institution 2010, U.S. Department of Health and Human Services 2010).[1] Many cash or in-kind assistance programs have expanded in recent years to meet rising poverty in suburban areas. For example, half the recent growth in EITC filings has occurred in suburban communities, where more workers are qualifying for the tax credit (Kneebone 2008). SNAP and UI caseloads increased at a faster rate in suburban communities than in central cities during the first year of the Great Recession (Kneebone and Garr 2010a). Similarly, the largest increases in UI receipt during the Great Recession occurred in lower-density suburbs (Kneebone and Garr 2010a).

Equally important are social or human service programs that provide more than $150 billion annually in specialized services for low-income populations such as job training, adult education, child care, substance abuse or mental health services, and emergency assistance (Allard 2009a). Most social service programs are funded by the federal, state, or local government but delivered by community-based nonprofit organizations. Even though they often get overlooked in policy discussions, social service programs provide essential help to millions of low-income Americans, including many who may not be eligible for cash assistance. As is the case with cash assistance programs, there is evidence that more families are seeking help from such organizations in recent years (Allard and Roth 2010). For example, visits to food pantries are up 46 percent since 2005, and the number of sheltered homeless families has increased by 30 percent since 2007 (Mabli, Cohen, Potter and Zhao 2010, U.S. Department of Housing and Urban Development 2010).

Unlike many cash assistance programs, which are available to those who meet eligibility criteria, there is no entitlement to social service programs or guarantee that programs will be offered in one's community. Instead, social service provision in suburbs, as well as in cities and rural communities, is inherently local and heavily reliant on the capacity of community-based nonprofit organizations to deliver publicly funded social service programs through contracts with state or local government agencies. The availability of nonprofit social service programs varies from place to place, however, determined by levels of federal, state, and local government funding; substantive orientation of local nonprofits; the engagement of local civic leadership and entrepreneurs with issues of poverty; and the presence of private philanthropy (Allard 2009a).

Rising demand upon local nonprofit social service providers has occurred at a time when many providers also are experiencing decreases in public and philanthropic funding. Nearly half of nonprofit service organizations in urban and rural areas also reported a decrease in revenue in recent years. These funding cuts led about three-quarters of urban and rural social service providers to cut programs, staff, client caseloads, or close temporarily (Allard 2009a, 2009b, 2009c). Fiscal

---

1   This estimate does not separate out UI benefits received by low-income households, which compose just 22 percent of all households receiving UI. Also, this estimate only includes the refundable portion of the CTC, which tends to target low-income tax filers.

strain on service providers exacerbates spatial mismatch problems, where providers are not always most accessible to the neighborhoods and populations most in need (Allard, Tolman and Rosen 2003, Allard 2009a, Murphy and Wallace 2010).

Spatial mismatches in social service provision have become a mounting concern in suburbs as the number of poor persons in these areas continues to grow. Poverty rates are less severe in suburbs than in cities, but poverty is more diffuse; this creates unique challenges for policymakers and service providers to meet the needs of poor residents (Holliday and Dwyer 2009, Allard and Roth 2010). With the devolution of federal and state welfare programs, the burden to respond to these needs has increasingly fallen on the shoulders of local suburban municipalities and counties, yet local suburban governments are not necessarily prepared or equipped to provide services that meet the diverse and dynamic needs of the poor (Orfield 2002, Allard 2009a, Allard and Roth 2010).

Although there is a growing body of research on the social services infrastructure in suburbs (e.g., Hendrick and Mossberger 2009, Murphy and Wallace 2010), many questions are left unanswered regarding suburban poverty, demand for safety net assistance, and the capacity of suburban safety nets. In particular, there is little research addressing the challenges that confront suburban providers amidst changing needs in their communities and the strategies they use to address these challenges. To better understand suburban safety net responses to the changing geography of poverty, we examine the responses of 100 suburban social service providers through a series of four telephone and web-based surveys that we completed between June 2009 and April 2010 in the suburbs of three major metropolitan areas: Chicago, Illinois; Los Angeles, California; and, Washington, DC. Complementing these survey data, we also draw upon findings from in-depth interviews with 17 nonprofit providers in these three metros. With surveys and interviews we gathered detailed information about services offered and organizational capacity. Providers discussed the challenges they face in providing services in the suburbs, as well as their organizational strategies for managing those challenges. Finally, surveys and interviews explored the effects of the Great Recession on the operations and financial positions of suburban social service providers.

Although there are many different ways to classify or categorize areas as urban or suburban, we follow the convention of much recent research and define *suburbs* as the counties and municipalities neighboring the largest city or cities in a metropolitan area (U.S. Office of Management and Budget (OMB) 2000). We favor conceiving of suburbs as county and municipal entities in this chapter because much of the social assistance landscape outside of big cities is tied to county and municipal boundaries. Most cash and in-kind assistance programs are funded by the federal and state government but are administered through county-level offices of state health and human service agencies. Similarly, it is common for an individual only to be eligible for public assistance and social service programs delivered within his or her particular county of residence. Many suburban municipalities administer modest safety net programs, such as food pantries, through own-source revenues. Philanthropic foundations also typically define their impact areas along county and municipal lines, limiting their grant-making to specific urban and suburban jurisdictions. Nonprofit social service providers, whether drawing on public or private revenue streams, often will work closely with county and municipal governments when making decisions about how to develop and site new programs. In fact, nonprofit service organizations often seek endorsement or support from local government to help connect to provider networks in communities, attract clients, and cultivate collaborations. Suburban responses to rising poverty, therefore, are most likely to be filtered through efforts at the county and municipal level.

Understanding Suburban Poverty

The popular conception of suburbia as non-Hispanic White and middle class is a legacy from the post-World War II era, when construction of extensive interstate and roadway systems, along with inexpensive land and rapid development, hastened the growth of suburbs at the cost of disinvestment in central cities (Jackson 1985). Working- and middle-class White families flocked to suburban communities seeking to escape the racialized problems associated with urban living (Baldassare 1986). The work of early suburban scholars did little to dispel the myth of the suburbs as a non-Hispanic White, middle-class "utopia" (Kruse and Sugrue 2006), although by the late 1980s some demographers were beginning to provide evidence that the suburbs are not as racially and economically homogeneous as many people believed (Logan and Alba 1993).

The spatial distribution of poverty and opportunity between cities and suburbs—and within suburbs themselves—has begun to change more noticeably since the late 1990s.[2] Not only did concentrated poverty decline in central city areas during the 1990s, but poverty rates increased in many suburbs, particularly in inner-ring areas (Kingsley and Pettit 2007). While poverty increased in 38 percent of U.S. cities from 1990 to 2000, it did so in 42 percent of U.S. suburbs (Berube and Frey 2002). The geography of poverty continued to shift in the following decade. From 2000 to 2009, cities saw a 16.7 percent increase in the number of poor persons, yet the number of poor people in the suburbs of the nation's 100 largest metro areas increased by over twice that amount—37.4 percent—from 1999 to 2009 (Kneebone 2010).

---

2   Poverty is defined here as income below the Federal poverty line or the official income threshold. This threshold is calibrated by family size and composition and adjusted each year according to the Consumer Price Index (CPI), but it is not adjusted for geographic differences in the cost of living. The federal poverty line in 2009 for a family of four (two adults with two children under 18 years old) is $21,756. Families with an income below this threshold are defined as "poor," regardless of geographic location (Fisher 1992, U.S. Bureau of the Census 2009)

Recent research has developed various typologies intended to capture the economic and demographic heterogeneity across suburban municipalities (Orfield 2002, Mikelbank 2004, Holliday and Dwyer 2009, Murphy 2010). For example, Orfield's (2002) classification scheme highlights "at-risk communities," which are suburban clusters composed of municipalities with sagging tax bases, deteriorating infrastructure, aging housing stock, and struggling schools. Others classify poor suburbs using a neighborhood-level rather than municipal-level analysis, which identifies pockets of poverty nested within more affluent suburban communities (Holliday and Dwyer 2009, Murphy 2010). Regardless of the level of analysis, these typologies underscore that suburban poverty is not confined to the inner-tier regions closest to the urban core and that its form varies within and across suburbs.

In addition to growing rapidly throughout the suburbs, suburban poverty is an important object of study because it has features that distinguish it from urban poverty. Holliday and Dwyer (2009) find that poor suburban neighborhoods have fewer welfare recipients and female-headed households than their high-poverty urban counterparts. The suburban poor are more likely to be non-Hispanic White and Latino, while poor urban neighborhoods have larger percentages of African American residents. There is evidence that low-skilled immigrants—many of them Latino—are increasingly settling in the suburbs, drawn by jobs in construction, landscaping, and the service industry (Massey and Capoferro 2008). Finally, poor suburban areas tend to have higher rates of overcrowding, a greater number of people lacking English proficiency, and fewer college graduates or professionals than urban centers (Holliday and Dwyer 2009).

Emerging research has begun to identify shifting patterns of suburban poverty and how suburban context shapes the well-being of low-income suburban residents (Duchon, Andrulis and Reid 2004, Andrulis and Duchon 2007, Felland, Lauer and Cunningham 2009). These studies establish the connection between place, poverty, and access to key resources such as employment and health care. Job growth since 2000 has been uneven across suburban communities, benefitting affluent suburbs more than poorer suburbs (Kneebone 2009). Such patterns may have exacerbated existing spatial mismatches between the locations of jobs and the suburban locations where people of color and low-skill populations are most likely to live (Holzer and Stoll 2007). Access to health care in the suburbs is also patterned by geography. Felland et al. found that low-income individuals in the suburbs of five cities—Boston, Cleveland, Indianapolis, Miami, and Seattle—face barriers to accessing care that include transportation and language barriers (Felland et al. 2009). They conclude that the spatial mismatch between where the poor live and the location of health care providers is compounded by the geographic dispersion of the suburban poor.

Less research has explored the relationship between place, poverty, and the safety net (Allard 2009a). Existing research on suburban poverty does not adequately consider the demands placed upon suburban nonprofit social service organizations or the capacity of suburban safety nets to respond to increased demand for assistance, particularly at a time of fiscal austerity. In many instances it appears that suburban safety net providers are barely getting by in this current economic and fiscal environment, rather than providing support adequate to ensure working poor populations and job seekers are able to get ahead. Given the critical role of nonprofit social service organizations in providing assistance to the poor today, we argue that a careful assessment of these organizations is an important step toward a more complete understanding of how poverty is affecting suburbs and which policy interventions may be most effective in addressing rising need.

In this chapter we examine the strength and adaptability of the suburban nonprofit social service sector by asking several research questions that explore the relationship between suburbs, poverty, and social service provision:

- What is the demand for social services in the suburbs, and how is it changing?
- What challenges do service providers encounter to operating programs in the suburbs?
- How do nonprofits respond to these challenges?

Our findings provide a view of the nonprofit safety net in select suburban places that are now home to an increasing share of America's poor, and answers to these questions will help suburban social service providers and suburban community leaders identify solutions that may improve the effectiveness and efficiency of local safety net programs. Although this is an exploratory study, we believe our findings reflect conditions that will persist in many suburbs over time and provide an important starting point for continued research in this area.

Data and Study Sites

To better understand the current context for social service provision in suburbs and the challenges that providers face in those communities, we collected detailed information on the operations and fiscal health of 100 diverse nonprofit social service organizations operating in suburbs of three metropolitan areas: Chicago, Los Angeles, and Washington, DC. Nonprofit organizations were included in this study if they delivered one of the following direct services to low-income persons: substance abuse and mental health services; employment assistance; food; housing; children and youth services; family services; emergency assistance; and homeless centers. We define the suburban areas in metropolitan Chicago to include municipalities outside the city of Chicago in Cook County, as well as DuPage, Lake, Kane, McHenry, and Will counties. Los Angeles suburbs are defined in this study to include municipalities in Los Angeles County outside the city of Los Angeles, as well as Riverside and San Bernardino counties east of Los Angeles.[3]

---

3   Riverside and San Bernardino counties technically comprise a separate metropolitan area (Riverside-San Bernardino-Ontario, CA), but in practice they contain many bedroom

Finally, Washington, DC suburbs include Prince George's and Montgomery counties in Maryland; Arlington, Loudoun, Fairfax, and Prince William counties; and Alexandria in northern Virginia.

Our data come from four different surveys we conducted with nonprofit service providers over an 11-month period, June 2009 to April 2010.[4] A survey sample of 225 nonprofit social service providers in the three study sites was purposively selected to ensure adequate variation by organizational size, location, and service mission.[5] In order to gain a more textured understanding of the everyday operation of social services in these three metropolitan areas, we conducted site visits and in-depth interviews with 17 agencies that participated in the initial telephone survey.[6]

Organizations included in this study offer a diversity of services across all three suburban metropolitan areas (see Table 11.1). More than half of the respondents in our sample offer some sort of food support (68.4 percent) or services related to job searching or training (54.6 percent), but fewer provided GED or ESL programs (32.7 percent) or out-patient substance abuse services (19.4 percent).

Because of the nature of this sample of nonprofit service organizations, we are cautious in our interpretation of the findings that follow. While our data affirm other research, suggesting that there is heterogeneity within and across suburban areas (Orfield 2002, Mikelbank 2004), our findings may not be generalizable to suburbs in other metro areas. Our sample varies in geography, organizational size,

---

communities for workers in Los Angeles County. In 2000, roughly 150,000 workers in these counties regularly commuted to Los Angeles County.

4   One initial telephone survey and three follow-up web-based surveys were completed. Verification calls were made to each provider to confirm location and services offered, as well as identify an executive director or program manager who could answer longer survey questions. Telephone surveys collected detailed information on client characteristics, services available, funding, changes in demand, shifts in program funding, and strategies for coping with the impact of the recession. About two months after completing the phone survey, a web survey collected information on changing client populations and needs, as well as information about reserve funds and expectations of public program cuts. A third web survey focused on community collaboration was completed in February 2010. A final web survey was completed in April 2010 that asked organizations to revise their expectations about program funding for the coming fiscal year. Sixty-one organizations completed all four waves and 82 completed three of four waves.

5   An initial sampling frame of 225 providers was identified and calls to verify operations were completed with 198 organizations (response rate of 88 percent). All 198 organizations were invited to participate in a longer initial telephone survey; 100 completed this 25-minute telephone follow-up survey (response rate of 53 percent). Organizations were contacted at least four times by phone to complete the interview. Six nonprofits completing the verification call refused to participate in the telephone survey. Nine organizations were removed from the survey sample during the course of the study, as six proved to be located outside the study area and three were no longer operational.

6   These visits were between 90 minutes and four hours long. Five site visits were conducted in suburban Washington, DC, five in Chicago, and seven in Los Angeles.

**Table 11.1   Characteristics of Nonprofit Suburban Social Service
Providers Surveyed in Metropolitan Chicago, Los Angeles,
and Washington, DC**

Location:	
• Metropolitan Los Angeles (%)	29.6
• Metropolitan Chicago (%)	33.7
• Metropolitan Washington, DC (%)	36.7
Size, Type, and Budget:	
• Religious Nonprofit (%)	26.0
• Secular Nonprofit (%)	74.0
• Median Adult Monthly Caseload	310
• Median Child Monthly Caseload	200
Annual Budget	%
• More than $1 million	45.7
• $1 million to $200,000 (%)	28.7
• $200,000 to $50,000 (%)	20.2
• Less than $50,000 (%)	5.3
Services Offered	%
• Food Assistance or Meals	68.4
• Family or Individual Counseling	57.1
• Job Training, Search, or Placement	54.6
• Youth Programs	54.1
• Clothing or Household Items	53.1
• Assistance Finding Affordable Housing	49.0
• Emergency Cash or Utility Assistance	48.0
• Assistance Paying Rent	43.9
• GED, ESL, or High School Completion	32.7
• Temporary Shelter or Housing	31.6
• Senior Programs	30.6
• Outpatient Mental Health	27.6
• Programs for Ex-offenders	21.4
• Outpatient Substance Abuse	19.4
• Physical and/or Developmental Disability	14.3
• Offer 2–5 different services (%)	28.6
• Offer 6 or more different services (%)	50.0
N = 98	

Source: Survey of Suburban Social Service Providers (2010).

Table 11.2   Demographic Characteristics: Population by Race and Ethnicity, Metropolitan Los Angeles, 2005–09

County/Municipality	Population	Percent Non-Hispanic White	Percent African American	Percent Asian	Percent Latino
Los Angeles County:	**9,785,295**	**50.7%**	**8.8%**	**13.0%**	**47.3%**
• City of Los Angeles	3,796,840	50.3%	9.8%	10.7%	48.5%
• Long Beach	462,823	45.0%	13.6%	12.9%	40.0%
• Glendale	195,876	71.2%	2.0%	16.0%	17.8%
• Santa Clarita	168,538	71.9%	2.7%	7.0%	28.2%
• Pomona	151,552	47.0%	8.0%	7.2%	70.8%
• Pasadena	142,013	58.8%	11.4%	12.3%	33.6%
Riverside County:	**2,036,304**	**64.3%**	**6.1%**	**5.2%**	**43.2%**
• Riverside	291,094	60.2%	7.0%	6.2%	47.8%
• Moreno Valley	184,039	40.2%	17.7%	5.6%	51.6%
• Corona	148,000	64.7%	6.2%	8.9%	42.0%
• Murrieta	94,342	68.1%	5.3%	9.0%	25.7%
• Temecula	93,474	71.9%	3.8%	8.2%	24.7%
San Bernardino County:	**1,986,635**	**61.2%**	**8.9%**	**5.8%**	**46.6%**
• San Bernardino	198,464	50.0%	16.3%	3.8%	57.3%
• Fontana	184,152	58.5%	9.7%	6.3%	65.6%
• Ontario	170,734	45.8%	8.0%	4.4%	64.3%
• Rancho Cucamonga	169,062	63.9%	8.1%	8.9%	33.3%
• Victorville	102,666	60.4%	16.4%	3.9%	44.1%

Source: 2005–09 American Community Survey.

and mission, but it is small and purposively selected. Therefore, our data are better suited for exploring organizational behavior than for hypothesis testing.

Although we worked hard to include a representative set of nonprofit providers, our sampling frame relied on listings of providers and IRS 990 data, which may omit or overlook some organizations. First, organizations with revenues under $25,000 may not have filed a 990 form.[7] Second, organizations do not always file

---

7   Although nonprofits with revenues under $25,000 have been required to file a 990 form to the IRS since 2006, these organizations may not be aware of this new requirement.

Table 11.3   Demographic Characteristics: Population by Race and Ethnicity, Metropolitan Chicago, 2005–09

County/Municipality	Population	Percent Non-Hispanic White	Percent African-American	Percent Asian	Percent Latino
Cook County:	**5,257,001**	**53.9%**	**25.5%**	**5.7%**	**22.5%**
• City of Chicago	2,824,064	41.9%	34.1%	4.9%	27.4%
• Cicero	80,550	30.5%	3.4%	0.5%	84.7%
• Evanston	76,599	68.2%	18.5%	7.3%	7.6%
• Arlington Heights	73,334	88.7%	1.0%	7.3%	5.2%
• Schaumburg	70,698	74.0%	3.3%	16.9%	7.6%
• Palatine	66,537	81.0%	3.0%	10.6%	15.9%
DuPage County:	**925,530**	**80.9%**	**4.3%**	**9.7%**	**11.9%**
• Naperville	141,644	79.4%	4.0%	13.3%	5.0%
• Wheaton	54,341	89.2%	2.9%	4.2%	4.6%
• Downers Grove	48,849	89.4%	3.1%	4.7%	4.3%
• Elmhurst	45,670	89.8%	1.3%	5.4%	8.2%
• Lombard	42,666	81.0%	4.4%	10.6%	7.2%
Kane County:	**494,371**	**76.8%**	**5.5%**	**3.0%**	**27.7%**
• Aurora	172,501	59.6%	11.2%	6.0%	39.0%
• Elgin	102,590	68.0%	6.6%	4.6%	40.5%
• Carpentersville	37,162	68.6%	4.6%	5.0%	47.3%
• Saint Charles	32,952	91.6%	1.6%	3.2%	8.9%
• Batavia	27,154	90.8%	3.8%	1.7%	4.2%
Lake County:	**702,558**	**78.1%**	**6.5%**	**5.7%**	**18.6%**
• Waukegan	90,393	51.3%	17.0%	4.3%	52.5%
• North Chicago	32,993	47.7%	31.3%	3.4%	31.0%
• Mundelein	32,832	75.7%	1.6%	9.4%	27.4%
• Highland Park	31,129	94.5%	0.4%	1.9%	5.1%
• Gurnee	30,237	76.7%	5.7%	11.3%	9.5%
McHenry County:	**312,946**	**90.9%**	**0.9%**	**2.7%**	**10.6%**
• Crystal Lake	41,094	91.4%	1.7%	2.1%	10.8%
• Algonquin	30,464	90.3%	0.8%	6.2%	7.1%
• Lake in the Hills	29,421	86.1%	0.8%	5.9%	12.8%
• McHenry	26,057	90.4%	0.2%	1.8%	13.0%
• Woodstock	23,231	83.3%	1.8%	1.6%	22.6%

Will County:	**664,361**	**77.9%**	**10.6%**	**3.8%**	**14.0%**
• Joliet	143,008	67.6%	17.0%	2.0%	26.7%
• Bolingbrook	69,594	56.1%	18.7%	9.5%	23.0%
• Romeoville	37,499	71.9%	9.2%	4.2%	28.0%
• Plainfield	33,714	85.3%	4.2%	6.3%	9.6%
• Homer Glen	25,654	95.7%	0.8%	1.9%	4.0%

Source: 2005–09 American Community Survey.

a 990 form in time for their entity to be listed for the year in which they file. Third, there is no guarantee that organizations that file will remain in operation a month later. Finally, some entities that offer social services may not identify as providers with the IRS and therefore would not be considered for our sample. For example, a church that runs a limited food pantry once a month for congregants may not wish to be publicly listed as a food pantry. Despite these sampling limitations, we are confident that our survey data accurately capture the nonprofit landscape in these three suburban areas. The site visits we conducted with providers enhance and corroborate the survey data, and the multiple time points of the surveys allow us to capture the volatility of the nonprofit sector over time.

It also is important to note that the suburban areas of Los Angeles, Chicago, and Washington, DC are representative of the considerable demographic and socioeconomic diversity present in suburban America (Orfield 2002, Mikelbank 2004). For instance, Latinos compose more than 40 percent of the population in many parts of suburban Los Angeles, and several suburban municipalities in Los Angeles, Riverside, and San Bernardino counties are majority or near-majority Latino (see Table 11.2).[8] By contrast, most suburban communities outside of Chicago are predominantly non-Hispanic White, although municipalities such as Cicero, Elgin, Aurora, and Waukegan have sizable Latino populations (see Table 11.3). Many suburban Washington, DC communities have substantial African American and Asian populations. Prince George's County, Maryland, is nearly two-thirds African American (63.8 percent), whereas about 20 percent of the population in Alexandria and Prince William County, Virginia, are African American. More than 15 percent of the population in suburban Fairfax, Virginia, and parts of suburban Montgomery County, Maryland, is Asian (see Table 11.4).

The suburban populations of these three metro areas also differ in their share of immigrants and the rate at which the immigrant population has grown since 2000.[9] All counties across the three metro areas experienced an increase in the

---

8   Unless otherwise indicated, all demographic data are from five-year 2005–09 American Community Survey (ACS) estimates.

9   We define "immigrant" as individuals born abroad who were not U.S. citizens at birth. This is consistent with the U.S. Census definition of foreign-born populations and includes naturalized U.S. citizens, lawful permanent residents, temporary migrants, refugees, and undocumented residents of the U.S.

**Table 11.4   Demographic Characteristics: Population by Race and
Ethnicity, Metropolitan Washington, DC, 2005–09**

County/Municipality	Population	Percent Non-Hispanic White	Percent African American	Percent Asian	Percent Latino
Washington, DC	588,433	35.9%	55.2%	3.0%	8.5%
Montgomery County:	**946,172**	**60.2%**	**16.3%**	**13.2%**	**15.1%**
• Silver Spring	76,335	46.6%	24.8%	7.8%	26.6%
• Germantown	61,345	53.5%	21.6%	13.3%	21.1%
• Rockville	59,825	66.2%	8.2%	18.5%	13.1%
• Wheaton-Glenmont	59,815	42.8%	19.4%	12.8%	35.4%
• Gaithersburg	58,632	55.9%	13.1%	17.3%	23.3%
Prince George's County:	**834,986**	**23.3%**	**63.8%**	**3.9%**	**12.4%**
• Bowie	53,572	48.3%	43.9%	3.5%	5.5%
• Chillum	34,828	15.0%	54.3%	0.7%	37.2%
• College Park	27,202	66.2%	14.1%	11.1%	10.1%
• Clinton	26,629	15.8%	78.2%	2.0%	3.3%
• Fort Washington	25,620	18.9%	63.8%	9.3%	8.0%
Alexandria	**142,131**	**64.5%**	**21.8%**	**5.2%**	**13.9%**
Arlington	**206,405**	**71.3%**	**8.1%**	**8.4%**	**16.7%**
Fairfax County:	**1,012,751**	**66.7%**	**9.2%**	**16.0%**	**14.0%**
• Burke	55,831	72.5%	6.1%	13.9%	13.7%
• Centreville	53,876	57.2%	9.3%	25.8%	12.5%
• Reston	53,759	73.2%	9.2%	10.7%	9.7%
• Annandale	53,686	65.2%	7.5%	19.6%	19.2%
• Chantilly	46,419	66.8%	6.1%	19.4%	11.0%
Loudoun County:	**277,465**	**73.2%**	**7.8%**	**12.2%**	**10.1%**
• Leesburg	38,394	72.8%	12.0%	6.7%	12.0%
• Purcellville	4,964	88.0%	3.8%	2.4%	5.8%
• Lovettsville	1,187	90.2%	4.6%	0.3%	9.4%
• Hamilton	823	80.8%	17.5%	0.0%	2.4%
• Middleburg	386	73.8%	26.2%	0.0%	0.8%
Prince William County:	**360,910**	**60.9%**	**19.4%**	**6.9%**	**18.5%**
• Dale City	63,910	46.4%	28.0%	7.3%	24.5%
• Woodbridge	34,778	47.5%	23.3%	7.8%	31.2%
• Lake Ridge	30,396	69.3%	18.8%	5.8%	10.8%
• Linton Hall	20,921	70.4%	7.6%	12.8%	11.6%
• Montclair	18,785	68.2%	18.4%	5.0%	10.1%

Source: 2005–09 American Community Survey.

Table 11.5 Proportion and Number of Immigrant Population, Suburban Los Angeles Counties and Select Cities, 2005–09

County/Municipality	Proportion Immigrant	Origin (proportion of all immigrants)				Number of Immigrants		
		Asia	Africa	Latin America		2000	2005–9	Percent Change
Los Angeles:								
• Los Angeles County	35.5%	31.8%	1.4%	60.4%		3,449,444	3,468,597	0.6%
• Riverside County	22.0%	16.7%	1.3%	73.4%		293,712	447,647	52.4%
• San Bernardino County	21.1%	19.6%	1.7%	73.1%		318,647	419,202	31.6%
Chicago:								
• Cook County	20.5%	22.9%	2.8%	48.4%		1,064,703	1,079,102	1.4%
• DuPage County	17.9%	39.4%	2.2%	29.6%		138,656	165,433	19.3%
• Kane County	17.3%	13.1%	0.8%	73.3%		63,516	85,367	34.4%
• Lake County	18.0%	23.8%	1.1%	52.0%		95,536	126,094	32.0%
• McHenry County	10.0%	19.0%	2.1%	50.5%		18,764	31,306	66.8%
• Will County	11.2%	25.9%	3.1%	49.9%		35,715	74,681	109.1%
Washington, DC:								
• Montgomery County, MD	29.6%	37.1%	13.8%	36.3%		232,996	280,379	20.3%
• Prince George's County, MD	18.2%	16.2%	25.5%	53.4%		110,481	151,703	37.3%
• Fairfax County, VA	27.1%	50.7%	8.8%	30.8%		237,677	274,249	15.4%
• Loudoun County, VA	19.9%	52.1%	5.3%	29.0%		19,116	55,082	188.1%
• Prince William County, VA	19.7%	28.3%	10.9%	53.5%		32,186	70,919	120.3%

Note: We use the term "immigrant" interchangeably with "foreign born." The U.S. Bureau of the Census defines "foreign born" as anyone who is not a U.S. citizen at birth.

Sources: 2000 Census and 2005–09 American Community Survey.

Table 11.6   Characteristics of Immigrant Population, Select Cities in Three Metro Areas, 2005–09

Metro/Municipality	Origin (proportion of all immigrants)				Number of Immigrants		
	Proportion Immigrant	Asia	Africa	Latin America	2000	2005–9	Percent Change
Los Angeles Metro:							
• Glendale	53.6%	75.7%	1.1%	16.4%	106,119	105,004	-1.1%
• Ontario	29.1%	10.7%	0.6%	86.5%	48,789	49,670	1.8%
• Indio	27.9%	3.3%	0.3%	91.3%	16,322	22,160	35.8%
• Long Beach	27.8%	31.0%	1.4%	61.5%	132,168	128,467	-2.8%
• Rialto	27.7%	4.9%	1.0%	92.5%	20,439	27,267	33.4%
• Santa Clarita	19.8%	27.5%	3.0%	57.5%	24,727	33,312	34.7%
• Rancho Cucamonga	16.6%	40.2%	4.1%	45.4%	17,644	28,081	59.2%
• Victorville	16.6%	17.3%	2.1%	74.5%	7,937	17,027	114.5%
• Temecula	15.2%	36.7%	1.7%	44.6%	6,897	14,215	106.1%
• Murrieta	13.7%	42.3%	2.7%	41.3%	3,829	12,902	237.0%
Chicago Metro:							
• Cicero	43.7%	1.1%	0.0%	96.5%	37,343	35,170	-5.8%
• Waukegan	33.4%	10.0%	1.0%	85.0%	26,556	30,161	13.6%
• Carpentersville	32.4%	11.7%	0.1%	78.7%	8,006	12,023	50.2%

• Bolingbrook	22.7%	34.1%	6.3%	50.1%	8,108	15,785	94.7%
• Arlington Heights	17.0%	28.7%	1.5%	13.6%	10,546	12,441	18.0%
• Lake in the Hills	15.6%	28.3%	0.6%	34.3%	1,999	4,577	129.0%
• Naperville	15.4%	60.0%	3.5%	11.9%	14,963	21,868	46.1%
• Joliet	15.0%	9.3%	1.1%	81.9%	11,566	21,492	85.8%
• Highland Park	11.5%	23.9%	2.5%	22.5%	4,798	3,570	-25.6%
• Batavia	4.6%	33.2%	3.3%	26.4%	1,242	1,261	1.5%
Washington DC Metro:							
• Chillum	42.4%	1.6%	27.1%	69.7%	13,030	14,750	13.2%
• Silver Spring	34.6%	18.7%	19.2%	55.1%	26,904	26,404	-1.9%
• Germantown	32.7%	32.6%	16.8%	44.2%	11,134	20,042	80.0%
• Chantilly	27.5%	62.3%	6.3%	22.8%	9,095	12,741	40.1%
• Dale City	25.2%	22.1%	15.1%	55.5%	7,298	16,115	120.8%
• Alexandria, VA	23.9%	27.5%	29.4%	33.1%	32,600	33,945	4.1%
• Reston	21.7%	44.6%	12.1%	28.0%	12,413	11,681	-5.9%
• Linton Hall	19.3%	49.8%	9.6%	34.5%	514	4,035	685.0%
• Leesburg	15.0%	34.9%	3.3%	46.9%	2,439	5,746	135.6%
• Fort Washington	14.4%	44.1%	13.8%	37.1%	2,955	3,691	24.9%

Sources: 2000 Census and 2005–09 American Community Survey.

number of immigrants from 2000 to 2009 (see Table 11.5), but the growth in suburban counties was much greater than in core urban counties.[10] For example, the immigrant populations in Riverside and McHenry counties climbed by over 50 percent; Will County's foreign-born population jumped by 109 percent; and in Loudon County, Virginia, immigrants grew by 188 percent to represent nearly 20 percent of the county's total population.

Growth in the number of immigrants also ranges between suburban municipalities (see Table 11.6). By the second half of the last decade, the immigrant population more than doubled in some places, particularly those with a relatively small number of immigrants in 2000. The immigrant population of Lake in the Hills, a small Chicago suburb in McHenry County, increased by 129 percent from 2000 to 2009. Similarly, in Linton Hall, Virginia, immigrants now represent 19.3 percent of the population after increasing by 685 percent (from 514 to 4,035) since 2000.[11]

As with immigrant settlement patterns, poverty rates vary across the suburban landscape (see Tables 11.7, 11.8, and 11.9).[12] County poverty rates range widely from 2.8 percent in Loudoun County, Virginia, to 14.3 percent in San Bernardino County, California, and to an even greater degree across suburban municipalities. The poverty rate is 5 percent in the western San Bernardino County community of Rancho Cucamonga but more than twice that in nearby Ontario (12.3 percent) and nearly four times as high in Victorville (19.2 percent). Similar variation in poverty can be seen in Chicago. Rates of poverty exceed 12 percent in Joliet, Waukegan, and Aurora—relatively large municipalities ringing the metro area—while many of their neighboring municipalities have much lower poverty rates.[13]

The number of poor people increased in most of the suburban study sites between 2000 and 2009, yet some communities saw a greater increase than others. Although poverty rates remain well below 10 percent in most of suburban Chicago, every suburban county and nearly every one of the largest suburban

---

10   This is in keeping with trends throughout the U.S., as new immigrants bypass central cities, settling instead in suburbs and small towns (Singer 2008, Katz, Creighton, Amsterdam and Chowkwanyun 2010).

11   Perhaps most striking is the increase in foreign-born residents in places that already had a large number of immigrants in 2000. For example, while over 11,000 immigrants lived in Joliet, Illinois, in 2000, this number climbed to nearly 21,500 (an 85.8 percent increase) by the latter half of the decade. Similarly, Victorville's immigrant population—now at 17,027—grew by 114.5 percent during this period.

12   Differences in number of poor persons are calculated from 2000 Census and 2005–09 five-year American Community Survey (ACS) estimates. Combined ACS estimates could mute some of more recent increases in poverty given there are recession years grouped together with years characterized more by growth. We do not control for margin of error here.

13   This variation in suburban poverty rates may reflect patterns of residential settlement, affordable housing, and segregation, as well as proximity to the central city and high-poverty neighborhoods within the urban core.

Table 11.7   Demographic Characteristics: Population below the Federal Poverty Line, Metropolitan Los Angeles, 2005–09

County/Municipality	Poverty Rate		Number of Poor Persons		
	2000	2005–9	2000	2005–9	Percent Change
Los Angeles County:	**17.9%**	**15.4%**	**1,674,599**	**1,486,783**	**-11.2%**
• City of Los Angeles	22.1%	19.1%	801,050	713,149	-11.0%
• Long Beach	22.8%	18.8%	103,434	85,755	-17.1%
• Glendale	15.5%	12.3%	29,927	23,868	-20.2%
• Santa Clarita	6.4%	7.6%	9,552	12,569	31.6%
• Pomona	21.6%	15.7%	31,149	23,513	-24.5%
• Pasadena	15.9%	13.7%	20,909	18,968	-9.3%
Riverside County:	**14.2%**	**12.3%**	**214,084**	**245,454**	**14.7%**
• Riverside	15.8%	13.1%	39,060	37,235	-4.7%
• Moreno Valley	14.2%	14.8%	20,141	26,962	33.9%
• Corona	8.3%	8.3%	10,244	12,272	19.8%
• Murrieta	4.3%	5.6%	1,915	5,269	175.1%
• Temecula	6.7%	6.8%	3,864	6,378	65.1%
San Bernardino County:	**15.8%**	**14.3%**	**263,412**	**278,582**	**5.8%**
• San Bernardino	27.6%	26.1%	49,691	50,597	1.8%
• Fontana	14.7%	12.1%	18,676	22,199	18.9%
• Ontario	15.5%	12.3%	24,133	20,835	-13.7%
• Rancho Cucamonga	7.1%	5.0%	8,955	8,205	-8.4%
• Victorville	18.7%	19.2%	11,885	18,881	58.9%

Source: 2005–09 American Community Survey.

municipalities in the Chicago metro area saw dramatic increases in the number of poor in the 2000s. Poverty rates declined across the suburban counties of metropolitan Los Angeles, yet many suburban municipalities in the Los Angeles metro area experienced sizable increases in the number of poor persons. Although metropolitan Washington, DC is home to some of the most affluent communities and lowest unemployment rates in the country, there are significant and growing pockets of poverty. Portions of Montgomery County and Prince George's County in Maryland, and Fairfax, Loudoun, and Prince William counties in Virginia, saw more than 40 percent increases in the number of poor from 2000 to 2009, with several municipalities experiencing more than a 100 percent increase in the number of poor.

Table 11.8   Demographic Characteristics: Population below the Federal Poverty Line, Metropolitan Chicago, 2005–09

County/Municipality	Poverty Rate		Number of Poor Persons		
	2000	2005–9	2000	2005–9	Percent Change
Cook County:	**13.5%**	**15.1%**	**713,040**	**781,017**	**9.5%**
• City of Chicago	19.6%	20.8%	556,791	576,344	3.5%
• Cicero	15.5%	16.1%	13,187	12,912	-2.1%
• Evanston	11.1%	9.7%	7,518	6,751	-10.2%
• Arlington Heights	2.5%	3.6%	1,878	2,616	39.3%
• Schaumburg	3.0%	4.5%	2,209	3,156	42.9%
• Palatine	4.8%	7.5%	3,100	4,951	59.7%
DuPage County:	**3.6%**	**5.3%**	**32,163**	**48,317**	**50.2%**
• Naperville	2.2%	3.3%	2,809	4,538	61.6%
• Wheaton	3.6%	4.8%	1,847	2,353	27.4%
• Downers Grove	2.3%	3.8%	1,096	1,802	64.4%
• Elmhurst	2.5%	3.2%	1,041	1,423	36.7%
• Lombard	3.8%	3.3%	1,560	1,375	-11.9%
Kane County:	**6.7%**	**8.8%**	**26,587**	**43,091**	**62.1%**
• Aurora	8.5%	12.1%	12,034	20,654	71.6%
• Elgin	8.1%	10.9%	7,414	10,990	48.2%
• Carpentersville	8.5%	9.4%	2,578	3,487	35.3%
• Saint Charles	3.4%	4.9%	925	1,602	73.2%
• Batavia	3.6%	5.9%	836	1,571	87.9%
Lake County:	**5.7%**	**6.7%**	**35,714**	**46,040**	**28.9%**
• Waukegan	13.9%	13.0%	12,058	11,422	-5.3%
• North Chicago	15.1%	16.0%	3,596	4,051	12.7%
• Mundelein	4.6%	4.0%	1,395	1,294	-7.2%
• Highland Park	3.8%	4.3%	1,182	1,324	12.0%
• Gurnee	3.0%	5.1%	867	1,531	76.6%
McHenry County:	**3.7%**	**5.6%**	**9,446**	**17,334**	**83.5%**
• Crystal Lake	3.5%	4.5%	1,324	1,815	37.1%
• Algonquin	1.7%	3.8%	387	1,163	200.5%
• Lake in the Hills	2.1%	4.2%	503	1,223	143.1%
• McHenry	4.6%	6.7%	975	1,736	78.1%
• Woodstock	7.2%	10.2%	1,431	2,331	62.9%

Will County:	4.9%	6.4%	24,225	41,864	72.8%
• Joliet	10.8%	12.2%	10,946	17,080	56.0%
• Bolingbrook	4.1%	5.7%	2,310	3,916	69.5%
• Romeoville	1.9%	6.0%	387	2,171	461.0%
• Plainfield	1.8%	2.8%	229	923	303.1%
• Homer Glen	–	3.3%	–	842	–

Source: 2005–09 American Community Survey.

These findings underscore the diverse starting points for suburban communities in terms of needs and changes in need but also portend some of the likely variation we might expect to see in the suburban social service infrastructure. As we will show in the sections that follow, unevenness in the social service infrastructure has implications for nonprofit providers' capacity to adapt and sustain their programs—a mounting concern in these rapidly changing suburban communities where the demand for help is escalating.

Changes, Demands, and Challenges for Social Service Providers

Rising poverty creates new demands for suburban nonprofit social service providers. Using survey data and in-depth interviews, we examine the responsiveness of the suburban nonprofit social service safety net in these three metropolitan areas. In particular, we explore changes in client characteristics and the challenges of providing services in today's suburban context. Where appropriate, we highlight similarities across the three metropolitan areas, but the discussion below also underscores the considerable differences between and within suburbs in Los Angeles, Chicago, and Washington, DC.

Increased and Shifting Demand

Driven in part by the impact of the Great Recession, rising rates of poverty have escalated need across a wide range of suburban communities. Nine out of ten suburban nonprofits interviewed reported increases in the number of persons seeking assistance in the previous 12 months. About eight in ten providers reported serving larger numbers of clients than a year ago. The typical nonprofit reporting increases in demand for assistance has seen demand rise by about 30 percent between 2008 and 2009. However, nearly one-fifth of nonprofits reporting an increase in help-seeking indicated that they had experienced more than a 50 percent increase in the number of clients seeking assistance during that time.

Not only is need increasing in suburban communities, but nearly all suburban nonprofit service providers interviewed report that the types of needs of their client base are changing in response to the prolonged economic downturn. For

Table 11.9   Demographic Characteristics: Population below the Federal Poverty Line, Metropolitan Washington, DC, 2005–09

County/Municipality	Poverty Rate 2000	Poverty Rate 2005–9	Number of Poor Persons 2000	Number of Poor Persons 2005–9	Percent Change
Washington, DC:	**20.2%**	**18.3%**	**109,500**	**102,142**	**-6.7%**
Montgomery County:	**5.4%**	**5.3%**	**47,024**	**49,830**	**6.0%**
• Silver Spring	9.3%	7.4%	7,072	5,595	-20.9%
• Germantown	4.6%	6.5%	2,511	3,981	58.5%
• Rockville	7.8%	3.7%	3,555	2,207	-37.9%
• Wheaton-Glenmont	8.5%	10.0%	4,844	5,903	21.9%
• Gaithersburg	7.1%	8.1%	3,718	4,707	26.6%
Prince George's County:	**7.7%**	**7.4%**	**60,196**	**60,237**	**0.1%**
• Bowie	1.6%	2.9%	805	1,521	88.9%
• Chillum	10.2%	13.5%	3,427	4,476	30.6%
• College Park	19.9%	19.8%	3,154	3,145	-0.3%
• Clinton	3.4%	2.2%	856	578	-32.5%
• Fort Washington	3.7%	4.1%	881	1,037	17.7%
Alexandria	**8.9%**	**7.1%**	**11,279**	**10,059**	**-10.8%**
Arlington	**7.8%**	**7.2%**	**14,371**	**14,545**	**1.2%**
Fairfax County:	**4.5%**	**5.1%**	**43,396**	**51,480**	**18.6%**
• Burke	2.3%	2.7%	1,306	1,496	14.5%
• Centreville	3.0%	5.2%	1,452	2,769	90.7%
• Reston	4.5%	5.2%	2,527	2,774	9.8%
• Annandale	7.0%	5.8%	3,833	3,082	-19.6%
• Chantilly	2.3%	4.4%	944	2,017	113.7%
Loudoun County:	**2.8%**	**2.8%**	**4,637**	**7,823**	**68.7%**
• Leesburg	3.6%	5.4%	1,002	2,027	102.3%
• Purcellville	4.2%	3.0%	150	150	0.0%
• Lovettsville	2.9%	1.4%	25	17	-32.0%
• Hamilton	3.3%	2.3%	19	19	0.0%
• Middleburg	9.9%	9.6%	63	37	-41.3%
Prince William County:	**4.4%**	**5.1%**	**12,182**	**18,022**	**47.9%**
• Dale City	4.4%	5.3%	2,452	3,376	37.7%
• Woodbridge	5.5%	7.7%	1,741	2,649	52.2%

• Lake Ridge	2.3%	1.9%	710	566	-20.3%
• Linton Hall	2.8%	2.5%	248	518	108.9%
• Montclair	2.6%	2.0%	408	371	-9.1%

Source: 2005–09 American Community Survey (combined).

example, specific issues directly related to unemployment are more apparent now in many suburban communities. Fifty-one percent of nonprofits interviewed reported seeing more clients seeking help finding employment compared to a year ago. Nearly 80 percent of providers also indicate that an increasing number of clients are seeking help after having exhausted their unemployment insurance. One workforce development organization in suburban Chicago reported that the number of clients seeking assistance in the past year increased tenfold, from 50 per month to 500 per month.

Other needs are emerging in suburban communities that are directly related to unemployment and lost work earnings due to the recession. More than three-quarters of suburban nonprofits report seeing families with food needs more often than a year ago. Sixty-five percent of nonprofits report more frequent requests for assistance paying utility bills, and nearly 60 percent report more frequent requests for help with mortgage or rent payments. The director of a suburban Chicago organization stated that they are getting thousands of calls a month for utility and rental assistance—many more than the previous year—but stated, "there are only two other agencies in this area that provide utility/rental assistance." Eight of every ten providers interviewed reported seeing more clients who have been evicted as homeowners or as renters in a foreclosed property. Compounding the problem of rising housing need is the lack of affordable housing options for low-income households in suburbs. As one provider noted, "the trend in the last five years is to renovate housing, and low-income housing is being squeezed out. Our families are looking for shelter or piling up with other people."

Changes in the type of need and demand for services have proven challenging for service providers, but equally as difficult has been the change in the *type of client* seeking help. Forty-five percent of providers report that many clients come from households where one or both adults are working, but their earned income is insufficient to make ends meet or lift them over the poverty line. A similar percentage of providers we interviewed indicated that more two-parent households were coming for help compared to previous years. One executive from a suburban office of a large faith-based service provider in Chicago stated, "the face of the poor has changed, it is working families, people that are working and somebody is working two jobs or more—and they still can't make ends meet."

A significant change in the type of people seeking help has been the shift from lower-skilled individuals to clients of

> … mid-to-upper skill level, looking for funds to retrain and some networking opportunities … . The lower-skilled individuals are not seeking services to the

degree they had before, because service centers are saturated with dislocated workers collecting unemployment, [while] low-skilled workers may have exhausted unemployment and are going to other social service organizations for help with basic needs.

Seventy-three percent of nonprofits surveyed indicated that they are seeing many more clients with no previous connection to safety net programs compared to the prior year. A suburban food bank manager noted that the organization was "seeing different clients this year—people who had been working 10 to 20 years that now don't have work." Such sentiments were echoed by an administrator from a small community-based organization outside of Washington, DC that provides emergency assistance and domestic violence services: "we're seeing middle-class clients who are not used to seeking services. We're seeing people who used to be donors who are no longer able to give and are now seeking help."

Few families seeking help for the first time know much about government assistance or community-based nonprofit sources of support. Forty-five percent of nonprofits indicate that they are seeing more clients who are eligible for government assistance such as SNAP or Medicaid but have not applied for such help due to lack of awareness or concern about stigma. A survey respondent in suburban Chicago observed that, "there is a new group of people who don't know where to go for help, they are newly poor and don't know what to do."

Eventually, however, many such families do find their way to local nonprofit organizations. A suburban Los Angeles provider noted that they were serving more families that hesitate to "seek help right away; they don't know where to start. We're getting referrals from churches and schools, trying to get individuals who've been laid off into the office sooner rather than later to get help with food and gas vouchers, so they can pay the rent or mortgage." An executive from another suburban nonprofit organization described rising demand in the second half of 2009 and then noted that people not accustomed to receiving services "are becoming familiar with the fact that there are services available; they are going to county [human service] agencies and they are getting referred to us." Delays in getting help, however, can exacerbate the economic hardships faced by low-income families.

Immigrant Communities

Immigrants—particularly those from Mexico and Central America—are a fast-growing group in many of the suburbs in our three study sites. Yet, immigrants may be the population subgroup most at risk of having their needs go unmet. Consistent with increases in immigrant residents across the suburbs of all three metro areas, 40 percent of nonprofit organizations interviewed provide services for immigrants more often than they did one year ago.[14] Many organizations report serving immigrant groups, but few organizations focus on the special needs of immigrant populations or provide relevant services in a culturally sensitive manner. For example, the director of a suburban nonprofit in Chicago that serves foreign-born Latinos stated,

> we are the only agency of our kind in the suburbs with a bilingual, bicultural staff tailored to the Hispanic community. We have people coming to us from [throughout the suburban metropolitan area]. For our immigration services they come in from Wisconsin and Indiana ... There are no inter-agency coalitions among Latino-serving or immigrant-serving organizations in the suburbs.

The director from an LA-based suburban organization made a similar observation: "There are no other organizations with cultural/language delivery for the Korean population [in this region]." With few organizations equipped to serve a diverse and growing immigrant population, suburban organizations that focus on the immigrant community must stretch their resources to meet demand. A lack of such organizations also means that some immigrants must rely on other programs that may be less equipped to meet their linguistic and cultural needs. In both situations, suburban providers that serve low-income immigrants experience considerable strain to meet the need.

Nonprofits in our study that worked with Latino immigrants also described concern about the potential impact of anti-immigrant sentiment on immigrant-serving providers. One director in Chicago referred to an agency in a neighboring suburb

> whose main problem is that they have an organized anti-immigrant group [in their community]. I don't know how [the agency] can work when there is a rally outside their door saying they shouldn't help undocumented immigrants—that they should all be deported—and blocking funding, going to the city council. ... Thank God that's not happening here.

Even if it is not overt, anti-immigrant sentiment sometimes lies just beneath the surface. Upon completing a large fund-raising event in the community, this same director noticed a series of anti-immigrant comments posted online in response to news coverage of the event. "People were saying 'these undocumented should all go back' and 'they like everything for free because they're parasites,'" she said. "It's scary. We know the sentiment is there."

---

14   Our survey data are limited and unable to provide detailed information about the characteristics of the immigrant populations served by the providers in our sample. There is some evidence that different immigrant groups may have differential access to social service providers (see Allard and Roth 2012).

Combined with the small number of organizations working with expanding immigrant communities, the "chilling effect" that anti-immigrant sentiment can have on suburban social service organizations is cause for concern. The "chilling effect" can soften the support that these nonprofits receive from non-immigrant community members and local institutions. It can also make it difficult for these agencies to provide direct services to working poor immigrant families because it disrupts their ability to conduct outreach and serve as advocates—important components of their service missions to strengthen immigrant communities and neighborhoods. Building trust may not be difficult for nonprofits that have a long history of involvement with the immigrant community, but newer organizations or those that are only recently adapting to the needs of an emerging immigrant population may not as easily gain the trust they need to effectively serve the foreign-born community.

The Search for Affordable Office Space

It seems intuitive that nonprofit providers could respond to changes in poverty by locating services in places that are experiencing significant increases in poverty and/ or places accessible to the people who need them. Quality, affordable office space, however, is not readily available in all suburban areas, and many nonprofit service organizations are restricted in the types of space they can afford or that is suitable for their needs. Often operating on shoestring budgets, nonprofit service providers cannot afford to buy or rent expensive commercial or office space. Among those nonprofits we surveyed, slightly less than half own office space (49.4 percent), nearly 61 percent rent at least some of their office space, and almost half of nonprofits (47 percent) report using office space donated to them by other organizations or government agencies (see Table 11.10). Forty-two percent of nonprofits that rent office space report paying rent lower than the market rate. Local government is the most frequent connection to donated space for nonprofit providers (67.6 percent), but slightly more than one-third of nonprofit providers receive space from another nonprofit organization (37.8 percent) and nearly one-third receive space from a church (32.4 percent). Many nonprofits indicated that they have the option to obtain donated space from a local church if they need it, and several indicate having relied on religious institutions for donated space in the past.

The difficulty finding suitable affordable office space leads many suburban nonprofits to share space with one another. Almost 30 percent of respondents that own their building lease or rent some portion of their space to other social service organizations or community-based nonprofits (28.2 percent). Forty percent of renters lease their space from other nonprofit social service organizations. Roughly half of survey respondents indicated that they have partnered with other organizations to colocate or share office space in the previous year (not shown in Table 11.10). Efforts to colocate not only solve a fiscal puzzle for service providers, they also can make services more accessible to clients in need of a range of supports. A relatively large agency in Maryland states,

Table 11.10   Survey Respondents' Space Usage in 2010

Own:	**49.4%**
% of owners that purchased space since late 2007	15.4%
% of owners that lease or rent to other nonprofits	28.2%
Rent:	**60.8%**
% of renters that rent from other nonprofit	39.6%
% of renters that rent from local government	8.3%
% of renters that rent at subsidized or below market rate	41.7%
Donated:	**46.8%**
% of entities using donated space from other nonprofit	37.8%
% of entities using donated space from religions congregation	32.4%
% of entities using donated space from local government	67.6%

Notes: N = 98; percentages (Own, Rent, Donated) do not add up to 100 percent because some organizations have multiple spaces secured under different types of agreements.
Source: Survey of Suburban Social Service Providers (2010).

> we partner with a large number of other nonprofits, and work to attract complementary services into our office complex. We currently have ten other NGOs [nongovernmental organizations] here either full- or part-time. Clients are able to access mental health, primary care, emergency assistance, food, clothing, and transitional housing from the providers here.

Compounding the challenge of finding affordable office and program space, suburban providers often have to serve wider geographic areas than their urban counterparts. We found that 33 percent of our study respondents operate programs for low-income populations in more than one *county*, and 62 percent have programs in more than one *municipality*. Those that operate in more than one site often have a main office in one community, with satellite programs operating in schools, churches, an apartment converted to office space, or community centers in neighboring areas. The distances between these places can be several hours by car. This creates logistical challenges for workers who travel between multiple sites and for managers who coordinate an array of programs, each in a different place under a different space arrangement.

Multisite organizations in the suburbs are able to address some of the spatial mismatch between low-income residents and the services they need, yet not all of these locations are full-day program sites, and some are only used for single-session community events. The director of a large, multisite organization in suburban Los Angeles explains that, "In addition to locations where full-time services are provided, we also provide our services at multiple locations on a part-time basis (1–2–3 days a week)." The same Los Angeles director continues, "Additionally, we have a multitude of arrangements whereby we will use someone's space to provide one service only," such as an immigration workshop, a parent education program, or a community event. This illustrates the enormous effort of suburban providers to locate services—even if temporarily—in places that are more convenient for the suburban poor. However, it also underscores that the suburban safety net is fragmented and irregular, both across time and space.

Funding

At the same time that need and demand for services are rising, suburban providers in our study report many threats to their program funding. Our data indicate that suburban nonprofit service providers—like those in central-city areas—piece together program funds from a few primary sources (Smith and Lipsky 1993, Allard 2009a). More than eight of every ten nonprofits that responded to our survey received funding from government grants or contracts. Often providers were managing several different grants or contracts for services from several different state, county, or local government agencies. In addition, over 90 percent reported funding from either charitable philanthropic organizations or from private individual giving (cash or in-kind). Fewer than 15 percent of nonprofits interviewed received Medicaid reimbursements for services, and Medicaid composed only a small share of funding for most of those providers (Allard and Smith 2009).[15] Despite the mix of revenues, most suburban nonprofits were highly dependent on public funding. For example, the typical nonprofit service provider surveyed received roughly half of its operating budget from government grants or contract accounts, with charitable philanthropy and private giving contributing fairly evenly to the remaining balance.

At the time of the survey most state governments—critical sources of funding for social service programs—were facing substantial budget deficits and imposing cuts to human service budgets. For example, Illinois was facing an estimated $14 billion deficit, while California was grappling with an $18 billion deficit. Each state cut social service program funding by several billion dollars in fiscal year 2009/10, and more significant cuts were expected in the following fiscal year. Deficits in Maryland ($2.8 billion) and Virginia ($3.6 billion) were smaller by comparison but still posed a threat to social service program funding (McNichol, Oliff and Johnson 2010).

---

15   Consistent with evidence of the rising importance of Medicaid as a source of social service funding, however, a few providers we interviewed indicated they were exploring ways to begin providing services for Medicaid-eligible clients. As state governments continue to resolve budget deficits, Medicaid may become increasingly seen as the most stable or predictable source of government funding for social services.

Nonprofits interviewed were clearly aware of the threat that state budget deficits posed to ongoing operations. A large, multisite provider in the Chicago suburbs stated,

> We are already seeing the effects of the State's poor budgeting on our programs for the current fiscal year. From all that we have heard, we anticipate cuts from 16–50% for the next year. Already, we know some of the funding we receive from DHS will remain the same. In essence, this is a decrease as each year, our costs go up but the revenue decreases. We have not seen a cost of doing business increase in over 5 years.

Similarly, a director of a workforce development organization said,

> The committed state funding for one of our major programs is once again expected to be delayed by months. This will mean a significant impact to the agency budget which in turn will affect operating decisions. The state will still require delivery of program service hours as agreed upon in the contract irregardless [sic] of whether the agency has available resources or not to keep programs operating.

The uncertainty of state budgets affected small organizations as well. The director of a food pantry in suburban Los Angeles explained that "In 2007 and 2008 we operated with a deficit, decreasing our reserve account by $40,000, leaving a balance of $65,000. If we were to continue depleting our reserve account we would close our doors in two years."

Program funding cuts have become a common annual event for many nonprofit providers, compounding during the years since the Great Recession began. No one source of funding is more durable than any other. Nearly half of survey respondents reported a drop in funding from any one of four key revenue sources in the fiscal year prior to the survey—Medicaid reimbursements, government grants and contracts, grants from charitable organizations and foundations, and private giving—and about 25 percent experienced cuts across *all four* funding streams from 2009 to 2010.[16] Although a handful of providers in our surveys reported substantial cuts in funding of more than 75 percent in fiscal year 2009–10, most of the reductions in program funding reported were less than 10 to 15 percent. Lost funding over any amount has been difficult to replace in the current economic and fiscal environment. Less than 40 percent of providers who reported cuts in one source of funding were able to find additional funding from another source.

---

16   Such figures are consistent with other recent studies of the nonprofit sector. See Foundation Center (2010); Lawrence and Mukai (2010); Nonprofit Finance Fund (2010); Schroeter-Deegan (2010); United Way Metropolitan Chicago and Chicago Community Trust (2007).

Many of the nonprofits in our study are located in suburban communities with few potential corporate partners and few networks through which to connect to private philanthropy. As one nonprofit director in a high-poverty suburb of Chicago stated, "the level of begging and groveling you have to do is just different [here] because you don't go to church with those people or you're not in school with them. ... We put a lot more time and effort into it, and the fruit is just not there."

Limited access to foundations and corporate partnerships was a common refrain among providers in suburban Los Angeles, Chicago, and Washington, DC. Providers often referred to these limitations in spatial terms. An executive director of a large faith-based nonprofit in suburban Los Angeles explained the difficulty organizations that operate inland from the city of Los Angeles face when trying to access philanthropic support:

> The inland counties received one-tenth of the charitable giving relative to other areas in southern California. The point is that we have tremendous needs, but we don't have the economic base to meet the need. We don't have a coast. In Los Angeles, where there's a coast there's money—that's where CEOs want to live. Foundations, particularly local foundations, get their money from the local community.

An administrator from an emergency assistance provider in suburban Maryland shared her efforts to raise support from county government in light of the fact that many clients came from far outside the organization's immediate community:

> Our county [and catchment area] extends to the fringe of DC. We had people driving all the way from there. ... We asked if county councilpersons are willing to help their constituents. They haven't been willing to pitch in, however. ... I give new clients outside of [our catchment area] the number of their county councilperson and tell them to call.

Thus, gaps in suburban social services may arise in part due to the challenges providers face in securing sufficient public and philanthropic dollars given their physical location in the suburbs and the large service areas that characterize the suburban context.

Responding to Need

Rising need, fragmented availability of services, and unstable revenue streams place great strain on suburban nonprofit social service providers. To respond to these pressures and maintain operations, suburban nonprofits were considering a number of responses to cope with increased need amid stretched program resources in the spring of 2010. Among the providers in our sample, 45.6 percent

Table 11.11   Type of Coping Strategy Being Considered for Coming Year

	Percentage of Organizations
Prioritizing Clients by Degree of Need	50.0%
Referring a Greater Number of Clients Out	45.6%
Reducing FT and/or PT Staff	41.7%
Reducing Overhead Costs	41.3%
Expanding Waitlist	35.6%
Reducing Services Available	33.3%
Reducing Number of Clients Served	27.5%
Reducing Salaries	16.1%
Reducing Hours of Operation	14.1%
Merging with Another Organization	8.6%
Anticipate Closing Down	4.6%

Note: N = 77.

Source: Survey of Suburban Social Service Providers (2010).

were considering referring a larger number of clients to other organizations in the community and 27.5 percent anticipated juggling rising demand by reducing the number of clients served. Just over 14 percent of providers were considering reducing their hours of operation (see Table 11.11). A nonprofit service organization in San Bernardino County that has experienced significant increases in adult clients seeking help with employment, food, and housing described the challenge of rising caseloads: "We've had to turn away more clients than ever before. With the number of people calling for help, the only way to be really fair is to set up a day of the week when people can call in."

Another common strategy used to manage rising demand for help is to expand client waiting lists. Over one-third of all suburban nonprofits interviewed were thinking of placing larger numbers of clients on waiting lists and increasing the length of time clients must wait before getting help. In such an environment it is not surprising that nonprofit service providers feel compelled to make determinations about the severity of need across applicants for assistance. Fifty percent of nonprofits indicated they were weighing strategies to "triage" clients, prioritizing those with more severe or acute needs. One respondent explained, "This is why our client numbers remain the same—more people are seeking services, but we can only help a certain number." A nonprofit operating emergency assistance and employment-related programs in northern Virginia explained, "We have not turned anyone away—but there are waitlists for certain programs." This same provider later noted that "anyone who has emergency needs is seen, but other programs—like our self-sufficiency program—have lengthening wait times."

Providers are also responding to increased pressures and demands by relying more on technology in order to improve services, outreach, and billing. For example, a suburban Chicago provider is "enhancing the use of technology to reach more individuals in an effective and efficient manner—web page improvements, Facebook accounts, Twitter accounts." An agency in suburban Los Angeles is working closely with the Social Security Administration to better serve the homeless:

> We work closely with [the] Social Security Administration in helping our clients get public assistance. ... They have developed a new way to [help us] keep in touch with clients—Community Voice Mail—and we are experimenting with them to see if it improves communication with homeless individuals.

A call center for rent and utility assistance in Chicago's suburbs has made communication and resource distribution more efficient. "This has dramatically streamlined the process for distributing financial resources to those in need," a director explained. "A very large number of agencies throughout the suburban portion of Cook County are participating." A suburban food bank in Washington, DC is revamping its website to facilitate online ordering. The same food bank is also delivering its services to low-income neighborhoods, loading up vans with food and driving these mobile pantries to areas that are underserved.

Increased collaboration with other nonprofit organizations is another common strategy for coping with the strain of heightened demand in an uncertain economic environment. Fifty-seven percent of providers surveyed reported that they collaborate with other local nonprofit organizations, and nearly 40 percent stated that collaboration is a frequent activity. For example, a large nonprofit organization in suburban Los Angeles has worked to cultivate collaborative relationships with other local organizations as a way to provide better quality services to clients. In doing so, this organization "has strengthened partnerships with other businesses and organizations to maximize delivery of services and assistance to clients."

In Chicago, one respondent explained, "we have expanded services to Faith-based and community based organizations, and we are leveraging resources and expertise of the local community colleges." Particularly in suburbs where there are few other providers to partner with, these collaborations can be essential. An executive director of a nonprofit in suburban Washington, DC explains the mutually beneficial nature of these collaborations: "We are involved in a 3-way partnership: A local church provides office space to our agency as part of their outreach efforts. Adjacent to our office, the church hall is being used as a stand-alone classroom for 10 special needs high school students. They attend academic classes in the hall, and work repairing our clients' homes as part of their building skills training." In this example, the collaboration provides affordable office space for the provider, increases the efficiency of service provision, and potentially lowers barriers to access for immigrant groups who may be more willing to seek services from a program that is housed in a church.

Many of the agencies in our study spoke of building ties to local and nonlocal institutions in order to recruit or dispatch volunteer workers. For example, an agency providing services to families in Montgomery County, Maryland, collaborates with community colleges and graduate programs to recruit interns. The director of another organization in suburban Washington, DC—a large multisite provider—explained that she has forged new partnerships in response to the recession: "Our construction training program has taken a big hit because there are no jobs in the commercial sector. Our placement rates are down to 25%, [so] we pursued a relationship with a local community college to shift our focus to building maintenance." Other organizations we interviewed are relying more heavily on Americorps volunteers for what one director termed "non-professional program delivery," or drawing on the growing pool of unemployed workers as a volunteer source. One employment-related agency in suburban Chicago reported that it "set up a volunteer network for the unemployed individuals to keep them engaged and gaining skills while they are looking for new employment opportunities."

Collaboration as a coping strategy emerged as a theme among immigrant- and Latino-serving organizations as well. Immigrant-serving respondents spoke of the need to foster a more inclusive environment for working poor immigrant families. Building alliances and coalitions with local law enforcement, politicians, community-based organizations, and immigrant-serving organizations are all potential steps toward creating such an environment.[17] One suburban Chicago provider described a new initiative to better connect organizations in order to provide a broader range of services for immigrants across a larger area. Another suburban nonprofit executive in Chicago described "a Latino coalition in the community—there are banks and libraries and other agencies like churches, and attorneys. We meet once a month [to discuss emergent issues concerning the Latino immigrant community]."

While collaboration is an effective coping strategy for these (and other) reasons, survey respondents were careful to explain that it is not adequate to offset the challenges of providing services in the suburbs. While funding limitations can sometimes be minimized by interagency collaborations, these collaborative opportunities are circumscribed in suburbs where there are few other nonprofits. Our survey respondents often describe a thinness or fragility to the local nonprofit sector that makes it difficult to find partners or collaborators and better serve the changing needs of the community. An executive from an emergency shelter program in suburban Virginia noted the dilemma created when demand exceeds capacity and there are no programs for referrals. Her shelter is "turning away 300 people per month ... [which is a big problem because] we're the only

---

17   These alliances can be difficult to build, particularly in communities that have not been altogether welcoming to immigrant newcomers.

shelter in the area, so we have no one to refer them to." Another suburban Los Angeles nonprofit in our study receives several thousand calls inquiring about emergency cash assistance each month, leading an administrator to observe, "the problem is that there are only two other agencies in this area that provide utility or rental assistance—one of the major requests [from clients]."

The fragility of the local nonprofit sector can lead to program closures that ultimately place even greater strain on the programs that remain. Thirty-one percent of nonprofits interviewed indicated that they had experienced increased demand for help due to program cutbacks or agency closures elsewhere in their community. Many nonprofit service providers recognize that inquiries for assistance are driven in part by caseload management choices made in other organizations. As one provider put it, "most of our programs get clients through referrals. We're at the end of the chain of a series of decision makers. We see things that are happening [in the community], but someone else is sending us the clients." Even with organizations working to fill gaps across multiple suburban jurisdictions, the relatively limited number of suburban providers means that the assistance available to low-income households may be determined simply by where they reside, with some suburban communities receiving a more generous or more balanced bundle of social service programs than others.

Indeed, many survey respondents provided examples of their creative resilience in the face of new and difficult challenges, yet nearly all of them also spoke about "getting by" rather than "getting ahead." Regarding the latter, some larger nonprofits have been able to hire a grant director or absorb other nonprofits to help their organizations be more competitive. "We have hired a Fund Development position so we hope we see some results," explained one director. "We hope the new position will take us into larger gifts and a planned giving campaign—[it's a] spend money to make money concept." This does not come without its risks, however, and concerns for long-term sustainability loom large.

Many organizations we spoke with are confident that they can remain solvent in the short run, but planning further ahead is much less certain. "I have some indication that supporting foundations will pick up the slack from government agencies," stated one provider. "The challenge is that many of the foundations do not want us to become too dependent upon them in the long run." The director of a youth-serving organization in suburban Los Angeles noted, "Fewer new grants will be issued and competition for the ones that are will be greater ... . One of the Foundations that supported us for a number of years actually closed down." This uncertainty is common in suburban Chicago as well. One nonprofit there was able to secure funding in 2009 and 2010, but "it isn't always certain how foundations and organizations will reassess their guidelines as (or when) funding ability changes." Not all organizations are experiencing uncertainty to this degree, but even the most confident are preparing for more difficult times to come. The director of a suburban Los Angeles organization—a food bank— explained, "The foundations that support us are very stable and we do not expect a decrease. However we are increasing the number of foundation that we are applying to."

Conclusion

Our examination of suburban communities outside of Chicago, Los Angeles, and Washington, DC reveals suburbs to be quite diverse in terms of poverty, race, and ethnic composition. Over the course of the past decade, many suburbs have experienced unprecedented increases in their poor populations, yet the nonprofit social service sector—so critical to providing help to the poor—is faced with numerous obstacles in its effort to keep up with these demographic shifts. This creates a dilemma for social service providers: to find new and adaptive ways to fulfill their mission in serving the poor even as the challenges of providing services in the suburbs makes it increasingly difficult to do so. The Great Recession has exacerbated this dilemma by further accentuating the demand for services and destabilizing the financial security of the organizations that provide them. Indeed, all suburban nonprofit service organizations we interviewed reported increased demand for help and expanded client caseloads from a year or two ago.

Suburban service providers are coping with this strain by employing an array of strategies. Collaboration with a variety of stakeholders—other nonprofits, religious institutions, and schools—was an important coping strategy that emerged from our survey. These relationships can help service providers overcome obstacles such as finding affordable space, recruiting volunteers, and making services more accessible to clients in a variety of places. However, although partnerships are useful for these (and other) reasons, they are not a panacea for the complex challenges of service provision in the suburbs. Depending on the suburb, it may be unreasonable to expect that suburban nonprofits can build collaborations that enable them to overcome these obstacles. Quite simply, the possibilities for collaboration are limited in many places because there are few (or no) other organizations in these areas. Furthermore, depending on the mission and capacity of the organizations that *do* operate in a given community, a partnership may not be adequate to meet the particular needs of the low-income families who live there.

Additional research on the suburban safety net is necessary to understand the role of nonprofit organizations in metropolitan safety nets. Research needs to expand to additional suburbs, gather different types of data, and examine how components of the nonprofit service sector interact with variable suburban contexts to meet the needs of the poor. Suburbs with a rapid growth of low-skilled immigrants provide one such area in need of more research. How do service providers manage the challenges of working with immigrants in places that are unwelcoming to newcomers? How is capacity to provide services affected when suburban nonprofits work with multiple immigrant groups representing different nationalities, cultures, and languages? What partnerships are most effective in these environments?

The absence of nonprofit service providers or the presence of inadequately resourced nonprofits will make it difficult for communities to respond to rising need and continued changes within suburban labor markets, even after local economies recover from the recent downturn. To the extent that nonprofit organizations cannot sustain funding or replace lost funds, many may be forced to close programs and doors. Suburban families in need will have a harder time finding help, possibly leading many to experience more serious economic hardship. Not only is there the prospect of less safety net help for low-income populations in the near term, but also there may be fewer sources of support in the future. Without a more resilient funding structure and the institutional supports necessary to improve capacity, nonprofit providers may continue to get by without getting ahead for years to come, making it difficult for suburban communities to respond to permanent shifts in need.

So what does this mean for these suburban communities moving forward? First, the need for the safety net in the suburbs will persist. As of the writing of this chapter, the number of poor persons in the suburbs has risen steadily for over a decade. Indeed, even during times of strong economic growth during the early 2000s, the number of poor people living in the suburbs continued to rise. In other words, even as the economy rebounds, the demand for services in the suburbs will not soon disappear. Second, nonprofit social service providers will remain critical to the local safety net for years to come. As the safety net has evolved it has gradually, yet decisively, come to rely on local nonprofits to distribute important services and resources for low-income adults, and there is no indication that nonprofit social service providers themselves will become any less important to help seekers.

Therefore, given that demand for social services in the suburbs will persist and that nonprofits are essential components of the safety net, we should be concerned for the resilience, diversity, and accessibility of suburban service providers. To be sure, there are examples of large social service providers in our sample who are strategically expanding operations to meet the rising demand for services. Yet the predominant story across our sample is that nonprofits are struggling to keep their doors open. In the long run, this suggests that the geography of the suburban safety net will continue to become more uneven. Communities with an established nonprofit sector, a strong tax base, a history of support from local and county governments, and reliable provider networks are at an advantage relative to neighboring suburbs that lack these characteristics. To the extent that providers are constrained by funding or reliant on local government for support, they may be unable to serve low-income individuals and families outside their immediate geography. Ultimately, this will result in a suburban geography that is increasingly unequal, exacerbating the difficulties for the poor who happen to live in areas where the suburban safety net does not reach.

If there is a silver lining, it is that nonprofit organizations are accustomed to unexpected changes in funding patterns. This means that many of the smaller entities are lithe enough to adapt to new challenges, and the largest nonprofits have enough resources to expand service delivery to areas where need is the greatest. These are resilient, mission-driven organizations. The nonprofit providers in our sample are fully aware that their services are of critical importance for the families they serve, and they know that if they close their doors there may not be any other provider who can meet the need. Therefore, we expect that nonprofit service organizations will continue to innovate, collaborate, and fund-raise in order to maintain operations, even if it means scaling down programs in the face of rising need.

Acknowledgements

This project was supported by the Metropolitan Policy Program at the Brookings Institution, the Population Research Center at NORC and the University of Chicago, and National Institute of Child Health and Human Development (NICHD) Grant #5R24HD051152-07. The authors thank Alan Berube and Elizabeth Kneebone for comments on previous drafts.

References

Allard, S.W. and Roth, B.J. 2012. *The Uneven Geography of Immigrant Settlement and Social Services*. Working Paper presented at the University of Chicago Doctoral Theory Workshop. 1 March.

Allard, S.W. and Roth, B.J. 2010. *Strained Suburbs: The Social Services Challenges of Rising Suburban Poverty*. Washington DC: Brookings Institution.

Allard, S.W. 2009a. *Out of Reach: Place, Poverty, and the New American Welfare State*. New Haven, CT: Yale University Press.

Allard, S.W. 2009b. *State Dollars, Nonstate Support: The Complexity of Local Nonprofit Welfare Provision in the United States*. Paper presented at the Harvard Academy for International and Area Studies, Harvard University. 8–9 May.

Allard, S.W. 2009c. Mismatches and unmet needs: Access to social services in urban and rural America, in *Welfare Reform and its Long-Term Consequence for America's Poor*, edited by James P. Ziliak. Cambridge: Cambridge University Press.

Allard, S.W. and Smith, S.R. 2009. *Medicaid and the Funding of Nonprofit Service Organizations*. Paper presented at the 2009 American Political Science Association Meetings. 3–6 September.

Allard, S.W., Tolman, R. and Rosen, D. 2003. Proximity to service providers and service utilization among welfare recipients.' *Journal of Policy Analysis and Management* 22(4), 599–613.

Andrulis, D. and Duchon, L. 2007. The changing landscape of hospital capacity in large cities and suburbs: Implications for the safety net in Metropolitan America. *Journal of Urban Health*, 84(3), 400–414.

Andrulis, D., Duchon, L. and Reid, H. 2004. *Before and After Welfare Reform: The Uncertain Progress for Poor Families and Children in the Nation's 100*

Largest Cities and Their Suburbs. New York, NY: SUNY Downstate Medical Center.

Baldassare, M. 1986. *Trouble in Paradise: The Suburban Transformation of America.* New York, NY: Columbia University.

Berube, A. and Kneebone, E. 2006. *Two Steps Back: City and Suburban Poverty Trends, 1999–2005.* Washington, DC: Brookings Institution.

Berube, A. and Frey, W.H. 2002. *A Decade of Mixed Blessings: Urban and Suburban Poverty in Census 2000.* Washington, DC: Brookings Institution.

Center on Budget and Policy Priorities. 2010. *Policy Basics: Introduction to the Food Stamp Program.* Washington, DC: Center on Budget and Policy Priorities.

Danziger, S. and Gottschalk, P. 1993. *Uneven Tides: Rising Inequality in America.* New York, NY: Russell Sage Foundation.

Duchon, L., Andrulis, D. and Reid, H. 2004. Measuring progress in meeting healthy people goals for low birth weight and infant mortality among the 100 largest cities and their suburbs. *Journal of Urban Health,* 81(3), 323–39.

Farley, R. 1964. Suburban persistence. *American Sociological Review,* 29(1), 38–47.

Felland, L.E., Lauer, J.R. and Cunningham, P.J. 2009. *Suburban Poverty and the Health Care Safety Net.* Washington, DC: Center for Studying Health System Change.

Fisher, G.M. 1992. The development and history of the poverty thresholds. *Social Security Bulletin,* 55(4), 3–14.

Foundation Center. 2010. Foundation Support Declined in 2008 for Half of Major Funding Areas. New York, NY: Foundation Center.

Gottschalk, P. and Danziger, S. 2005. Inequality of wage rates, earnings and family income in the United States, 1975–2002. *Review of Income and Wealth,* 51(2), 231–54.

Hendrick, R. and Mossberger, K. 2009. *Uneven Capacity and Delivery of Human Services in the Chicago Suburbs: The Role of Townships and Municipalities.* Chicago, IL: Chicago Community Trust.

Holliday, A.L. and Dwyer, R.E. 2009. Suburban neighborhood poverty in U.S. Metropolitan Areas in 2000. *City & Community,* 8(2), 155–76.

Holzer, H. and Stoll, M. 2007. *Where Workers Go, Do Jobs Follow? Metropolitan Labor Markets in the U.S., 1990–2000.* Washington, DC: Brookings Institution.

Isaacs, J.B., Vericker, T., Macomber, J. and Kent, A. 2009. *Kids' Share: An Analysis of Federal Expenditures through 2008.* Washington, DC: Urban Institute and Brookings Institution.

Jackson, K. 1985. *Crabgrass Frontier: The Suburbanization of the United States.* New York, NY: Oxford University Press.

Katz, B., Creighton, M., Amsterdam, D. and Chowkwanyun, M. 2010. Immigration and the new Metropolitan geography. *Journal of Urban Affairs,* 32(5), 523–47.

Kingsley, T.G. and Pettit, K.L.S. 2007. *Concentrated Poverty: Dynamics of Change.* Washington, DC: Urban Institute.

Kneebone, E. 2010. *The Great Recession and Poverty in Metropolitan America.* Washington, DC: Brookings Institution.

Kneebone, E. and Garr, E. 2010a. *The Landscape of Recession: Unemployment and Safety Net Services across Urban and Suburban America.* Washington, DC: Brookings Institution.

Kneebone, E. and Garr, E. 2010b. *The Suburbanization of Poverty: Trends in Metropolitan America, 2000 to 2008.* Washington, DC: Brookings Institution.

Kneebone, E. 2009. *Economic Recovery and the EITC: Expanding the Earned Income Tax Credit to Benefit Families and Places.* Washington, DC: Brookings Institution.

Kneebone, E. 2008. *Bridging the Gap: Refundable Tax Credits in Metropolitan and Rural America.* Washington, DC: Brookings Institution.

Kruse, K.M. and Sugrue, T.J. 2006. The new suburban history, in *The New Suburban History*, edited by K.M. Kruse and T.J. Sugrue. Chicago, IL: The University of Chicago Press.

Lawrence, S. and Mukai, R. 2010. *Foundation Growth and Giving Estimates.* New York, NY: Foundation Center.

Logan, J.R. and Alba, R. 1993. Locational returns to human capital: Minority access to suburban community resources. *Demography, 30*(2), 243–68.

Logan, J.R. and Schneider, M. 1981. The stratification of Metropolitan suburbs, 1960—1970. *American Sociological Review*, 46(2), 175–86.

Mabli, J., Cohen, R., Potter, F. and Zhao, Z. 2010. *Hunger in America 2010: National Report Prepared for Feeding America.* Princeton, NJ: Mathematica Policy Research, Inc.

Massey, D.S. and Capoferro, C. 2008. The geographic diversification of American immigration, in *New Faces in New Places*, edited by D.S. Massey. New York, NY: Russell Sage Foundation.

Massey, D.S. and Denton, N. 1993. *American Apartheid.* Cambridge, MA: Harvard University Press.

McNichol, E., Oliff, P. and Johnson, N. 2010. *Recession Continues to Batter State Budgets; State Responses Could Slow Recovery.* Washington, DC: Center on Budget and Policy Priorities.

Mikelbank, B.A. 2004. A typology of suburban places. *Housing Policy Debate*, 15(4), 935–64.

Murphy, A.K. 2010. The symbolic dilemmas of suburban poverty: Challenges and opportunities posed by variations in the contours of suburban poverty. *Sociological Forum*, 25(3), 541–69.

Murphy, A.K. and Wallace, D. 2010. Opportunities for making ends meet and upward mobility: Differences in organizational deprivation across urban and suburban poor neighborhoods. *Social Science Quarterly*, 91(5), 1164–86.

Nonprofit Finance Fund. 2010. *2010 State of the Nonprofit Sector Survey.* New York, NY: Nonprofit Finance Fund.

Orfield, M. 2002. *American Metro Politics: The New Suburban Reality.* Washington, DC: Brookings Institution.

Pitti, S.J. 2003. *The Devil in Silicon Valley: Northern California, Race, and Mexican Americans*. Princeton, NJ: Princeton University Press.

Schroeter-Deegan, J. 2010. *Economic Outlook 2010: Illinois Nonprofits and Grantmakers Still Reeling After Rough Year*. Chicago, IL: Donors Forum.

Simms, M.C. 2008. *Weathering Job Loss: Unemployment Insurance*. Washington, DC: Urban Institute.

Singer, A. 2008. Twenty-first-century gateways: An introduction, in *Twenty-First Century Gateways*, edited by A. Singer, S.W. Hardwick and C.B. Brettell. Washington, DC: Brookings Institution.

Smith, S.R. and Lipsky, M. 1993. *Nonprofits for Hire: The Welfare State in the Age of Contracting*. Cambridge, MA: Harvard University Press.

Tax Policy Center, Urban Institute, and Brookings Institution. 2010. *Spending on the EITC, Child Tax Credit, and AFDC/TANF, 1976—2010* [Online]. Available at www.taxpolicycenter.org [accessed: 15 August 2010].

United Way Metropolitan Chicago and Chicago Community Trust 2007. *A Report on the Chicago Region's Health and Human Services Sector*. Chicago, IL: United Way Metropolitan Chicago and Chicago Community Trust.

U.S. Bureau of the Census. *2009 Census*. Washington, DC: U.S. Bureau of the Census.

U.S. Department of Health and Human Services. 2010. *TANF Financial Data*. Washington, DC: U.S. Department of Health and Human Services.

U.S. Department of Housing and Urban Development, Office of Community Planning and Development. 2010. *The 2009 Annual Homeless Assessment Report to Congress*. Washington, DC: U.S. Department of Housing and Urban Development.

U.S. House of Representatives, House Committee on Ways and Means. 2004. *Green Book*. Washington, DC: U.S. House of Representatives.

U.S. Office of Management and Budget (OMB). 2000. *Standards for Defining Metropolitan and Micropolitan Statistical Areas*. Washington, DC: U.S. Office of Management and Budget.

Wiese, A. 1999. The other suburbanites: African American suburbanization in the North before 1950. *The Journal of American History*, 85(4), 1495–524.

Wilson, W.J. 1987. *The Truly Disadvantaged*. Chicago, IL: The University of Chicago Press.

Index

Bold page numbers indicate figures, italic numbers indicate tables.

abandonment crisis 7, 42, 60, 62, 69, 72, 136, 177–9, 185, 201, 229
affordable housing 2, 35, 40, 42, 52, 70, 72, 74–5, 134, 139, 177, 181, 229–30, 243, 254, 262, 267
American Community Survey (ACS) 6, 16, 19, 39, 41, *41*, 43, **45**, 46, *47*, *48*, *49*, *50*, **51**, *51*, *54*, *55*, 56, *57*, **58**, **59**, **60**, **61**, **63**, *64*, *65*, **66**, *67*, **68**, **71**, *72*, **73**, *114*, *115*, 158, 195, 213, *255*, *257*, *258*, *259*, *261*, *262*, *263*, *265*
Anacker, K.B. 1, 3, 4, 60, 62, 80, 81, 82, 123, 136, 154, 155, 188
anchor institution 227, 233–5, 239
anti-immigrant 126, 269–70
appreciation 4, 17
Arizona, immigration policy in 84, 117–18, 136, 177, 219
Asian 4, 90, 94, *255*, *256*, 257, *258*
assets 3, 17, 226, 234, 243, 245
assimilation 7, 116, 123
at-risk suburbs 2–3

Baldassare, M. 1, 2, 250
Baltimore County 7, 140, **141**, 142, 146, 155, 187–9, **190**, 190–6, 202, 208
    Black/African American communities in 188–95, **190**
Bel Air Road, Baltimore County, Maryland 188–9, **190**, 195, *197*, *198*, 201
Berube, A. 1, 3–4, 15–16, 20, 26, 29, 42–3, 52, 82, 120, 135, 230–1, 234, 247, 250, 281
Bier, T.E. 1–2, 4, 155, 172, 180
Black/African communities in Baltimore County 2–4, 7, *33*, *34*, 45, 48, *49*, 62, 64, 67, **68**, 69, 74, 82, 84, 86,

88, **90**, 90, **91**, 91, **92**, 92, **93**, 93–6, **99**, 99, 100–2, 104–9, *114*, *115*, 140, *147*, 148, 180, 183, 187–92, 194–200, 202, 205–8, 221–2, 228
blockbusting 62, 187, 189, 190–1, 194, 196, 198, 227
Brettell, C.B. 113, 118
Build a Better Burb competition 138

Carpentersville, Illinois 7, 113, *115*, 116–18, 120–7, *260*, *264*
censuses, decennial 6, 16, 19, **21**, *21*, *23*, *24*, *25*, *27*, *28*, *31*, *33*, *114*, *115*, 158, *see also* decennial census
Charles, S.L. 140, 148
Chester, Pennsylvania 214, 220, 222–3, **224**, **225**, 225–33, 235–9, 241–3
Chicago, Illinois 33, 74, 82, 84, 97, 134, 140, 148, 190, 195, 249, 252, 253, *254*, *256*, 257, *259*, *260*, 262–3, *264*, 265, 267–9, 281
city models 85–6, *see also* Traditional model of urban form
Civil Rights Act 227
civil rights 119, 187, 190, 191, 192, 193, 194, 199, 208, 227
class 3–5, 34, 84, 86, 87, 93, 108–9, 117, 118, 120, 124, 136, 148, 163, 182, 193–5, 203, 205, 215, 228, 238, 243, 247, 250, 268, *see also* middle-class, working class
Cleveland, foreclosures in 178–9
Cleveland, Ohio 3, 4, 7, 26, *30*, 59, 155, 177–80, 182, 183, 185, 234, 240, 251
Cleveland Heights, Ohio 180–4
color, of 4, 39–40, 46, 48, 62, 65, **66**, 66–7, 70, 74, 82, 84, 86–7, 93, 101,

107, 109, 124, 136, 158, 160, *162*,
   163, 165, *166*, 167, 171, 187–9,
   192, 195, 199, 200–1, 204, 219,
   227, 251
common size ratio 224, **225**, 225–6
community development 5, 179, 227,
   228–30, 233, 241
Community Development Block Grant
   (CDBG) 5–6, 181, 220, 228, 230,
   243
concentrated poverty 2, 6, 16, 19, 20, 22,
   24, *25*, 26, 29, *30*, 32, 33, 34, 35,
   36, 227, 230, 232, 233, 247, 250,
   see also poverty, extreme poverty,
   high poverty
Congress, *see* U.S. Congress
Cook County, Illinois 134, 252, *256*, *259*,
   264, 276
Core Based Statistical Area (CBSA)
   157–8, *159*, *160*, **161**, *162*, 163,
   164, 165, *166*, 167, *168*, **169**,
   170, 218, *see also* Metropolitan
   Statistical Area (MSA)
crime rates 15, 16, 40, 69, 121, 125, 234,
   247
Cuyahoga County 3, 178–80, 182–5, 229,
   235, 240

decennial censuses 6, 16, 19, **21**, *21*, *23*,
   24, *25*, *27*, *28*, *31*, *33*, *114*, *115*,
   158, *see also* Census, decennial
decline of suburbs 1–7, 70, 121–2, 124,
   127, 139, 142, 153–8, 162, 165,
   167, 171–2, 179–80, 183, 189,
   198, 199, 201, 208, 215–16, 218,
   222, 237, 263, *see also* urban
   decline
demographic 1, 3, 7–8, 32, 34–5, 40, 46,
   53, 81, 86–7, 101, 116, 120, 126,
   135–7, 149, 208, 213, 216, 218,
   220, 230, 251, *255*, *256*, 257, *258*,
   263, *264*, *266*, 279
developing suburb 3–4, *see also* outer
   suburb
displacement 135, 140–1
distressed, older suburbs 2, 3, 8, 16,
   213–15, 217–20, 230, 232, 234,
   237, 238, 239, 241–4

Chester, Pennsylvania 214, 220,
   222–3, **224**, **225**, 225–33, 235–9,
   241–4
East Cleveland, Ohio 180, 214,
   220–3, **224**, **225**, 225–9, 234–41, 244
Inkster, Michigan 214, 220–3, **224**,
   225, 225–9, 233–4, 236, 239–43
Prichard, Alabama 214, 222–3, **224**,
   225, 225–9, 230–33, 236–7,
   240–3
diversity 1–4, 40, 60, 62, 74, 104, 134,
   180, 182, 215, 217, 222, 238, 253,
   257, 280
Dunham-Jones, E. 137
DuPage County, Illinois 252, *256*, *259*,
   264
Dwyer, R.E. 82, 155, 249, 251

East Cleveland, Ohio 180, 214, 220–3,
   224, **225**, 225–9, 234–41, 244
economic crisis, *see* Great Recession,
   recession
education 1, 16, 35–6, 87, 121, 182, 185,
   207, 216, 227, 236, 248, 272
ethnicity, *49*, 61–2, *65*, **66**, 85, 87–8, 109,
   215, 227, *255*, *256*, *258*, *see also*
   race
extreme poverty 17, 19, 20–2, *21*, **21**,
   23, *24*, *25*, 26, *27*, *28*, 29, 32–6,
   33, *34*, 216, *see also* poverty,
   concentrated extreme poverty,
   high poverty
exurb 3, 18, *28*, 29, 56–8, **58**, **59**, **60**, 74,
   101, 134, 136, 143, **157**, 179, 189

Farmers Branch, Texas 7, 113, *114*, 116,
   117, 118, 120, 121, 122, 123, 124,
   125, 126, 127
federal government 5, 83–4, 117–19, 125,
   177, 244
financial crisis 135, 149, *see also* Great
   Recession
flags 123
foreclosure 6, 7, 42, 69, 74, 136, 175,
   177–85, 188, 202, 205–8, 214,
   217–18, 228
Frey, W.H. 39–40, 43–4, 47, 57, 67, 188,
   250

Great Recession 42, 188–9, 248–9, 265,
    273, 279
growth of suburbs 3, 6, 7, 15, 20, 29,
    60–1, 81, 134, 136, 143, 153, 156,
    157, 157–8, 159, 165, *166*, 171,
    195, 216, *219*, 231, 250, 262

Hamtramck, Michigan 241
Hanlon, B. 3, 6, 7, 81–3, 85–7, 92, 102,
    106, 113, 133, 135, 139, 142–3,
    154–5, 179–80, 214–16
Hazleton, Pennsylvania 118
health and concentrated poverty 15–17,
    42, 81, 121, 193, 215, 234, 244,
    248, 249, 251–2, *254*, 271
high-poverty 2, 6, 16, 17, 19, 20, 33–5, 34,
    41–4, 49–50, 50, 51, 52–3, 54, 55,
    56–60, 57, 58, 59, 60, 61, 65, 66–7,
    69–70, 72–3, 75, 155, 168, 228,
    257, 262, *see also* concentrated
    poverty, extreme poverty
Hill, E. 7, 214, 237–8
Hispanic, *see* Latino
homeowner's association 200–1
homeownership 2, 4, 7, 34, 40, 41, 41–6,
    47, 48, 49, 50, 51, 53, 56, 62, 65,
    66, 69, 70, 72, 74–5, 116, 123,
    125–6, 181, 223, 230
house price 17, 69, 136, 188–9, 196, *see
    also* property value
Housing and Economic Recovery Act
    (HERA) 177
Hudnut, W.H. 1–2, 5, 154

Illegal Immigration Reform and Immigrant
    Responsibility Act (IIRIRA) 119
Illegal Immigration Relief Act (IIRA) 118
immigrants 2, 4, 7, 48, 52, 82, 85–6, 97–8,
    113, 116–19, 120–7, 155, 230, 251,
    257, *259*, *260*, 260, 262, 268–9,
    270, 277, 279
immigration 7, 113, 116–27, 155, 219,
    227, 230, 269, 272
Immigration Reform and Control Act
    (IRCA) 119
income 1–7, 17, 19, 20, 35–6, 39–40, 42,
    45, 52, *55*, 56, 59, 61–2, **63**, *64*, 64,
    65, 66–7, 72, 74–5, 81, 85, 87, 92,

108, *114*, *115*, 116, 136, 139–41,
    147, 148–9, 153–6, 158, *160*, **161**,
    162, *166*, 167–8, **169**, 171, 179,
    181–2, 185, 187–91, 193–7, *198*,
    198–9, 208, 216, 229–30, 232,
    238, 242–4, 247–8, 250–2, 267,
    269, 271, 276, 278–80 *see also*
    household income
individual responsibility 194, 207
infill 138, 140–1, 183
Inkster, Michigan 214, 220–3, **224**, **225**,
    225–9, 233–4, 236, 239–43
inner suburb 1, 7, 82, 106, 133–5, 149,
    158, 178–80, 185, *see also* inner-
    ring suburb, mature suburb
inner-ring suburban decline
inner-ring suburb 1, 3, 6–7, 74, 121, 140,
    153, **154**, 154–6, **157**, 157–8, *160*,
    161, *162*, 162–3, **163**, *164*, **165**,
    165, *166*, 167–8, **169**, **170**, 171–2,
    214–16, 223, 241, 250, *see also*
    inner suburb, mature suburb
integration 36, 70, 81, 126, 180, 227Kahn,
    M.E. 138

Kane County, Illinois 252, *256*, *259*, *264*
Keating, W.D. 7, 155, 172, 177, 179, 180,
    182, 227
Kneebone, E. 1, 3, 4, 6, 15, 16, 26, 29,
    40–3, 52, 82, 104, 135, 230, 247,
    248, 250, 251, 281

Lake County, Illinois 74, 252, *256*, *259*,
    264
Lang, R.E. 87
Latino 4, 32, *33*, 33–4, 40, 45, 47, 48, 67,
    69, 74, 82, 88, 90, **94**, 94, **95**, 95,
    96, 96, **97**, 97–8, 101, 104–8, *114*,
    115, 116, 120, 124, 129, 140, 148,
    205, 221–2, 251, *255*, *256*, 257,
    258, 269, 277
Lee, S. 7, 153, **154**, 154, 156–7, **157**, 158,
    172
Leigh, N. 153, **154**, 154, 157–8, 172
Leinberger, C. 4, 42
Liberty Road, Baltimore County, Maryland
    187–9, **190**, 192, 195–6, *197*, *198*,
    198–9, 201–2

local government 17, 113, 116, 118–19,
    121, 137, 143, 227, 232, 237, 248,
    250, 270, *271*, 272, 280
Los Angeles, California 8, 26, *31*, 81–3,
    97, 249, 252, 253, *254*, *255*, 257,
    259, *260*, *263*, 263, 265, 268,
    271–4, 276, 278, 279
Lucy, W.H. 1, 2, 136, 154

mansion 136, 140, **141**, 141, 180, 182
Maryland, Priority Funding Area (PFA)
    program **142**, 143, 148
mature suburb 1, 3–4, 18, *28*, 29, 56, *see
    also* inner ring suburb
McHenry County, Illinois 252, *256*, *259*,
    262, *264*
McMansion 136, 140, 141
Metropolitan Statistical Area (MSA) 1, 8,
    18, 39–50, *41*, *49*, 52–53, 56–9, **58**,
    59, **60**, 61–2, **63**, *64*, 64, *65*, 66, **66**,
    67, 69–70, 73–5, 81, 89, 157, 219
Mikelbank, B.A. 2, 7, 155, 213–15, 251,
    257
Millennials, *see* young workers
minority, *see* color, of
Montgomery County, Maryland 73, 97,
    253, 257, *258*, *259*, 263, *266*, 277
Moos, M. 156
Morrow-Jones, H.A. 60, 81–2, 154–6
multifamily housing 48, 70, 75

Neighborhood Change Database (NCDB)
    43, *49*, *54*, 220
Neighborhood Stabilization Program
    (NSP) 7, 177–9, 181–5, 217,
    228–30, 234
Nelson, A.C. 136, 158
neoliberalism 116, 120–2, 126, 187–8,
    190, 193–6, 207
New Metropolitan Reality model 3
New Urbanism 137
Non-Hispanic White 1, 4, 7, 33, 34–5,
    39–41, *41*, 44–7, *48*, 48, *49*, *51*, 62,
    64, 65, **66**, 67, **68**, 69, 74, 82, 87–8,
    90, 94, 98–9, 101–2, 104, 107–9,
    114, *115*, 116, 136, 180, 182, 188–
    9, 191–2, 195, 197–9, 200, 202–3,
    205–8, 215, 217, 219, 221–2, 228,
    250–1, *255*, *256*, 257, *258*

older suburb 1–2, 6, 8, 29, 52, 96, 134,
    136, 139–40, 142–3, 155–6,
    158, 178, 213–15, 217, *see also*
    distressed, older suburbs, mature
    suburb
Orfield, M. 1–3, 5–6, 154–5, 172, 214–16,
    249, 251, 253, 257
outer-ring suburb 45, 154, 156–8, *160*,
    161, *162*, 162–3, **163**, *164*, **165**,
    165, *166*, 167, 171, 216, *see also*
    developing suburb
outer suburb 5, 98, 108, 127, 136, 156, *see
    also* developing suburb

per capita income 7, *114*, *115*, 158, *160*,
    160, **161**, 167, **169**, 171, *see also*
    income, household income
Phillips, D.L. 1–2, 135, 154
polarization 5, 156
policy 1–2, 4–7, 18–20, 36, 113, 116–17,
    119–21, 123–4, 126–7, 134, 143–4,
    148–9, 155, *159*, *166*, 167, 171,
    180, 183, 185, 187, 194, 211,
    213–14, 216, 220, 240, 243, 247–8,
    252, 281, *see also* public policy
poverty 1–6, 8, 13, 15–22, *21*, **21**, *23*, *24*,
    25, 26, *27*, *28*, 29, *30*, 32–6, *33*, *34*,
    39–44, 49–50, *50*, *51*, **51**, 52–3, 54,
    55, 56–7, *57*, **59**, 59–60, **60**, **61**, 64,
    65, 66–67, **68**, 69–70, 72–6, 81–82,
    106, *114*, *115*, 120, 135, 154–5,
    158, *160*, **161**, 162–3, *166*, 167–8,
    171, 179, 214, 216–18, 221–3,
    227–8, 230–3, 244, 247–52, 262–3,
    263, *264*, 265, *266*, 267, 270, 274,
    279, *see also* concentrated poverty,
    extreme poverty, high poverty
predatory lending 136, 205, 207
Prichard, Alabama 214, 222–3, **224**, **225**,
    225–9, 230–33, 236–7, 240–3
Prince George's County, Maryland 92–3,
    107–9, 253, 257, *258*, *259*, 263, *266*
Priority Funding Area (PFA) program **142**,
    143, 148
property value 4, 7, 40, 42, 60–2, 64,
    66–7, 69, 73–5, 139–41, 156,
    187–91, 194–6, 197, 197–9, 200–1,
    208, 239, *see also* house price
public policy 1, 4, 213, *see also* policy

Puentes, R. 1, 82, 96, 106, 214, 216
punctuated equilibrium 187, 205, 208

race 3–4, *49*, 61–2, *65*, **66**, 85, 87–8, 94,
    102, 109, 120, 191, 194–7, 204,
    215–16, 221, 227–8, 247, 255, 256,
    258, 279, *see also* ethnicity
Randallstown, Baltimore County,
    Maryland 187–9, 191, 196, 199,
    200, 202
real estate 40, 62, 136, 177, 190, 192,
    203
Real Estate Owned (REO) 181
recession 35, 42, 57, 138, 177, 181, 248,
    249, 253, 262, 265, 267, 273, 277,
    279, *see also* Great Recession
redevelopment 6, 133–5, 137–8, 140–3,
    143, **144**, 144–6, *147*, 148–9, 156,
    179, 228, 241–2
regional 1, 2, 3, 5, 8, 22, 29, 36, 41–2, 45,
    75–6, 133–4, 139, 144, 155–6, 158,
    159, 172, 181, 215–6, 218, 227,
    231, 234, 237, 239–40, 243
Reisterstown Road, Baltimore County
    188, 189, **190**, 195–6, *197*, *198*,
    198, 201
rental housing 6, 70, 72, 74, 180–2, 185
retrofit 133, 135, 137–41, 148–9
revitalization 5, 7, 87, 139, 155–6, 172,
    230
Riverside County, California 26, 252, *255*,
    257, *259*, 262, *263*
Rusk, D. 5, 17, 62, 66

safety net 6, 8, 36, 40, 194, 247, 249,
    251–2, 265, 268, 272, 279–80
San Bernardino County, California 252,
    255, 257, *259*, 262, *263*, 275
SB 1070, Arizona 117–18
segregation 62, 64, 67, 69, 86, 108,
    191–2, 198, 227, 247, 262
Shaker Heights, Ohio 178, 180, 182–3
single-family 1–2, 39, 41, *41*, 42, 44–5,
    48, 49, 57–8, 69–70, 72–5, 117,
    124, 133, 139–41, **143**, **144**, **145**,
    145–6, 148, 181–3, *197*
smart growth 134, 143, 148, 153, 172
social services 2, 4, 39, 87, 118, 233, 249,
    252, 253, 257, 274, 280

socioeconomic 1, 3, 6–8, 40, *114*, *115*,
    116, 120–2, 126, 153, 156–7, 213,
    220, 230, 257
South Euclid, Ohio 178, 180, 182–3, 185
spatial mismatch 8, 17, 249, 251, 271
sprawl 5, 7, 39, 133–6, 138, 149, 155–6,
    157, 158–9, 167, *168*, 168, **169**,
    170, 171, 189, 215
state government 244, 249, 272
steering 62, 204
sustainability 7, 133–5, 138–40, 149, 178

Traditional model of urban form 7, 81–3,
    85–8, 92–3, 96, 102, 104, 106–7,
    109
typology 3, 40, *41*, 43–6, 74, 214–15

underclass 32, 34–5
unemployment 42, 75, *114*, *115*, 142,
    193–4, 198, 214, 217–8, 222–3,
    227, 242, 247, 263, 267, 268
urban containment 7, 153, 156–8, *159*,
    166, 167–8, **169**, **170**, 171–2
urban model 81–2, 98
    see also Traditional model of urban
    form

U.S. Congress 84

Vicino, T.J. 1, 3, 7, 82, 113, 139, 142,
    154–5, 195

Walker, K.E. 120, 126
Warren, D. 216–17
Washington, DC 5, 7–8, 42, 81–5, 87,
    89, 89, **90**, 90, **91**, **92**, 92–4, **93**,
    94, **95**, **96**, **97**, 97–9, **98**, **99**, **102**,
    105, **106**, 106, **107**, 108–9, 195,
    240, 249, 252–3, *254*, 257, *258*,
    261, 263–5, *266*, 268, 274, 276–7,
    279
wealth 3, 17, 66, 74, 81, 85, 86, 156,
    193–4
Will County, Illinois 257, *259*, 262, *265*
Williamson, J. 137, 138
Woldoff, R. 191, 197
Wolfson, Emily 198–9

younger workers 87, 104–6, **107**, 108